THE LANGUAGE OF THE LAW

THE
LANGUAGE
OF
THE LAW

AN ANTHOLOGY OF LEGAL PROSE

SELECTED AND EDITED BY
LOUIS BLOM-COOPER

ASSISTED BY
EDWARD JACKSON

WITH A FOREWORD BY
LORD RADCLIFFE

THE MACMILLAN COMPANY
NEW YORK

Library of Congress Catalog Card Number: 67-12653

First Printing

THE MACMILLAN COMPANY, NEW YORK
Printed in the United States of America

Contents

Foreword, ix

Introduction, xvii

Acknowledgments, xxiii

1. ON AND OFF THE BENCH, 1

Francis Bacon: *From* Essays or Counsels Civil and Moral *: Of Judicature*, 3

Serjeant Sullivan: *The Last Forty Years of the Irish Bar*, 7

Judge Parry: *A Day in My Life in the County Court*, 16

Lord Asquith: *Some Aspects of the Work of The Court of Appeal*, 29

Mr Justice Cardozo: *A Ministry of Justice*, 47

2. CRIME AND PUNISHMENT, 61

Mr Justice Stephen: *The Punishment of Convicts*, 63

Lord Inglis: *A Simple Statement*, 82

Lord Macnaghten: *White Collar Crime*, 86

Lord Cooper: *An Admonition*, 91

Lord Pearce: *Counsel of Deception*, 93

Judge Frank: *Police Practices*, 100

Mr Justice Holmes and Mr Justice Brandeis: *Evidence from Eavesdropping*, 107

Mr. Justice Frankfurter: *Dirty Business*, 118

3. FAMILY RELATIONS, 123

Lord Stowell: *The Marriage Union*, 125

v

Lord Justice James: *Illegitimate Insularity*, 136
Lord O'Brien: *The Enfant Gâté of Roscarberry*, 139
Mr Justice Isaacs: *A Woman's Place*, 143
Mr Justice Hiemstra: *Wounded Feelings*, 152
Lord Justice Harman: *The Lay-About*, 155

4. SLAVES AND CITIZENS, 159
Mr Justice McLean: *The Black Goes Free*, 161
Mr Justice Harlan: *No Caste Here*, 166
Mr Justice van den Heever: *Entrenched Clauses*, 173
Mr Justice Holmes: *Freedom for Thought*, 181

5. P.P.E., 183
Lord Bowen: *Laissez-Faire*, 185
Mr Justice Rich: *Free Trade*, 194
Mr Justice Black: *Pyrrhic Victory*, 198
Mr Justice Holmes: *The Authorised Voice*, 204
Mr Justice Evatt: *Marxism at Law*, 206
Judge Learned Hand: *Point of Danger*, 209
Mr Justice Douglas: *McCarthy Redivivus?*, 216
Mr Justice Holmes: *Limits of Tolerance*, 219
Mr Justice Holmes: *Incitement*, 224

6. WORDS, WORDS, WORDS..., 227
Judge Augustus Hand and Judge Manton: *Art for Art's Sake*, 229
Mr Justice Millin: *Speaking Up for Hitler*, 235
Mr Justice Blagden: *Anglo-Indian Privilege*, 243
Lord Atkin: *The Meaning of Money*, 254
Mr Justice Price: *Cows and Bitches*, 256

Sir Kenneth Gresson: *Nymphet on Trial*, 261

Sir Jocelyn Simon: *English Idioms from the Penal Law*, 266

7. JUDICIAL RESTRAINT, 293

Chief Justice Crewe: *Name and Dignity*, 295

Chief Justice Pratt and Mr. Justice Fortescue: *Right to be Heard*, 297

Mr. Justice Holmes: *Common Law*, 301

Mr Justice Krause: *Lawyers as Judges*, 305

Viscount Radcliffe: *The Unbranded Order*, 310

Lord Denning: *No Well-tuned Cymbal*, 315

Lord Devlin: *Non-conformity No Disgrace*, 319

The Supreme Court of Israel: *A Judge's Duty*, 323

Mr Justice Frankfurter and Mr Justice Douglas: *Judicial Silence – Public Noise*, 324

8. JUDICIAL FELICITIES, 329

Lord Macnaghten: *Mrs Bunch's Baggage*, 331

Mr Justice O'Brien: *Common Carrier*, 335

Mr Justice Cardozo: *The Reasonable Rescuer*, 339

Lord Thomson: *Round in Bogey*, 343

Lord O'Brien: *Wicklow Picnic*, 345

Mr Justice Dysart: *Night Thoughts*, 349

Mr Justice G. N. Holmes: *Ambidextrous Sheriff*, 352

Mr Justice van den Heever: *Time and Space*, 354

Mr Justice Frankfurter: *Advice to a Young Man interested in going into Law*, 357

Mr D. F. Wilson: *This Charm of Endearment*, 358

Mr John Watson: *In the Lands Tribunal*, 361

Professor Richard Field: *Envoi—Judicial Infelicity*, 373

Notes on Contributors, 379

Foreword

By VISCOUNT RADCLIFFE

ALL ANTHOLOGIES REPRESENT an individual choice from a
mass of underlying material. You approve or disapprove according to your familiarity with that material and your reaction to the
personal selections that have been made. But then it is not easy
to be fair to the anthologist and his very considerable labours
unless one has some light upon the principles of his choice and
the theme upon which the separate extracts are strung. Here, I
think, we must be guided by the actual words of the title that
Mr Blom-Cooper has assigned to his book, *The Language of
the Law*, and by the avowals that he has made in his interesting
Introduction.

This then is not a collection of the 'beauties' of legal writing,
and I am glad of that. Nor does it set out to inform the reader,
lay or professional, what has been laid down to be the law on
various important aspects of human relations. Indeed, as the
reader will see, it is peppered with dissenting judgments, in which
the still waters of judicial expression are troubled by a breeze of
indignation that seems sometimes to be distributed impartially
between the wrongness of the majority conclusion and the obtuse-
ness of the speaker's colleagues. This, as Mr Blom-Cooper says,
helps to good forthright expression. Nor, again, is the collection designed to show that there is anything specially wise or
specially enlightened or specially humane about the judicial
character, though I will observe in passing that some of the
speakers do sound as if they were quite good men. No, what we
are to attend to, if we are to get the best out of the book, is the
form and style in which judges have expressed themselves when
speaking judicially, the apparatus of their prose, in fact. It is this
that is to count. When they speak without their robe, they are
mere lecturers or essayists, ununiformed like other men, and,
like other men, they are apt to need a lot of words to reach their

point. But what is said from the Bench is rather a different matter.

This is to me a new line of approach, and I find it productive of some fascinating enquiries. Is there really something of a common style of expression among the judges, past and present, who sit or have sat in what I will call, quite inadequately and inappropriately, Anglo-Saxon Courts of Justice? If so, why? Because of a common method of training? Because of something inherent in the respective legal systems? Because they are systems of precedent, which is another way of saying that judges are always reading each other's opinions. And, if there is a common style, what are its qualities, and, if they are identifiable, do they express anything that is illuminative of the system of law they expound?

I feel that the law is entitled to an anthology of this type. When one turns to that great treasure house, the *Oxford Book of English Prose*, it is plain that Sir Arthur Quiller-Couch did not face up to the legal judgment as one of his abundant sources. So far as I can remember, this whole collection contains only three extracts from the law courts, and these are no more than short snippets from well-known pieces of elegance. I do not blame him for his lack of adventure—the ocean that he would have had to explore is wide and deep, and only professional navigators, I think, can chart their course among its currents. Nevertheless it is not to be ignored that ever since the English language took shape men of a fairly high level of education have been making it their instrument to express lucidly, coherently and, they hope, convincingly, their conclusions on questions of great personal moment. It would be singular if out of all this there had not been wrought much that invites the attention and merits the respect of the general connoisseur of English prose.

Q. himself felt the necessity of asking the question, What is the cardinal virtue that one should require in assessing the merits of prose style? He came up with the answer that that virtue was Persuasion. Considering the rich variety of the forms and purposes of prose writing, his answer seems to me almost capricious. Indeed, for judicial prose, I would much prefer A. Clutton-Brock's word Justice, which Q. rejects. But the passage from *Modern Essays* that he gives us in the Oxford Book (p. 1028) appears to me so apt to express what I have in mind that I take leave to quote a sentence or two from the whole fine context. 'The cardinal virtue of prose', says Clutton-Brock, 'is Justice, and . . . Justice needs inquiry, patience, and a control even of the noblest passions . . . a habit of Justice in all the processes of thought, a style tranquillised and a form moulded by that habit. The master of prose is not cold, but he will not let any word or image inflame him with a heat irrelevant to his purpose. Unhasting, unresting, he pursues it, subduing all the riches of his mind to it, rejecting all beauties that are not germane to it; making his own beauty out of the very accomplishment of it, out of the whole work and its proportions . . .'

There is much more of value in the rest of the passage that I have not quoted, but I think that even what I have should stand as a measuring rod for the qualities of judicial speech. Applied, it might record some readings substantially different from those that are current today. But Clutton-Brock is, after all, outlining a classical ideal, and in this country we have got rid of the stigma of classicism.

There are, of course, certain classes of legal judgment that must be excluded in the interests of the general reader. Mr Blom-Cooper has rightly spared us jargon, unavoidable as it sometimes is; and there are branches of what I may call the more technical aspects of law, such as patent and taxation law, which, though yielding some of the most elegant examples of judicial exposition and demonstration, are perhaps caviar reserved for the palate of the specialist alone. We must dispense too with those rather weary pilgrimages through a long list of decided cases, to be 'noticed', 'distinguished' and in the end either explained or explained away, in which the judge succeeds in reconciling his piety with his learning.

Within these limitations, however, I know of no reason why we should not find a high quality of prose in any such anthology as this, whether it is persuasion, justice or, perhaps, conviction that is to be looked for as its cardinal virtue. It should be capable of challenging comparison with the best that has been written in other fields. That wise and delightful letter which Mr Justice Frankfurter wrote to his twelve-year-old correspondent and legal aspirant (see p. 357) explains how a lawyer ought to prepare himself for the mastery of his craft. 'No one can be a truly competent

lawyer unless he is a cultivated man. . . . The best way to prepare
for the law is to come to the study of the law as a well-read person.
Thus alone can one acquire the capacity to use the English
language on paper and in speech and with the habits of clear
thinking which only a truly liberal education can give. No less
important for a lawyer is the cultivation of the imaginative faculties by reading poetry, seeing great paintings, . . . and listening to
great music. Stock your mind with the deposit of much good
reading . . .' I do hope that law teachers in this country realise
the truth of this.

Every reader who grubs about in *The Language of the Law*
must make up his own mind what qualities he finds in its material.
It is not for me to prompt, and I am probably prejudiced anyway.
But, if ordinary conceptions are a good guide, there are certain
graces that he is at any rate entitled to expect: lucidity of thought
and expression, compression (I hope that the lawyers are not
going to let us down there), and a power to pursue an argument
in a way that does relate conclusions to facts and principles that
are relevant to them. Whether a reader will find these or more I
do not know. What I think may strike him as he reads is that
there is a certain strangeness in the language, a formality even in
the choicest pieces that removes it a little distance from ordinary
writing or ordinary speech. The natural sequence of words
suffers curious inversion, and there are those little archaisms,
'vouchsafe', 'apprehend', 'recuse', 'transgression', 'kinsman',
into which it is all too easy to slip. He may observe too a
strangeness in the process of thought itself, so that the judge
seems sometimes to take a long and difficult path to reach
a fairly obvious conclusion, and again he seems to insist on
treating as simple what is inherently complicated. That is to say,
I think, that by the very nature of law its expounders cannot
be quite free from resort to a hieratic tongue or from thinking
rather by categories than particulars. The real masters, let us
say Lord Macnaghten and Mr Justice Holmes, transcend these
limitations.

It is only fair to realise that to speak from the Bench implies the
observance of some special conditions: I do not call them restraints or handicaps, but they do influence the resulting form.
First and foremost, a judge must speak with authority and

authority calls for certain abnegations. Let us notice one or two of the more important.

He must submit to strict reticence about his personality. What he says from the Bench has weight and deserves obedience because he is a judge, no less, not because he is brilliant or witty or has a tender heart or a lovable character. These qualities may peep through but, essentially, he speaks from behind a mask, and it is not his business to drop it.

It is his business, on the other hand, to show that he is a learned man, because his learning links him up with the great body and process of the law to which the case before him must be subjected. Besides, the public nowadays expects the judge to show his paces, as it were. We have passed from those simpler times when 'Because I say so' was sufficient warrant for a judicial decision. Personally, I envy the airy brevity of many earlier judgments; just as I envy the dignified certainties on moral or social issues, eloquent of the eighteenth century, with which Lord Stowell, for instance, disposed of Mrs Evans's marital complaints (see p. 125). But a democracy, which takes little for granted in its officers, requires other ways, and the judge now must reason his conclusions and must convince as well as decide. His learning then brings him weight, and one can only pray that it will not leave him ponderous. Here Mr Blom-Cooper has been considerate to his readers in his selections. For the great masters upon whom he has rightly drawn the judgment delivered is only the tip of a massive iceberg of experience and learning. They do not need to recount at length the list of their qualifications. A glance here, a pounce there, and then the hammer stroke that pins the conclusion so surely to its base. It is the pinning, I think, that counts.

There are, alas, graces that we welcome in others but look at askance in the trimmings of a judge. Take the qualities of eloquence and wit, for instance. Can we allow a judge to be eloquent in the delivery of his opinion, or do we feel uneasily that he is, as it were, forcing a card and making an illegitimate assault upon our reason? An austere and workmanlike eloquence we may perhaps accept without embarrassment or suspicion. Those indignant dissenting opinions for which Mr Blom-Cooper has, I fancy, a special fondness, are entitled to and do indeed achieve a convincing breath of eloquence. Turn, please, to Mr Justice McLean in *Re John*

Anderson (p. 161) or Mr Justice Harlan in *Plessy* v. *Ferguson* (p. 166) or Mr Justice Holmes in *Abrams* v. *U.S.* (p. 219), and ask whether the law cannot in truth express a sober eloquence of its own. But the limits are strict. One hint that the judge is enjoying the sound of his own voice, an innocent pleasure enough, or that he is palming off emotion as reason, and authority has flown out of the window. And, Ichabod, who will ever sound again from a judicial seat the wild poetry of Chief Justice Crewe's famous 'For where is Bohun? Where's Mowbray? Where's Mortimer? Nay, which is more, and most of all, where is Plantagenet? They are intombed in the urnes and sepulchres of mortality' (see p. 296). But then we do not anyway write today in the tongue of Sir Thomas Browne.

'Judges,' said Francis Bacon, 'ought to be more learned than witty', and Bacon knew much better how other people ought to behave than how to behave himself. We all know very well what he meant, and I am sure that he was right. Heaven defend us from the funny judge or the flippant judge or, for that matter, from the 'with it' judge. The last causes me the same sort of discomfort as those Prime Ministers who select public honours for popular entertainers. They should recall Horace Walpole's remark to Lady Ossory about the pomp of Garrick's funeral: 'It is confounding the immense space between pleasing talents and national services.'

The truth is, I think, that the funny judge is a contradiction in terms. No doubt human beings involve themselves in ridiculous situations and behave in ridiculous ways enough, and their goings on appear the more absurd when they are suddenly reviewed under the cold eye of the law. But their follies are exposed to the judge in trust for the public, that justice may be done, and it is outrageous that he should ever seem to entertain them for his personal amusement. I do not altogether acquit some of the felicities that appear in this book. Certainly, it is largely a matter of taste, but I believe that a judge who is going to employ the weapon of wit should always realise that in doing so he is departing from a valuable general rule.

I am sure that there are justifiable exceptions. We should all go mad with solemnity if one could not detect an occasional lift of the eyebrow or a gleam behind the spectacles. The Irish Courts,

again, are and always have been a law to themselves, and I
suspect that in their precincts Bench, witnesses and litigants
understand each other with a sympathy that is denied to people
of more rigid structure. Lord Macnaghten was an Irishman,
though he graced the English Courts. Is his handling of Mrs
Bunch at Paddington and the loss of her Gladstone bag (see p. 331)
witty? I do not know, though I do know that it is convincing and
delightful and that it contains nothing that could wound even the
most sensitive of parties. But then perhaps his wit is directed at
the weighty formulae of the law, when they are wheeled into
place to measure the minor incidents of ordinary life, and not at
Mrs Bunch herself or her 'ephemeral and evanescent porter'.
That in itself is a solemn thought.

Introduction

IN A previous anthology, *The Law as Literature*, the editor of this volume tried to bridge the gulf of incomprehension between lawyer and layman. A number of glimpses of the law, as seen from the Bench, the Bar, the dock, the litigant's uncomfortable seat, and the press-box, were singled out for public appreciation. Only what was 'literature' in the broadest permissible sense qualified for inclusion: too-technical and mundane contributions from lawyers were rejected, leaving only a nucleus of legal judgments—readily applauded by the legal profession—as against a mass of excellent writing from non-lawyers which in the main did no more than confirm the suspicion that the law has little to do with justice. The result was an imbalance in the relative literary merits of the legal and lay contributions. Mr Stephen Potter, speaking on the B.B.C. programme, *The Critics*,* commented that the judicial selections reminded him of Dr Johnson's gibe: 'Sir, a woman preaching is like a dog's walking on his hind legs. It is not done well; but you are surprised at finding it done at all.'

Writing about the law, the layman has a freedom of expression denied to the judge, speaking on or off the Bench. While the form of English judgment lends itself readily to literary exposition, there is still the overriding limitation that a judicial decision has primarily a serious functional purpose: the facts of the case must be set out, the arguments fairly presented—the truth, Lord Eldon said, is best discovered by powerful statements on both sides of the question—and the reasons supporting the judge's decision must be spelt out. This, incidentally, is a major reason why literary excellence is more often found in a dissenting judgment, when the judge can dispense with the deadening preliminaries and come straight to the heart of his protest.

The living law, moreover, is an endless attempt to lay down

* 17 December 1961.

xvii

immutable principles and logic (*pace* Mr Justice Holmes's 'the life of the law has not been logic; it has been experience') on the shifting sands of the custom and prejudice of the community. On the one hand the law is always striving, and never quite managing, to keep pace with the march of events; the more it lags behind social demands the more anachronistic it appears and the more it hardens into pedantry. On the other hand, the law is constantly threatened by anarchy and individualism; hence the judge moves forward only pragmatically, and in reshaping any legal principle treads warily for fear that the social structure may be in jeopardy. In a constant attempt to compromise between the temper of the law and the temper of the moment, the courts set out deliberately to bring classical objectivity to their judgments. But in the very subduing of subjectivity the written judgment tends to be stripped of emotional and expressive content. Only the great, and on rare occasions the less than great, judges combine with this classical objectivity that unmistakable passion for justice, restrained or un-restrained, which alone produces the true fusion between law and literature. The ideal legal anthology would contain nothing else, and nothing less.

But it is almost impossible for a judge to remain on these heights for any sustained period of time. This opening of one of Lord Macnaghten's speeches suffices as an example*:

'My Lords, in the office of Grace, Smith & Co., a firm of solicitors in Liverpool of long standing and good repute, the appellant Emily Lloyd, a widow woman in humble circumstances, was robbed of her property. It was not much, just a mortgage for £450 bequeathed to her by her late husband, and two freehold cottages at Ellesmere Port which she bought herself without legal assistance for £540 after her husband's death. But it was all she had, and after the order of the Court of Appeal reversing a judgment of Mr Justice Scrutton (who tried the case with a special jury) she was compelled to appeal to this House as a pauper.'

The effect of this simple opening is magnificent: it anticipates the judge's conclusion, after setting out the story of the easy-going solicitor, Smith ('a gentleman "devoted" as he says, "to public works", meaning by that, I suppose, that his proper business as a solicitor was a matter of secondary consideration with him') and of his clerk Sandles, who tricked Mrs Lloyd into conveying her property to himself,

* *Lloyd* v. *Grace, Smith & Co.* [1912] A.C. 716, 732

'that it would be absolutely shocking ... if Mr Smith were not held liable for the fraud of his agent in the present case. When Mrs Lloyd put herself into the hands of the firm, how was she to know what the exact position of Sandles was? Mr Smith carries on business under a style or firm which implies that unnamed persons are, or may be, included in its members. Sandles speaks and acts as if he were one of the firm. He points to the deed boxes in the room and tells her that her deeds are quite safe in "our" hands. Naturally enough she signs the documents he puts before her without trying to understand what they were. Who is to suffer for this man's fraud? The person who relied on Mr Smith's accredited representative, or Mr Smith, who put this rogue in his own place and clothed him with his own authority?'

But between the two passages cited lie over four thousand words which, while they are caviare to the lawyer, hold nothing but unrelieved tedium for the layman.

So too it was possible for Lord Justice Harman to begin a judgment* deliciously with

'To reach a conclusion on this matter involved the court in wading through a monstrous legislative morass, staggering from stone to stone and ignoring the marsh gas exhaling from the forest of schedules lining the way on each side. I regarded it at one time, I must confess, as a slough of despond through which the court would never drag its feet but I have, by leaping from tussock to tussock as best I might, eventually, pale and exhausted, reached the other side where I find myself, I am glad to say, at the same point as that arrived at with more agility by Lord Denning M.R.'

But it was quite impossible for him or for anyone to attempt to maintain this felicitous vein when struggling with the legal issues posed by the fuliginous obscurity of certain Acts of Parliament.

It is even clearer that no isolated phrase or witticism, however elegant, will lift the judgment that contains it out of its legal rut and into the class of 'literature'; this is a separate mine which has been fruitfully worked by Mr R. E. Megarry Q.C.† Such gems as Lord Devlin's

'If a person wakes up in the middle of the night and finds an escaping tiger on top of his bed and suffers a heart attack, it would be nothing to the point that the intentions of the tiger were quite amiable.'‡

* *Davy* v. *Leeds Corporation* [1964] 1 W.L.R. 1218, 1224.
† Miscellany-at-law.
‡ *Behrens* v. *Bertram Mills Circus Ltd* [1957] 2 Q.B. 1, 17-18.

therefore fall within the Rule in Megarry's Case, but not within that of the present volume. One must equally exclude the whole of one of Lord Hewart's cruellest judgments* which, after a languid 'We need not trouble you, Mr Valentine Holmes', ran on to compete in the Mr Bumble stakes:

'Mr Meston puts his case, such as it is, very clearly. It really comes to this: that if this case were different from what it is, he might succeed; but, as this case is what it is, this appeal must be dismissed.'

What, then, is the common factor in all the pieces in this anthology? The object was to concentrate on the human and essentially literate side of the law, and so attempt to explain, and hope to justify, lawyers' ways to laymen. Each contribution had therefore to possess both human interest and real pretensions to being 'literature'; and it was necessary to find a satisfactory definition of 'literature' to make selection easier. Writing which manages to move, to instruct, or to entertain in such a way as wholly to engross a reader will, for him, be 'literature': and the more profound the emotion, the wiser and the more informative the instruction, the more entrancing the entertainment, the greater—or at least better—the literature. When, in addition, the author, whether consciously or unconsciously, uses words which by their sound, style, rhythm and juxtaposition actively enhance the power of what they mean, then one has more than mere literature: one has a flash of poetry. Such flashes will from time to time, one hopes, illumine the receptive reader of these pages: and what Shaw called 'word music' will ring in his ears as he reads, for example, Mr Justice Holmes's noble dissent in favour of freedom of thought.† The sceptic is invited to experiment in altering the sequence of the words, or their rhythm, in any of that great judge's most moving periods. The effect will be what was so well illustrated by the late Lord Birkett, who said that the difference between 'Great is Diana of the Ephesians!' and 'Diana of the Ephesians is great!' was the difference between a call to arms and a peaceful protest.

That at least is the theory behind the anthologist's eclecticism. But in these matters everyone is blessed with what may be called

---

* *Sidcup Building Estates Ltd* v. *Sidery* (1940) Traffic Cases 164.

† *U.S.* v. *Schwimmer*, 299 U.S. 644, 653 (1929); *infra.*, p. 182.

a built-in 'literatometer': an automatic device which enables a reader—and especially a re-reader—instinctively to tell whether this or that piece passes or fails the acid test: and it is by this means, rather than by any carefully distilled definition that the present anthology of legal literature has been chosen and is now, with mingled diffidence, affection and pride, presented to the public. It is not claimed that every piece merits an alpha plus: and perhaps voices will be heard, in echo of Chief Justice Crewe, crying 'Where is Sumner, where is Macmillan; and where, oh where, is Mansfield?' The editorial answer is an unrepentant '*proxime accesserunt*', coupled with a threat—should response to the present volume prove kind—to hunt out and publish in due course a further selection of the best achievements of lawyers in moving, in instructing, and in entertaining their fellow human beings.

Acknowledgments

GRATEFUL ACKNOWLEDGMENT IS made to the following for permission to reprint copyright material:

The Incorporated Council of Law Reporting for England and Wales for judgments reported in the official English Law Reports; the U.S. Government Printing Office for judgments reported from the U.S. Federal Courts; W. Green & Son Ltd., Edinburgh, for judgments reported in the Scots Law Times; the Department of Law, State of New York, for the judgment of Judge Cardozo in *Wagner* v. *International Railway*, 232 N.Y. 176 (1921); the Canada Law Book Company Ltd. for the judgment of Mr Justice Dysart in *Mitchell* v. *Martin & Rose* [1925] 1 D.L.R. 260; the South African Law Reports and Juta & Co. Ltd. for judgments reported from the South African Supreme Court; the Commonwealth Law Reports and the Law Book Company of Australasia Pty. Ltd. for judgments reported in the Commonwealth Law Reports; Butterworth & Co. (New Zealand) Ltd. for the judgment of Sir Kenneth Gresson in *Re Lolita* [1961] N.Z.L.R. 542, 548; the Incorporated Council of Law Reporting, Dublin, for judgments reported in the Official Irish Law Reports; the Harvard Law Review Association for Judge Cardozo's essay *A Ministry of Justice* and Professor Field's verses *Frankfurter J. Concurring*; Christy & Moore Ltd. for Judge Parry's essay, *A Day in my Life in the County Court*; the Society of Public Teachers of Law and the Hon. Luke Asquith for Lord Asquith's essay, *Some Aspects of the Work of the Court of Appeal*; William Hodge & Co. Ltd. for parts of the speech of Lord Inglis in defence of Madeleine Smith; the Southdown Press Pty., Melbourne, for Mr D. F. Wilson's judgment in a case reported in *Truth*, 24 June 1961; Harcourt, Brace & World Inc. for Mr Justice Frankfurter's letter to a twelve-year-old correspondent, from *Of Law and Men*; the Ministry of Justice, Israel, for a short passage in the judgment of the Supreme Court of Israel in *Eichmann* v. *Attorney-General of Israel*; the personal representatives of the estate of Serjeant Sullivan and the editors of the Cambridge Law Journal for the address to the Cambridge Law Society, *The Last Forty Years of the Irish Bar*; the Government of West Bengal for the judgment of Mr Justice Blagden in *Mayr* v. *Rivaz* [1943] I.L.R. 1 Cal. 750; the Law Quarterly Review for Sir Jocelyn Simon's essay, *English Idioms from the Penal Law*; John Arthur Fergus Watson for judgments delivered by him in the Lands Tribunal.

On and Off the Bench

Essays or Counsels Civil and Moral:
Of Judicature

JUDGES OUGHT TO remember that their office is *jus dicere*, and not *jus dare;* to interpret law, and not to make law, or give law. Else will it be like the authority claimed by the church of Rome, which under pretext of exposition of Scripture doth not stick to add and alter; and to pronounce that which they do not find; and by shew of antiquity to introduce novelty. Judges ought to be more learned than witty, more reverend than plausible, and more advised than confident. Above all things, integrity is their portion and proper virtue. *Cursed* (saith the law) *is he that removeth the landmark.* The mislayer of a mere-stone is to blame. But it is the unjust judge that is the capital remover of landmarks, when he defineth amiss of lands and property. One foul sentence doth more hurt than many foul examples. For these do but corrupt the stream, the other corrupteth the fountain. So saith Solomon, *Fons turbatus, et vena corrupta, est justus cadens in causa sua coram adversario.** The office of judges may have reference unto the parties that sue, unto the advocates that plead, unto the clerks and minsters of justice underneath them, and to the sovereign or state above them.

First, for the causes or parties that sue. *There be* (saith the Scripture) *that turn judgment into wormwood;* and surely there be also that turn it into vinegar; for injustice maketh it bitter, and delays make it sour. The principal duty of a judge is to suppress force and fraud; whereof force is the more pernicious when it is open, and fraud when it is close and disguised. Add thereto contentious suits, which ought to be spewed out, as the surfeit of courts. A judge ought to prepare his way to a just sentence, as God useth to prepare his way, by raising valleys and taking down

---

* A righteous man losing his case is like a troubled fountain or a corrupt spring.

hills: so when there appeareth on either side an high hand, violent prosecution, cunning advantages taken, combination, power, great counsel, then is the virtue of a judge seen, to make inequality equal; that he may plant his judgment as upon an even ground. *Qui fortiter emungit, elicit sanguinem,** and where the wine-press is hard wrought, it yields a harsh wine, that tastes of the grape-stone. Judges must beware of hard constructions and strained inferences; for there is no worse torture than the torture of laws. Specially in case of laws penal, they ought to have care that that which was meant for terror be not turned into rigour; and that they bring not upon the people that shower whereof the Scripture speaketh, *Pluet super eos laqueos†* for penal laws pressed are a *shower of snares* upon the people. Therefore let penal laws, if they have been sleepers of long, or if they be grown unfit for the present time, be by wise judges confined in the execution: *Judicis officium est, ut res, ita tempora rerum, &c.‡* In causes of life and death, judges ought (as far as the law permitteth) in justice to remember mercy; and to cast a severe eye upon the example, but a merciful eye upon the person.

Secondly, for the advocates and counsel that plead. Patience and gravity of hearing is an essential part of justice; and an over-speaking judge is no well-tuned cymbal. It is no grace to a judge first to find that which he might have heard in due time from the bar; or to show quickness of conceit in cutting off evidence or counsel too short; or to prevent information by questions, though pertinent. The parts of a judge in hearing are four: to direct the evidence; to moderate length, repetition, or impertinency of speech; to recapitulate, select, and collate the material points of that which hath been said; and to give the rule or sentence. Whatsoever is above these is too much; and proceedeth either of glory and willingness to speak, or of impatience to hear, or of shortness of memory, or of want of a staid and equal attention. It is a strange thing to see that the boldness of advocates should prevail with judges; whereas they should imitate God, in whose seat they sit; who *represseth the presumptuous, and giveth grace to the modest.*

---

* He who blows violently will suffer a nose-bleed.
† He shall rain snares upon them.
‡ The office of judge requires regard for time as well as for merit.

But it is more strange, that judges should have noted favourites; which cannot but cause multiplication of fees, and suspicion of bye-ways. There is due from the judge to the advocate some commendation and gracing, where causes are well handled and fair pleaded; especially towards the side which obtaineth not; for that upholds in the client the reputation of his counsel, and beats down on him the conceit of his cause. There is likewise due to the public a civil reprehension of advocates, where there appeareth cunning counsel, gross neglect, slight information, indiscreet pressing, or an over-bold defence. And let not the counsel at the bar chop with the judge, nor wind himself into the handling of the cause anew after the judge hath declared his sentence; but on the other side, let not the judge meet the cause half way, nor give occasion for the party to say his counsel or proofs were not heard.

Thirdly, for that that concerns clerks and ministers. The place of justice is an hallowed place; and therefore not only the bench, but the foot-pace and precincts and purprise thereof, ought to be preserved without scandal and corruption. For certainly *Grapes* (as the Scripture saith) *will not be gathered of thorns or thistles*; neither can justice yield her fruit with sweetness amongst the briars and brambles of catching and polling clerks and ministers. The attendance of courts is subject to four bad instruments. First, certain persons that are sowers of suits; which make the court swell, and the country pine. The second sort is of those that engage courts in quarrels of jurisdiction, and are not truly *amici curiae*, but *parasiti curiae* in putting a court up beyond her bounds, for their own scraps and advantage. The third sort is of those that may be accounted the left hands of courts; persons that are full of nimble and sinister tricks and shifts, whereby they pervert the plain and direct course of courts, and bring justice into oblique lines and labyrinths. And the fourth is the poller and exacter of fees; which justifies the common resemblance of the courts of justice to the bush whereunto while the sheep flies for defence in weather, he is sure to lose part of his fleece. On the other side, an ancient clerk, skilful in precedents, wary in proceeding, and understanding in the business of the court, is an excellent finger of a court; and doth many times point the way to the judge himself.

Fourthly, for that which may concern the sovereign and estate.

Judges ought above all to remember the conclusion of the Roman Twelve Tables; *Salus populi suprema lex*, and to know that laws, except they be in order to that end, are but things captious, and oracles not well inspired. Therefore it is an happy thing in a state when kings and states do often consult with judges; and again when judges do often consult with the king and state: the one, when there is matter of law intervenient in business of state; the other, when there is some consideration of state intervenient in matter of law. For many times the things deduced to judgment may be *meum* and *tuum*, when the reason and consequence thereof may trench to point of estate: I call matter of estate, not only the parts of sovereignty, but whatsoever introduceth any great alteration or dangerous precedent; or concerneth manifestly any great portion of people. And let no man weakly conceive that just laws and true policy have any antipathy; for they are like the spirits and sinews, that one moves with the other. Let judges also remember, that Solomon's throne was supported by lions on both sides: let them be lions, but yet lions under the throne; being circumspect that they do not check or oppose any points of sovereignty. Let not judges also be so ignorant of their own right, as to think there is not left to them, as a principal part of their office, a wise use and application of laws. For they may remember what the apostle saith of a greater law than theirs; *Nos scimus quia lex bona est, modo quis ea utatur legitime.**

* We know that the law is sound so long as a man uses it lawfully.

The Last Forty Years of the Irish Bar*

FORTY YEARS AGO in my old country the legal world was in a state of transition. The Judicature Act had just got into swing and although four Courts still opened in the hall beside the Liffey they were soon to be fused into one. These were at that time the Court of Chancery, the Court of Queen's Bench, the Court of Exchequer, and the Court of Common Pleas, and the doors of these four opened on the Central Hall and their names stood over them. The Court of Chancery stood by itself, but it was thought in those days that you had your choice of three Common Law Courts in which to have your case tried. If you had some merit on your side but thought that the law was against you, you issued your writ in the Queen's Bench, which was presided over by Mickey Morris, as he was invariably called although he was a lord, because Mickey had a good deal of common sense, a great deal of humanity, but his ideas of jurisprudence were peculiarly his own. On the other hand, if you were strongly of opinion that however iniquitous your client was, he had the law on his side, you issued your writ in the Court of Exchequer, presided over by Christopher Palles, the greatest judge before whom I have ever appeared. Christopher Palles decided according to what he believed to be the law, and would pay no attention to any other consideration that might be advanced before him. On the other hand there was a third course: if you had neither law nor merits you went to the Court of Common Pleas, which in that day was presided over by Chief Justice May, before whom no case was certain and no case was hopeless.

There were other changes coming into vogue. The practice of law had been, one might almost say, the property of the wealthier classes. There was one good thing about the legal profession during the whole of the nineteenth century in Ireland, and certainly in the last forty years: it was not a money-making trade, and there

* An address delivered to the Cambridge University Law Society, 23 November 1926, published in Volume 3, Cambridge Law Journal (1927).

were never in my recollection discussions of a bitter character either in public or in private as to the enormous fortune that might be made at the Bar, because fortunes were not to be made.

A new regime was making its appearance in the country. Litigation was no longer indulged in by the landed gentry, except the litigation that was forced upon them by the unfortunate agrarian agitation and the state of affairs that prevailed in the enforcement of the payment of rent; but the squireen class that figured so largely in the pictures of Ireland drawn by Charles Lever and the storytellers of his day, and the small landed gentry had been completely wiped out of existence by the Land Acts of 1881 and 1887, which had created a peasantry permanently fixed in their holdings and in their farms, endowed with property by law, and endowed with the spirit of litigation by a beneficent nature.

To meet this state of affairs there had been instituted some years before, and there was in full swing with us, the County Court system. It was a great blessing to the country. The great thing about it was that litigation was cheap, incredibly cheap to one who lives in this country, because recent discussion would seem to imply that in order that justice may be good it should be enormously expensive. I do not subscribe to that, and in the County Courts in Ireland litigation was so cheap that the natural proclivity of a gay man to settle disputes by breaking his neighbour's head was curbed by the economy and effectiveness of bringing a County Court action instead; for a dispensary doctor, a pleasant climate and a good constitution might mend the neighbour's head for nothing, but if he swore a right of way across his farm it would blister him and his heirs for ever. A suit could be brought for £5 in the County Court for about 12s 6d. Up to £10 – which is an immense amount – a fully-blown 'counsellor' could be had for 10s 6d or a guinea; or if people were gambling extravagantly for enormous sums of £20 or upwards they would have to pay their counsel two guineas and then, whatever their County Court judge did, they had the right of appeal to the Lords Justices of Assize, one of whom would try the case over again. Of course the County Court sat at the people's doors, and witnesses were no expense, and even at the assizes these cases would be tried before men of the eminence of Christopher Palles and Fitzgibbon, as good judges as could be found anywhere, and the cases tried at a cost of less than £5 a side. I think it was a good thing that such a profession held out little chance of a man making a fortune. It attracted no man for the purpose of making money, and the attraction of a profession ought to be itself, and not its money-earning capacity, for any man fit to march in its ranks.

One thing, which even the new world and the new generation and the new class speedily learned from the old tradition, ought to be learned by every man who contemplates the law as his profession, is that the barrister is an independent officer in the administration of justice. His office and his dignity are no less than the office and dignity of the judge. He functions for a different purpose, but he contributes as much to doing right and to maintaining law and social stability as any other officer, no matter in what position in court he sits and no matter what his emoluments may or may not be; and the independence of the Bar and the appreciation of the independence of the Bar is the bedrock foundation of public confidence in the true administration of justice, and the position of the barrister is one to which any man should be proud to attain, and in the practice of which any man should be proud to spend his life even though he lived and died a poor man.

It was a peculiarity of the Irish Bar that we had no chambers and we had no clerks. The life of the Bar was a life of intimacy which I think members of the University would appreciate. Having no chambers in the High Court of Justice in Dublin, if you were long enough at the profession you might prescribe to a desk in the Law Library and when you were not actually engaged in court you sat at your desk in an immense chamber in which the walls were lined with books and all the reports and textbooks required for professional work were available. At the door was a man in a pulpit, who shouted out the name of any barrister who was summoned to the door by a solicitor to receive a brief. He dealt with the solicitor direct without the intervention of a clerk. The junior barristers, even if they were not engaged in a case, went into the courts in their wigs and gowns and spent their days in the courts learning their business – a practice which is not followed in England as much as it ought to be. For it is only in watching business being conducted and in that alone, not through books, that the practice of the law and the meaning of the law can be learned.

Life in the library was in theory absolutely demoralising. How a man could work with the incessant buzz and noise of conversation – sometimes directed to himself – might appear to be a puzzle, but somehow or other you get used to anything and your ear gets trained to shut out all sounds but the one it wants to hear, and you can carry on a conversation and write an opinion at the same time when you have practised doing this for a sufficiently long period of years. Generally you could go and work there with people reciting the latest gossip, and even speaking to yourself, without hearing a sound. But there was one sound you never missed: what John Stuart Mill might have called your enlightened self-interest always detected the sound of your own name, with the hope of a brief behind it.

Then in the County Court life was extremely intimate among the members of the Bar who followed the court from place to place. Even in the Law Library when a certain amount of dignity might be expected to attach to persons of age and title, the youngest junior called you by the same name that your oldest chum called you by, and if you had not a nickname you were called by your Christian name: but that he addressed you in any formal manner was absolutely unknown, and from end to end of the profession the terms on which we lived were terms of intimacy. Every man had to sit and listen to a criticism of himself, and he might not resent anything which was said to him whether it was half jest or wholly earnest. He knew what his profession was thinking about him, and he did not lead the Irish Bar if the Irish Bar did not choose to be led by him – a very good thing which helps a man to maintain the same constancy and size with his hat on.

The first thing for a junior to do was to attach himself to the County Court, because there the relations between the two branches of the profession were so close that a junior barrister was always given a chance to display his ability in court. It was a tradition of both branches of the profession that new juniors were to be given an opportunity of showing themselves when first they appeared at Quarter Sessions. Accordingly, if they made good they got on, and if they did not, certainly no blame attached to their colleagues at the Bar, who always were ready to give a trial to the newest recruit who joined the Quarter Sessions: a very excellent rule that developed many a good man in my day.

Of course the sort of law you got in the County Court depended on the judge, and in my early days the County Court system had taken over as a going concern a certain number of old gentlemen who had been chairmen of Quarter Sessions, and there were three or four whom I remember very well. Whenever a man got a job in Ireland, with a salary attached to it, he kept it as long as he could – no one ever resigned a salaried position; and thus it was. I remember very well that the County Court of Clare was presided over by a most charming and delightful old gentleman. He had about eighty or ninety days' work in the year, he was paid £1,600 and allowances, which made it about £1,800, he was allowed to appoint any junior relative, no matter how small and however incompetent, to be his Registrar, and he lived in France when he was not discharging his duties as a County Court judge in Clare. When I first appeared before him he was only ninety-one years old: he was quite good except for one thing; he was so short-sighted that though he could write beautifully he could not see beyond the edge of his desk, but that really did not much matter. When you go into the courts you often hear people talking about the advantage of seeing and hearing the witness. He could hear the witness, but he had not seen a witness for years. When I appeared before him, to make up for that, he had as his Registrar a Clerk of the Peace who was the Civil Officer, a gentleman who supplied his defects, because what used to happen was this. The Clerk of the Peace, whom we will call Henry, would see a friend of his in court. Henry, when I was there, had a large wastepaper basket full of apples and a jack knife which he used for peeling the apples and putting large chunks into his mouth. During a case this is what happened. Henry would say, 'That's all your Honour – fine 12s 6d, that's good enough.' The judge would say, 'A very small amount: make it £1, Henry.' Henry would say, 'Let's make it 15s, your Honour.' The Clerk of the Peace would look through the list and say, "Mr Mulcahy, why are you waiting there, what is your case?' The judge would say, 'What's that?' Henry would say, 'I said that the next case was No. 97,' but the judge would say, 'But Henry you said the last case was No. 23.' Henry, 'Yes, your Honour, but the next case is No. 97.' And Mr Mulcahy would come up and be sworn and the judge would say, 'Henry, who is this?' Henry, 'Your Honour knows him very well. He is an excellent man, your Honour, you can trust every word he says.' Then Mr Mulcahy would state his case, and Henry would say, 'Who is defending this case?' and a little gentleman would say, 'I am defending.' Henry would say, 'Who is the defendant?' 'The defendant is Peter Scanlan.' 'Sure I know that.' 'He lives at Dessart.' 'I can see that from the Civil Bill book. Is he that fellow with the slant eye.' 'Yes.' 'Tell me, is he that fellow that gave evidence about a goat at the last Assize?' 'He is.' 'Has that chap the impudence to come into this Court again? Well he can get on with it.' But he would not get off with it. All cases were conducted on a similar basis. For Henry was an excellent judge!

The County Court judge in the adjoining county was named Purcell: he had not reached the age of ninety. His peculiarity was he used to appear to be asleep all the time he was doing his business, but when some unusual form of perjury was introduced by a witness he delivered a shrill whistle. He was under the delusion that the State entitled him to be called 'My Lord': if you addressed him as 'Your Honour,' he whistled again as if he did not believe you.

The County Court judge of Tipperary, which was next to Limerick, was a gentleman named Ryan. I have never practised before him, but Lord Carson used to do so, and he told me that one day he met Ryan on a platform at Tipperary Station and said, 'Well, Judge, had you an interesting case in court today?' Now poor Judge Ryan was stone deaf. 'Eh?' he said. Carson shouted the question again.' Oh, yes, a very interesting case. I am not certain what it was about, I think it was a choral society complaining about an instrument: I suppose it was a harmonium.' The next morning Carson discovered that it was an action about the price of a Singer's sewing machine.

Well, in the county of Cork was Sir John Chute Nelligan. He had been in nine different counties and had been brought up on replies, rejoinders and bills of exception, and things of that kind which sound like antediluvian reptiles. But Nelligan was extremely careful in the way in which he discharged his duty. Always piously inclined and prefacing his judgment with the ejaculation 'God bless my soul!' he used to say, 'If I exceed my jurisdiction some man will bring an action against me.' The first thing he would be sure of was that the Civil Bill process had been served. Now of course if it was served personally on a man, Nelligan could pick no quarrel with the process server, but if it was served in any other way he used to spread himself to find out whether he had jurisdiction in this particular case and you would hear a colloquy between the Recorder and the process server, and the process server would stand up and say he had served the process on the defendant's wife and the judge would say, 'You swear that the lady is his wife.' 'I believe so.' 'But you have just sworn it.' 'Well, your Honour, it is the way she had the appearance of being his wife.' 'What appearance is that? How do you know that she was not his twin sister?' 'Sure, your Honour, he has no twin sister.' 'How do you know? Were you present at his birth?' 'I was not, your Honour, but I am sure she is his wife.' 'Well, the responsibility is on your shoulders and we will proceed.'

As the old Chairmen of the Quarter Sessions were transferred to the new courts they were allowed to continue their practice at the Bar, and Sir Francis Brady had been appointed as Crown Prosecutor of Cork while he was still holding the position of County Court judge in North Tyrone which was off my circuit. He was a charming old gentleman, and just at about the age of eighty-five or eighty-six took a new lease of life and a new wife, and for about twelve or thirteen years more he was kept in decorative order and repair. He was a great musician and used to whistle extremely well selections from the classic works and operas while he was conducting a prosecution. He was so intent on whistling them correctly that he did not always pay close attention to what was going on in court, and Henry Wright, the Crown Solicitor, would give him a nudge during the trial and he would break off in the middle of a bar to discover that it was necessary for him to examine a witness. He would rise, turn over his brief, and say, 'Your name is John Flaherty?' 'It is not, sir.' 'And you are a painter?' 'I am not, sir.' 'And you live at 19, Donovan's Quay?' 'I have never heard of the place, sir.' 'Henry, what is this man saying?' Henry would screw in his monocle and say, 'He appears to be contradicting you, sir.' Then he would start again, 'Your name is John Flaherty?' 'It is not, sir.' 'And you are a painter?' 'I have never had a painter in my family. I drive a car.' 'I must ask your Lordship's permission to cross-examine this witness.' His Lordship would observe that this gentleman when sworn had said that his name was Peter Riley. Then Sir Francis would say, 'Oh, I have turned over two pages, my lord.'

Criminals, of course, had to be tried by jury and at the Quarter Sessions, and in some courts it was absolutely unheard of that any criminal was convicted by these juries, because whatever the evidence might be, a Limerick court would acquit anybody. In acquitting a man of stabbing in spite of the evidence, on one occasion, the judge, Adams, stood up, and pointing to the jury on his left said: 'These twelve gentlemen on my left say you are not guilty, so I have to discharge you, and I would invite you, Michael, to take a good look at them so that you will know them afterwards, because I will promise you this: if you treat any one of them as you have treated the prosecutor in this case, you will not receive one day's imprisonment from me even if you are convicted of it.'

I was present at a trial in Kerry when there were two ladies put into the dock charged with stealing the wallet of a cattle dealer, and it was an extremely hot day, and one member of the jury was a very stout red-faced gentleman, and as I looked at him this round red face of his began to set, like the sun before a storm; it went down slowly and gradually behind the edge of the jury box. Apparently he found comfortable quarters under the jurors' bench. As no more was seen of him the other eleven went out and acquitted the prisoners as usual. Right in the middle of the next case the sun rose again, and this worthy pushed up his face and sat on the knees of two gentlemen behind him, and the puzzled expression on his face was delightful. He could not co-ordinate what he heard with the evidence he had been listening to before he went to sleep, and it did not strike him that it was a different case. Then he took his hat and shook it violently at the judge. 'My Lord, I want to speak.' 'Be quiet.' 'But I have not spoken yet.' 'Well, what do you want to say?' 'My Lord, I want to let the girls go and give the boy back his money.' The judge could not make out what he was talking about, and when eventually he appealed to the Clerk of the Crown, he had also been asleep, and he thought it was a wise and excellent suggestion. He did not at first see what the trouble was about, but the prisoners were fetched back and the word 'not' was struck out of the sentence and the girls were imprisoned. Then they proceeded with the next case. . . .

The division of the country meant the end of the old Irish Bar. There were set up in Ireland two totally different systems of law and administration, and it was to one whose heart and soul were buried in the practice of his profession a great loss and a great misery. The recollection of the old time is very very acute with me, and I hope the recounting of the memories of the past has not been altogether uninteresting to you.

A Day in My Life in the County Court

We take no note of time
But from its loss.
                    Young's *Night Thoughts*

[Judge Parry spent nearly twenty years, at the turn of the century, as the judge sitting at Manchester County Court. He had been struck by how much the public image of the law in action was derived simply from the cases reported in the High Court. He was concerned that too little of the life of the community, as reflected in the daily work of the county court judge, was known to outsiders. The daily parade of the judgment debtors summoned for non-payment of their commercial debts, the small bankruptcies, the everyday problems of neighbours, of landlords and their tenants – all had an immediate bearing upon the social welfare of the mass of the community. Little – far too little – attention had been directed to the County Courts, where a mass of the humdrum disputes and social problems are handled, sometimes sympathetically and sometimes simply with dispatch.

Judge Parry's reflections on his work are taken from pages 52 to 74 in *Judgments in Vacation* by E. A. Parry, published by Smith, Elder & Co. in 1911.]

... [53] THE PRACTICE IN Manchester is to have special days for the bigger class of cases, and to try to give clear days for the smaller matters where most of the parties appear in person. The former are printed in red on the Court Calendar, and the latter in black, and locally the days are known as red-letter days and black-letter days. On a black-letter day counsel and solicitors indeed often appear – for it is a practical impossibility to sort out the cases into two exact classes – but the professions know that on a black-letter day they have no precedence, and very cheerfully acquiesce in the arrangement, since it is obvious that to the community at large it is at least as important that a working woman should be home in time to give her children their dinner as that a solicitor should return to his office or a barrister lunch at his club.

Let me try, then, to bring home to your mind what happens on a black-letter day.

We are early risers in Manchester, and the court sits at ten. I used to get down to my court about twenty minutes earlier, as on a black-letter day there are sure to be several letters from debtors who are unable to be at court, and these are always addressed to me personally. Having disposed of the correspondence there is generally an 'application in chambers' consisting of one or more widows whose compensation under the Workmen's Compensation Act remains in court to be dealt with for their benefit. [54] [56] You will see groups of women making their way down to the court, many with a baby in one arm and a door key slung on the finger. The wife is the solicitor and the advocate of the working-class household, and very cleverly she does her work as a rule. The group of substantial-looking men chatting in the street are debt-collecting agents and travelling drapers discussing the state of trade. These are the Plaintiffs and their representatives, the women are the Defendants. Here and there you will see a well-dressed lady, probably summoned to the Court by a servant or a dressmaker. There will always be a few miscellaneous cases, but the trivial round and common task of the day is collecting the debts of small tradesmen from the working class.

I have no doubt that a County Court Judge gets an exaggerated view of the evils of the indiscriminate credit given to the poor. They seem to paddle all their lives ankle-deep in debt, and never get a chance of walking the clean parapet of solvency. But that is because one sees only the seamy side of the debt-collecting world, and knows nothing of the folk who pay without process. At the same time, that indiscriminate credit-giving as practised in Manchester is an evil, no one, I think, can doubt, and it seems strange that social reformers pay so little attention to the matter.

The whole thing turns, of course, upon imprisonment for debt. Without imprisonment for debt there would be little credit given, except to persons of good character, and good character would be an asset. As it is, however, our first business in the morning will be to hear a hundred judgment summonses in which creditors are seeking to imprison their debtors. There are some ten thousand judgment summonses in Manchester and Salford in a year, but they have to be personally served, and not nearly that number come for trial. We start with a hundred this morning, of which say sixty are served. It is well to sit punctually, and we will start on the stroke of ten.

A debt collector enters the Plaintiff's box, and, refreshing his memory from a note-book, tells you what the Defendant's position is, where he works, and what he earns. The minute book before you tells you the amount of his debt, that he has been ordered to pay 2s a month, and has not paid anything for six months. His wife now enters into all the troubles of her household, and makes the worst of them. One tries to sift the true from the false, the result being that one is generally convinced that the Defendant has had means to pay the 2s a month, or whatever the amount may be, since the date when the order was made. The law demands that the debtor should be imprisoned for not having paid, but no one wants him to go to prison, so an order is made of seven or fourteen days, and it is suspended, and is not to issue if he pays the arrears and fees, say in three monthly instalments. The wife is satisfied that the evil day is put off and goes away home, and the creditor generally gets his money. He may have to issue a warrant, but the Defendant generally manages to pay by hook or by crook, rather than go to Knutsford Gaol, where the debtors are imprisoned, and as a matter of fact only a few actually go to gaol. Of course, the money is often borrowed or paid by friends, which is another evil of the system. The matter is more difficult when, as often happens, the Defendants do not appear. It is extraordinary how few people can read and understand a comparatively simple legal notice or summons. Mistakes are constantly made. A collier once brought me an official schedule of his creditors, in which in the column for 'description', where he should have entered 'grocer', 'butcher', etc., he had filled in the best literary description he could achieve of his different creditors, and one figured as 'little lame man with sandy whiskers'. There are of course many illiterates, and they have to call in the assistance of a 'scholard'. An amusing old gentleman came before me once, who was very much perturbed to know if, to use his own phrase, he was 'entaitled to pay this 'ere debt'. The incident occurred at a time when the citizens of Manchester were being polled to vote on a 'culvert scheme' of drainage, which excited much popular interest.

'I don't deny owing the debt,' he said, 'and I'll pay reet enow, what your Honour thinks reet, if I'm entaitled to pay.'

I suggested that if he owed the money he was clearly 'entitled' to pay.

'Well,' he continued, 'I thowt as I should 'ave a summons first.'

'But you must have had a summons,' I said, 'or how did you get here?'

''E towd me case wor on,' he said, pointing to the Plaintiff, 'so I coom.'

I looked up matters and discovered that service of the summons was duly reported, and informed the Defendant, who seemed much relieved.

'You see,' he said, 'I'm no scholard, and we got a paaper left at our 'ouse, and I took it up to Bill Thomas in our street, a mon as con read, an' 'e looks at it, an' says as 'ow may be it's a coolvert paaper. "I'm not certain," 'e says, "but I think it's a coolvert paaper." So I asks him what to do wi' it, and he says, "Put a cross on it, and put it in a pillar box," and that wor done. But if you say it wor a summons, Bill must a bin wrong.'

One can gather something from this poor fellow's difficulties of the trouble that a summons of any kind must cause in a domestic household, and one can only hope for the day when England will follow the example of other civilised countries and at least do away with the judgment summons and imprisonment for debt.*

The hundred judgment summonses will have taken us until about eleven o'clock, and meanwhile in an adjoining court the Registrar has been dealing with a list of about four hundred cases. The bulk of these are undefended, and the Registrar enters up judgment and makes orders against the Defendant to pay the debt by instalments, at so much a month. A small percentage – say from five to ten per cent. of the cases – are sent across to the Judge's court for trial, and small knots of folk come into court to take the seats vacated by the judgment debtors and wait for the trials to come on.

* A committee under the chairmanship of Mr Justice Payne is at present sitting to consider the law relating to the enforcement of judgments.

The trial of a County Court action on a black-letter day, where Plaintiff and Defendant appear in person, where neither understands law, evidence, or procedure, and where the main object of each party is to overwhelm his opponent by a reckless fire of irrelevant statements, is not easy to conduct with suavity and dignity. The chief object of a County Court Judge, as it seems to me – I speak from many years' experience – should be to suffer fools gladly without betraying any suspicion that he considers himself wise. Ninety-nine per cent. of the cases are like recurring decimals. They have happened, and will happen again and again. The same defence is raised under the same circumstances. To the shallow-witted Defendant it is an inspiration of mendacity, to the Judge it is a commonplace and expected deceit. All prisoners in a Police Court who are found with stolen goods upon them tell you that they have bought them from a man whose name they do not know. There is no copyright in such a defence, and it sounds satisfactory to each succeeding publisher of it. No doubt it is disappointing to find that the judge and jury have heard it before and are not disposed to believe it. In the same way in the County Court there are certain lines of defence that I feel sure students of folk-lore could tell us were put forward beneath the oak trees when the Druids sat in County Courts in prehistoric times. The serious difficulty lies in continuing to believe that a Defendant may arise who actually has a defence, and in discovering and rescuing a specimen of a properly defended action from a crowded museum of antique mendacities. Counter-claims, for instance, which of course are only filed in the bigger cases, are very largely imaginative. The betting against a valid counter-claim must be at least ten to one. It is, of course, in finding the one that there is scope for ingenuity. It is the necessity for constant alertness that makes the work interesting.

The women are the best advocates. Here, for instance, is a case in point.

A woman Plaintiff with a shawl over her head comes into the box, and an elderly collier, the Defendant, is opposite to her. The action is brought for nine shillings. I ask her to state her case.

'I lent yon mon's missus my mon's Sunday trousers to pay 'is rent, an' I want 'em back.'

That seems to me, as a matter of pleading, as crisp and sound as can be. If the trousers had been worth five hundred pounds, a barrister would have printed several pages of statement of claim over them, but could not have stated his case better. My sympathies are with the lady. I know well the kindness of the poor to each other, and, won by the businesslike statement of the case, I turn round to the Defendant and ask him why the trousers are not returned and what his defence may be.

He smiles and shakes his head. He is a rough, stupid fellow, and something amuses him. I ask him to stop chuckling and tell me his defence.

'There's nowt in it all,' is his answer.

I point out that this is vague and unsatisfactory, and that the words do not embody any defence to an action of detinue known to the law.

He is not disturbed. The lady gazes at him triumphantly. He is a slow man, and casually mentions 'The 'ole street knows about them trousers.'

I point out to him that I have never lived in the street, and know nothing about it. He seems to disbelieve this and says with a chuckle. 'Everyone knows about them trousers.'

I press him to tell me the story, but he can scarcely believe that I do not know all about it. At length he satisfies my curiosity.

'Why yon woman an' my missus drank them trousers.'

The woman vociferates, desires to be struck dead and continues to live, but bit by bit the story is got at. Two ladies pawn the husband's trousers, and quench an afternoon's thirst with the proceeds. The owner of the Sunday trousers is told by his wife a story of destitution and want of rent, and the generous loan of garments. Everyone in the street but the husband enjoys the joke. The indignant husband, believing in his wife, sues for the trousers and sends his wife to court. The street comes down to see the fun, and when I decide for the Defendant there is an uprising of men, women, and babies, and the parties and their friends disappear while we call the next case. These are the little matters where it is easy to make a blunder, and where patience and attention and a knowledge of the ways and customs of the 'ole street' are worth much legal learning.

One must learn to sympathise with domestic frailties. I was rebuking a man, the other day, for backing up his wife in what was not only an absurd story, but one in which I could see he had no belief.

'You should really be more careful,' I said, 'and I tell you candidly I don't believe a word of your wife's story.'

'You may do as yer like,' he said, mournfully, 'but I've got to.'

The sigh of envy at the comparative freedom of my position as compared with his own was full of pathos.

A case of a workman who was being sued for lodging money gave me a new insight into the point of view of the clever but dissipated workman. His late landlady was suing for arrears run up when, as she said, he was 'out of work'.

The phrase made him very angry.

'Look 'ere,' he said, 'can that wumman kiss the book agen? She's swearin' false. I've never been out o' wark i' my life. Never.'

'Tummas,' says the old lady, in a soothingly irritating voice. 'Think, Tummas.'

'Never been out o' wark i' my life,' he shouts.

'Oh, Tummas,' says the old lady, more in sorrow than in anger. 'You remember Queen's funeral. You were on the spree a whole fortneet.'

'Oh, ay!' says Thomas unabashed; 'but you said out o' wark. If you're sayin' on the spree I'm with yer, but I've never been out o' wark i' my life.'

It was a sad distinction for a clever working man to make, but a true one and to him an important one, and I rather fancy the nice old lady knew well what she was doing in her choice of phrase and hoped to score off Thomas by irritating him into an unseemly exhibition by the use of it.

A class of case that becomes very familiar arises out of the sale of a small business. A fried-fish shop is regarded by an enterprising widow who does not possess one as a mine of untold gold. She purchases one at a price above its value, fails from want of knowledge to conduct it successfully, and then brings an action for fraudulent misrepresentation against the seller. Of course, there are cases of fraud and misrepresentation; but, as a rule there is nothing more than the natural optimistic statements of a seller followed by incompetence of the purchaser and the disgust of old customers. In a case of this sort, in which up to a point it was difficult to know where the truth lay, owing to the vague nature of the evidence, a graphic butcher gave a convincing account of the reason of the failure of the new management. He had come down to the court in the interests of justice, leaving the abattoir – or as he called it 'habbitoyre' – on his busiest morning.

'Yer see,' he said, 'I knew the old shop well. I was in the 'abit of takin' in a crowd of my pals on Saturday neet. So when the old Missus gave it up, I promised to give it a try wi' the new Missus. Well, I went in twice, an' there wor no sort o' choice at all. There worn't no penny fish, what there wor, wor 'a-penny fish, and bad at that, an' the chips wor putty.'

It was obvious that the Plaintiff had started on a career for which Nature did not intend her, and that the cause of the failure of the business was not the fraud of the Defendant, but the culinary incompetence of the Plaintiff.

It is amazing how, apart altogether from perjury, two witnesses will give entirely different accounts of the same matter. No doubt there is a great deal of reckless evidence given and some perjury committed, but a great deal of the contradictory swearing arises from 'natural causes', as it were. A man is very ready to take sides, and discusses the facts of a case with his friend until he remembers more than he ever saw. In 'running down' cases, where the witnesses are often independent folk and give their own evidence their own way, widely different testimony is given about the same event. One curious circumstance I have noticed in 'running down' cases is that a large percentage of witnesses give evidence against the vehicle coming towards them. That is to say, if a man is walking along, and a brougham is in front of him and going the same way as he is, and a cab coming in the opposite direction collides with the brougham, I should expect that man to give evidence against the cab. I suppose the reason of that is that to a man so situated the brougham appears stationary and the cab aggressively dangerous, but whatever the reason may be the fact is very noticeable.

On the whole the uneducated man in the street is a better witness of outdoor facts than the clerk or warehouseman. The outdoor workers have, I fancy, a more retentive memory for things seen, and are more observant than the indoor workers. They do not want to refresh their memory with notes.

A story is told of a blacksmith who came to the farriery classes

held by the Manchester Education authorities. The clerk in charge
gave him a notebook and a pencil.

'Wot's this 'ere for?' asks the blacksmith.

'To take notes,' replied the clerk.

'Notes? Wot sort o' notes?'

'Why, anything that the lecturer says which you think important and want to remember, you make a note of it,' said the clerk.

'Oh,' was the scornful reply, 'anything I want to remember I
must make a note of in this 'ere book, must I? Then wot do you
think my blooming yed's for?'

It is the use and exercise of the 'blooming yed' that makes the
Lancashire workman the strong character he is. May it be long
before the mother wit inside it is dulled by the undue use of the
scholastic notebook.

Witnesses are often discursive, and the greatest ingenuity is
devoted to keeping them to the point without breaking the thread
of their discourse. Only long practice and a certain instinct which
comes from having undergone many weary hours of listening can
give you the knack of getting the pith and marrow of a witness's
story without the domestic and genealogical details with which he
– and especially she – desires to garnish it.

I remember soon after I took my seat on the bench having an
amusing dialogue with a collier. He had been sued for twelve
shillings for three weeks' rent. One week he admitted, and the
week in lieu of notice, which leads to more friction between
landlord and tenant than any other incident in their contract, was
duly wrangled over and decided upon. Then came the third week,
and the collier proudly handed in four years' rent books to show
nothing else was owing. The landlord's agent pointed out that
two years back a week's rent was missing, and sure enough in the
rent book was the usual cross instead of a four, showing that no
rent had been paid for that week.

'How did that week come to be missed?' I asked the collier.

'I'll never pay that week,' he said, shaking his head stubbornly.
'Not laikely.'

'But,' I said, 'I'm afraid you'll have to. You see you admit it's
owing.'

'Well, I'll just tell yer 'ow it was. You see we wor 'aving rabbit
for supper, an' my wife –'

He looked as if he was settling down for a long yarn, so I interposed: 'Never mind about the rabbit, tell me about the rent.'

'I'm telling yer. Yer see we wor 'aving rabbit for supper, an' my wife 'ad got a noo kettle, an' we don't 'ave rabbit every –'

'Oh, come, come,' I said impatiently, 'just tell me about the rent.'

He looked at me rather contemptuously, and began again at the very beginning.

'I'm telling yer, if yer'll only listen. We wor 'aving rabbit for supper, an' my wife 'ad got a noo kettle, an' we don't 'ave rabbit every neet for supper, an' my wife 'ad just put the kettle, the noo kettle –'

'Oh, never mind about the kettle, do please get to the rent,' I said, and was immediately sorry I had spoken.

'I'm getting to it, ain't I?' he asked, rather angrily. 'We wor 'aving rabbit for supper' – I groaned inwardly and resolved to sit it out without another word – 'an' my wife 'ad got a noo kettle, an' we don't 'ave rabbit every neet for supper, an' my wife 'ad just put the kettle – the noo kettle with the rabbit – on to th' fire, when down coom chimley an' aw into middle o' room. Was I going to pay rent for that week? Not laikely!'

It turned out that I was wholly in the wrong, and that the destruction of the rabbit was a kind of equitable plea in defence to the action for rent. When I am tempted now to burst in too soon upon an irrelevant story, I think of the rabbit and am patient. Of course all rabbit stories are not even equitable defences, but the diagnosis of what is purely domestic and dilatory and of what is apparently anecdotal but in reality relevant gives a distinct charm to one's daily work.

One day of my life every month is given up to the trial of Yiddish cases. The Yiddisher is a litigious person, and his best friend would not describe him as a very accurate witness. One ought to remember, however, that he has not had generations of justice administered to him, that he is a child and beginner in a court of law, and that the idea of a judge listening to his story and deciding for him upon the evidence is, in some cases from personal experience and in all cases from hereditary instinct, an utterly unfamiliar thing. The fact, too, that he speaks Yiddish, or very broken English, and never answers a question except by asking another, always gives his evidence an indirect flavour. One strong point about a Yiddisher is his family affection, and he swears in tribes, so to speak. A Christian in a family dispute will too often swear anything against his brother, and is often wickedly reckless in his sworn aspersions. A Yiddisher, on the other hand, will swear anything for his brother, and most Yiddish evidence could be discounted by an accurate percentage according to the exact relationship by blood or marriage of the witness to the Plaintiff or Defendant.

It is needless to say a foreign-speaking race such as this gives one some anxiety and trouble in a small-debt court. One of my earliest Yiddish experiences was a case in which two Yiddishers each brought his own interpreter. A small scrap of paper cropped up in the case with some Hebrew writing on it. One interpreter swore it was a receipt, the other that it was an order for a new pair of boots. Without knowing anything of Hebrew, it occurred to me that these divergent readings were improbable. The case was adjourned. I applied to some of my friends on that excellent body, the Jewish Board of Guardians, a respectable interpreter was obtained, and the Hebrew document properly translated. There is now an official interpreter attached to the Manchester Court, and I think I can safely congratulate the Yiddish community on a distinct improvement in their education in the proper use of English law courts.

That some of them have the very vaguest notions of the principles on which we administer justice may be seen from the following story which happened some years ago. A little flashy Yiddish jeweller, who spoke very bad English, had taken out a judgment summons against an old man who appeared broken down in health and pocket. I asked the little man for evidence of means which would justify me in committing the debtor to prison.

'Vell,' he says, 'I vill tell you. He ish in a very larsh vay of pizness indeed. He has zree daughters working for him and several hands as vell, and zare is a great deal of monish coming into ze house.'

The old man told a sad story of ill health, loss of business, and said that his daughters had to keep him. It turned out that there was a Yiddish gentleman in court, Mr X, who knew him, and Mr X corroborated the defendant's story in every particular. He had had a good business, but was now being kept by his daughters, having broken down in health.

I turned to the little jeweller and said: 'You have made a mistake here.'

'It ish no mishtake at all,' he cried excitedly. 'Mr X ish a very bad man. He and the Defendant are both cap makers, and are vot you call in English a long firm.'

This was too much for Mr X – a most respectable tradesman – and he called out: 'My Lorts, may I speak?' Without waiting for leave, he continued very solemnly: 'My Lorts, I have sworn by Jehovah that every vord I say ish true, but I will go furder than that. I vill put down ten pounds in cash, and it may be taken avay from me if vot I say ish not true.'

The offer was made with such fervour and sincerity that I thought it best to enter into the spirit of the thing.

Turning to the little man, I asked: 'Are you ready to put down ten pounds that what you say is true?'

He looked blank and lost, and, shaking his head, murmured sadly, 'No, it ish too motch.'

I pointed out to him how his attitude about the ten pounds went to confirm the evidence for the Defendant, and seeing his case slipping away from under his feet, he cried out, as if catching at the last straw, 'My Lorts thish ish not mine own case, thish ish mine farder's case, and I vill put down ten pounds of mine farder's monish that vot I say ish true.'

The offer was not accepted, and the Defendant was not committed. But the story throws light on the rudimentary ideas that some Yiddishers have of the administration of justice.

And now we have finished the list of cases, but there are a few stragglers left in court. Some of them have been in the wrong court, or come on the wrong day; some have applications to make, or advice to ask. I always make a point now of finding out what these folk want before leaving the bench. I remember in my early days a man coming before me the first thing one morning, and saying he had sat in my court until the end of yesterday's proceedings.

'Why didn't you come up at the end of the day,' I asked, 'and make your application then?'

'I was coming,' he replied, 'but at the end of last case you was

off your chair an' bolted through yon door like a rabbit.' I think
his description was exaggerated, but I rise in a more leisurely way
nowadays, though I am still glad when the day's work is over.

I do not know that what I have written will convey any clear
idea of the day of my life that I have been asked to portray. I
know it is in many respects a very dull grey life, but it has its
brighter moments in the possibilities of usefulness to others. I
am not at all sure that the black-letter jurisdiction of a big urban
County Court ought not to be worked by a parish priest rather
than by a lawyer. I know that it wants a patience, a sympathy,
and a belief in the goodness of human nature that we find in
those rare characters who give up the good things in this world
for the sake of working for others. I am very conscious of my
own imperfections; but I was once greatly encouraged by a
criticism passed upon me which I accidentally overheard, and
which I am conceited enough to repeat. I was going away from
the court, and passed two men walking slowly away. I had
decided against them, and they were discussing why I had
done so.

'Well, 'ow on earth 'e could do it I don't see, do you, Bill?'
''E's a fool.'
'Yes, 'e's a fool, a — fool, but 'e did 'is best.'
'Ay. I think 'e did 'is best.'

After all, coming from such source or indeed from any source,
the suggestion contained in the conversation was very gratifying.
I have often thought that one might rest beneath an unkinder
epitaph than this:

HE WAS

A —— FOOL,

BUT

HE DID HIS BEST.

Some Aspects of the Work of The Court of Appeal*

I HAVE CHOSEN this theme partly because much of the raw material necessary for its treatment is wafted to me unsought, as a by-product of professional routine: but partly also because the subject itself is so very unevenly explored. I know of no treatise dealing comprehensively with the functions of the English Court of Appeal. If such a thing exists, I would bless anyone who would bring it to my notice: it is always refreshing to discover what one's functions are. There is of course much diffused information. There are the debates in Parliament when the Judicature Acts of the 1870's were in the crucible. There are decisions of the Court itself and of the House of Lords. There are penetrating articles in learned reviews, dealing with patches of the subject. Nor will those who heard or have read the address on this subject of the present Master of the Rolls† to students of London University, while appreciating its happy amalgam of wit and erudition, fail to deplore its brevity. Again there is the bleak, bloodless outline contained in Order 58 of the Orders of the Supreme Court. This is quite admirable for its appointed purpose. But it no more gives, nor pretends to give, a picture of the working of the Court, than an ordnance survey map gives a picture of the English countryside. My copy of Salmond's *Jurisprudence* devotes two pages to the Court of Appeal – Holdsworth, perhaps six. The late Mr Theobald Mathew – *clarum et venerabile nomen* – with his inimitable gift of condensation, has summarised once and for all the functions of a judge of first instance. He should be 'quick, courteous and wrong'. '*Wrong*', because otherwise there would

---

* Address delivered before the Society of Public Teachers of Law at its Annual Meeting on Saturday 15 July 1950, in The Law Society's Hall, Chancery Lane when the author, then Lord Justice Asquith, was a member of the Court of Appeal.

† Sir Raymond Evershed.

be nothing left for the Court of Appeal to do. I wish Mr Mathew could have found time to embalm the functions of a judge of the Court of Appeal in some equally compact formula. Do not let us, however, jump to the conclusion that a Lord Justice should be 'quick, courteous and right'. This would run counter to Mr Mathew's own principle since no work would then be left for the House of Lords. The Lords of Appeal in Ordinary must not lightly be defrauded of their statutory prey.

One reason for the nakedness of the land – the dearth of systematised learning in this field – is no doubt that the Court of Appeal is too young to have attracted a literature of its own. It is an upstart – a creature of statute and of recent statute, for the Acts of Parliament of the 1870's are mere striplings. It lacks pride of ancestry. It cannot trace its pedigree, as the King's Bench Division somewhat deviously contrives to do, to Plantagenet sources: nor even to either of the old Exchequer Chambers, courts of respectable antiquity. Indeed the Court of Appeal, framed by two great Equity lawyers, was not even modelled on the Exchequer Chamber as recast in 1830, but on a different nineteenth-century institution – the Chancery Court of Appeal: from which indeed it drew its first and amongst its most distinguished incumbents. We all know the early history of the Court of Appeal: a story of great expectations defeated. How it was projected by the 1873 Act as the upper division of a court of judicature which would be 'Supreme' in fact as well as in name, destined to absorb the appellate jurisdiction both of the House of Lords and of the Judicial Committee of the Privy Council. How these bodies were, largely owing to the objection of Scottish and Irish members of the House of Lords, reprieved by the Act of 1875; and finally how by the Appellate Jurisdiction Act 1876, the House of Lords was reinstated and reinforced with two Lords of Appeal in Ordinary. From this familiar tale there hangs a less familiar pendant. It was apparently realised that the new Court of Appeal was being emasculated in its cot; and a solatium was devised, which operated in relief not only of the Court of Appeal but of the High Court. More resonant titles were conferred on their judicial officers. By the 1873 Act – or was it by the Judicature Commission? One or the other – the judicial officers of the High Court had been designated simply 'Justices', and those of the Court of Appeal simply 'Judges': by supplementary and consolatory provisions the 'Justices' broadened down into 'Judges' of the High Court, and the Judges of the Court of Appeal into 'Lords Justices of Appeal'.

Yes, the story of the Court of Appeal's early demission from the exalted role originally assigned to it has often been told. But information is far harder to come by in any coherent form of the subsequent history, development and practical working of this truncated entity. Indeed the philosophic theory of appellate jurisdiction itself has developed at a slow tempo. For instance it was not until the 1930's that the principles were deliberately reviewed and marshalled which an appellate court should apply in dealing with three important classes of appeals:

(a) appeals on quantum of damages only;
(b) appeals on questions of fact from a judge sitting alone;
(c) appeals from a judge in chambers exercising a judicial discretion.

Nor in regard to the problem of the binding character of precedents can our most august appellate court be charged with precipitancy. If the Court of Appeal, born yesterday, did not frame a comprehensive theory as to the operation of its own previous decisions until 1944, it can console itself with the reflection that the House of Lords, which was sitting as a supreme Court of Error as far back as the fourteenth century, did not perform a roughly corresponding operation till nearly the end of the nineteenth (1898).

But enough of prolegomena. The object of this paper is twofold. First, I would like, so far as decorum permits, to expose some of the actual machinery of the Court of Appeal as it functions *de die in diem* behind its uninformative façade: in other words to invest the skeleton of O.58 with a modicum of flesh and blood. I cannot do this without drawing largely on my own personal experience and I apologise in advance if this imparts – as to some extent it must – an egotistical complexion to what I say.

Secondly, I would like to consider one or two tough impersonal problems which confront the court: in particular – some of the puzzles which the theory of precedents involves in and for any appellate body consisting, as our appellate courts do, of several members.

May I begin by noting, as one who passed to the Court of Appeal after some eight years in the King's Bench Division, some of the contrasts – the very vivid contrasts – subsisting between these two spheres? These contrasts relate first to the nature of the work – its character, range and severity; secondly to the setting and atmosphere in which that work is done; and thirdly, to the technique ruling in regard to work in each sphere.

(1) *The nature of the work*

In the King's Bench Division, not much less than half of a judge's time is (or was when I was there) given to crime, either at the Assizes, or at the Old Bailey or in the Court of Criminal Appeal. The judge accumulates a certain silt of criminal experience in these courts. That deposit whether shallow or deep is of course wholly wasted when he arrives in the Court of Appeal, a purely civil tribunal. Of the King's Bench Division civil work more than half then consisted (and I think still consists) of personal injury cases, usually 'running down'. These of course furnished and still furnish a quota of appeals; but it is the merest fraction of appeals as a whole. So most of his civil experience viewed as a possible qualification or training for appellate work is wasted also. In the result, the great bulk of the appellate work must of necessity be new to him. The new work concerns branches of the law which he has either never encountered, or with which at best he contracted a nodding acquaintance when doing his Bar exams, an acquaintance which he perhaps hoped would not ripen into closer intimacy.

Just consider the variety and range of appeals to the Court of Appeal. Such appeals include (I take them in haphazard order):

(a) Revenue appeals. Revenue law is a world of its own, vast, self-contained, new to most judges, forbidding in proportion to its novelty.

(b) Probate appeals, trailing in their wake an unfamiliar jargon about 'scripts', the 'substance of the case' – and what not.

(c) Admiralty appeals; of which it has been justly said that there are enough of them to make one feel at sea, but not enough to enable one to find one's sea legs.

(d) Divorce appeals. Divorce is a subject of which, as regards mainly undefended cases, puisne judges who have been on circuit know something; but hardly enough for appellate work.

(e) Chancery appeals. Of these I will say nothing. My heart is too full. In time, conceivably, my feelings towards them may 'mellow into indifference'.*

(f) Patent and trade mark appeals.

(g) Perhaps worst: Rent Restriction Act appeals, again a complete, but hardly a brave, new world – though I feel for the Rent Restriction Acts the reluctant respect one feels for an old tough sparring partner whom one has never been able to knock out.

It follows from what has been said that the neophyte in the Court of Appeal is compelled, at an age when his intellectual arteries are beginning to harden, to go back to school: to get up new branches of the law; to brush up many which he has forgotten: and to do all this 'ambulando'. I mean while he is notionally already trying appeals on the false assumption that he has completed the process of self-education or re-education. I say 'notionally', for in practice the situation is eased and lubricated by common sense: which prescribes an appropriate composition for any division of the Court which has to deal with appeals of a particular type. In dealing with Chancery appeals the majority of the Court, including as a rule its president, will be Chancery men, and correspondingly all along the line in any specialised field.

Before leaving this branch of the comparison – that which concerns the nature of the work – I would like to add something which, while not commonly realised, accords with the views of most of my colleagues who have reached the Court of Appeal via the mill of the King's Bench Division. When we sat at the Assizes, as we often did, till six and seven in the evening and worked Saturdays, we all thought this hard work at the time. We agree now, nevertheless, that work in the Court of Appeal is about 50 per cent. more exacting – indeed in the case of the presiding Lord Justice, who gives the leading judgments, back-breaking, and in the case

* Mr. Birrell's phrase. He hoped (somewhere in *Obiter Dicta*) that his feelings towards the works of (I think) Hannah More, would undergo this mollificative process.

of the Master of the Rolls, who presides over the whole machine and has a dozen other irons in the fire, herculean. Lord Bowen, when still Bowen, J., in 1886, in an article in the second volume of the *Law Quarterly Review*, which is extremely interesting in the light of what has happened since, says much the same thing in relation to the work of the Court of Appeal as it existed at that time.

(2) *Setting and atmosphere*

The personal atmosphere of the Court of Appeal today is instinct with comity and friendliness. One's colleagues are such nice and accomplished men that it is almost a pleasure to be dissented from by them. But the intellectual climate is severe. More particularly to one accustomed to browse in the lowlands of the King's Bench Division and to inhale its crass air, is the intellectual atmosphere of the Court of Appeal, one of extreme, of almost Himalayan, rarefaction. One would hardly be surprised if an 'abominable snowman' entered the Court and applied for security for costs or a stay of execution.

The general setting of the Court is sober, drained of colour, and devoid of excitement, contrasting in this regard with the high pomps of circuit. When I say 'devoid of excitement', I do not forget that the Court was once pelted with tomatoes by a frustrated appellant: but one cannot bank on the recurrence of a colourful incident like this, and must resign oneself to the prevalence, as a rule, of a drab dignity. No red robes, no javelin men or trumpeters. no cathedral services, no Rolls-Royce provided by a thoughtful and lavish High Sheriff, no fuss or drama, no headlines (though of course no good judge will either provoke or miss those last), plain black robes, grinding work and no circuit allowance!

(3) *Technique*

The technique of the Court of Appeal is wholly different – as that of any court consisting of three or more judges must necessarily be – from the technique of a court of first instance where a judge sits alone. It is as though a man accustomed to solitary exercise were relegated to an unending three-legged race – (logically a *four*-legged race, since three runners are involved). What a puisne judge feels, on first being appointed such, is his solitude, and he feels it acutely. The give and take, or, to give it a grand name, the 'cross-fertilisation of minds' which a barrister's chambers afforded, is gone. No one to consult, immediate decisions to be taken (e.g. rulings on objections to the admissibility of a question to a witness), no possibility of sharing, spreading and thus lightening his responsibilities or of picking any brain but his own. In the Court of Appeal, all this is reversed. Sharing, pooling, communication and consultation are the life blood of the Court. At first the change of gear is difficult; indeed it is more than a change of gear, it is putting the engines in reverse. Mutual dependence supplants a hard-earned, carefully cultivated self-sufficiency. One of the greatest difficulties (if I may recur to the metaphor of the four-legged race) is for each member of the Court to keep in step with the other two. A judge of first instance, sitting alone, can adjust the tempo of the proceedings to his own rate of intake, and indeed to his own standard of hearing. If he fails to hear or to understand something, he can say 'stop'; 'repeat'; 'elucidate'. But when he is sitting with two others as an appellate judge, particularly if the other two are (as my companions have invariably been), quicker witted than himself, he feels a good deal of delicacy about halting the proceedings, when that means reducing the pace of the whole convoy to that of its slowest ship. But if he does not, he may drop an essential stitch and never pick it up again.

The curious thing is how hitchlessly, notwithstanding this and many similar difficulties I could mention, the system on the whole works. Dissent in particular is far less common than I at least had anticipated. In four years and a half for instance, I think I myself have only given three minority judgments; and I am sure my conformity has not been due to mere sloth. In the great majority of cases the three minds, after a period of oscillation and fluctuation while material is being fed into them and argument is proceeding, settle down into a parallel course and advance smoothly to a common conclusion.

Consultation, as I have indicated, is as imperative in appellate work as it is, generally speaking, impossible in work of first instance. But in appellate work, it is often conducted under many handicaps. The three put their heads together – in a purely geographical as well as a metaphorical sense (I have known the physical impact of skull on skull) – they put their heads together to see if they can agree whether the respondent is to be called on, or whether judgment should be reserved or given forthwith, or, in the latter case, on what lines it should proceed. But the colloquy is embarrassed, hurried, furtive and transacted in an exchange of stage whispers which the whisperers hope rather than believe will not be overheard in counsel's front row. It is possible that better results might be obtained by more frequent adjournments before delivering unreserved judgments, or by reserving judgment oftener. Probably three-quarters of the judgments of the Court of Appeal are given *ex tempore*. I believe all – certainly the vast majority – of those of the House of Lords are reserved. No doubt the Court of Appeal, which is a final court of appeal for over 90 per cent. of the cases which come before it, would have reserved many more judgments in the last few years if it had not been engaged in a ceaseless battle against time and arrears. This battle is for the time being won. I say 'for the time being' advisedly. The pressure on the Court may revive at any moment. The immediate position, however, may be judged from the fact that the number of appeals awaiting hearing at the beginning of this term was 118. A few years ago it was nearer 400. An appeal now comes on for hearing on the average within two months after being set down, as opposed to six or more months after. This has not been achieved without effort. The Court has sat habitually in three divisions, and often in four, for lengthened hours and with vacations voluntarily reduced.

Still under the head of *technique* – two further questions suggest themselves: (1) Is it right that our Court of Appeal should review findings of fact, as it does in all except certain special classes of appeal, e.g., those from County Courts? (2) Is it right that it should hear appeals by way of oral argument only? In both these respects it contrasts with many if not most foreign appellate courts.

Many foreign courts of appeal limit their purview to points of law; many also proceed wholly, or almost wholly, on written 'briefs'. The relative advantages of their practice and ours are under consideration by the Evershed Committee and I will not dwell on the topic beyond saying as regards the first point, that I believe that what limited County Courts appeals to points of law was not a counsel of perfection but a counsel of necessity. Unless that limitation had been imported the system would have been un-workable. County Court judges simply could not get through their work or fulfil their appointed function if they were saddled with the labour (and incidentally litigants of modest means with the expense) involved in taking a note of the evidence sufficient to enable an appellate court to review their findings of fact. As to oral as opposed to written argument on appeal, the first method has certain obvious advantages. It enables counsel to confront and answer any objection to their argument which springs to the mind of the tribunal in the course of it. The best written argument drafted by the most prescient advocate cannot forecast, and answer proleptically, all of these objections.

On the other hand such a system as ours necessarily involves a good deal of interruption of counsel by the court, and this is sometimes condemned out of hand. It can admittedly be carried too far.* But discrimination is here, surely, necessary. Interruptions which prevent counsel from developing his argument are poles removed from interruptions which, once it has been developed, require him to elucidate and enable him to defend it. The first are a source of unmixed disadvantage and have been reprobated since the days of Bacon. It is a platitude that the worst counsel knows as a rule better than the best judge how best to present the material of a case with which he is entirely familiar and of which the judge is wholly ignorant. At this stage the only interruptions which seem justified are those which are necessary because the court either does not hear what counsel says, or does not follow the thread of his argument. But once counsel has fully deployed his material and his submissions, there is in my view far more to be gained than lost by the heckling which follows. No doubt it is irksome to counsel: but a litigant with a strong case has everything to gain and nothing to lose by this process. In its absence, both sides would be left in ignorance of what is passing in the tribunal's mind, and, where what is so passing is fallacious, would be denied the opportunity of correcting it.

Before passing finally from this topic of 'technique' I would

* A small girl was taken to see Mr Haldane (as he then was) arguing an appeal before the House of Lords. Asked what were her impressions, she said "it was very nice, but who was the old man who was trying the whole time to interrupt the judges?'

mention three suggestions* which in my view would make the work of the Court of Appeal easier: (1) At present appellants from County Courts in their notice of appeal are compelled to state its grounds. This is the rule also in respect of the Crown paper, and some other classes of appeals. In ordinary appeals from a judge sitting alone in the High Court there is no such requirement or practice. Why not assimilate High Court practice to County Court practice in this respect? Or insist that appellants and respondents in the Court of Appeal should, like parties to an appeal to the House of Lords or Privy Council, file the reasons on which they rely and be limited to these 'reasons'? This would not only canalise the court's attention and so economise its time, but save expense by limiting the documents to be copied to those which are relevant to the particular grounds stated. (2) Again why should not any judgment of the Court of Appeal reversing or overruling any decision of an inferior tribunal be circulated to that tribunal? This is done by the House of Lords when reversing the Court of Appeal (sometimes indeed when affirming it). It certainly used to be done (I think it is still) when the Court of Criminal Appeal quashes a conviction on the ground of misdirection. High Court judges in civil cases are not automatically informed, but their clerks have the means of finding out when and why they are being reversed. On the other hand at present a County Court judge who is reversed, may, unless the case is reported, never be disabused of his error.† (3) Why should not shorthand writers be attached to the Court of Appeal to take a shorthand note of the judgments? Such a shorthand writer is attached to every court in the High Court and takes down not only the judgment but the evidence, which may be vastly more voluminous. This omission in the case of the Court of Appeal has to my knowledge led to endless inconvenience and has been the subject of repeated but unavailing protest on the part of successive Masters of the Rolls. I am not suggesting that more Court of Appeal decisions should be reported. I am suggesting that, in the case of its unreported decisions, a shorthand transcript

* Though I did not know it when these lines were written, I have since been informed that the Evershed Committee have reported in favour of all three of these suggestions.

† This has now been remedied.

should be kept of the judgment giving the Court's reasons. As it is, in the Record Office you will find (along with the pleadings) nothing relating to the actual decision preserved but the formal order, and this may throw no light on the reasons on which it was based. When in a later case these reasons are canvassed, counsel who were not engaged in the previous case are naturally ignorant of them. Counsel who were in the case may have forgotten them: oftener they remember something, but their recollection of the reasons genuinely differs.* Quite a long book could be written about anomalies in our judicial system which no one defends, but which (through pure inertia) no one corrects. If I live long enough, I may try to *write* it.

I now turn to the second section of this paper. It concerns problems which, although they present themselves to courts of first instance, assume of necessity in reference to appellate courts of multiple membership a more complicated texture. What I have particularly in mind is the doctrine of precedent – of the binding character of previous decisions of courts of superior or co-ordinate authority: and this with special reference to the enucleation of the *ratio decidendi* from the husk in which it may be embedded. I must tread warily in this matter –

> Incedo per ignes
> Suppositos cineri doloso

for it would clearly be improper for me to express any opinion on any outstanding controversial question of law which might come up for decision before a court of which I might be a member. I must therefore confine myself on the one hand to what is not in controversy – to unchallenged fact and history: and on the other, as regards what *is* in controversy, to defining the problem, analysing its factors or tracing its development; leaving you to provide the solution. Even within these limits, there is much to be said.

Among the special difficulties which may attend the doctrine of ‘*stare decisis*’ in the case of an appellate tribunal of multiple membership, four stand out:

First, those which may arise when the court consists of an even number of judges and they are equally divided.

---

* This has now been remedied.

Secondly, those which arise where the court (or its majority) reaches the same conclusion for different and inconsistent reasons.

Thirdly, those which arise where the court (or its majority) bases its conclusion on two or more reasons which are consistent and cumulative, and the question is whether some one or more of these reasons, and if so which, are part of the *ratio decidendi*, or whether some, and which, are *obiter dicta*.

And fourthly, those which arise where a court bound by its own previous decisions finds these irreconcilable either with each other or with the decision of a superior court. It is obvious that I can only skim the surface of these topics.

(1) And first as to an equal division of judicial opinion. Our own appellate courts as a rule avoid an equal division by sitting in unequal numbers, though in my early years at the Bar this did not apply to the Divisional Court which often sat two strong: nor in much earlier times to the old common law courts sitting in banc, generally four strong. But in other jurisdictions, in Australia, for example, it appears to be quite usual today for the High Court to sit six strong. Equal divisions are there not uncommon. In Australia the result of an equal division would seem to vary according to the nature of the appeal. In all classes of appeal the result is to affirm the judgment *a quo*: but in one class, it has been questioned whether the effect of this affirmation is to create a precedent binding on the High Court itself, as opposed to the court appealed from. In another class of appeal that half of the Court prevails which includes the Chief Justice; whose vote, one may assume, is the object of a struggle like that for the body of Patroclus in Homer. As I have said, as a rule we 'by-pass' this difficulty, since the Court of Appeal commonly sits three strong and the House of Lords five or three. It is true that two members of the Court of Appeal can by consent hear a final appeal. But a special rule provides that when they do so and are equally divided there shall be a rehearing before three. In the rare cases where the House of Lords is evenly divided the result is the dismissal of the appeal, and the affirmation of the decision appealed from; which *does* thereupon become a decision of the House of Lords, binding on that House as such.

(2) And next as to the second problem, that which arises when different members of the court arrive at the same conclusion for

different and discrepant reasons. Many instances of this are given in a most valuable article in 63 L.Q.R. 461, by Professor Paton and Mr Sawer, mainly from Australia. But I would select as almost ideal for illustrative purposes a decision of the House of Lords cited by the Master of the Rolls in a recent address. I'm not sure it is not imaginary but this detracts nothing from its force. It could happen tomorrow. Let us imagine an appeal from the Court of Appeal to the House of Lords is allowed by a majority of three to two. The appeal was based on three grounds, A, B and C, any one of which, if established, would entitle the appellant to succeed. The three who were for allowing the appeal differed in their opinions of the three grounds on which it was based. Of the majority judges, No. 1 allowed the appeal on ground A, rejecting grounds B and C; No. 2 allowed it on ground B, rejecting grounds A and C; No. 3 allowed it on ground C, rejecting A and B. The minority of two, of course, rejected all three grounds, A, B and C. In the result, while the appellant won, yet each of the three grounds on which he had relied had been rejected by a majority of four to one of the Law Lords. What 'in the Resurrection' did the case decide? No doubt, at least, that where grounds A, B and C recur in combination the same result should follow. But what ought the Court of Appeal and the High Court to do, if, after the decision, a litigant before them based himself solely on ground A, or on grounds A and B combined, or on grounds A and C? I advisedly leave the answer in the air.*

(3) Thirdly comes the problem, arising where the court or its majority bases its conclusion on two or more reasons which are consistent and cumulative: the problem whether all, or if not all, which, of the reasons are part of the *ratio decidendi*. I consulted on the general problem of *ratio* and *dictum* one of our greatest judicial luminaries – one who has made classic contributions to this

* Since writing the above it has come to my knowledge that this precise illustration was put to counsel by Lord Simonds during the argument before the Judicial Committee of the Privy Council in *Commonwealth of Australia* v. *Bank of New South Wales* [1949] 2 All E.R. 755. See 66 L.Q.R. p. 298 and 23 Australia L.J. (1949) 355, for this and a most interesting comment by Lord Normand, from which it appears that in a Scottish appellate court the antinomy would have been obviated and the appellant would, in the circumstances assumed, have failed.

problem. I caught him in a light vein, and he told me this: 'the rule is quite simple: if you agree with the other bloke you say it's part of the *ratio*; if you dont, you say it's '*obiter dictum,*' with the implication that he is a congenital idiot.' And this may well, as a matter of pure psychological fact, have more underlying truth than we know, or care to avow. The theory, however, in cases of this sort is of course different and much more decorous. It has been notably expounded by the House of Lords in its recent decision in *Jacobs* v. *L.C.C.* [1950] 1 All E.R. 737. In that case the question arose whether in its previous decision in *Fairman* v. *Perpetual Investment Trust* [1923] A.C. 74, the House of Lords decided, as had been assumed generally, that a person lodging with the tenant of a flat, was as against the landlord of the flats a licensee and not an invitee. Three of the five Law Lords had expressed the view that he or she was. But the opinion has since sporadically found expression that this conclusion was 'unnecessary to the decision' of the appeal and was therefore *obiter*. Such doubts were ventilated for instance by the late Lord Justice Scott in *Hazeldine* v. *C. A. Daw & Son Ltd.* [1941] 2 K.B. 343; by Mr Justice Black, in an Irish case, *Boylan* v. *Dublin Corporation* [1949] Irish Rep. 60; and by the Court of Appeal in a passage (which unquestionably was *obiter* in the strictest sense of the word) in *Pearson* v. *Lambeth Borough Council* [1950] 1 All E.R. 682, to which decision I must tremblingly confess that I was a party. The explanation of the doubts shared by myself, and now authoritatively and peremptorily dispelled, lies, I think, in an ambiguity involved in the familiar formula 'necessary' or 'unnecessary to the decision' (a formula originating, I think, from a seventeenth-century judgment).

Absurd consequences (so the reasoning proceeds) follow if it can validly be argued that where there are two independent reasons either of which justifies a decision, both are *obiter* because neither is 'necessary' having regard to the existence of the other. If 'having an umbrella' means 'having a necessary umbrella' then a man who has two umbrellas has no umbrella at all. But let Lord Simonds be heard on this point in his own language: 'However this may be, there is in my opinion no justification for regarding as an *obiter dictum* a reason given by a judge for his decision, because he has given another reason also. If it were a proper test to ask whether the decision would have been the same apart from the proposition alleged to be *obiter*, then a case which *ex facie* decides two things would decide nothing.' Professor Wambaugh, in *The Study of Cases*, 2nd edn. 1894, p. 17, had propounded as a general test for *obiter dicta* the following formula: 'reverse the meaning of the proposition and then see whether it would affect the decision; if the answer is in the negative then the proposition is not part of the *ratio*.' This test as has been pointed out (in the L.Q.R. January 1948, p. 31) seems to have been based on a statement of Chief Justice Vaughan in *Bole* v. *Horton* (1673), Vaughan 360 at 382:

'An opinion given in court, if not necessary to the judgment given of record, but that it might have been as well given if no such, or a contrary opinion had been broached, is no judicial opinion, nor more than a *gratis dictum*.' Wambaugh's test seems now to have been either rejected by the House of Lords or held inapplicable to the case before it. If applied in *Fairman*'s case it would have worked out in this way: reverse the proposition 'the landlord is a licensor not an invitor,' so that it becomes 'the landlord is an invitor and not a licensor.' Would this affect the decision? No, because then the plaintiff would equally have failed. *Ergo* the proposition that the landlord is a mere licensor is *obiter*. Professor Paton and Mr Sawer, in L.Q.R. Vol. 63 at p. 475, show prescience of the objections which this test has since evoked from the highest tribunal, for in language foreshadowing that of Lord Simonds, they comment as follows: 'But where the Court bases its decision on two alternative grounds, neither would be part of the *ratio* if we applied Wambaugh's test to each of the propositions in turn.'

Lord Simonds points out that the principle now affirmed by the House of Lords had been applied by the Court of Appeal in *London Jewellers Ltd.* v. *Attenborough* [1934] 2 K.B. 206. The question in that case was how far the Court of Appeal was bound by its own previous decision in *Folkes* v. *King* [1923] 1 K.B. 282, a case in which the Court of Appeal had given two reasons for its decision. In *Attenborough*'s case it was argued that, since in *Folkes*' case two reasons were given, the first reason being sufficient the second was *obiter*. The Court rejected this contention. The Court, by Lord Justice Greer, said of *Folkes*' case, 'In that case two reasons were given by all the members of the Court of Appeal for their decision, and we are not entitled to pick out the first reason as the *ratio decidendi*, and neglect the second, or to pick out the second as the *ratio decidendi* and neglect the first: we must take both as forming the grounds of the judgment.' Lord Simonds further cites Lord Justice Pickford in *Cheater* v. *Cater* [1918] 1 K.B. 247.

Where, of course, a court decides a case on ground A, and goes on to say that it is therefore unnecessary to consider ground B, but that if it had been necessary to consider it, the court might have been disposed to take a certain view of that ground: then indeed it would seem that, as regards ground B, we have definitely moved out of the zone of *ratio* into that of *dictum*. But where the problem is not so simplified by fool-proof language on the part of the judge – language saying almost in terms that he is emitting a *dictum* – there must yet be cases in which he is in fact doing no more. It would be convenient to possess a criterion of *dicta* not labelled as such. The term 'unnecessary to the decision' has so often been used in this connection that while it is now clear what its application would be in such a case as *Fairman*'s it would be an advantage to know whether it is in any modified (and so if what) sense, still a valid touchstone at all for the purpose in hand. It is quite clear from Lord Simonds' language that an observation can be *obiter* though not proclaimed in terms to be such, and he has himself said that the dividing line from *ratio* may be a difficult one in such cases. Perhaps the result of *Jacobs*' case is that where a judge gives two reasons for his decision *prima facie* he is affirming both as part of the *ratio*, but that this presumption can be rebutted where expressly or by implication his language negatives this. Lord Sumner's language in *Fairman*'s case comes pretty near doing so, but apparently not near enough.

(4) There remains the fourth class of problem; that which arises where a court, bound by its previous decisions, finds that they are irreconcilable with each other or with the decision of a superior court.

Here I must again remind myself of the danger of expressing an opinion on matters which might come up for judicial decision before a division of the Court of Appeal of which I might happen to be a member. This particular problem is always coming up. I will therefore once more limit myself on the one hand to stating what no one disputes, and on the other to propounding as opposed to answering questions. Under the first head it is indisputable that *Young* v. *Bristol Aeroplane Co.* (*supra*) decides what I take from its headnote in [1944] K.B. 718:

> The Court of Appeal is bound to follow its own decisions and those of courts of co-ordinate jurisdiction, and the 'full' court is in the same position in this respect as a division of the court consisting of three members. The only exceptions to this rule are: – (1) The Court is entitled and bound to decide which of two conflicting decisions of its own it will follow; (2) the Court is bound to refuse to follow a decision of its own which, though not expressly overruled, cannot in its opinion, stand with a decision of the House of Lords; (3) the Court is not bound to follow a decision of its own if it is satisfied that the decision was given *per incuriam*, e.g., where a statute or a rule having statutory effect which would have affected the decision was not brought to the attention of the earlier court.

So much is beyond controversy. But so much else arising from the decision has been and is the subject of acute debate in the profession, in the L.Q.R., the *Cambridge Law Journal* and elsewhere that I propose to embody one or two of these outstanding questions in an imaginary examination paper. The Public Teachers of English Law, hardened by experience and habit, may perhaps be induced to look with a more indulgent eye than others on the medium adopted, which consorts with the non-committal attitude which I feel bound to assume.

QUESTIONS

(1) If tomorrow before the Court of Appeal a case were cited (*X* v. *Y*), decided by the Court of Appeal before the *Bristol* case and in flagrant conflict with it: would the Court of Appeal be free to perform the process, which the *Bristol* case itself authorises and enjoins, of choosing between the two: and if it so elected, to prefer the earlier decision? If not, why not?

(2) How far, if at all, would the answer depend on whether *X* v. *Y* had been cited to the Court of Appeal at the hearing of the *Bristol* case itself?

(3) If a decision of the House of Lords, according to its headnote decided on the face of it that A equals B, and the Court of Appeal decided that on its true construction this meant 'A does not equal B'; would this decision of the Court of Appeal,

as to what the House of Lords meant, be binding on the Court of Appeal in future? Or would it be a decision which 'cannot stand' with a decision of the House of Lords?

(4) Is a decision of the Court of Appeal that two previous decisions of its own are reconcilable, less or more binding on it, than a decision of the Court of Appeal that two previous decisions of its own are irreconcilable?

(5) How far if at all do the effects on a Court of Appeal decision of a House of Lords decision *ex facie* inconsistent with it, differ, according as the House of Lords decision (a) precedes or (b) follows that of the Court of Appeal? Does it matter, where the House of Lords decision comes first, whether it was cited in the Court of Appeal, when the latter made its decision?

(6) What does '*per incuriam*' –
   (a) Cover
   (b) Not cover?

Candidates are requested to attempt all six questions and to forward their answers to the Court of Appeal. No doubt they will take full advantage of an article by Prof. A. L. Goodhart, K.B.E., in L.Q.R. for July 1950, which appeared a few days after this address was given.

A Ministry of Justice

[Ever since a Labour victory at the last election seemed possible, and was later translated by the electorate into reality, law reform has been a catch-phrase of every lawyer-politician. Most bandied about has been the machinery for reforming the law; if the law is to match the needs of a twentieth-century democracy the means to achieve those needs, it was strenuously urged upon us all, must first be provided. No one person or body has ever had in England the sole task of keeping English law under constant review and of recommending changes in the law. But if an institution of law reform had hitherto eluded the British, the idea for a body mediating between the courts and the legislature is not new in the English-speaking world.

Mr Justice Cardozo in this lecture, which first appeared in the *Harvard Law Review* in December 1921 and was later reproduced as a chapter in *Law and Literature* (1930), not only shows his own partiality for a Ministry of Justice but also alludes to the history of such advocacy.]

THE COURTS ARE not helped as they could and ought to be in the adaptation of law to justice. The reason they are not helped is because there is no one whose business it is to give warning that help is needed. Time was when the remedial agencies, though inadequate, were at least in our own hands. Fiction and equity were tools which we could apply and fashion for ourselves. The artifice was clumsy, but the clumsiness was in some measure atoned for by the skill of the artificer. Legislation, supplanting fiction and equity, has multiplied a thousand-fold the power and capacity of the tool, but has taken the use out of our own hands and put it in the hands of others. The means of rescue are near for the worker in the mine. Little will the means avail unless lines of communication are established between the miner and his rescuer. We must have a courier who will carry the tidings of distress to those who are there to save when signals reach their ears. Today courts and legislature work in separation and aloofness. The penalty is paid both in the wasted effort of production and in the lowered quality of the product. On the one side, the judges, left to fight against anachronism and injustice by the methods of judge-made law, are distracted by the conflicting promptings of justice and logic, of consistency and mercy, and the output of their labours bears the tokens of the strain. On the other side, the legislature, informed only casually and intermittently of the needs and problems of the courts, without expert or responsible or disinterested or systematic advice as to the workings of one rule or another, patches the fabric here and there, and mars often when it would mend. Legislature and courts move on in proud and silent isolation. Some agency must be found to mediate between them.

This task of mediation is that of a ministry of justice. The duty must be cast on some man or group of men to watch the law in action, observe the manner of its functioning, and report the changes needed when function is deranged. The thought is not a new one. Among our own scholars, it has been developed by Dean Pound with fertility and power.* Others before him, as he reminds us, had seen the need, and urged it. Bentham made provision for such a ministry in his draft of a Constitutional Code.† Lord Westbury renewed the plea.‡ Only recently, Lord Haldane has brought it to the fore again. || 'There is no functionary at present who can properly be called a minister responsible for the subject of Justice.'** 'We are impressed by the representations made by men of great experience, such as the President of the Incorporated Law Society, as to the difficulty of getting the attention of the government to legal reform, and as to the want of contact between those who are responsible for the administration of the work of the commercial courts and the mercantile community, and by the evidence adduced that the latter are, in consequence and progressively, withdrawing their disputes from the jurisdiction of the

---

* POUND, *Juristic Problems of National Progress*, 22 Am. J. of Sociology (May, 1917), 721, 729, 731; POUND, *Anachronisms in Law*, 3 J. Am. Judicature Soc. (February 1920), 142, 146.
† *Works*, IX, 597–612.
‡ NASH, *Life of Lord Westbury*, 191, quoted by Pound, *supra*.
|| *Report of Lord Haldane's Committee on the Machinery of Government* (1918).
** *Ibid.*, p. 63.

courts.'* In countries of continental Europe, the project has passed into the realm of settled practice. Apart from these precedents and without thought of them, the need of such a ministry, of someone to observe and classify and criticise and report, has been driven home to me with steadily growing force through my own work in an appellate court. I have seen a body of judges applying a system of case law, with powers of innovation cabined and confined. The main lines are fixed by precedents. New lines may, indeed, be run, new courses followed, when precedents are lacking. Even then, distance and direction are guided by mingled considerations of logic and analogy and history and tradition which moderate and temper the promptings of policy and justice. I say this, not to criticise, but merely to describe. I have seen another body, a legislature, free from these restraints, its powers of innovation adequate to any need, preoccupied, however, with many issues more clamorous than those of courts, viewing with hasty and partial glimpses the things that should be viewed both steadily and whole. I have contrasted the quick response whenever the interest affected by a ruling untoward in results had some accredited representative, especially some public officer, through whom its needs were rendered vocal. A case involving, let us say, the construction of the Workmen's Compensation Law, exhibits a defect in the statutory scheme. We find the Attorney General at once before the legislature with the request for an amendment. We cannot make a decision construing the tax law or otherwise affecting the finances of the state without inviting like results. That is because in these departments of the law, there is a public officer whose duty prompts him to criticism and action. Seeing these things, I have marvelled and lamented that the great fields of private law, where justice is distributed between man and man, should be left without a caretaker. A word would bring relief. There is nobody to speak it.

For there are times when deliverance, if we are to have it – at least, if we are to have it with reasonable speed – must come to us, not from within, but from without. Those who know best the nature of the judicial process, know best how easy it is to arrive at an impasse. Some judge a century or more ago, struck out upon a path. The course seemed to be directed by logic and analogy. No

* *Ibid.*, p. 64.

milestone of public policy or justice gave warning at the moment that the course was wrong, or that danger lay ahead. Logic and analogy beckoned another judge still farther. Even yet there was no hint of opposing or deflecting forces. Perhaps the forces were not in being. At all events, they were not felt. The path went deeper and deeper into the forest. Gradually there were rumblings and stirrings of hesitation and distrust, anxious glances were directed to the right and to the left, but the starting point was far behind, and there was no other path in sight.

Thus, again and again, the processes of judge-made law bring judges to a stand that they would be glad to abandon if an outlet could be gained. It is too late to retrace their steps. At all events, whether really too late or not, so many judges think it is that the result is the same as if it were. Distinctions may, indeed, supply for a brief distance an avenue of escape. The point is at length reached when their power is exhausted. All the usual devices of competitive analogies have finally been employed without avail. The ugly or antiquated or unjust rule is there. It will not budge unless uprooted. Execration is abundant, but execration, if followed by submission, is devoid of motive power. There is need of a fresh start; and nothing short of a statute, unless it be the erosive work of years, will supply the missing energy. But the evil of injustice and anachronism is not limited to cases where the judicial process, unaided, is incompetent to gain the mastery. Mastery, even when attained, is the outcome of a constant struggle in which logic and symmetry are sacrificed at times to equity and justice. The gain may justify the sacrifice; yet it is not gain without deduction. There is an attendant loss of that certainty which is itself a social asset. There is a loss too of simplicity and directness, an increasing aspect of unreality, of something artificial and fictitious, when judges mask a change of substance, or gloss over its importance, by the suggestion of a consistency that is merely verbal and scholastic. Even when these evils are surmounted, a struggle, of which the outcome is long doubtful, is still the price of triumph. The result is to subject the courts and the judicial process to a strain as needless as it is wearing. The machinery is driven to the breaking point; yet we permit ourselves to be surprised that at times there is a break. Is it not an extraordinary omission that no one is charged with the duty to watch machinery or output, and to notify the master of the works when there is need of replacement or repair? In all this, I have no thought to paint the failings of our law in lurid colours of detraction. I have little doubt that its body is for the most part sound and pure. Not even its most zealous advocate, however, will assert that it is perfect. I do not seek to paralyse the inward forces, the 'indwelling and creative' energies,* that make for its development and growth. My wish is rather to release them, to give them room and outlet for healthy and unhampered action. The statute that will do this, first in one field and then in others, is something different from a code, though, as statute follows statute, the material may be given from which in time a code will come. Codification is, in the main, restatement. What we need, when we have gone astray, is change. Codification is a slow and toilsome process, which, if hurried, is destructive. What we need is some relief that will not wait upon the lagging years. Indeed, a code, if completed, would not dispense with mediation between legislature and judges, for code is followed by commentary and commentary by revision, and thus the task is never done. 'As in other sciences, so in politics, it is impossible that all things should be precisely set down in writing; for enactments must be universal, but actions are concerned with particulars.'† Something less ambitious, in any event, is the requirement of the hour. Legislation is needed, not to repress the forces through which judge-made law develops, but to stimulate and free them. Often a dozen lines or less will be enough for our deliverance. The rule that is to emancipate is not to imprison in particulars. It is to speak the language of general principles, which, once declared, will be developed and expanded as analogy and custom and utility and justice, when weighed by judges in the balance, may prescribe the mode of application and the limits of extension. The judicial process is to be set in motion again, but with a new point of departure, a new impetus and direction. In breaking one set of shackles, we are not to substitute another. We are to set the judges free.

I have spoken in generalities, but instances will leap to view. There are fields, known to us all, where the workers in the law

* BRYCE, *Studies in History and Jurisprudence*, 609.
† ARISTOTLE, *Politics*, Bk. II (Jowett's translation).

are hampered by rules that are outworn and unjust. How many judges, if they felt free to change the ancient rule, would be ready to hold today that a contract under seal may not be modified or discharged by another and later agreement resting in parol?* How many would hold that a deed, if it is to be the subject of escrow, must be delivered to a third person, and not to the grantee?† How many would hold that a surety is released, irrespective of resulting damage, if by agreement between principal and creditor the time of payment of the debt is extended for a single day?‡ How many would hold that a release of one joint tortfeasor is a release also of the others? How many would not prefer, instead of drawing some unreal distinction between releases under seal and covenants not to sue,‖ to extirpate, root and branch, a rule which is today an incumbrance and a snare? How long would Pinnel's case** survive if its antiquity were not supposed to command the tribute of respect? How long would Dumpor's case†† maintain a ghostly and disquieting existence in the ancient byways of the law?

I have chosen extreme illustrations as most likely to command assent. I do not say that judges are without competence to effect some changes of that kind themselves. The inquiry, if pursued, would bring us into a field of controversy which it is unnecessary to enter. Whatever the limit of power, the fact stares us in the face that changes are not made. But short of these extreme illustrations are others, less glaring and insistent, where speedy change is hopeless unless effected from without. Sometimes the inroads upon justice are subtle and insidious. A spirit or a tendency, revealing itself in a multitude of little things, is the evil to

---

* 3 WILLISTON, *Contracts*, §§ 1834–1837; Harris v. Shorall, 230 N. Y. 343 (1921).

† Blewitt v. Boorum, 142 N. Y. 357, 37 N. E. 119 (1894).

‡ N.Y. Life Ins. Co. v. Casey, 178 N. Y. 381, 70 N. E. 916 (1904).

‖ Gilbert v. Finch, 173 N. Y. 455, 66 N. E. 133 (1903); Walsh v. N. Y. Central R. R. Co., 204 N. Y. 58, 97 N. E. 408 (1912); cf. 21 Columbia L. Rev. 491.

** 5 COKE, 117; cf. Jaffray v. Davis, 124 N. Y. 164, 167, 26 N. E. 351 (1891); Frye v. Hubbell, 74 N. H. 358, 68 Atl. 325 (1907); 1 WILLISTON, *Contracts*, § 121; ANSON, *Contracts*, Corbin's edn., p. 137; FERSON, *The Rule in Foakes v. Beer*, 31 Yale L. J. 15.

†† 2 COKE, 119.

be remedied. No one of its manifestations is enough, when viewed alone, to spur the conscience to revolt. The mischief is the work of a long series of encroachments. Examples are many in the law of practice and procedure.* At other times, the rule, though wrong, has become the cornerstone of past transactions. Men have accepted it as law, and have acted on the faith of it. At least, the possibility that some have done so, makes change unjust, if it were practicable; without saving vested rights. Illustrations again may be found in many fields. A rule for the construction of wills established a presumption that a gift to issue is to be divided, not *per stirpes*, but *per capita*.† The courts denounced and distinguished, but were unwilling to abandon.‡ In New York, a statute has at last released us from our bonds,‖ and we face the future unashamed. Still more common are the cases where the evil is less obvious, where there is room for difference of opinion, where some of the judges believe that the existing rules are right, at all events where there is no such shock to conscience that precedents will be abandoned, and what was right declared as wrong. At such times there is need of the detached observer, the skilful and impartial critic, who will view the field in its entirety, and not, as judges view it, in isolated sections, who will watch the rule in its working, and not, as judges watch it, in its making, and who viewing and watching and classifying and comparing, will be ready, under the responsibility of office, with warning and suggestion.

I note at random, as they occur to me, some of the fields of law where the seeds of change, if sown, may be fruitful of results. Doubtless better instances can be chosen. My purpose is not advocacy of one change or another, but the emphasis of illustration that is concrete and specific.

* In jurisdictions where procedure is governed by rules of court, recommendations of the ministry affecting the subject-matter of the rules may be submitted to the judges.
† I state the law in New York and in many other jurisdictions. There are jurisdictions where the rule is different.
‡ Petry *v.* Petry, 186 App. Div. 738, 175 N. Y. Supp. 30 (1919), 227 N. Y. 621, 125 N. E. 924 (1919); Matter of Durant, 231 N. Y. 41, 131 N. E. 562 (1921).
‖ Decedent's Estate Law, § 47a; L. 1921, c. 379.

It is a rule in some jurisdictions that if A sends to B an order for goods, which C, as the successor to B's business, takes it on himself to fill, no action at the suit of C will lie either for the price or for the value, if A in accepting the goods and keeping them believed that they had been furnished to him by B, and this though C has acted without fraudulent intent.* I do not say that this is the rule everywhere. There are jurisdictions where the question is still an open one. Let me assume, however, a jurisdiction where the rule, as I have stated it, prevails, or even one where, because the question is unsettled, there is a chance that it may prevail. A field would seem to be open for the declaration by the lawmakers of a rule less in accord, perhaps, with the demands of a 'jurisprudence of conceptions',† but more in accord with those of morality and justice. Many will prefer to turn to the principle laid down in the French Code Civil:

L'erreur n'est une cause de nullité de la convention que lorsqu'elle tombe sur la substance même de la chose qui en est l'objet. Elle n'est point une cause de nullité, lorsqu'elle ne tombe que sur la personne avec laquelle on a intention de contracter, à moins que la considération de cette personne ne soit la cause principale de la convention.‡

Much may be said for the view that in the absence of bad faith, there should be a remedy in quasi contract.‖

It is a rule which has grown up in many jurisdictions and has become 'a common ritual'** that municipal corporations are liable for the torts of employees if incidental to the performance or non-performance of corporate or proprietary duties, but not if incidental to the performance or non-performance of duties public or governmental. The dividing line is hard to draw.

Building a drawbridge, maintaining a health department, or a charitable institution, confining and punishing criminals, assaults by policemen, operating an elevator in a city hall, driving an ambulance,

---

* Boulton v. Jones, 2 H. & N. 564 (1857); I WILLISTON, Contracts, § 80; cf. Boston Ice Co. v. Potter, 123 Mass. 28 (1877); Kelly Asphalt Co. v. Barber Asphalt Paving Co., 211 N. Y. 68, 71, 105 N. E. 88 (1914).

† POUND, Mechanical Jurisprudence, 8 Columbia L. Rev., 605, 608, 610; Hynes v. N. Y. Central R. R. Co., 231 N. Y. 229, 235, 131 N. E. 898 (1921).

‡ Code Civil, Art. 1110.

‖ ANSON, Contracts, Corbin's edn., 31; KEENER, Quasi Contracts, 358–360.

** 34 Harv. L. Rev., 66.

sweeping and cleaning streets, have been held governmental acts. Sweeping and cleaning streets, street lighting, operating electric light plants, or water works, maintaining prisons, have been held private functions.*

The line of demarcation, though it were plainer, has at best a dubious correspondence with any dividing line of justice. The distinction has been questioned by the Supreme Court of the United States.† It has been rejected recently in Ohio.‡ In many jurisdictions, however, as, for example in New York, it is supported by precedent so inveterate that the chance of abandonment is small. I do not know how it would fare at the hands of a ministry of justice. Perhaps such a ministry would go farther, and would wipe out, not merely the exemption of municipalities, but the broader exemption of the state.‖ At least there is a field for inquiry, if not for action.

It is a rule of law that the driver of an automobile or other vehicle who fails to look or listen for trains when about to cross a railroad, is guilty of contributory negligence, in default, at least, of special circumstances excusing the omission. I find no fault with that rule. It is reasonable and just. But the courts have in some jurisdictions gone farther. They have held that the same duty that rests upon the driver, rests also upon the passenger.** The friend whom I invite to ride with me in my car, and who occupies the rear seat beside me, while the car is in the care of my chauffeur, is charged with active vigilance to watch for tracks and trains, and is without a remedy if in the exuberance of jest or anecdote or reminiscence, he relies upon the vigilance of the driver to carry him in safety. I find it hard to imagine a rule more completely unrelated to the realities of life. Men situated as the guest in the case I have supposed, do not act in

* *Ibid.*, 67.

† Workman *v.* The Mayor, 179 U. S. 552, 574 (1900).

‡ Fowler *v.* City of Cleveland, 100 Ohio St. 158, 126 N. E. 72 (1919).

‖ Smith *v.* State, 227 N. Y. 405, 125 N. E. 841 (1920).

** Read *v.* N.Y. C. & H. R. R. Co., 123 App. Div. 228, 107 N.Y. Supp. 1068 (1908): S. C. 165 App Div. 910, 150 N. Y. Supp. 1108 (1914), aff'd., 219 N. Y. 660, 114 N. E. 1081 (1916); Noakes *v.* N. Y. C. & H. R. R. Co., 121 App. Div. 716, 106 N.Y. Supp. 522 (1907), 195 N. Y. 543, 88 N. E. 1126 (1909). For the true rule see Weidlich *v.* N. Y., N. H., & H. R. R., 93 Conn. 438, 106 Atl. 323 (1919); 31 Yale L. J. 101.

the way that this rule expects and requires them to act. In the first place, they would in almost every case make the situation worse if they did; they would add bewilderment and confusion by contributing multitude of counsel. In the second place, they rightly feel that, except in rare emergencies of danger known to them, but unknown to the driver, it is not their business to do anything. The law in charging them with such a duty has shaped its rules in disregard of the common standards of conduct, the everyday beliefs and practices, of the average man and woman whose behaviour it assumes to regulate. We must take a fresh start. We must erect a standard of conduct that realists can accept as just. Other fields of the law of negligence may be resurveyed with equal profit. The law that defines or seeks to define the distinction between general and special employers is beset with distinctions so delicate that chaos is the consequence. No lawyer can say with assurance in any given situation when one employment ends and the other begins. The wrong choice of defendants is often made, with instances, all too many, in which justice has miscarried.

Illustrations yet more obvious are at hand in the law of evidence. Some of its rules are so unwieldy that many of the simplest things of life, transactions so common as the sale and delivery of merchandise, are often the most difficult to prove. Witnesses speaking of their own knowledge must follow the subject-matter of the sale from its dispatch to its arrival. I have been told by members of the bar that claims of undoubted validity are often abandoned, if contested, because the withdrawal of the necessary witnesses from the activities of business involves an expense and disarrangement out of proportion to the gain. The difficulty would be lessened if entries in books of account were admissible as *prima facie* evidence upon proof that they were made in the usual course of business. Such a presumption would harmonise in the main with the teachings of experience. Certainly it would in certain lines of business, as, e.g., that of banking, where irregularity of accounts is unquestionably the rare exception. Even the books of a bank are not admissible at present without wearisome preliminaries.* In England, the subject has for many years been

* Ocean Bank v. Carll, 55 N. Y. 440 (1874); Bates v. Preble, 151 U. S. 149 (1894).

regulated by statute.* Something should be done in our own country to mitigate the hardship. 'The dead hand of the common-law rule . . . should no longer be applied to such cases as we have here.'†

We are sometimes slow, I fear, while absorbed in the practice of our profession, to find inequity and hardship in rules that laymen view with indignation and surprise. One can understand why this is so. We learned the rules in youth when we were students in the law schools. We have seen them reiterated and applied as truths that are fundamental and almost axiomatic. We have sometimes even won our cases by invoking them. We end by accepting them without question as part of the existing order. They no longer have the vividness and shock of revelation and discovery. There is need of conscious effort, of introspective moods and moments, before their moral quality addresses itself to us with the same force as it does to others. This is at least one reason why the bar has at times been backward in the task of furthering reform. A recent study of the Carnegie Foundation for the Advancement of Teaching deals with the subject of training for the public profession of the law.‡ Dr Pritchett says in his preface:‖

There is a widespread impression in the public mind that the members of the legal profession have not, through their organisations, contributed either to the betterment of legal education or to the improvement of justice to that extent which society has the right to expect.

The Centennial Memorial Volume of Indiana University contains a paper by the Dean of the Harvard Law School on the Future of Legal Education.**

'So long as the leaders of the bar,' he says,†† 'do nothing to make the materials of our legal tradition available for the needs of the twentieth century, and our legislative lawmakers, more zealous than well instructed in the work they have to do, continue to justify the words of the chronicler – 'the more they spake of law the more they did unlaw' –

---

* 42 & 43 VICT. C. 11; STEPHEN, *Digest of the Law of Evidence*, Art. 36.
† Rosen *v.* United States, 245 U. S. 467 (1918).
‡ *Bulletin No. 15*, Carnegie Foundation.
‖ *Ibid.*, p. xvii.
** POUND, *The Future of Legal Education*, 259.
†† *Ibid.*, 268.

so long the public will seek refuge in specious projects of reforming the outward machinery of our legal order in the vain hope of curing its inward spirit.'

Such reproaches are not uncommon. We do not need to consider either their justification or their causes. Enough for us that they exist. Our duty is to devise the agencies and stimulate the forces that will make them impossible hereafter.

What, then, is the remedy? Surely not to leave to fitful chance the things that method and system and science should order and adjust. Responsibility must be centred somewhere. The only doubt, it seems to me, is where. The attorneys-general, the law officers of the states, are overwhelmed with other duties. They hold their places by a tenure that has little continuity, or permanence. Many are able lawyers, but a task so delicate exacts the scholar and philosopher, and scholarship and philosophy find precarious and doubtful nurture in the contentions of the bar. Even those qualities, however, are inadequate unless reinforced by others. There must go with them experience of life and knowledge of affairs. No one man is likely to combine in himself attainments so diverse. We shall reach the best results if we lodge power in a group, where there may be interchange of views, and where different types of thought and training will have a chance to have their say. I do not forget, of course, the work that is done by Bar Associations, state and national, as well as local, and other voluntary bodies. The work has not risen to the needs of the occasion. Much of it has been critical rather than constructive. Even when constructive, it has been desultory and sporadic. No attempt has been made to cover with systematic and comprehensive vision the entire field of law. Discharge of such a task requires an expenditure of time and energy, a single-hearted consecration, not reasonably to be expected of men in active practice. It exacts, too, a scholarship and a habit of research not often to be found in those immersed in varied duties. Even if these objections were inadequate, the task ought not to be left to a number of voluntary committees, working at cross-purposes. Recommendations would come with much greater authority, would command more general acquiescence on the part of legislative bodies, if those who made them were charged with the responsibilities of office. A single committee should be organised as a ministry of justice.

Certain at least it is that we must come to some official agency unless the agencies that are voluntary give proof of their capacity and will to watch and warn and purge – unless the bar awakes to its opportunity and power.

How the committee should be constituted, is, of course, not of the essence of the project. My own notion is that the ministers should be not less than five in number. There should be representatives, not less than two, perhaps even as many as three, of the faculties of law or political science in institutes of learning. Hardly elsewhere shall we find the scholarship on which the ministry must be able to draw if its work is to stand the test. There should be, if possible, a representative of the bench; and there should be a representative or representatives of the bar.

Such a board would not only observe for itself the workings of the law as administered day by day. It would enlighten itself constantly through all available sources of guidance and instruction; through consultation with scholars; through study of the law reviews, the journals of social science, the publications of the learned generally; and through investigation of remedies and methods in other jurisdictions, foreign and domestic. A project was sketched not long ago by Professor John Bassett Moore, now judge of the International Court, for an Institute of Jurisprudence.* It was to do for law what the Rockefeller Institute is doing for medicine. Such an institute, if founded, would be at the service of the ministers. The Commonwealth Fund has established a Committee for Legal Research which is initiating studies in branches of jurisprudence where reform may be desirable. The results of its labours will be available for guidance. Professors in the universities are pointing the way daily to changes that will help. Professor Borchard of Yale by a series of articles on the Declaratory Judgment† gave the impetus to a movement which has brought us in many states a reform long waited for by the law.‡ Dean Stone of Columbia has disclosed inconsistencies and weaknesses in decisions that deal with the requirement of mutuality of remedy in cases of specific performance.‖ Professor

* *Report of Dean of Columbia University Law School for 1916.*
† 28 Yale L. J., 1.
‡ Harv. L. Rev. 34, 697.
‖ *The 'Mutuality' Rule in New York*, 16 Columbia L. Rev. 443.

Chafee in a recent article* has emphasised the need of reform in the remedy of interpleader. In the field of conflict of laws, Professor Lorenzen has shown disorder to the point of chaos in the rules that are supposed to regulate the validity and effect of contracts.† The archaic law of arbitration, amended not long ago in New York through the efforts of the Chamber of Commerce,‡ remains in its archaic state in many other jurisdictions, despite requests for change. A ministry of justice will be in a position to gather these and like recommendations together, and report where change is needed. Reforms that now get themselves made by chance or after long and vexatious agitation, will have the assurance of considerate and speedy hearing. Scattered and uncoordinated forces will have a rallying point and focus. System and method will be substituted for favour and caprice. Doubtless, there will be need to guard against the twin dangers of overzeal on the one hand and of inertia on the other – of the attempt to do too much and of the willingness to do too little. In the end, of course, the recommendations of the ministry will be recommendations and nothing more. The public will be informed of them. The bar and others interested will debate them. The legislature may reject them. But at least the lines of communication will be open. The long silence will be broken. The spaces between the planets will at last be bridged.

The time is ripe for betterment. 'Le droit a ses époques,' says Pascal in words which Professor Hazeltine has recently recalled to us. The law has 'its epochs of ebb and flow'.‖ One of the flood seasons is upon us. Men are insisting, as perhaps never before, that law shall be made true to its ideal of justice. Let us gather up the driftwood, and leave the waters pure.

---

* 'Modernizing Interpleader,' 30 Yale L. J. 814.
† 30 Yale L. J. 565, 655; 31 *id.*, 53.
‡ Matter of Berkovitz, 230 N. Y. 261, 130 N. E. 288 (1921).
‖ H. D. HAZELTINE, 1 Cambridge, L. J. 1.

Crime and Punishment

The Punishment of Convicts*

THE NOT VERY dignified panic which was excited some few weeks ago by the garotters† has, like most other subjects which raise the same sort of popular discussion, a great number of roots. As a rule, the public at large accept with considerable equanimity the existence of many evils which they appear to think it impossible to remedy, but from time to time the existence of these evils makes itself disagreeably prominent. It is brought home to the sympathies, or, it may be, to the fears of the mass of the well-to-do part of the community, and a sort of effervescence ensues, which may or may not produce permanent results, but which at any rate gives an opportunity of seeing what a very intricate matter it is to deal with any one of the questions which, in the half-articulate phraseology of the day, are called social.

The vehement clamour which still exists upon the subject of convicts and their discipline leads, when it is systematically examined, to a great variety of subjects, of the existence of some of which, in any shape, the public hardly seems to be aware, whilst their connection with each other seems to be altogether unsuspected. It is the object of this paper to point out the relation of some of these questions to each other. The general problem to be discussed is, How are criminals punished, and how ought they to be punished? The answer to the first of these questions is usually given in more or less graphic descriptions of the interior of such establishments as Portland and Dartmoor, but in order to begin at the beginning, it is necessary to go a step farther

* From the Cornhill Magazine, vol. vii (1863), page 189.

† Garotting is attempting to choke or strangle the victim of a robbery. There had been an outbreak of robbery with violence in London in the latter part of 1862, and in a number of cases the violence took the form of garotting. This outbreak caused great public alarm, quite out of proportion to the volume of crime. It led, contrary to the advice of the Home Secretary, to the Garotting Act 1863 which provided the penalty of whipping. The Home Secretary called it 'panic legislation after the panic had subsided'.

back, and to ask how the inmates of the establishments come to be sent there. There are not many of our institutions which attract or, in some respects, deserve more notice than the criminal law. Reports of trials are always popular, and an assize court presents to curiosity greater attractions than a theatre. We have endless Acts of Parliament, judges of first-rate ability, an elaborate system of procedure, and careful rules of evidence; but it must always strike a person practically conversant with the subject, as one of the most curious of all anomalies, that whereas the sole object of all this apparatus is the infliction of punishment, there is no part of the whole matter to which so little attention is paid by those who are principally concerned in it. If the elucidation of a point of law is required – if the question is, whether a particular fraud exactly comes up to what the law calls a false pretence, or crosses the invisible boundary between embezzlement and breach of trust – if it becomes necessary to ascertain, whether a question may lawfully be put to a witness in a particular shape – the machinery for obtaining an answer is almost redundant; counsel will speak and judges will listen till the force of nature can go no further. If a question of fact is raised, it will be sifted with a degree of ingenuity which leaves little to be desired; but when the judge has laid down the law, and the jury have found the facts, the interest of the case is over. The rest is matter of mere personal discretion. The judge looks at the prisoner for a few moments, makes him a little speech, and pronounces his sentence, often with a good deal of solemnity, but apparently with singularly little principle. It may be six, nine, or twelve months' imprisonment, or penal servitude for any term, from three years upwards. No one who has not tried knows the sense of helplessness which enters the mind of a man who has such a function to perform even in the humblest degree. It is just as easy to say nine as to say six months – to say six years' penal servitude as to say four; and the question which of the two is to be said has to be settled in a very short time, without consultation, advice, or guidance of any description whatever. Yet the sentence is the gist of the proceeding. It is to the trial what the bullet is to the powder.* Unless it is what it ought

* Cf. Stephen's 'The Criminal Law stands to the passion of revenge in much the same relation as marriage to the sexual appetite.' – *General View of the Criminal Law of England*, p. 99.

to be, the counsel, the witnesses, the jury, and the summing up, to say nothing of the sheriff with his coach, javelin-men and trumpeters, are a mere *brutum fulmen* – they might as well have stayed at home but for the credit of the thing.

It is an old reproach against the criminal law of this country that it considers prisoners in the light of game, protected for the amusement and profit of the gentlemen sportsmen by elaborate rules of evidence and procedure, which give them as large a chance of escape as is necessary to keep up the interest of the pursuit. This, which has been called the 'sporting theory of criminal justice', is no doubt susceptible of a good deal of illustration; but nothing can set it in so clear a light as the comparative importance attached to the trial and the punishment. A pack of hounds, and a number of men, dogs, and horses will spend hours in hunting a fox, which, when caught, is abandoned to the dogs without an observation. The criminal, when fairly run down, is sentenced by the judge, and turned over to another set of authorities utterly unconnected with and unrelated to him, as if the law had nothing whatever to do with a man after asserting its right to punish him. Between the judges who sentence and the gaolers and managers of convict prisons who punish, there is no sort of relation. They act upon different principles, and constantly pull different ways. The judge, struck by some special act of malignity or cruelty in a prisoner's conduct, gives him six or eight years' penal servitude instead of four. When the prisoner gets to the convict prison, the special reason which caused the sentence is unknown. The man is considered simply as a prisoner under an eight years' sentence, and is put through a course of discipline to which his offence may have, and often has, absolutely no relation whatever. Some years ago, a young man, infuriated at an assault, committed either on himself, or his brother, ran home, got a swordstick, and ran it through the aggressor's heart. He was convicted of manslaughter, and sentenced to fifteen years' penal servitude. Apart from this unhappy outbreak, he was a person of excellent character, and, in particular, he was thoroughly honest and industrious. Yet he would have to be passed through Sir Joshua Jebb's mill for reforming professional thieves and robbers, as if his crime had been one of idleness and dishonesty.

There is every reason to believe that much of the dissatisfaction which exists as to the treatment of convicts arises from this complete want of connection between those who assess, and those who inflict the punishment. The effect would no doubt be produced, more or less, wherever the cause existed; but the cause in England acts with peculiar energy, on account of features of the criminal law with which people in general are not acquainted. Probably, no system in the world leaves so wide a discretion to the judges in the matter of the amount of punishment, and none renounces more completely the attempt to adapt in any way whatever the kind of punishment to the nature of the offence.

A few words on the history and present condition of the criminal law will not only illustrate the fact, but show the cause of it. The criminal law has gone through three principal phases or stages. The first may be said to have been ended with the Stuarts; the second lasted till the time of George IV; and the third has lasted from that time to the present day. The law was first reduced to something like a settled condition in the times of Henry III and Edward I. In the four following centuries parts of its procedure – trial by battle, for instance – became obsolete, and other parts, such as trial by jury, underwent a great change of character; but the definitions of crimes, and the punishments allotted to them, underwent surprisingly little alteration. They might be divided into three principal classes – political offences, felonies, and misdemeanours. It would be no easy matter to draw the lines by which these classes were distinguished from each other with any approach to accuracy, or to show what were their legal relations to each other. Indeed, political offences never were technically distinguished from other felonies and misdemeanours; their general nature, as far as regarded punishment, is easily understood. The distinction between felonies and misdemeanours was probably originally meant to divide crimes which were levelled against the security of life and property, such as murder, robbery, and arson, from those which partook rather of the nature of private injuries, like libel, or a private assault, or a riot.

The punishments for political offences were either death in the most horrible form, or ruinous fines, often accompanied by the utmost severities, in the way of imprisonment, and even mutilation. The punishment for felony, in almost every instance, was death. The punishment for misdemeanour was fine and imprison-ment, both or either, to which might be added whipping or the pillory, at the discretion of the court. The heedless and wanton severity of this barbarous system was considerably mitigated by exceptions as irrational and capricious as itself. The law of benefit of clergy reduced the punishment for many felonies to a short imprisonment, or burning in the hand by branding the brawn of the thumb – a punishment of which the severity de-pended principally on the temper of the executioner. The general result was that for nearly 400 years criminals ran a considerable chance of being hung; but if they escaped that, they escaped, in cases which did not affect the government, with something like practical impunity. In the latter part of the seventeenth and throughout the whole of the eighteenth, and even in the begin-ning of the nineteenth century, this barbarous system – which, amongst other defects, had that of being so meagre that it left many most serious crimes unpunished, and so technical that it constantly allowed criminals to escape through the most ridicu-lous quibbles – was adapted to the altered circumstances of society by some of the clumsiest, most reckless, and most cruel legis-lation that ever disgraced a civilised country. Every sort of trifle was erected into a 'felony without benefit of clergy'; a crime, that is, for which the culprit was immediately, and on the first offence, to be put to death; and this was varied by provisions affixing in some instances the punishment of transportation for various terms, differing in the most arbitrary manner, to particular offences, created not with any general views at all, but because the fancy of the public was struck by some particular case for which no special provision happened to have been made. If this blood-thirsty and irrational code had been consistently carried out, it would have produced a reign of terror quite as cruel as that of the French Revolution, and not half so excusable. It owed its existence to the fact that its administration was as capricious as its provisions were bloody. Not a twentieth part of the persons capitally con-victed were executed. Some were imprisoned, many transported to various parts of the world, principally to the American colonies, from which they seldom returned, and not a few were compelled to serve in the army and navy, probably to encourage the others.

For between forty and fifty years this cruel and reckless system has been gradually superseded by one which leaves nothing to be desired on the score of humanity, but which is as deeply tainted with the original vice of recklessness and utter want of system as the older laws which it has superseded. The punishment of death was superseded by transportation, which in its turn has given place to penal servitude, and imprisonment and hard labour have taken the place of the old-fashioned inprisonment in the common gaol – one of the stupidest penalties that ever was devised. Numerous and costly experiments have been made as to the best way of inflicting these punishments, with an eye both to the punishment and to the reformation of those who undergo them. In pursuance of these schemes, establishments have been set up which are models of organisation, intelligence, and patience; but no one appears to have noticed the fact that these schemes, admirably intended, and most ingeniously executed, are so many unconnected experiments, and that the criminal law, by which their principles ought to be ascertained and regulated, has itself no principles whatever.

One of the minor defects of the criminal legislation of the last century was the incoherent, irrational, and incredibly intricate variety of its secondary punishments. When a judge was not compelled to sentence a man to death, he was, generally speaking, obliged to transport or imprison him for not less than some specified term, and these minimum punishments not only varied in degree in the most arbitrary manner, but were frequently far too severe for cases which fell within the definitions of crimes to which they were affixed. In order to meet this evil, an Act was passed which does away with all minimum punishments whatever (except in one or two cases of little practical importance), and empowers the judges in every case whatever to give as little penal servitude and as little imprisonment, either with or without hard labour, as they think fit. The latitude of their discretion in the other direction is not quite so great, but it does not happen in one case in a hundred that a judge is restrained by the law from giving as much punishment as he thinks the case deserves. The general result of these circumstances is that the punishments which the law awards are determined in amount solely by the individual impression of the judge at the time of trial, and in kind are confined in the common run of cases to penal servitude, and imprisonment with or without hard labour. The infliction of death for murder is almost, if not quite, the only instance in which any attempt has been made to observe any peculiar proportion between the punishment and the crime.

It follows from this that the whole subject of legal punishments must be regarded as one on which we have almost everything to learn from experience. It is by no means uncommon to read statements to the effect that the system of deterring punishments has been tried and has failed, and that we are therefore committed by past experience to confine ourselves to punishments intended solely or principally to reform. This is far from being the case. Our mode of punishing has been so reckless and unsystematic that we have never given any system a full trial. We did indeed at one time punish a certain proportion of prisoners selected almost at random with barbarous severity, but the severity was so capricious, and the law so uncertain, that the severity had not a fair chance. It cannot be said to have failed, for it never was consistently tried. On the other hand we have never thoroughly tried the reforming system. If it is essential to the true theory of punishment that prisoners should undergo a sort of semi-collegiate education at the public expense, we ought at least to detain our pupils long enough, and superintend them afterwards with sufficient care to have a reasonable security that we really have moulded their character into the desired shape; but we have not done this. The whole system of short sentences is opposed to the reforming theory. It proceeds on the notion that punishment is intended to deter, and that in cases of an ordinary kind a short sentence will have sufficient deterring effect. Hence our practice is contradictory and halts between two opinions. The sentences are passed upon one principle, and the discipline under them is arranged upon another.

The bad, and, indeed, absurd effects of this state of things will be made clear by a short enumeration of the commoner kinds of crimes. We are apt to talk as if crime was a single, definite habit, and as if criminals formed a well-defined class, all the members of which were addicted to the same practices. In point of fact, this is utterly unlike the truth. There are several well-defined classes of crimes, and to punish them all in the same way, even though they may be punished in a different degree, is as absurd as to prescribe

the same treatment for every kind of disease. All offences against
the law are crimes in the general sense of the word. It is as much a
crime – as much a violation of law – not to sweep the snow from
the pavement in front of one's house as to commit murder, for
the law enjoins the one act as expressly as it forbids the other. The
crimes, however, which people generally mean by the word 'crime'
are those offences against the law which are also grave offences
against morality, and are besides of common occurrence. They
may be broadly but accurately classed under a small number of
heads. They are either the infliction of bodily injury, mortal or
not; theft under various forms, accompanied or not with violence
to the person or to the habitation; malicious injuries to property
by fire or otherwise; forgery in various forms, and offences
against the coin. This enumeration, short as it is, will be found to
include very nearly every offence that occurs in the ordinary
routine of business in the criminal courts. Anyone who will take
the trouble of consulting the five or six Acts of Parliament which
now define the various forms of these crimes, and determine the
punishments to which those who commit them are liable, may
satisfy himself not only as to the extraordinary amount of the discretion entrusted to the judges in the matter of punishment, but
also as to the necessity for giving them that discretion in the
existing state of the law. Offences of the most widely different
character are included in the same definition. Burglary, for instance, includes not merely the breaking open of a carefully secured house by a gang of ruffians armed to the teeth with all sorts
of deadly weapons, and fully prepared to use them, but also the
breaking of a baker's window at five minutes past nine on a summer's evening by a hungry boy who wants to steal a penny loaf.
Manslaughter includes shooting dead a policeman who arrests
without a warrant a person who has been guilty of a conspiracy
to murder. It also includes the case of killing by negligent driving,
or by throwing a stone in a foolish joke. In these and some other
cases the definitions of the crimes might be improved, but in
others no skill in defining will give much clue as to the punishment. Bigamy, for instance, may be a very venial offence if the
second wife is not deceived, or if the first has been long missing.
It may be a crime more deliberate than rape, and not less injurious to the victim. Perjury may be little worse than a deliberate lie.

It may be the instrument of the worst kind of murder, or of robbery far more malignant and injurious than is committed by the most audacious garotter. It is clear from this that the law as it stands gives no security at all for anything approaching to uniformity of punishments, and it never can give such a security until it has provided means for performing and combining the results of three independent processes. These are, the classification of crimes, the classification of criminals, and the classification of punishments. When these three operations have been performed it will be possible to bestow upon the punishment of offenders a degree of care bearing some sort of proportion to that which is at present expended, wisely and properly, on the proof of the fact that they are criminals. The criminal law is at present in the condition in which medical practice would be if, after bestowing the utmost possible care on the diagnosis of a disease, a physician took no trouble at all about his prescription. The judge who sentences a man to penal servitude after a trial which is a model of patience and impartiality, is just like a doctor who, after spending half the morning in finding out that his patient was consumptive, should politely show him the door, saying as he did so, 'Go and spend 25*l* in drugs at such a chemist's.' It would be impossible within the limits of an article, and if it were possible it would not be interesting to general readers, to point out the way in which the performance of these different operations could be practically ensured; but some of the principles on which they ought to proceed may be indicated. The classification of crimes ought to be based on the moral sentiment which the crime would excite in the public at large if it were an isolated act in the life of a man otherwise unobjectionable. The moral sentiment depends partly on the consequences of the act, partly on the character which it presupposes on the part of the person guilty of it. Crimes which not only involve disastrous consequences to others, but afford evidence of odious qualities in those who commit them, should form the first class. Crimes which involve disastrous consequences to society, but do not afford evidence of especially odious qualities in the criminal, would form the second class; and crimes which afford evidence of odious qualities in the criminal, but do not involve disastrous consequences to society, the third. The odious qualities which most frequently display themselves in crime are malignity – whether in the form of cruelty or vengeance; lust; and recklessness – the quality which would lead a man to carry out his own purposes with perfect indifference to the interests of others, though he might not feel any active or individual ill-will to them: the temper which would lead a man to upset a railway train for the pleasure of seeing the confusion. Combine any one of these tempers of mind with an act highly injurious to others, and the worst form of crime is the result. Murder; the intentional infliction of great bodily injury; robbery or burglary, accompanied by bodily violence, or by the use of weapons, or by the display of the physical force of numbers; rape; arson; extortion by threats; perjury, with intent to procure the punishment of innocent persons:– are crimes of this kind, and would form the most prominent members of the first class in a classification of crimes. The second class in such a classification would be composed of crimes injurious to the public, but showing no specially odious qualities in the criminal. It would include the largest number of offences, and those which occur far more frequently than any others; those, namely, which arise from the love of gain, especially forgery, coining, and theft in its various forms. The third class – crimes which are not injurious to the public, or in which the injury to the public is a subordinate feature, the principal feature being the odious nature of the qualities which they display – are uncommon, though a few instances might be mentioned, if it were desirable to do so. The offence of cruelty to animals is one of them. There are others on which it is better not to be too explicit. These crimes are of rare occurrence, and will need no further notice.

Such being the classification of crimes, how are criminals to be classified? Considered with reference to the particular crimes of which they are guilty, they may act either with or without deliberation and special provocation; and considered with reference to their habits of life, they may be either professional or occasional criminals.

In order to arrive at a proper classification of punishments, it is necessary to compare these classifications of crimes and criminals with certain well-established principles as to the object of punishment. These principles are that the object of punishment is the prevention of crime, which is effected partly by the effects produced on the criminal, and partly by the effects produced on the public. The effect on the criminal may be either to take from him the power or the will to repeat his offence. He is deprived of the power by death, or by imprisonment as long as it lasts. He is deprived of the will either by terror, or by reformation. The effect on the public is to produce in the minds of those who are predisposed to commit crimes terror of the consequences, and in those who are not, hatred of the crime itself, which gradually becomes a prevailing sentiment in the majority of every civilised community, and so holds them back from yielding to the temptation of entertaining the question whether or not they shall commit crimes. This secondary effect of punishment, though often overlooked, is most important. If any person of ordinary decency and morality will honestly ask himself what is the real reason why he would not commit a murder, however great might be the gain, and however small the risk, he will find that no small part of his reluctance to do so arises from the horror in which the crime is universally held, and which he as one of the public shares. If he asks why the public universally hold murder in horror, he will find that it is to a great extent due to the fact that murder is a capital crime. If the law excluded certain forms of murder from the definition of that offence – duelling, for instance – the public disapproval of them would be greatly diminished. The ways, then, in which punishment operates are by disabling or reforming, which affects only the convicted criminal; by terror, which affects the convicted criminal and all persons likely to commit similar crimes; and by association, which affects the public at large. What, then, are the means which society has at its disposal for the production of any one of these results? There is, first, the punishment of death; secondly, imprisonment or penal servitude in its various forms; and, lastly, the infliction of bodily pain, of which flogging is the only form now employed or suggested. Death is disabling, and also terrifying in the highest degree. Imprisonment and penal servitude are disabling while they last, and combine the deterrent and reforming elements in different degrees, according to the nature of the discipline to which the convicts are subjected. Bodily pain is highly deterrent, and may or may not be reforming, according to the character of the person punished. By combining these observations with the preceding ones, it may be shown what criminals it is necessary to disable, to terrify, or to reform, and in respect of what sort of crimes, and also what are the cases in which it is important to sanction and gratify public indignation against particular practices. In other words, these principles and classifications afford the first steps towards the solution of the problem, How ought convicts to be dealt with? This is closely connected with another question, which must be considered with it: How far is it possible, regard being had to the means at the disposal of the legislature, and to the average permanent condition of the public mind, to deter men by terror, to disable them from crime, to sanction and to gratify public indignation against particular offences, and to reform by discipline?

First, then, how far is it possible to deter men from crime by terror? If the public sentiment permitted it, there can be no doubt that they might be deterred to any extent. No man would pick a pocket if he saw a pistol pointed at his head, and knew that he would be shot dead the instant he had seized the coveted article, and there can be no doubt that if theft were punished with instant death whenever it was detected, and if the public used every effort to detect it, men would not steal. Unsparing persecution, carried out with relentless determination, will put down even what men hold most sacred. It is perfectly possible to put down a religious or political movement even when it is supported by the strongest public sympathy and the highest abstract principles. There can be no doubt that the same course might be taken with crime, and that if criminality were hunted as vigorously in England as heterodoxy used to be in Spain, there would in course of time be as few criminals here as there were heretics there. The weak point of Draconian systems is the uncertainty and compassion of their administration. Hang every thief, and there will be no theft. Reprieve some ignorant lad or starving woman who has committed a theft, and the efficiency of the law is gone. Hence the real limit to deterrent punishment is public feeling. A certain amount of deterrent punishment the public in its average moods will endure. The introduction of any further amount destroys the certainty of the law, and so weakens its effect indefinitely. How far, then, will the public allow deterrent punishment to be carried? The answer to this question must depend upon individual experience and observation. There are, however, some facts to go upon. Little or no general objection has been shown for some years past to the

infliction of capital punishment in bad cases of murder, and on the
last occasion when a man was hung for attempting to commit murder
his execution produced general satisfaction. He had done his very
utmost to kill a woman and thought that he had succeeded in
doing it. Upon any great emergency, when strong sentiments of
vengeance or horror are excited, the public will not only tolerate,
but demand great severity. Little or no remonstrance was made
against the wholesale executions by which the Indian Mutiny
was avenged and put down. On the whole, it appears highly probable that the public would both tolerate or approve deterrent
punishments of considerable severity in cases in which their
moral sympathies were greatly interested, or their fears vividly
appealed to, and no doubt such punishments might be so managed
as to have a great effect on persons disposed to commit crimes.
Suppose, for instance, that the public would allow a man convicted of some specially brutal and cruel assault on a woman to
be kept for two years in solitary confinement and on low diet, and
to receive during that period a dozen lashes from a cat-and-nine-
tails every six weeks, there can be no doubt that if he survived
the punishment he would never forget it as long as he lived. If
some such discipline formed an indispensable preface to all reformatory punishments, it could hardly fail to terrify criminals.
How far in point of fact the public would go in this direction it is
of course impossible to say; but there can be little doubt that by
careful selection both of the crimes to be subjected to such
punishments, and of the particular cases in which they should be
inflicted, the deterring force of the law might be very greatly increased. This incidentally answers the question as to the cases in
which public indignation can be directed against particular crimes
and gratified by their punishment. Wherever the feeling exists it
can be deepened and intensified by legislation in accordance with
it. Where it does not exist legislation can hardly create it. The
horror which murder excites is deepened by hanging murderers,
because it has an independent source of its own; but if men were
hung for obtaining goods by false pretences, the law, and not the
crime, would be the subject of horror.

The cases in which disabling punishments would be permitted
by public feeling are not very numerous, but they are most
important. Death, the most disabling of all punishments, will no

doubt continue to be confined to murder; though it is to be regretted that the power of inflicting it for attempts to murder, and possibly also for the most aggravated forms of burglary and highway robbery, should have been altogether given up; but imprisonment for very long terms, in some cases even for life, would no doubt be not only tolerated, but cordially approved of by the public, in cases of crimes committed by professional criminals, even if the crimes themselves were not specially repulsive in a moral point of view. A man who, after some four or five convictions for felony, is convicted once more, and who has been for years living upon crime, is like a pirate – *hostis humani generis*. Legislators may be sure that in shutting up for life rogues of this description they would have the public voice fully and justly on their side.

The question how far and how criminals can be reformed is one which there is some difficulty in discussing fairly when the public are in a state of panic. It would, however, be a pitiful thing if the brutalities of a few scoundrels were allowed to undo all that has been effected in favour of a very miserable part of the human race for the last half century. By attending to the classification of crimes and criminals, and to the nature of the means at the disposal of philanthropic governors of convict prisons – and notwithstanding the floods of ridicule poured on Sir Joshua Jebb, he may well be proud of that honourable title – it is easy to see in general what are the limits within which criminals can be reformed. The means, and the only effective means of reform which the best managed prison can supply, are discipline and enforced industry. To some extent it may give good habits, but it cannot purify the heart, and no one ought to expect it to do so. When, therefore, the criminal has yielded to great temptation, or has been led astray by bad company, by bad education, or, as may be sometimes the case, by misdirected notions of courage, independence, or love of adventure, there are great hopes that he may be reformed. There is a relation, and there might and ought to be a close relation, between the treatment and the disease; but there is a sort of corruption which this kind of discipline has no tendency at all to affect. The shameless rogue who has deliberately and systematically taken up crime as his business, and looks upon periods of penal servitude as intervals of bad luck; and still more, the infamous wretches who are stained with crimes which are perhaps even more loathsome than dangerous – the murderer, the ravisher, the man who extorts by false accusations, the robber who habitually uses violence – are not people whom discipline will affect at all. They belong to another class, and ought to be treated on a different principle from common criminals. The horrible consequences of mixing up all these men in one mass are beginning to make themselves felt; and it should be fully understood that the true remedy is to be found in varying the kinds as well as the periods of punishment to which men are subjected. Look, for instance, at the frightful case, which occurred last summer, of the Fordingbridge murder. A man commits a rape. He is sentenced to a certain term of penal servitude, during which he has to work, say, nine hours a day, is well fed, and has nine hours' sleep every night in a sufficiently warm and comfortable bed. When he comes out he repeats his first offence, this time with the addition of murder. Would any reasonable man have expected any other result? What was there in his previous sentence either to deter or to reform him? Sharp physical pain, the lowest diet, the hardest lodging, might have had some chance of taming him, and if these hardships had shattered his constitution and even shortened his life, he would have had no right to complain. The knowledge that he had to suffer these evils would at any rate have been a warning to others, and if he had been imprisoned, as he ought to have been for many years, he would have been harmless to everyone except himself. Our heedless and unsystematic way of punishing which puts such a crime as his on a level, say, with passing a forged note, was the cause in this case of the sacrifice of two lives, his victim's and his own.

The general result of the whole is that crimes involving great moral atrocity as well as great public mischief should be met by deterrent and also by disabling punishments – that crimes of less magnitude committed by professional criminals should be visited with disabling punishments, and that the punishments in use at present should be confined to cases in which there is reasonable ground to hope for real reform.

It would be no very difficult matter to carry out some parts, at all events, of this scheme. The law is now brought into a shape and size in which it would be comparatively easy to say which crimes should be made the objects of what might be called exemplary punishment, nor would it be really difficult to ascertain whether a man convicted of some offence which did not fall under this category deserved to be treated as a professional criminal. As matters stand at present, previous convictions can generally be charged in indictments for felony, in order to render a man liable to aggravated punishment. There is no real reason why power should not be given to indict a man so convicted for being a professional criminal. It might be provided that if it was shown by evidence that he had been convicted a certain number of times, and that he was in the habit of associating with persons known to be thieves or bad characters, the burden of proving that he got his living honestly should be thrown upon him. He might be examined as to his life, his companions, his means of earning wages, and the like, and evidence might be admitted of his character. If, as the result of the whole inquiry, the jury were satisfied that he lived by crime, and was a habitual criminal, he ought to be imprisoned for life, and prevented at all events from doing further mischief. Probably the jury will not feel much difficulty in knowing what to think of a man who, being convicted of a burglary, committed in a thoroughly skilful professional way, appeared to have been previously convicted of various offences as often as twelve or fifteen times; yet this is not an imaginary case. It actually happened in one of the Midland counties less than a year ago. The prisoner was sentenced to eighteen years' penal servitude, whatever that may mean, but he will probably be revisiting his old haunts long before the year 1879.

In addition to these alterations, it would be no doubt desirable to examine closely the state of the existing convict prisons. There is probably a good deal of ignorance and prejudice in the universal chorus of indignation raised against them, but without entering at large into the subject, a few remarks upon it may be permitted. In the first place it might be foretold with certainty that the system would err on the side of indulgence. To a humane and educated man, the task of inflicting pain must always be odious in comparison with that of regulating a sort of system of education. There is also a natural love in all officials, especially in all military men, for the system, completeness, and organisation

of a great establishment, and the combination of these considerations forms a strong temptation to any manager to try to make his
convict establishment in a sense cheerful and comfortable. A man
whose life is passed in managing, providing for, and regulating
convicts, comes inevitably, if he is a kind-hearted and good-
natured man, to forget their worst features, and look upon them
more or less as his dependants. The worst that can fairly be said of
Sir Joshua Jebb seems to be, that he may have been too sanguine
and liberal in his philanthropy. It is, however, fair to him to call
attention to the fact that he has expressly admitted that the English convict system is not suited for the worst class of rogues. In a
statement published in a condensed form in this Magazine,*
after quoting from *The Times* an observation that the professional
criminals 'constitute the ugly percentage of the convicts – with
which nothing can be done – the true blackamoors of the system
who can never be washed white,' he adds, 'Here it is, and perhaps
here only, we fail.' In other words, the system is, on his own showing, quite unfit for the very class whom of all others it is most
important to punish effectually. Some sixty or seventy thoroughly
hardened professional footpads and garotters are enough to throw
all London into a panic, and when the public ask why this is so,
they are told that penal servitude is not intended for gentlemen of
this persuasion. It would be well to make an effort to meet their
peculiar views. Even if it should seem too extensive and difficult
an undertaking to devise new classifications of crime and new
systems of punishment for special cases, and if, as there is great
reason to fear, it is true that the objections to transportation are
really conclusive, it is the greatest of all mistakes to make convicts too comfortable. To honest poverty it is the most cruel
insult, to the criminals themselves it is cruel kindness, for their
crimes are due in almost every case to 'the lust of the flesh, the
lust of the eye, and the pride of life'. It would be an outrage on
decency to paint with any approach to truth the inside of the
minds of prisoners. If their habitual language is the best index
to them, they must contain abysses of blasphemy and filth which
can hardly be imagined. Take a man of this kind, feed him well,
work him lightly, let him have plenty of sleep in a soft and warm
bed, and confine him for years to the society of persons of his

* Cornhill Magazine, vol. iv (1861), page 240.

own class and sex, and you expose him to temptations far greater than libraries of tracts and armies of chaplains can encounter. Monkish austerities had their meaning. It was not for nothing that the monks recommended fasting and bodily austerities, and though the subject cannot well be fully discussed, no one who thinks upon it can fail to see that hard work and spare diet would be in the highest degree necessary to men in the circumstances of convicts, even if the matter of punishment were out of the question.

One simple mode of securing this result suggests itself to ob-servers from the outside. Why should these men be provided for in all respects merely because they are criminals? Why might they not work for their living, and suffer all the hardships that honest men suffer in the daily struggle for subsistence. Suppose that on his introduction to Dartmoor or Portland the convict were addressed thus: 'There is the quarry, and there is a pickaxe. The terms are so much for every ton of stone; and if you work uncommonly hard, you will be able to earn, say, 6s a week. Honest labourers have to support a family on 9s or 10s. Out of that you must find yourself. The rent of your cell is so much, and will be stopped out of your wages: and there will also be a weekly stoppage to pay for your clothes. Everything else you can buy at stated prices at shops in the prison. Now work or be idle, just as you please; but observe, you do not get one penny beyond what you earn. If you are ill, you may go into hospital, but you will have to pay so much a week, and you must work out your debts before you leave the prison. If you refuse to work, you may settle the question with your own stomach; but if you rebel, or steal from the other convicts, or are disobedient to, or assault the warders, there is a court in the nature of a drumhead court-martial constantly sitting, which will do justice upon you with surprising promptitude, and in the same way in which soldiers and sailors are punished.' If this kind of remedy were applied, we should hear little of either luxurious living or idleness. The con-victs would have no right to complain. They would be merely undergoing the common lot – working for their living like honest men – subject only to such special restraints as their own mis-conduct had rendered necessary. In this way good and bad fortune would apportion itself in prison pretty much as it does in the rest of the world. The active man would be moderately comfortable, the idle one would be wretched; and the calamities and personal advantages which do not depend upon morality would fall, as it pleased Providence, as they do on the rest of mankind. This suggestion might be applied to every sort of punishment; to persons subjected to deterrent or disabling imprisonment, as well as to those who have to undergo that which is more directly reformatory. It would substitute for an artificial discipline, which it is hardly possible to regulate in a satisfactory manner, a natural discipline, which would regulate itself with no trouble at all.

A Simple Statement

*The opening and peroration of the final speech to the
jury at the trial of Madeleine Smith for murder**

[This address on 8 July 1857 by Lord Inglis, when at the Scottish
Bar and Dean of Faculty of Advocates, is widely regarded as a
classic in defence speeches. Lord Inglis later became a distinguished judge as Lord President of the Court of Session]

GENTLEMEN OF THE jury, the charge against the prisoner is
murder, and the punishment of murder is death; and that simple
statement is sufficient to suggest to us the awful solemnity of the
occasion which brings you and me face to face. But, gentlemen,
there are peculiarities in the present case of so singular a kind –
there is such an air of romance and mystery investing it from
beginning to end – there is something so touching and exciting
in the age, and the sex, and the social position of the accused –
ay, and I must add, the public attention is so directed to the trial,
that they watch our proceedings and hang on our very accents
with such an anxiety and eagerness of expectation, that I feel
almost bowed down and overwhelmed by the magnitude of the
task that is imposed on me. You are invited and encouraged by
the prosecutor to snap the thread of that young life, and to con-
sign to an ignominious death on the scaffold one who, within a
few short months, was known only as a gentle and confiding
and affectionate girl, the ornament and pride of her happy home.
Gentlemen, the tone in which my learned friend, the Lord Advocate, addressed you yesterday could not fail to strike you as most
remarkable. It was characterised by great moderation – by such
moderation – as I think must have convinced you that he could
hardly expect a verdict at your hands – and in the course of that
address, for which I give him the highest credit, he could not resist
the expression of his own deep feeling of commiseration for the

* Notable British Trial Series.

position in which the prisoner is placed, which was but an involuntary homage paid by the official prosecutor to the kind and generous nature of the man. But, gentlemen, I am going to ask you for something very different from commiseration; I am going to ask you for that which I will not condescend to beg, but which I will loudly and importunately demand – that to which every prisoner is entitled, whether she be the lowest and vilest of her sex or the maiden whose purity is as the unsunned snow. I ask you for justice; and if you will kindly lend me your attention for the requisite period, and if heaven grant me patience and strength for the task, I shall tear to tatters that web of sophistry in which the prosecutor has striven to involve this poor girl and her sad, strange story.

*

I have thus laid before you, as clearly as I could, what I conceive to be all the important branches of this inquiry separately, and as calmly and deliberately as I could; and I now ask you to bring your judgment – to bring the whole powers with which God has endowed you – to the performance of your most solemn duty. I have heard it said that juries have nothing to do with the consequences of their verdicts, and that all questions of evidence must be weighed in the same scale, whether the crime be a capital one or merely penal in a lower degree. I cannot agree to that proposition. I cannot too indignantly repudiate such a doctrine. It may suit well enough the cramped mind of a legal pedant, or the leaden rules of a heartless philosophy; but he who maintains such a doctrine is entirely ignorant of what materials a jury is, and ought to be, composed. Gentlemen, you are brought here for the performance of this great duty, not because you have any particular skill in the sifting or weighing of evidence – not because your intellects have been highly cultivated for that or similar purposes – not because you are a class or caste set apart for the work; but you are here because, as the law expresses it, you are indifferent men – because you are like, not because you are unlike, other men; not merely because you have clear heads, but because you have warm and tender hearts – because you have bosoms filled with the same feelings and emotions, and because you entertain the same sympathies and sentiments as those whose lives, characters, and fortunes are placed in your hands. To rely, therefore, upon your reason only, is nothing less than impiously to refuse to call to your aid, in the performance of a momentous duty, the noblest gifts that God has implanted in your breasts. Bring with you then to this service, I beseech you, not only your clear heads, but your warm hearts – your fine moral instincts, and your guiding and regulating consciences – for thus, and thus only, will you satisfy the oath which you have taken. To determine guilt or innocence by the light of intellect alone is the exclusive prerogative of infallibility; and when man's presumptuous arrogance tempts him to usurp the attribute of Omniscience, he only exposes the weakness and frailty of his own nature. Then, indeed,

> Man, proud man,
> Dressed in a little brief authority,
> Most ignorant of what he's most assured,
> Plays such fantastic tricks before high Heaven,
> As make the angels weep.*

Raise not, then, your rash and impotent hands to rend aside the veil in which Providence has been pleased to shroud the circumstances of this mysterious story. Such an attempt is not within your province, nor the province of any human being. The time may come – it certainly will come – perhaps not before the Great Day in which the secrets of all hearts shall be revealed – and yet it may be that in this world, and during our own lifetime, the secret of this extraordinary story may be brought to light. It may even be that the true perpetrator of this murder, if there was a murder, may be brought before the bar of this very court. I ask you to reflect for a moment what the feelings of any of us would then be. It may be our lot to sit in judgment on the guilty

---

* The correct version of these Shakespearean lines from *Measure for Measure* (Act II, Scene 2, line 117) are:

> . . . ; but man, proud man,
> Drest in a little brief authority,
> Most ignorant of what he's most assur'd,
> His glassy essence, like an angry ape,
> Plays such fantastic tricks before high heaven,
> As make the angels weep; who with our spleens,
> Would all themselves laugh mortal.

man. It may be the lot of any one of you to be empanelled to try the charge against him. Would not your souls recoil with horror from the demand for more blood? Would not you be driven to refuse to discharge your duty in condemning the guilty, because you had already doomed the innocent to die? I say, therefore, ponder well before you permit anything short of the clearest evidence to induce or mislead you into giving such an awful verdict as is demanded of you. Dare any man hearing me – dare any man here or elsewhere say that he has formed a clear opinion against the prisoner – will any man venture for one moment to make that assertion? And yet, if on anything short of clear opinion you convict the prisoner, reflect – I beseech you, reflect – what the consequences may be. Never did I feel so unwilling to part with a jury – never did I feel as if I had said so little as I feel now after this long address. I cannot explain it to myself, except by a strong and overwhelming conviction of what your verdict ought to be. I am deeply conscious of a personal interest in your verdict, for if there should be any failure of justice I could attribute it to no other cause than my own inability to conduct the defence; and I feel persuaded that, if it were so, the recollection of this day and this prisoner would haunt me as a dismal and blighting spectre to the end of life. May the Spirit of all Truth guide you to an honest, a just, and a true verdict! But no verdict will be either honest, or just, or true, unless it at once satisfies the reasonable scruples of the severest judgment, and yet leaves undisturbed and unvexed the tenderest conscience among you.*

* The jury returned the peculiar Scottish verdict of Not Proven.

White Collar Crime

*Speech in Gluckstein v. Barnes (Official Receiver and
Official Liquidator of Olympia Ltd.)**

MY LORDS, Mr Swinfen Eady argued this appeal with his
usual ability, but the case is far too clear for argument. The learned
counsel for the appellant did not, I am sure, raise the slightest
doubt in the mind of any of your lordships as to the propriety of
the judgment under appeal; the only fault to be found with the
learned judges of the Court of Appeal, if I may venture to criticise their judgment at all, is that they have treated the defences
put forward on Mr Gluckstein's behalf with too much ceremony.
For my part, I cannot see any ingenuity or any novelty in the trick
which Mr Gluckstein and his associates practised on the persons
whom they invited to take shares in Olympia Ltd. It is the old
story. It has been done over and over again.

The gentlemen set about forming a company to pay them a
handsome sum for taking off their hands a property which they
had contracted to buy with that end in view. They bring the
company into existence by means of the usual machinery. They
appoint themselves sole guardians and protectors of this creature
of theirs, half-fledged and just struggling into life, bound hand
and foot, while yet unborn, by contracts tending to their private
advantage, and so fashioned by its makers that it could only act
by their hands and only see through their eyes. They issue a
prospectus representing that they had agreed to purchase the
property for a sum largely in excess of the amount which they had
in fact to pay. On the faith of this prospectus they collect subscriptions from a confiding and credulous public. And then
comes the last act. Secretly, and therefore dishonestly, they
put into their own pockets the difference between the real and the
pretended price. After a brief career the company is ordered to be
wound up. In the course of the liquidation the trick is discovered.

* [1900] A. C. 240, 248.

Mr Gluckstein is called upon to make good a portion of the sum which he and his associates had misappropriated. Why Mr Gluckstein alone was selected for attack I do not know any more than I know why he was only asked to pay back a fraction of the money improperly withdrawn from the coffers of the company.

However that may be, Mr Gluckstein defends his conduct, or rather I should say, resists the demand, on four grounds, which have been gravely argued at the bar. In the first place, he says that he was not in a fiduciary position towards Olympia Ltd. before the company was formed. Well, for some purposes he was not. For others he was. A good deal might be said on the point. But to my mind the point is immaterial, for it is not necessary to go back beyond the formation of the company.

In the second place, he says, that if he was in a fiduciary position he did in fact make a proper disclosure. With all deference to the learned counsel for the appellant, that seems to me to be absurd. 'Disclosure' is not the most appropriate word to use when a person who plays many parts announces to himself in one character what he has done and is doing in another. To talk of disclosure to the thing called the company, when as yet there were no shareholders, is a mere farce. To the intended shareholders there was no disclosure at all. On them was practised an elaborate system of deception.

The third ground of defence was that the only remedy was rescission. That defence, in the circumstances of the present case, seems to me to be as contrary to common sense as it is to authority.

The last defence of all was that, however much the shareholders may have been wronged, they have bound themselves by a special bargain, sacred under the provisions of the Companies Act 1862, to bear their wrongs in silence. In other words, Mr Gluckstein boldly asserts that he is entitled to use the provisions of an Act of Parliament, which are directed to a very different purpose, as a shield and shelter against the just consequences of his fraud.

My Lords, I am afraid I must call your Lordships' attention for a moment to the prospectus of Olympia Ltd. In my opinion it is the cardinal point of the case, and I do not think full justice has been done to it. The prospectus, I am sorry to find, was prepared in the office of a well-known solicitor. I wish I could say that it displays the simplicity and candour which some persons perhaps might expect from such an origin. Now this is what the self-constituted guardians of Olympia Ltd. and its shareholders tell those whom they invite to join with them in their enterprise: 'The promoters of this company, hereinafter called the vendors, who constitute the entire board of the company which lately produced "Venice in London", recently entered into a contract on behalf of a syndicate of which they themselves are members, for the purchase of the entire Olympia property. The vendors effected this purchase on 8 February 1893, at competition before the chief clerk of Mr Justice North in the Chancery Division of the High Court of Justice, for the sum of £140,000 payable in cash and they will, acting on behalf of such syndicate, be the vendors of that property to this company. ... Any other profits made by the syndicate from interim investments are excluded from the sale to the company. A printed form of the memorandum of agreement which was signed by each member of that syndicate may be inspected by intending applicants for shares or debentures at the offices of the solicitors of the company. The vendors have agreed to resell to the company the whole of the property purchased by them on 8 February 1893 for the sum of £180,000 (being nearly £18,000 less than the amount of Messrs Driver & Co's valuation) payable as to £155,000 in cash, and the balance in cash or shares of the company . . . Out of the profit to be made by the vendors on behalf of the syndicate the vendors have agreed to pay interest at the rate of 5 per cent per annum upon the amount for the time being paid up on the shares and debentures until the opening of the first entertainment. They will also provide all the preliminary expenses of the formation and bringing out of the company, and the issue of its capital up to and including allotment, and all costs including stamp duty in connection with the completion of the purchase of the property and the mortgage to secure debentures. The conveyance will be made direct to the company by direction of the vendors.'

My Lords, it is a trite observation that every document as against its author must be read in the sense which it was intended to convey. And everybody knows that sometimes half a truth is no better than a downright falsehood. Is the statement in the prospectus which I have just read as to the price which the vendors had to pay for the property true or false? In the letter it is true. The vendors had bid £140,000 for the property, and had formally agreed to pay that sum for it. But for all that, the sum of £140,000 was not the sum they were going to pay, and they knew that well enough. They had provided themselves with counters, obtained at little cost, which in reckoning the price would be taken, as they knew, at their face value, so that the price of the property to them would be only about £120,000. Is that what Mr Gluckstein and his associates meant the public to understand? Surely ordinary persons reading the prospectus, and attracted by the hopes of profit held out by it, would say to themselves: 'Here is a scheme which promises well. The Gentlemen who are putting the property on the market know something about it, for they were the sole directors and managers of "Venice in London" which was a very profitable speculation. They have had the whole property valued by well-known auctioneers, who say that it is worth more than is asked for it. True, they secure a profit of £40,000 for themselves, but then they disclose it frankly, and it is not all clear profit. There is interest to be paid, and all the expense of forming the company. And they have actually agreed to pay £140,000 down. That sum, they tell us, is "payable in cash".' You will observe those last words 'payable in cash'. Their introduction is almost a stroke of genius. That slight touch seems to give an air of reality and bona fides to the story. Would anybody after that suppose that the directors were only going to pay £120,000 for the property, and pocket the difference without saying anything to the shareholders? 'But then,' says Mr Gluckstein, 'there is something in the prospectus about "interim investments", and if you had only distrusted us properly and read the prospectus with the caution with which all prospectuses ought to be read, and sifted the matter to the bottom, you might have found a clue to our meaning. You might have discovered that what we call "interim investments" was really the abatement in price effected by purchasing charges on the property at a discount.' My Lords, I decline altogether to take any notice of such an argument. I think the statement in the prospectus as to the price of the property was deliberately intended to mislead the shareholders and to conceal the truth from them. [252]

*

[255] There are two things in this case which puzzle me much and I do not suppose that I shall ever understand them. I mention them merely because I should be very sorry if it were thought that in those two matters the House unanimously approved of what has been done. I do not understand why Mr Gluckstein and his associates were not called upon to refund the whole of the money which they misappropriated. What they did with it, whether they put it in their own pockets or distributed it among their confederates, or spent it in charity, seems to be absolutely immaterial. In the next place I do not understand why Mr Gluckstein was only charged with interest at the rate of 3 per cent. I should have thought it was a case for penal interest.

In these two matters Mr Gluckstein has been in my opinion extremely fortunate. But he complains that he may have a difficulty in recovering from his co-directors their share of the spoil, and he asks that the official liquidator may proceed against his associates before calling upon him to make good the whole amount with which he has been charged. My Lords, there may be occasion in which that would be a proper course to take. But I cannot think that this is a case in which any indulgence ought to be shown to Mr Gluckstein. He may or may not be able to recover a contribution from those who joined with him in defrauding the company. He can bring an action at law if he likes. If he hesitates to take that course or takes it and fails, then his only remedy lies in an appeal to that sense of honour which is popularly supposed to exist among robbers of the humbler type.

An Admonition

Judgment in Macleod v. Mackenzie†

IN THE HEART of the Island of Lewis near the head of Loch Erisort there is a clachan called Balallan, in which the complainer keeps the local store, selling articles of clothing, provisions and general merchandise. He also acts as merchant for the local Harris tweed, and he works a croft, and at certain times of the year, particularly in the spring and summer, he also works at cutting, weathering and ingathering peats. His must be a full life, for his activities touch current regulations at countless points. In May 1946 there penetrated into Balallan from Inverness two inspectors of the Price Regulation Committee, and, on visiting the complainer's shop, they either attempted to purchase or found exposed for sale there a curious assortment of articles; twenty hand towels, eleven pairs of knickers, one pair of boy's boots, and certain other goods. Seven months later there were served upon the complainer, not one, but five separate complaints. Under the first he was charged with having priced the towels at 4½d too much, the total excess being 7s 6d. Under charge (2) he was charged with having priced the knickers at 9d per pair too much, the total excess being 8s 3d and under the third with having priced the pair of boots at 22s 6d instead of 22s, the excess being 6d.

Under the fourth and fifth complaints the gravamen of the charge was that he had failed to preserve for a period of twelve months from the date of delivery the invoices relating to these and certain other miscellaneous goods. The maximum penalties stated (in some cases inaccurately) in the complaints are, as usual, Draconian, and a plea of guilty having been tendered by a solicitor on behalf of the accused, the learned Sheriff-Substitute has imposed under charges (1), (2) and (3) three fines of £10

* Then Lord Justice-General of Scotland.

† 1947 S. L. T. 335, 336.

and under charges (4) and (5) two fines of £15, making £60 in all.

It appears from the bill of suspension and answers to be abundantly plain that there was no question of dishonesty or of engaging in black market transactions, but at worst of an unsuccessful effort to comply with all the regulations. Indeed the inspectors on the occasion of their visit found various articles undercharged. Moreover, the facts indicate that the complainer made a full disclosure, and gave every assistance to the inspectors and the authorities, and that the truth of the matter is that he has been guilty under the first three complaints of a technical infringement involving relatively trivial sums, and under the fourth and fifth complaints of inability to do that which in the case of such a store in such a place must be far from easy of performance in the absence of skilled clerical aid.

There is this further consideration, that although the maximum penalties under the first three complaints differed from those applicable under the last two, though the articles and the number of articles differed in the different complaints, and though the amounts involved vary from 6d in the case of charge (3) to 8s 3d in the case of charge (2) the penalty is, as I have stated, the same under the first three charges and 50 per cent greater for the fourth and fifth. Counsel for complainer has satisfied me that this is a case which may fairly be described as one in which the penalty is not properly related to the offence, and taking the whole circumstances into consideration I feel that justice would be done by substituting under each of the five heads for the penalty imposed by the Sheriff-Substitute an admonition.

Counsel of Deception

Judgment in Meek v. Fleming†

THE PLAINTIFF APPEALS from the judgment of Mr Justice Streatfeild sitting with a jury given on 21 October 1960, after a trial lasting five days. The jury, after an absence of four hours, gave answers to certain questions on which the judge dismissed the action and entered judgment for the defendant. The plaintiff by his notice of appeal complains that the verdict was against the weight of evidence, and makes certain unsubstantial criticisms of the summing-up. These have not been stressed, and in my judgment no criticism can be made of the conduct of the judge or the verdict of the jury on the evidence before them. The real ground of this appeal is stated in the notice of appeal as follows: '(6) That at the trial the rank and status of the defendant was by implication represented to be that of a chief inspector when in fact between the date of the matters complained of in the action and the date of the trial he had been reduced to the rank of a station sergeant by reason of misconduct and that the credit of the parties was a crucial issue at the trial.' A further notice of motion for leave to give fresh evidence alleges that on the question of credit the defendant deceived or misled the court, and thereby occasioned a miscarriage of justice.

The plaintiff was claiming damages for assault and wrongful imprisonment in respect of an incident that happened on Guy Fawkes night, 5 November 1958. There was a disorderly crowd in Trafalgar Square, and many police officers had been detailed to deal with it. They made a number of arrests that night, and removed the arrested persons in a police tender to Cannon Row police station where they charged them and then, as a rule, released them. The defendant was the chief inspector at Cannon

---

* Then Lord Justice Holroyd Pearce, presiding over a division of the Court of Appeal.

† [1961] 2 Q.B. 366, 373.

Row police station, and was actively engaged in helping to control
the disorder in Trafalgar Square. The plaintiff, a press photo-
grapher with a good record, was there with his camera for the
purpose of taking photographs. At about 9.40 p.m. the defendant
arrested him on a charge of obstructing the police, and took him
in a tender to Cannon Row police station where he was kept in
a cell until 1.30 a.m.

If the plaintiff's story was correct, the defendant arrested him
without proper cause, used considerable violence to him which
caused physical injury, and without justification locked him up
for some hours instead of charging him straight away and releasing
him. If the defendant's story was correct, he acted with propriety;
he was justified in arresting the plaintiff, and the subsequent
violence (which was far less than the plaintiff alleged) was wholly
occasioned by the plaintiff's own violence and resistance.

On 17 November 1958, the plaintiff issued the writ in this
action. On 17 December he appeared at the magistrates' court
and was convicted of obstructing the police and fined £5.
Another charge was dismissed.

On 16 December 1959, while this action was pending, certain
events occurred which at the trial were unknown to the plaintiff's
advisers, and which they had no reason to know or to suspect.
These events were deliberately concealed at the trial by the defendant and his legal advisers. It is on this concealment that the
plaintiff relies in this appeal. He asks for a new trial in order that
these facts may be proved by fresh evidence.

The facts have been agreed between the parties for the purpose
of this appeal in the following terms:

(1) At the date when the defendant gave evidence at the trial of the
action, his true rank in the Metropolitan Police Force was station
sergeant. (2) The defendant was reduced from the rank of chief inspector to station sergeant on 16 December 1959. (3) On 16 December
1959, the defendant appeared before a disciplinary board on the following charges: (i) Acting in a manner prejudicial to discipline by being a
party to an arrangement with [a police constable] whereby that officer
purported to have arrested a street bookmaker on 26 October 1959,
when in fact you were the officer who made the arrest. (ii) Without
good and sufficient cause did omit promptly and diligently to attend to
a matter which was your duty as a constable, that is to say having
arrested ... for street betting on 26 October 1959, you did not attend

the hearing of the case against him at Thames Metropolitan Magistrates' Court on 27 October 1959.

The defendant was reduced in rank to station sergeant on each charge, but on appeal to the commissioner on 30 December, the punishment on the second charge was reduced to a reprimand, but there was no variation in the first punishment.

It is conceded that those facts were known to the defendant's legal advisers and his counsel, and that as matter of deliberate policy they were not put before the Court. A letter written by the defendant's solicitor on 21 November 1960, pending the appeal, says:

The learned Queen's Counsel instructed by me was throughout, as I believe you are aware, in full possession of all the facts relating to my client's past and present status and the reasons for his reduction in rank, and conducted the case in full knowledge of these facts in the manner he felt was consistent with his duty to his client and the court, and he is fully prepared to defend and justify his handling of the case at the proper time if called upon to do so.

It having been decided not to reveal these facts, the following things occurred at the trial. The defendant attended the trial not in uniform, but in plain clothes, whereas all the other police witnesses were in uniform. Thus there was no visible sign of the defendant's altered status. He was constantly addressed by his counsel as 'Mr' and not by his rank of sergeant. Counsel tells us that he would so address a sergeant in the normal case. When the defendant entered the witness-box, he was not asked his name and rank in the usual manner. No suspicions were aroused since no one had any reason to suspect. The plaintiff's counsel, however, and the judge frequently addressed the defendant, or referred to him, as 'inspector' or 'chief inspector', and nothing was done to disabuse them.

The defendant started his evidence with a brief summary of his career up to the time when he was chief inspector at Cannon Row police station, but no reference was made to his reduction in rank. In cross-examination he was asked: 'You are a chief inspector, and you have been in the force, you told us, since 1938? (A) Yes, that is true.' That answer was a lie. Later: '(Q) You realise, as chief inspector, the importance of the note being accurate? (A) The importance of it conveying to me what I want to give in evidence.' He was asked further: 'Let us understand this.

You are a chief inspector. How old are you? (A) I am forty-six years of age.' And again: '(Q) I am not asking you whether you took part in the inquiries, but whether you as a responsible and senior adult man – never mind about your being a chief inspector – had no anxiety about this case, no concern or interest? (A) No. I can only repeat that I have nothing to fear.'

The judge referred to the defendant as 'inspector' or 'chief inspector Fleming' many times in his summing-up to the jury. It is clear that he reasonably considered that the defendant's rank and status were relevant on credibility in a case where there was oath against oath, and where there was a question of the defendant's conduct in the course of his duty. . . .

Nor was the defendant's counsel prepared to forgo the advantage to be derived from the status in the police force of his witnesses in general. The parties have, fortunately, in the interests of economy been able to use the reports of the case in *The Times* newspaper. These show that in his opening speech for the defence, counsel stated that the jury had not yet had an opportunity of listening to persons against whom it was at times fashionable to make wild hysterical allegations, but who could not have reached their positions unless they had shown to those who controlled the Metropolitan Police a substantial degree of responsibility. They were not concerned here with some newcomer to the force who had only just finished his course, and was out on the street full of enthusiasm to arrest the first person he could.

The Times report of the final speech of defendant's counsel shows that he said in reference to the allegations of the plaintiff:

That was un-English, and not what the jury would expect of any police officer who had passed through the sieve, been trained and risen to any rank in the Metropolitan Police.

He then went on to contrast unfavourably the plaintiff's background in Fleet Street where

words come out in very large letters, and the range of adjectives and description is so wide as to make us callous.

I accept from counsel that he was intending to refer to the generality of his seven or eight witnesses, all of whom had attained some rank above that of constable. Nevertheless, such references must inevitably have connoted in the minds of judge and jury a reference to the status of the defendant, who was the leading person in the case, and held (in their erroneous belief) the highest rank of all the witnesses.

The fact that the defendant's advisers were prepared to act as they did showed the great importance which they attached to the facts concealed. If one leaves aside for the moment any question of ethics, the hazards of such a course were extremely great. With so many police witnesses who might well know the truth (since the defendant's demotion was circulated in police orders) the chance of somebody in cross-examination referring to the defendant by his present rank of sergeant, or letting the truth out in some other way, was not negligible. Had that occurred, or had the plaintiff's counsel known the facts, and elicited them in cross-examination, it seems very unlikely that the jury would accept the defendant's case when they found how they had been deceived. Even without knowing the facts, the jury took four hours for their deliberations, and since the plaintiff's evidence was, broadly speaking, that of one against so many, one must, I think, conclude that he did well in the witness-box.

How then does the matter stand now that the truth has come out? This court is rightly loth to order a new trial on the ground of fresh evidence. *Interest reipublicae ut sit finis litium.* The cases show that this court has given great weight to that maxim. There would be a constant succession of retrials if judgments were to be set aside merely because something fresh that might have been material has come to light. In the case of fresh evidence relating to an issue in the case, the court will not order a new trial unless such evidence would probably have an important influence on the result of the case, though such evidence need not be decisive. Such evidence must also, of course, be apparently credible and such that it could not have been obtained with due diligence. But in the present case the fresh evidence is agreed, and it could not have been found out with due diligence since there was no reason to suspect it. In the present case, therefore, these two latter considerations are not in issue.

Where, however, the fresh evidence does not relate directly to an issue, but is merely evidence as to the credibility of an important witness, this court applies a stricter test. It will only allow its admission (if ever) where the evidence is of such a nature and the circumstances of the case are such that no reasonable jury could be expected to act upon the evidence of the witness whose character had been called in question or where the court is satisfied that the additional evidence *must* have led a reasonable jury to a different conclusion from that actually arrived at in the case. [378]

*

[379] There is no authority where the facts have been at all similar to those of the present case, but in my judgment the principles on which we should act are clear.

Where a party deliberately misleads the court in a material matter, and that deception has probably tipped the scale in his favour (or even, as I think, where it may reasonably have done so), it would be wrong to allow him to retain the judgment thus unfairly procured. *Finis litium* is a desirable object, but it must not be sought by so great a sacrifice of justice which is and must remain the supreme object. Moreover, to allow the victor to keep the spoils so unworthily obtained would be an encouragement to such behaviour, and do even greater harm than the multiplication of trials.

In every case it must be a question of degree, weighing one principle against the other. In this case it is clear that the judge and jury were misled on an important matter. I appreciate that it is very hard at times for the advocate to see his path clearly between failure in his duty to the court, and failure in his duty to his client. I accept that in the present case the decision to conceal the facts was not made lightly, but after anxious consideration. But in my judgment the duty to the court was here unwarrantably subordinated to the duty to the client. It is no less surprising that this should be done when the defendant is a member of the Metropolitan Police Force on whose integrity the public are accustomed to rely.

It was argued that there were several other police witnesses against the plaintiff's story; that although part of the issue depended on the evidence of the parties alone, the greater part of the defence depended on other witnesses than the defendant, and that therefore the concealment did not have any substantial result. But since the defendant and his advisers thought fit to take so serious a step, they must, in the light of their own intimate knowledge of their case, have regarded the concealment as being of overwhelming importance to their success. Therefore I am not prepared to countenance their present argument that it may have made no difference to the result.

It was argued that the defendant was justified in that a party need not reveal something to his discredit; but that does not mean that he can by implication falsely pretend (where it is a material matter) to a rank and status that are not his, and, when he knows that the court is so deluded, foster and confirm that delusion by answers such as the defendant gave. *Suggestio falsi* went hand in hand with *suppressio veri.* It may well be that it was not so clear in prospect as it is in retrospect how wide the web of deceit would be woven before the verdict came to be given. But in the event it spread over all the evidence of the defendant. It affected the summing-up of the judge, and it must have affected the deliberations of the jury. The defendant and his legal advisers, and probably some at least of his witnesses, on the one hand, were aware of the facts, and intent not to reveal them, in order that on the other hand the plaintiff and his counsel and the jury and the judge might remain in ignorance, and that the defendant might be thereby enabled to masquerade as a chief inspector of unblemished reputation enjoying such advantage as that status and character would give him at the trial. It would be an intolerable infraction of the principles of justice to allow the defendant to retain a verdict thus obtained.

[*New trial ordered*]

JUDGE FRANK

Police Practices

*Judgment in U.S.; ex rel. Caminito v. Murphy**

[In 1942 three accused men, named Noia, Bonino and Caminito were convicted in a New York State court of murder in the course of an armed robbery; all three were sentenced to life imprisonment. None of them gave evidence at the trial, the only testimony against them being separate confessions which each had signed while in custody. Noia did not appeal, partly because he was unsure of the result and because he did not wish to dip further into his family's depleted funds; and partly because he feared that he might be sentenced to death – the trial judge had indicated that he had considered imposing the death penalty.

Bonino and Caminito did appeal. Initially they were unsuccessful. Although he had brought his case before the highest court of the State three times and the Supreme Court of the United States once, Caminito persisted. Twelve years after his conviction, on a petition for habeas corpus, the Federal District Court held that his confession to the murder had not been coerced, and thus no guaranteed rights had been violated. But, on appeal, the United States Court of Appeal reversed the decision. Although it found there had been no police brutality, there had been coercion. Caminito had been questioned almost continuously for 27 hours. He had been held incommunicado, though relatives and lawyers tried vainly to see him. The police detectives had falsely identified him.]

THE SOLE EVIDENCE of Caminito's guilt consisted of his signed pre-trial confessions. At the trial, his counsel timely objected to their admission; ... he also moved to dismiss the indictment on the ground that the State had not proved Caminito guilty. Caminito testified that the police had coerced the confessions. The trial judge left to the jury the question whether the confessions had

* 222 F. 2d 698 (1955).

100

been thus induced. The jury, by returning a verdict of guilt, found that they were voluntary.

Caminito testified that, before giving the confessions, the police had beaten him. As the police testified to the contrary, we shall ignore that part of his testimony. But the following facts are not disputed.

(1) Caminito was taken into custody by the police on Sunday, 11 May 1941 at 6 pm.

(2) Commencing about 9 pm Sunday, he was continuously interrogated by five or six police officers for a period of approximately five hours, until 2 am the following morning, Monday, 12 May.

(3) At 3 am on Monday, 12 May, he was locked in a cell in which there were no bed, blankets, spring or mattress, but only a wooden bench.* (He testified that the cell was unheated. A witness for the State testified that the cell was equipped with a radiator but that he 'did not know if the heat was on' during the time Caminito was there confined.)

(4) At 10 am on Monday, 12 May, the questioning was resumed. The interrogation continued all day, with several detectives taking turns.

(5) Members of Caminito's family, his friends and an attorney retained by the family, called at the station house where he was detained and tried to get information concerning his whereabouts. The police officers knew these facts, but kept him incommunicado. Other than the police and the District Attorney, no one was permitted to see him until he was arraigned forty hours after being taken into custody.

(6) During the afternoon of Monday, 12 May, two women and a man were brought in to face Caminito. He was not told that they were detectives. Each falsely pretended to identify him as the person who was sitting at the wheel of the automobile at the time of the shooting, which occurred in connection with the holdup.

(7) About 9 pm, Monday, 12 May, twenty-seven hours after having been taken into custody, he signed a confession. He

* Caminito testified that he was unable to sleep in the cell.

gave a second confession to a District Attorney a short time later.

(8) About 2.30 or 3 am the following morning, Tuesday, 12 May, he was first placed under arrest.

(9) He was brought before a magistrate later that same day, more than forty hours after having first been taken into custody. The arraignment could and should have been held long before that time. The police officers knew that the courts were open for that purpose.

(10) Caminito had never been previously arrested or convicted.

These facts make it clear that the trial did not measure up to the standards prescribed by the due process clause of the Fourteenth Amendment. The confessions obtained by these loathsome means were no more evidence than if they had been forged. Absent, then, any admissible evidence of guilt, the trial judge should have dismissed the indictment or directed a verdict of acquittal. To jail a man convicted without evidence of guilt is to impose 'involuntary servitude' which, 'except as a punishment for crime', the Thirteenth Amendment forbids. Only in Erewhon, which recognised 'the crime of being maligned unjustly',* could this conviction be justified.

Alone or together, neither the unlawful detention for many hours nor the deceit in confronting Caminito with disguised police officers who lied in identifying him would suffice to vitiate the confessions as unconstitutionally obtained. But those factors did aggravate the following unconstitutional practices which – even in the absence of those factors – rendered the confessions inadmissible: (a) The police interrogated him almost continuously for 27 hours, with but a brief interval for rest in a cell so badly equipped as to make sleep virtually impossible for a man already harried by the questioning. (b) During this long period, the police, in effect, kidnapped him: they kept him incommunicado, refusing to allow his lawyer, his family, and his friends to consult with him.

Accordingly, the writ of habeas corpus must issue.

All decent Americans soundly condemn satanic practices, like those described above, when employed in totalitarian regimes. It

---

* Samuel Butler, *Erewhon* (2nd edn. 1901), Chapter 11.

should shock us when American police resort to them, for they do
not comport with the barest minimum of civilised principles of
justice. It has no significance that in this case we must assume
there was no physical brutality. For psychological torture may be
far more cruel, far more symptomatic of sadism. Many a man who
can endure beatings will yield to fatigue. To keep a man awake
beyond the point of exhaustion, while constantly pummelling him
with questions, is to degrade him, to strip him of human dignity,
to deprive him of the will to resist, to make him a pitiable creature
mastered by the single desire – at all costs to be free of torment.
Any member of this or any other court, to escape such anguish,
would admit to almost any crime. Indeed, the infliction of such
psychological punishment is more reprehensible than a physical
attack: It leaves no discernible marks on the victim. (Perhaps it
is inaccurate to describe such punishment as not 'physical', since
pronounced fatigue may have hidden physiological consequences.)
Because it is thus concealed, it has, under the brutalitarian
régimes, become the favourite weapon of the secret police, bent
on procuring confessions as a means of convicting the innocent.

Caminito testified as follows as to why he confessed: At 10.30
pm on Monday, 12 May, the police allowed him to talk to Noia
who had been similarly subjected to prolonged questioning.
'He said, "Let us give them (the police) the same story they gave
us." He says, "It would not mean anything. . . . We can see a
lawyer this way. We will tell the lawyer what happened, and they
cannot do us nothing. We did not do it. You don't have to worry.
You can prove where you were, and I can prove also." I said "No,
it is not right." He said, "How long can I stand this? . . . Let us
make up the story they gave us and give them the same story and
get it over with." . . . So I told him the story that the detectives
had told me of what happened, as I had heard maybe fifty times,
so he said, "That is the story they told me." ' They then agreed to
confess. While confessing, when Caminito did not know the desired answer, the police captain told him what to say and he said
it. 'They put the words right in his mouth.' He 'gave those answers for fear'. We do not rest our decision on that testimony:
Even without it, we are bound to infer, on the undisputed facts,
that something of the sort actually happened. For his testimony in this respect closely resembles many reports of those

who, behind the Iron Curtain, after like treatment, confessed to crimes they had not committed.

Aristotle, thousands of years ago, wrote of torture 'that people under its compulsion tell lies quite as often as they tell the truth, sometimes persistently refusing to tell the truth, sometimes recklessly making a false charge in order to be let off sooner. We ought to be able to quote cases, familiar to the judges, in which this sort of thing has actually happened. We must say that evidence under torture is not trustworthy, the fact being that many men whether thick-witted, tough-skinned, or stout of heart endure their ordeal nobly, while cowards and timid men are full of boldness till they see the ordeal of these others; so that no trust can be placed in evidence under torture.' In the sixteenth century, Montaigne said that tortures 'seem to be a test of endurance rather than of truth. For why should pain rather make me say what is, rather than force me to say what is not? ... The effect is that the man whom the judge has put to the torture, that he may not die innocent, is made to die both innocent and tortured.'

It is imperative that our courts severely condemn confession by torture, the so-called 'Third Degree'. To treat it lightly, to condone it, encourages its continued use, with evil effects on the police: the official who utilises the Third Degree, since he violates statutes and the Constitution, is himself a criminal; and his infliction of torture on others brutalises him.

Hall remarks on the 'startling fact that there is hardly a single physical act of brutality inflicted by the ... N.K.V.D. which American policemen have not at some time perpetrated' (but adds that our police are less 'scientific' about torture). The important difference is that in Russia the coercion of confessions is (at least with respect to some subjects) legal and avowed while with us it is always illegal and secret. That difference is basic: it means that we have a principle of justice on which we can rely to bring such coercion into disrepute and disuse.

That principle the police traduce when they act on the theory that, to discharge their duty, they have the authority to dispense with a suspect's constitutional privileges because they believe him guilty. For it is not the function of the police in our democracy to determine a man's guilt.

Trials fairly conducted have, alas, led to the conviction of some innocent men. All such tragedies cannot be avoided even in the best contrived of legal systems. But surely we dare not permit tragedies of that sort to result from confessions by torture. One shudders to think what happens to an innocent man sent to jail. Bitter, resentful, he may become an apt student of the hardened professional criminals he meets in jail, and thereby be converted from innocence into real criminality. If he withstands such a conversion, he will, as a marked man, when released, have a hard struggle to earn an honest living. If again charged with crime, he will encounter a serious difficulty at a trial: if he takes the witness stand, his previous conviction will count against him; if, on that account, he does not testify, his silence will adversely affect him. And let it not be forgotten that police zeal to convict an innocent man means often that the guilty man escapes punishment.

We have here at some length expressed our abhorrence of confession by torture for this reason: that practice is unknown in England where, to our shame, they call it the 'American method'. There are those who say that American conditions compel such official resort to crime to catch and convict criminals. The absurdity of such a view is evidenced by the fact that our most effective American police force, the FBI, abjures this execrable method and, in its school for state and city police, teaches that the 'third degree' is both detestable and inefficient. Because proof, in court, of its use is most difficult, the only real hope for its eradication lies in the educative influences of such police as the FBI, so that all our American policemen will be trained to detest it. Repeated and emphatic judicial denunciations of that barbarism – whenever it is exposed, as in this case – can help to that end. Until that end is realised, the many decent police officers, in a police force generally addicted to that practice, will find themselves at so grave a disadvantage that sooner or later, they may, if they do not themselves indulge in it, at least acquiesce in it. For the accustomed ways of any group usually come to seem the right ways. As Chesterton said, 'The horrible thing about all legal officials, even the best, about all judges, magistrates, detectives and policemen, is not that they are wicked (some of them are good), not that they are stupid (several of them are quite intelligent); it is simply that they have got used to it.'

At any rate, as long as many policemen third-degree the helpless, the public will tend to believe that all police officers do likewise, that police brutality, although unfortunate, is normal. (That such a belief is widespread, anyone can see who reads the hundreds of popular, hard-boiled, detective novels.) As a consequence, the public suspects that almost all policemen deal brutally with suspects. Accordingly, the citizenry do not regard the police with respect, and fail adequately to co-operate with the police, a co-operation without which the police in a democracy cannot efficiently perform their lawful functions. Worst of all, public cynicism develops concerning the basic ideals expressed in our constitution.... [704]

[705] Recently many outstanding Americans have been much concerned – and justifiably – with inroads on the constitutional privileges of persons questioned about subversive activities. But concern with such problems, usually those of fairly prominent persons, should not blind one to the less dramatic, less publicised plight of humble inconspicuous men (like Caminito) when unconstitutionally victimised by officialdom. It will not do to say – as some do – that deep concern with such problems of the humble is the mark of an 'old-fashioned liberal'. For repeated and unredressed attacks on the constitutional liberties of the humble will tend to destroy the foundations supporting the constitutional liberties of everyone. The test of the moral quality of a civilisation is its treatment of the weak and powerless.

MR JUSTICE HOLMES and
MR JUSTICE BRANDEIS

Evidence from Eavesdropping

Dissenting opinions in Olmstead v. U.S.*

[The Supreme Court of the United States in 1928 ruled that
evidence of conversations, heard by the police through the device
of wiretapping, was admissible in evidence in federal prosecutions. Wiretapping, the majority of the Court held, did not
constitute 'unreasonable search and seizure' within the meaning
of the Constitution. Mr Justice Holmes and Mr Justice Brandeis
both dissented (as did Chief Justice Stone and Mr Justice Butler),
and demonstrated the evils of police practice in eavesdropping,
even for the purpose of catching the worst criminals.

In 1934 their dissent was upheld by Congress, which by Statute
made it unlawful for any person, unless authorised by the sender,
to 'intercept' any communication by wire or radio, or to 'divulge'
the contents of a communication so intercepted. Although this is
a federal rule, some States have followed suit. But those States
whose laws allow the admissibility of wiretapped evidence are
unaffected; and the Supreme Court has so far declined to disturb
a State conviction resulting from such evidence.

English law adheres to the simple, if somewhat morally reprehensible, rule that evidence, if otherwise admissible, is not
made inadmissible at a trial simply because the police have
obtained it illegally. Only this year, for the first time, the
Court of Criminal Appeal upheld the admissibility of tape-
recordings in evidence, and in doing so took no account of the
American experience. The English judges made no distinction
between human eavesdropping and eavesdropping by mech-
anised devices. Both were fair-game in the 'war' against 'criminals
who do not act in accordance with the Queensberry rules'; R. *v.*
Ali Maqsud [1965] 3 W.L.R. 229.]

* 277 U.S. 438, 469, 471 (1928).

MR JUSTICE HOLMES : My brother Brandeis has given this case so exhaustive an examination that I desire to add but a few words. While I do not deny it, I am not prepared to say that the penumbra of the Fourth and Fifth Amendments covers the defendant, although I fully agree that courts are apt to err by sticking too closely to the words of a law where those words import a policy that goes beyond them. But I think, as Mr Justice Brandeis says, that apart from the Constitution the Government ought not to use evidence obtained and only obtainable by a criminal act. There is no body of precedents by which we are bound, and which confines us to logical deduction from established rules. Therefore we must consider the two objects of desire, both of which we cannot have, and make up our minds which to choose. It is desirable that criminals should be detected, and to that end that all available evidence should be used. It also is desirable that the Government should not itself foster and pay for other crimes, when they are the means by which the evidence is to be obtained. If it pays its officers for having got evidence by crime I do not see why it may not as well pay them for getting it in the same way, and I can attach no importance to protestations of disapproval if it knowingly accepts and pays and announces that in future it will pay for the fruits. We have to choose, and for my part I think it a less evil that some criminals should escape than that the Government should play an ignoble part.

For those who agree with me, no distinction can be taken between the Government as prosecutor and the Government as judge. If the existing code does not permit district attorneys to have a hand in such dirty business it does not permit the judge to allow such iniquities to succeed. And if all that I have said so far be accepted it makes no difference that in this case wiretapping is made a crime by the law of the State, not by the law of the United States. It is true that a State cannot make rules of evidence for courts of the United States, but the State has authority over the conduct in question, and I hardly think that the United States would appear to greater advantage when paying for an odious crime against State law than when inciting to the disregard of its own. I am aware of the often repeated statement that in a criminal proceeding the court will not take notice of the manner in which papers offered in evidence have been obtained. But that somewhat rudimentary mode of disposing of the question has been over-thrown [by the courts]. I have said that we are free to choose between two principles of policy. But if we are to confine ourselves to precedent and logic the reason for excluding evidence obtained by violating the Constitution seems to me logically to lead to excluding evidence obtained by a crime of the officers of the law.

MR JUSTICE BRANDEIS: [471] The defendants were convicted of conspiring to violate the National Prohibition Act. Before any of the persons now charged had been arrested or indicted, the telephones by means of which they habitually communicated with one another and with others had been tapped by federal officers. To this end, a lineman of long experience in wiretapping was employed, on behalf of the Government and at its expense. He tapped eight telephones, some in the homes of the persons charged, some in their offices. Acting on behalf of the Govern-ment and in their official capacity, at least six other prohibition agents listened over the tapped wires and reported the messages taken. Their operations extended over a period of nearly five months. The typewritten record of the notes of conversations overheard occupies 775 typewritten pages. By objections season-ably made and persistently renewed, the defendants objected to the admission of the evidence obtained by wiretapping, on the ground that the Government's wiretapping constituted an unreasonable search and seizure, in violation of the Fourth Amendment; and that the use as evidence of the conversations overheard compelled the defendants to be witnesses against themselves, in violation of the Fifth Amendment.

The Government makes no attempt to defend the methods employed by its officers. Indeed, it concedes that if wiretapping can be deemed a search and seizure within the Fourth Amend-ment, such wiretapping as was practised in the case at bar was an unreasonable search and seizure, and that the evidence thus ob-tained was inadmissible. But it relies on the language of the Amendment; and it claims that the protection given thereby can-not properly be held to include a telephone conversation.

'We must never forget,' said Mr Chief Justice Marshall in *McCulloch* v. *Maryland*, 4 Wheat. 316, 407, 'that it is a constitu-tion we are expounding.' Since then, this Court has repeatedly sustained the exercise of power by Congress, under various clauses of that instrument, over objects of which the Fathers could not have dreamed. We have likewise held that general limitations on the powers of Government, like those embodied in the due process clauses of the Fifth and Fourteenth Amendments, do not forbid the United States or the States from meeting modern conditions by regulations which 'a century ago, or even half a century ago, probably would have been rejected as arbitrary and oppressive'. Clauses guaranteeing to the individual protection against specific abuses of power, must have a similar capacity of adaptation to a changing world. It was with reference to such a clause that this Court said in *Weems* v. *United States*, 217 U.S. 349, 373: 'Legislation, both statutory and constitutional, is enacted, it is true, from an experience of evils, but its general language should not, therefore, be necessarily confined to the form that evil had theretofore taken. Time works changes, brings into existence new conditions and purposes. Therefore a principle to be vital must be capable of wider application than the mischief which gave it birth. This is peculiarly true of constitutions. They are not ephemeral enactments, designed to meet passing occasions. They are, to use the words of Chief Justice Marshall "designed to approach immortality as nearly as human institutions can approach it". The future is their care and provision for events of good and bad tendencies of which no prophecy can be made. In the application of a constitution, therefore, our contemplation cannot be only of what has been but of what may be. Under any other rule a constitution would indeed be as easy of application as it would be deficient in efficacy and power. Its general principles would have little value and be converted by precedent into impotent and lifeless formulas. Rights declared in words might be lost in reality.'

When the Fourth and Fifth Amendments were adopted, 'the form that evil had theretofore taken', had been necessarily simple. Force and violence were then the only means known to man by which a Government could directly effect self-incrimination. It could compel the individual to testify – a compulsion effected, if need be, by torture. It could secure possession of his papers and other articles incident to his private life – a seizure effected, if need be, by breaking and entry. Protection against such invasion of 'the sanctities of man's home and the privacies of life' was provided in the Fourth and Fifth Amendments by specific language. But 'time works changes, brings into existence new conditions and purposes'. Subtler and more far-reaching means of invading privacy have become available to the Government. Discovery and invention have made it possible for the Government, by means far more effective than stretching upon the rack, to obtain disclosure in court of what is whispered in the closet.

Moreover, 'in the application of a constitution, our contemplation cannot be only of what has been but of what may be'. The progress of science in furnishing the Government with means of espionage is not likely to stop with wiretapping. Ways may some day be developed by which the Government, without removing papers from secret drawers, can reproduce them in court, and by which it will be enabled to expose to a jury the most intimate occurrences of the home. Advances in the psychic and related sciences may bring means of exploring unexpressed beliefs, thoughts and emotions. 'That places the liberty of every man in the hands of every petty officer' was said by James Otis of much lesser intrusions than these.* To Lord Camden, a far slighter intrusion seemed 'subversive of all the comforts of society'.† Can it be that the Constitution affords no protection against such invasions of individual security?

A sufficient answer is found in *Boyd* v. *United States*, 116 U.S. 616, 627–630, a case that will be remembered as long as civil liberty lives in the United States. This Court there reviewed the history that lay behind the Fourth and Fifth Amendments. We said with reference to Lord Camden's judgment in *Entick* v. *Carrington*, 19 Howell's State Trials, 1030: 'The principles laid down in this opinion affect the very essence of constitutional liberty and security. They reach farther than the concrete form of the case there before the court, with its adventitious circumstances; they apply to all invasions on the part of the Government and its employees of the sanctities of man's home and the privacies of life. It is not the breaking of his doors, and the rummaging of his

* Otis' Argument against Writs of Assistance. See TUDOR, *James Otis*, p. 66; JOHN ADAMS, *Works*, Vol. II, p. 524; MINOT, *Continuation of the History of Massachusetts Bay*, Vol. II, p. 95.
† *Entick* v. *Carrington*, 19 Howell's State Trials, 1030, 1066.

drawers, that constitutes the essence of the offence; but it is the invasion of his indefeasible right of personal security, personal liberty and private property, where that right has never been forfeited by his conviction of some public offence – it is the invasion of this sacred right which underlies and constitutes the essence of Lord Camden's judgment. Breaking into a house and opening boxes and drawers are circumstances of aggravation; but any forcible and compulsory extortion of a man's own testimony or of his private papers to be used as evidence of a crime or to forfeit his goods, is within the condemnation of that judgment. In this regard the Fourth and Fifth Amendments run almost into each other.'

In *Ex parte Jackson*, 96 U.S. 727, it was held that a sealed letter entrusted to the mail is protected by the Amendments. The mail is a public service furnished by the Government. The telephone is a public service furnished by its authority. There is, in essence, no difference between the sealed letter and the private telephone message. As Judge Rudkin said below: 'True the one is visible, the other invisible; the one is tangible, the other intangible; the one is sealed and the other unsealed, but these are distinctions without a difference.' The evil incident to invasion of the privacy of the telephone is far greater than that involved in tampering with the mails. Whenever a telephone line is tapped, the privacy of the persons at both ends of the line is invaded and all conversations between them upon any subject, and although proper, confidential and privileged, may be overheard. Moreover, the tapping of one man's telephone line involves the tapping of the telephone of every other person whom he may call or who may call him. As a means of espionage, writs of assistance and general warrants are but puny instruments of tyranny and oppression when compared with wiretapping.

Time and again, this Court in giving effect to the principle underlying the Fourth Amendment, has refused to place an unduly literal construction upon it. This was notably illustrated in the *Boyd* case itself. Taking language in its ordinary meaning, there is no 'search' or 'seizure' when a defendant is required to produce a document in the orderly process of a court's procedure. 'The right of the people to be secure in their persons, houses, papers, and effects, against unreasonable searches and seizures', would not be violated, under any ordinary construction of language, by compelling obedience to a subpoena. But this Court holds the evidence inadmissible simply because the information leading to the issue of the subpoena has been unlawfully secured. Literally, there is no 'search' or 'seizure' when a friendly visitor abstracts papers from an office; yet we held in *Gouled* v. *United States*, 255 U.S. 298, that evidence so obtained could not be used. No court which looked at the words of the Amendment rather than at its underlying purpose would hold, as this Court did in *Ex parte Jackson*, 96 U.S. 727, 733, that its protection extended to letters in the mails. The provision against self-incrimination in the Fifth Amendment has been given an equally broad construction. The language is: 'No person ... shall be compelled in any criminal case to be a witness against himself.' Yet we have held, not only that the protection of the Amendment extends to a witness before a grand jury, although he has not been charged with crime, *Counselman* v. *Hitchcock*, 142 U.S. 547, 562, 586, but that: 'It applies alike to civil and criminal proceedings, wherever the answer might tend to subject to criminal responsibility him who gives it. The privilege protects a mere witness as fully as it does one who is also a party defendant.' The narrow language of the Amendment has been consistently construed in the light of its object, 'to insure that a person should not be compelled, when acting as a witness in any investigation, to give testimony which might tend to show that he himself had committed a crime. The privilege is limited to criminal matters, but it is as broad as the mischief against which it seeks to guard.'

Decisions of this Court applying the principle of the *Boyd* case have settled these things. Unjustified search and seizure violates the Fourth Amendment, whatever the character of the paper; whether the paper when taken by the federal officers was in the home, in an office or elsewhere; whether the taking was effected by force, by fraud, or in the orderly process of a court's procedure. From these decisions, it follows necessarily that the Amendment is violated by the officer's reading the paper without a physical seizure, without his even touching it; and that use, in any criminal proceeding, of the contents of the paper so examined – as where they are testified to by a federal officer who thus saw the document or where, through knowledge so obtained, a copy has been procured elsewhere – any such use constitutes a violation of the Fifth Amendment.

The protection guaranteed by the Amendments is much broader in scope. The makers of our Constitution undertook to secure conditions favourable to the pursuit of happiness. They recognised the significance of man's spiritual nature, of his feelings and of his intellect. They knew that only a part of the pain, pleasure and satisfactions of life are to be found in material things. They sought to protect Americans in their beliefs, their thoughts, their emotions and their sensations. They conferred, as against the Government, the right to be let alone – the most comprehensive of rights and the right most valued by civilised men. To protect that right, every unjustifiable intrusion by the Government upon the privacy of the individual, whatever the means employed, must be deemed a violation of the Fourth Amendment. And the use, as evidence in a criminal proceeding, of facts ascertained by such intrusion must be deemed a violation of the Fifth.

Applying to the Fourth and Fifth Amendments the established rule of construction, the defendants' objections to the evidence obtained by wiretapping must, in my opinion, be sustained. It is, of course, immaterial where the physical connection with the telephone wires leading into the defendants' premises was made. And it is also immaterial that the intrusion was in aid of law enforcement. Experience should teach us to be most on our guard to protect liberty when the Government's purposes are beneficent. Men born to freedom are naturally alert to repel invasion of their liberty by evil-minded rulers. The greatest dangers to liberty lurk in insidious encroachment by men of zeal, well-meaning but without understanding.*

---

* The point is thus stated by counsel for the telephone companies, who have filed a brief as *amici curiae*: 'Criminals will not escape detection and conviction merely because evidence obtained by tapping wires of a public telephone system is inadmissible, if it should be so held; but, in any event, it is better that a few criminals escape than that the privacies of life af all the people be exposed to the agents of the Government, who will act at their own discretion, the honest and the dishonest, unauthorised and unrestrained by the courts. Legislation making wiretapping a crime will not suffice if the courts nevertheless hold the evidence to be lawful.'

Independently of the constitutional question, I am of opinion that the judgment should be reversed. By the laws of Washington, wiretapping is a crime. Pierce's Code, 1921, § 8976 (18). To prove its case, the Government was obliged to lay bare the crimes committed by its officers on its behalf. A federal court should not permit such a prosecution to continue.

The situation in the case at bar differs widely from that presented in *Burdeau* v. *McDowell*, 256 U.S. 465. There, only a single lot of papers was involved. They had been obtained by a private detective while acting on behalf of a private party; without the knowledge of any federal official; long before anyone had thought of instituting a federal prosecution. Here, the evidence obtained by crime was obtained at the Government's expense, by its officers, while acting on its behalf; the officers who committed these crimes are the same officers who were charged with the enforcement of the Prohibition Act; the crimes of these officers were committed for the purpose of securing evidence with which to obtain an indictment and to secure a conviction. The evidence so obtained constitutes the warp and woof of the Government's case. The aggregate of the Government evidence occupies 306 pages of the printed record. More than 210 of them are filled by recitals of the details of the wiretapping and of facts ascertained thereby. There is literally no other evidence of guilt on the part of some of the defendants except that illegally obtained by these officers. As to nearly all the defendants (except those who admitted guilt), the evidence relied upon to secure a conviction consisted mainly of that which these officers had so obtained by violating the State law.

As Judge Rudkin said below: 'Here we are concerned with neither eavesdroppers nor thieves. Nor are we concerned with the acts of private individuals. ... We are concerned only with the acts of federal agents whose powers are limited and controlled by the Constitution of the United States.' The Eighteenth Amendment has not in terms empowered Congress to authorise anyone to violate the criminal laws of a State. And Congress has never purported to do so. The terms of appointment of federal prohibition agents do not purport to confer upon them authority to violate any criminal law. Their superior officer, the Secretary of the Treasury, has not instructed them to commit crime on behalf of the United States. It may be assumed that the Attorney General of the United States did not give any such instruction.

When these unlawful acts were committed, they were crimes only of the officers individually. The Government was innocent, in legal contemplation; for no federal official is authorised to commit a crime on its behalf. When the Government, having full knowledge, sought, through the Department of Justice, to avail itself of the fruits of these acts in order to accomplish its own ends, it assumed moral responsibility for the officers' crimes. And if this Court should permit the Government, by means of its officers' crimes, to effect its purpose of punishing the defendants, there would seem to be present all the elements of a ratification. If so, the Government itself would become a lawbreaker.

Will this Court by sustaining the judgment below sanction such conduct on the part of the Executive? The governing principle has long been settled. It is that a court will not redress a wrong when he who invokes its aid has unclean hands. The maxim of unclean hands comes from courts of equity. But the principle prevails also in courts of law. Its common application is in civil actions between private parties. Where the Government is the actor, the reasons for applying it are even more persuasive. Where the remedies invoked are those of the criminal law, the reasons are compelling.

The door of a court is not barred because the plaintiff has committed a crime. The confined criminal is as much entitled to redress as his most virtuous fellow citizen; no record of crime, however long, makes one an outlaw. The court's aid is denied only when he who seeks it has violated the law in connection with the very transaction as to which he seeks legal redress. Then aid is denied despite the defendant's wrong. It is denied in order to maintain respect for law; in order to promote confidence in the administration of justice; in order to preserve the judicial process from contamination. The rule is one, not of action, but of inaction. It is sometimes spoken of as a rule of substantive law. But it extends to matters of procedure as well. A defence may be waived. It is waived when not pleaded. But the objection that the plaintiff comes with unclean hands will be taken by the court itself. It will be taken despite the wish to the contrary of all the parties to the litigation. The court protects itself.

Decency, security and liberty alike demand that government officials shall be subjected to the same rules of conduct that are commands to the citizen. In a government of laws, existence of the government will be imperilled if it fails to observe the law scrupulously. Our Government is the potent, the omnipresent teacher. For good or for ill, it teaches the whole people by its example. Crime is contagious. If the Government becomes a law-breaker, it breeds contempt for law; it invites every man to become a law unto himself; it invites anarchy. To declare that in the administration of the criminal law the end justifies the means – to declare that the Government may commit crimes in order to secure the conviction of a private criminal – would bring terrible retribution. Against that pernicious doctrine this Court should resolutely set its face.

Dirty Business

*Dissenting opinion in On Lee v. United States**

[A quarter of a century after *Olmstead* v. *United States*, the Supreme Court still declined to declare illegally acquired evidence inadmissible, despite the action of Congress and many State legislatures in excluding wire-tapped evidence from being admissible at a trial. The foreboding of continued unlawful police activity, predicted by Mr. Justice Brandeis, is restated by Mr. Justice Frankfurter.

On Lee owned a laundry in Hoboken, New York. During the time he was on bail pending trial on narcotics charges, an old acquaintance and former employee of On Lee's entered the customer's room of the laundry and engaged in conversation with On Lee. Unbeknown to On Lee the visitor was an 'undercover agent' for the Federal Bureau of Narcotics and had concealed on him a radio transmitter. On Lee, on that occasion and later during a street conversation, made incriminating statements to the 'undercover agent'. These conversations were 'audited' outside the laundry by another federal agent who gave evidence of the statement at On Lee's trial. The trial court admitted the evidence in face of On Lee's objection to its admissibility.]

The law of this Court ought not to be open to the just charge of having been dictated by the 'odious doctrine', as Mr Justice Brandeis called it, that the end justifies reprehensible means. To approve legally what we disapprove morally, on the ground of practical convenience, is to yield to a short-sighted view of practicality. It derives from a preoccupation with what is episodic and a disregard of long-run consequences. The method by which the state chiefly exerts an influence upon the conduct of its citizens, it was wisely said by Archbishop William Temple, is 'the moral qualities which it exhibits in its own conduct'.

* 343 U.S. 747, 758 (1952)

Loose talk about war against crime too easily infuses the administration of justice with the psychology and morals of war. It is hardly conducive to the soundest employment of the judicial process. Nor are the needs of an effective penal code seen in the truest perspective by talk about a criminal prosecution's not being a game in which the Government loses because its officers have not played according to rule. Of course criminal prosecution is more than a game. But in any event it should not be deemed to be a dirty game in which 'the dirty business' of criminals is outwitted by 'the dirty business' of law officers. The contrast between morality professed by society and immorality practised on its behalf makes for contempt of law. Respect for law cannot be turned off and on as though it were a hot-water faucet.

It is a quarter century since this Court, by the narrowest margin, refused to put wire-tapping beyond the constitutional pale where a fair construction of the Fourth Amendment should properly place it. Since then, instead of going from strength to strength in combatting crime, we have gone from inefficiency to inefficiency, from corruption to corruption. The moral insight of Mr. Justice Brandeis unerringly foresaw this inevitability. 'The progress of science in furnishing the Government with means of espionage is not likely to stop with wire-tapping. Ways may some day be developed by which the Government, without removing papers from secret drawers, can reproduce them in court, and by which it will be enabled to expose to a jury the most intimate occurrences of the home. Advances in the psychic and related sciences may bring means of exploring unexpressed beliefs, thoughts and emotions.' The circumstances of the present case show how the rapid advances of science are made available for that police intrusion into our private lives against which the Fourth Amendment of the constitution was set on guard.

It is noteworthy that, although this Court deemed wire-tapping not outlawed by the constitution, Congress outlawed it legislatively by the Communications Act of 1934. What is perhaps even more noteworthy is its pervasive disregard in practice by those who as law officers owe special obedience to law. What is true of the federal Act against wire-tapping and its violations is widely true of related state legislation and its disobedience.

Few sociological generalisations are more valid than that lawlessness begets lawlessness.

The members of this Court who so vigorously urged that wire-tapping is within the clear scope of the prohibition of the Fourth Amendment were no sentimentalists about crime or criminals. Mr Justice Holmes, Mr Justice Brandeis, Mr Justice Butler and Mr Chief Justice Stone were no softies. In all matters of social policy we have to choose, and it was the hardy philosophy of life that his years in the Army of the Potomac taught him that led Mr Justice Holmes to deem it 'a less evil that some criminals should escape than that the Government should play an ignoble part'.

Suppose it be true that through 'dirty business' it is easier for prosecutors and police to bring an occasional criminal to heel. It is most uncritical to assume that unless the Government is allowed to practise 'dirty business' crime would become rampant or would go unpunished.

In the first place, the social phenomena of crime are imbedded in the texture of our society. Equally deep-seated are the causes of all that is sordid and ineffective in the administration of our criminal law. These are outcroppings, certainly in considerable part, of modern industrialism and of the prevalent standards of the community, related to the inadequacy in our day of early American methods and machinery for law enforcement and to the small pursuit of scientific inquiry into the causes and treatment of crime.

Of course we cannot wait on the slow progress of the sociological sciences in illuminating so much that is still dark. Nor should we relax for a moment vigorous enforcement of the criminal law until society, by its advanced civilised nature, will beget an atmosphere and environment in which crime will shrink to relative insignificance. My deepest feeling against giving legal sanction to such 'dirty business' as the record in this case discloses is that it makes for lazy and not alert law enforcement. It puts a premium on force and fraud, not on imagination and enterprise and professional training. The third degree, search without warrant, wire-tapping and the like, were not tolerated in what was probably the most successful administration in our time of the busiest United States Attorney's office. This experience under Henry L.

Stimson in the Southern District of New York, compared with happenings elsewhere, doubtless planted in me a deep conviction that these short-cuts in the detection and prosecution of crime are as self-defeating as they are immoral.

Sir James Fitzjames Stephen brings significant testimony on this point:

'During the discussions which took place on the Indian Code of Criminal Procedure in 1872 some observations were made on the reasons which occasionally lead native police officers to apply torture to prisoners. An experienced civil officer observed, "There is a great deal of laziness in it. It is far pleasanter to sit comfortably in the shade running red pepper into a poor devil's eyes than to go about in the sun hunting up evidence." This was a new view to me, but I have no doubt of its truth.' 1 Stephen, A History of the Criminal Law of England (1883), 442, note. Compare §§ 25 and 26 of the Indian Evidence Act (1872).

And Fitzjames Stephen, who acted on this experience in drawing the Indian Evidence Act, was no softie, either before he became a judge or on the bench.

Accordingly I adhere to the views expressed in *Goldman* v. *United States*, 316 U.S. 129, 136, that the *Olmstead* case should be overruled for the reasons set forth in the dissenting opinions in that case. These views have been strongly underlined by the steady increase of lawlessness on the part of law officers, even after Congress has forbidden what the dissenters in *Olmstead* found the constitution to forbid.

Even on the basis of the prior decisions of this Court, however, I feel bound to dissent. The Court seems not content with calling a halt at the place it had reached on what I deem to be the wrong road. As my brother BURTON shows, the Court now pushes beyond the lines of legality heretofore drawn. Such encouragement to lazy, immoral conduct by the police does not bode well for effective law enforcement. Nor will crime be checked by such means.

Family Relations

The Marriage Union

Judgment in Evans v. Evans†

[35] THIS CAUSE HAS been carefully instructed with evidence by the practisers, who have had the conduct of it; and has been very elaborately argued by the counsel on both sides. It now devolves upon me to pronounce the legal result of the evidence, which has been thus collected, and of the arguments raised upon that evidence – a duty heavy in itself, from the quantity and weight of the matter; and extremely painful, from the nature and tendency of a great part of it, and from the inefficacy of this Court to give relief adequate to the wishes of both parties. Heavy and painful as it is, it is a duty which *must* be discharged; and which can only be discharged with satisfaction under a consciousness, that it is discharged with attention and impartiality, and under the reflection that if, after the endeavours which I have used in cleansing and in instructing my own conscience upon the subject, I should have taken what may be deemed an undue impression of the case, the laws of this country have not been deficient in providing a mode, by which the parties may be relieved against the infirmities of my judgment.

The humanity of the Court has been loudly and repeatedly invoked. Humanity is the second virtue of courts, but undoubtedly the first is justice. If it were a question of humanity simply, and of humanity which confined its views merely to the happiness of the present parties, it would be a question easily decided upon first impressions. Everybody must feel a wish to sever those who wish to live separate from each other, who cannot live together with any degree of harmony, and consequently with any degree of happiness; but my situation does not allow me to indulge the feelings, much less the *first* feelings, of an individual. The law has said that married persons shall not be *legally* separated upon

* Then Sir William Scott, judge of the Consistory Court of London.
† (1790) 1 Haggard Consistory Reports 34.

the mere disinclination of one or both to cohabit together. The disinclination must be founded upon reasons, which the law approves, and it is my duty to see whether those reasons exist in the present case.

To vindicate the policy of the law is no necessary part of the office of a judge: but if it were, it would not be difficult to shew that the law in this respect has acted with its usual wisdom and humanity, with that true wisdom, and that real humanity, that regards the general interests of mankind. For though in particular cases, the repugnance of the law to dissolve the obligations of matrimonial cohabitation, may operate with great severity upon individuals; yet it must be carefully remembered, that the general happiness of the married life is secured by its indissolubility. When people understand that they *must* live together, except for a very few reasons known to the law, they learn to soften by mutual accommodation that yoke which they know they cannot shake off; they become good husbands, and good wives, from the necessity of remaining husbands and wives; for necessity is a powerful master in teaching the duties which it imposes. If it were once understood, that upon mutual disgust married persons might be legally separated, many couples, who now pass through the world with mutual comfort, with attention to their common offspring and to the moral order of civil society, might have been at this moment living in a state of mutual unkindness – in a state of estrangement from their common offspring – and in a state of the most licentious and unreserved immorality. In this case, as in many others, the happiness of some individuals must be sacrificed to the greater and more general good.

That the duty of cohabitation is released by the cruelty of one of the parties is admitted, but the question occurs, *What is cruelty?* In the present case it is hardly necesssary for me to define it; because the facts here complained of are such as fall within the most restricted definition of cruelty; they affect not only the comfort, but they affect the health, and even the life of the party. I shall therefore decline the task of laying down a direct definition. This, however, must be understood, that it is the duty of courts, and consequently the inclination of courts, to keep the rule extremely strict. The causes must be grave and weighty, and such as shew an absolute impossibility that the duties of the married life can be discharged. In a state of personal danger no duties can be discharged; for the duty of self-preservation must take place before the duties of marriage, which are secondary both in commencement and in obligation; but what falls short of this is with great caution to be admitted. The rule of *per quod consortium amittitur* is but an inadequate test; for it still remains to be enquired, what conduct ought to produce that effect? whether the consortium is reasonably lost? and whether the party quitting has not too hastily abandoned the consortium?

What merely wounds the mental feelings is in few cases to be admitted, where they are not accompanied with bodily injury, either actual or menaced. Mere austerity of temper, petulance of manners, rudeness of language, a want of civil attention and accommodation, even occasional sallies of passion, if they do not threaten bodily harm, do not amount to legal cruelty; they are high moral offences in the marriage-state undoubtedly, not innocent surely in any state of life, but still they are not that cruelty against which the law can relieve. Under such conduct of either of the parties, for it may exist on one side as well as on the other, the suffering party must bear in some degree the consequences of an injudicious connection; must subdue by decent resistance or by prudent conciliation; and if this cannot be done, both must suffer in silence. And if it be complained that by this inactivity of the courts much injustice may be suffered, and much misery produced, the answer is, that courts of justice do not pretend to furnish cures for all the miseries of human life. They redress or punish gross violations of duty, but they go no farther; they cannot make men virtuous: and, as the happiness of the world depends upon its virtue, there may be much unhappiness in it which human laws cannot undertake to remove.

Still less is it cruelty, where it wounds not the natural feelings, but the acquired feelings arising from particular rank and situation; for the court has no scale of sensibilities, by which it can judge the quantum of injury done and felt; and therefore, though the court will not absolutely exclude considerations of that sort, where they are stated merely as a matter of aggravation, yet they cannot constitute cruelty where it would otherwise not have existed: of course, the denial of little indulgences and particular accommodations, which the delicacy of the world is apt to number among its necessaries, is not cruelty. It may, to be sure, be a harsh thing to refuse the use of a carriage, or the use of a servant; it may in many cases be extremely unhandsome, extremely disgraceful to the character of the husband; but the Ecclesiastical Court does not look to such matters: the great ends of marriage may very well be carried on without them; and if people will quarrel about such matters, and which they certainly may do in many cases with a great deal of acrimony, and sometimes with much reason, yet they must decide such matters as well as they can in their own domestic *forum*.

These are negative descriptions of cruelty; they shew only what is *not* cruelty, and are yet perhaps the safest definitions which can be given under the infinite variety of possible cases that may come before the court ... In the older cases of this sort, which I have had the opportunity of looking into, I have observed that the danger of life, limb, or health, is usually inserted as a ground upon which the court has proceeded to a separation. This doctrine has been repeatedly applied by the court in the cases that have been cited. The court has never been driven off this ground. It has been always jealous of the inconvenience of departing from it, and I have heard of no one case cited, in which the court has granted a divorce without proof given of a *reasonable apprehension* of bodily hurt. I say an *apprehension*, because assuredly the court is not to wait till the hurt is actually done; but the apprehension must be *reasonable*: it must not be an apprehension arising merely from an exquisite and diseased sensibility of mind. Petty vexations applied to such a constitution of mind may certainly in time wear out the animal machine, but still they are not cases of legal relief; people must relieve themselves as well as they can by prudent resistance – by calling in the succours of religion and the consolation of friends; but the aid of courts is not to be resorted to in such cases with any effect.

The libel states the marriage at *Calcutta*, in the East Indies, in the year 1778; and it proceeds to plead the character of the parties; *that he is a person morose, sullen, tyrannical,* and so on; and that *she is in every respect the reverse, a woman of mild and tender disposition.* These pictures are reversed, as is the usual manner, in the responsive allegation [40] ... [41] The case indeed is *civil*, as has been repeatedly observed, but the facts are undoubtedly criminal; or else why plead the bad disposition of the husband? Why plead it, except for the purpose of shewing that he has committed bad acts? Now I hardly know any case, in which it is allowed to create a presumption in favour of the probability of criminal facts having been done, where that presumption is founded upon the mere opinions of men concerning general disposition. Criminal facts must be tried by themselves. To try them by opinions ... is extremely dangerous for the court: to the individual, who is exposed to an enquiry of this kind, it is dangerous in the extreme; to place a man in this sort of legal pillory, where all who choose may pelt at him, is exposing an individual to the injustice of mankind, in such a way, as I am sure the justice of courts cannot relieve him from ... [42]

[48] [As to character,] the little that I have to say, is for the benefit of the parties; and it is this, that here again, if the matter rested simply upon the evidence given of character, yet after all the unhappy pains which have been taken to blacken each other, I see no reason why these two persons might not have passed through the world comfortably together, with a little discretion and management on their own side, and some discretion and management on the part of those who are mutually connected with them. To be sure, if people come together in marriage with extravagant expectations that all are to be halcyon days, the husband conceiving that all is to be authority with him, and the wife, that all is to be accommodation to her, everybody sees how that must end: but if they come together with the reflection, that, not bringing perfection in themselves, they have no right to expect it on the other side; that having respectively many infirmities of their own to be overlooked, they must overlook the infirmities in each other; then, if friends will be discreet enough to support them in the execution of their duty, there is a high probability that something like happiness might be produced ...[49]

[55] ... a very material fact in the cause is this – that, purely to gratify her wishes, and to consult her health, he quitted India: a country where he was almost naturalised, and where his prospects of avarice and ambition, at that period of time, were extremely inviting. ... But, say the gentlemen, there is no great merit in that, *he had got enough*. There is surely some merit in

knowing that; it is a merit everybody does not acquire; it is a proof of moderation, at least; and that he is not the mean and avaricious person which he has been represented to be: and, supposing that he was that mean and avaricious person, still there is more relative merit towards Mrs Evans, because, if he was a man extremely fond of his money and yet gave up his money on account of his wife, it is hard to say he had not some degree of fondness for his wife . . .

I am clear, therefore, that up to the time of the voyage nothing material had happened to cloud the happiness of the family . . . Till this time I see in the conduct of Mr Evans nothing to blame – I see much to approve. It is, however, upon this voyage, *mala ducta avi domum*, that a change of conduct in Mr Evans is first suggested to have taken place. It is not very well agreed what this change was, whether it was an indulgence of ungovernable sallies of ill temper, or whether it was a cool systematic plan of distressing his wife, by the most atrocious ill-usage; but certainly two things more inconsistent cannot be, than cool hypocrisy and wild passion. Now it is a strong presumption with me against the supposition of its being a case of ungovernable passions, that passions so inordinate appear to have developed themselves for the first time in the course of this voyage. If so, I think there must have been an alteration in the constitution of this man's mind; which is highly incredible. The material witnesses therefore resort to the other supposition . . .

One cannot help observing, that taking it to be a cool deep-laid plan, to be pursued and carried into effect in a secret way, the scene for the execution of such a plan is as unhappily chosen as can be. Everybody knows, that secrecy on board a ship is a thing not to be thought of. People cooped up in a ship live, and are forced to live, in that state of miserable intimacy, which makes almost everything which is done or said, known to every other person: there is for a time, a very unhappy circumstance it is, almost a suspension of everything like personal delicacy, every word and every act is known to almost everybody. Now, to suppose that man in such a situation should first think of opening a plan of secret violence, one must first suppose, not only that he left his temper in India, but that he left his common sense with it . . .

[68] [His Lordship discussed at length the conflicting testimony as to one incident on board, and concluded] that there was something of a struggle, how arising I don't know, but it was a struggle of no consequences; and that is the important point. If it had drawn consequences after it, there must have been other witnesses, and the witness who was there would have acted otherwise. It must have been therefore a trifle, and in being coloured as a matter of importance it has received an undue colour; the basis of the fact is extremely slight, and all beyond is colour – is exaggeration – is passion.

Having disposed of this great leading fact in the voyage, I shall dispatch in fewer words the other facts which are charged: in the first place, because they are, compared with this fact, very slight; in the next place, because they stand upon the single testimony of Mrs Hartle, who, in my opinion, has taken a very undue and extravagant impression of the whole business.

There is another charge, which is so strong a proof of this, that I shall notice it for no other purpose, than to exemplify the strong bias of this witness for making mountains out of molehills. I mean her evidence upon that article which charges the business of the noises. It is pleaded, that *while Mrs Evans was in a very weak and sickly state, Mr Evans accustomed himself, in the most unfeeling and cruel manner, to distress her and increase her pain, by making a violent noise with a hammer close to her.*

I had very great doubts about admitting this article. I admitted it upon an idea suggested naturally by the words, that this gentleman came, without any reason whatever, with a heavy massy instrument, to make a loud noise quite close to the head of a very sickly and infirm person. These are the ideas which that article, worded as it is, certainly excited in my mind. I do not believe that it could have entered the conception of the most ingenious person in this court, to have imagined how this would have ended – to have imagined that it should end in this gentleman's cracking almonds in an adjoining room with a hammer, which, being proper for such a purpose, could be no very ponderous instrument, and his afterwards coming to eat them in his wife's apartment. I do protest it is so singular a conceit, that if I did not see a great deal of unhappy seriousness in other parts of this cause, I might rather suspect that some levity was here intended against the court. I am sure of this, that if a man wanted to burlesque the Ecclesiastical Courts, he could not do it more effectually, than by representing that such a court had seriously entertained a complaint against a husband, founded upon the fact of his having munched almonds in the apartment of his wife . . .

[77] Upon the whole history of the voyage, and the facts contained in it, I find myself compelled to say, that I have no evidence which satisfies me, that Mr Evans has acted in this voyage in a manner inconsistent with the duties, and the rights, of a husband. If he had done so, it is impossible but that there must have been ample evidence; on the contrary, a great part of the evidence is absolutely irreconcilable with the notion of such mis-conduct having been practised. The evidence that does support it comes from the mouth of a person, who is in a great degree disabled by her prejudices. – But let me not be understood to insinuate, that this witness comes forward to deliver a false testi-mony. I am firmly persuaded that she believes every word she says; but she trusts to her resentments rather than to her recol-lections; she brings with her sincere intentions, but she does not bring a dispassionate mind; she does not bring that caution, and that sobriety of mind, which belong to a witness, deposing in a court of justice, upon matters by which the character of another individual may be so deeply affected . . .

[118] On 23 December, Mr Evans withdraws himself totally, taking with him the person of his eldest daughter; and offers to Mrs Evans, in a letter, which has my notice, because it has been noticed by the counsel on both sides, a settlement of £500 a year. The letter, although written in the height of irrita-tion, does not insinuate that species of misconduct with which she has been improperly charged in his allegation*; it only charges her with intolerable manners.

Here, I think, an impropriety, for the first time, attaches on the conduct of Mr Evans; for Mr Evans must be informed, that the law of this country, and of every Christian country, does not allow a man to use the language, '*I will be separated from my wife.*' If Mrs Evans had been guilty of any misconduct for which the law would decree a separation, he would be perfectly right in with-

* That Mrs Evans drank to excess.

drawing himself; but, in all cases where the law does not pretty positively allow, it pretty positively, I believe, condemns.

Marriage is the most solemn engagement which one human being can contract with another. It is a contract formed with a view, not only to the benefit of the parties themselves, but to the benefit of third parties; to the benefit of their common offspring, and to the moral order of civil society. To this contract is super-added the sanctity of a religious vow. Mr Evans must be told, that the obligations of his contract are not to be relaxed at the pleasure of one party. I may go farther; they are not to be lightly relaxed even at the pleasure of both. For if two persons have pledged themselves, at the altar of God, to spend their lives together, for purposes that reach much beyond themselves, it is a doctrine to which the morality of the law gives no coun-tenance, that they may, by private contract, dissolve the bands of this solemn tie, and throw themselves upon society, in the undefined and dangerous characters of a wife without a husband, and a husband without a wife.

There are, undoubtedly, cases for which a separation is pro-vided; but it must be lawfully decreed by public authority, and for reasons which the public wisdom approves. Mere turbulence of temper; petulance of manners; infirmity of body or mind, are not numbered amongst those causes. When they occur, their effects are to be subdued by management, if possible, or submitted to with patience; for the engagement was *to take for better, for worse*: and painful as the performance of this duty may be; painful as it certainly is in many instances, which exhibit a great deal of the misery that clouds human life, it must be attempted to be sweetened by the consciousness of its being a duty, and a duty of the very first class and importance . . .

[127] The truth of the case, according to the impression which the whole of it makes upon my mind, is this: two persons marry together; both of good moral characters, but with something of warmth, and sensibility, in each of their tempers; the husband is occasionally inattentive; the wife has a vivacity that sometimes offends and sometimes is offended; something like unkindness is produced, and is then easily inflamed; the lady broods over petty resentments, which are anxiously fed by the busy whispers of humble confidantes; her complaints, aggravated by their reports,

are carried to her relations, and meet perhaps with a facility of reception, from their honest, but well-intentioned, minds. A state of mutual irritation increases; something like incivility is continually practising; and, where it is not practised, it is continually suspected; every word, every act, every look, has a meaning attached to it; it becomes a contest of spirit, in form, between two persons eager to take, and not absolutely backward to give, mutual offence; at last the husband breaks up the family connection, and breaks it up with circumstances sufficiently expressive of disgust: treaties are attempted, and they miscarry, as they might be expected to do, in the hands of persons strongly disaffected towards each other; and then, for the very first time, as Dr Arnold has observed, a suit of cruelty is thought of; a libel is given in, black with criminating matter; recrimination comes from the other side; accusations rain heavy and thick on all sides, till all is involved in gloom, and the parties lose total sight of each other's real character, and of the truth of every one fact which is involved in the cause.

Out of this state of darkness and error it will not be easy for them to find their way. It were much to be wished that they could find it back again to domestic peace and happiness. Mr Evans has received a complete vindication of his character. Standing upon that ground, I trust he will act prudently and generously; for generosity is prudence in such circumstances. He will do well to remember, that the person he contends with is one over whom victory is painful; that she is one to whom he is bound by every tie that can fasten the heart of one human being to another; she is the partner of his bed! – the mother of his offspring! And, if mistakes have been committed, and grievous mistakes have been committed, most certainly, in this suit, she is still that person whose mistakes he is bound to cover, not only from his own notice, but, as far as he can, from that of every other person in the world.

Mrs Evans has likewise something to forget; mistakes have been made to her disadvantage too in this business: she, I say, has something to forget. And I hope she has not to learn, that the dignity of a wife cannot be violated by submission to a husband.

It would be happy indeed, if, by a mutual sacrifice of resentments, peace could possibly be re-established. It requires, indeed, great efforts of generosity, great exertions of prudence, on their own part, and on the part of those who are connected with them. If this cannot be done; if the breach is too far widened ever to be closed, Mrs Evans must find her way to relief; for, she must not continue upon her present footing, no, not for a moment: she must call in the intervention of prudent and respectable friends; and, if that is ineffectual, she must apply to the court, under the guidance of her counsel, or other persons by whom the matrimonial law of this kingdom is understood.

But, in taking this review, I rather digress from my province in giving advice: my province is merely to give judgment; to pronounce upon what I take to be the result of the facts laid before me. Considering, then, all those facts, with the most conscientious care, and with the most conscientious application of my understanding to their result, I am of opinion, that Mr Evans is exculpated from the charge of unmanly and unlawful cruelty. I therefore pronounce, *that Mrs Evans has failed in the proof of her libel, and dismiss Mr Evans from all further observance of justice in this behalf.*

Illegitimate Insularity

*Judgment in Re Goodman's Trusts**

I CONCUR IN the judgment of Lord Justice Cotton, both in the conclusion and reasoning. According to my view, the question as to what is the English law as to an English child is entirely irrelevant. There is, of course, no doubt as to what the English law as to an English child is. We have in this country from all time refused to recognise legitimation of issue by the subsequent marriage of the parents†, and possibly our peculiarity in this respect may deserve all that was said in its favour by Professor, afterwards Mr Justice, Blackstone, the somewhat indiscriminate eulogist of every peculiarity and anomaly in our system of laws.

But the question is, what is the rule which the English law adopts and applies to a non-English child? This is a question of international comity and international law. According to that law as recognised, and that comity as practised, in all other civilised communities, the status of a person, his legitimacy or illegitimacy, is to be determined everywhere by the law of the country of his origin – the law under which he was born. It appears to me that it would require a great force of argument, derived from legal principles, or great weight of authority clear and distinct, to justify us holding that our country stands in this respect aloof in barbarous insularity from the rest of the civilised world. On principle, it appears to me that every consideration goes strongly to show, at least, that we ought not so to stand. The family relation is at the foundation of all society, and it would appear almost an axiom that the family relation, once duly constituted by the law of any civilised country, should be respected and acknowledged by every other member of the great community of nations.‡

England has been for centuries a country of hospitality and

* (1881) 17 Ch. D. 296.
† This has since been remedied by two Acts, in 1926 and 1959.
‡ This paragraph was cited in a powerful dissent by Lord Justice Salmon in

commerce. It has opened its shores to thousands of political refugees and religious exiles, fleeing from their enemies and persecutors. It has opened its ports to merchants of the whole world and has by wise laws induced and encouraged them to settle in our marts. But would it not be shocking if such a man, seeking a home in this country, with his family of legitimated children, should find that the English hospitality was as bad as the worst form of the persecution from which he had escaped, by destroying his family ties, by declaring that the relation of father and child no longer existed, that his rights and duties and powers as a father had ceased, that the child of his parental affection and fond pride, whom he had taught to love, honour, and obey him, for whom he had toiled and saved, was to be thenceforth, in contemplation of the law of his new country, a fatherless bastard? Take the case of a foreigner resident abroad, with such a child. If that child were abducted from his guardianship and brought to this country, can anyone doubt that the courts of this country would recognise his paternal right and guardianship, and order the child to be delivered to any person authorised by him? But suppose, instead of sending, he were to come himself to this country in person, would it be possible to hold that he would lose his right to the guardianship of the child in this country because of the historical or mythical legend that the English barons and earls many centuries ago cried out in Latin, *Nolumus leges Angliae mutare*?* Can it be possible that a Dutch father stepping on board a steamer at Rotterdam with his dear and lawful child, should on his arrival at the port of London find that the child had become a stranger in blood and in law, and a bastard, *filius nullius*?

It may be suggested that that would not apply to a mere transient visit or a temporary commorancy, during which the foreign character of the visitor and his family would be recognised, with all its incidents and consequences, but that it would only apply

Re Valentine's Settlement [1965] 2 W.L.R. 1015, 1031, where the Court of Appeal declined to accept in England the adoption in South Africa of two children by parents domiciled in Southern Rhodesia whose courts recognised the adoption under the law of South Africa.

* The Statute of Merton 1235; the power influence against change held out until 1926!

to a man electing to have a permanent English domicil. But what could, in that view, be more shocking than that a man having such a family residing with him, perhaps for years, in this country as his lawful family, recognised as such by every court in the kingdom, being minded at last to make this country his permanent domicil, should thereby bastardise his children; and that he could re-legitimate them by another change of domicil from London to Edinburgh? And why should we on principle think it right to lay down a rule leading to such results? I protest that I can see no principle, no reason, no ground for this except an insular vanity, inducing us to think that our law is so good and so right, and every other system of law is naught, that we should reject every recognition of it as an unclean thing. . . .

The Enfant Gâté of Roscarberry

*Judgment in Barrett v. Irvine**

IF THIS CASE is deemed worthy of a place in our law books, or is made the subject of story in any metropolitan or local magazine, it may be well intituled 'The Enfant Gâté of Roscarberry'. A fond mother paid some money – the price of horses which her son, a spoilt boy, had bought, and it is argued that she thereby held him out to the world as, and constituted him, her general agent to buy horses on her credit to any extent his juvenile fancy might suggest. That, in fact, if another Waterloo was to be fought in defence of the liberties of Europe, this impulsive youth might horse, at her expense, a brigade of the Greys, Inniskillings, and 1st Royals, to add another page to the history of chivalry. If the law permits this, the man in the street, to whom I have so often referred as the embodiment of common sense, may well regard Mr Bumble's famous dictum not merely as historical, but true.

The defendant, Mrs Irvine, is sued for the price of a horse called 'Easter Boy' – her son, the spoilt lad I referred to, bought him from the plaintiff during the absence of his mother in Scotland. It is admitted she knew nothing about the transaction – about the purchase – that she did not in any way expressly authorise the purchase. Special authority to purchase the particular animal is admitted not to have existed, but it is said that she paid the price of some three or four other horses the boy bought, and that therefore in some way she held him out as her general agent to buy horses. This is an alarming doctrine. During the argument I put the following case to counsel. Take, I said, the instance of a father who has a daughter who hunts – who is fond of horses, and knows something about them – she buys some three or four horses, buying them during an interval of some years, and the father pays for the horses, and keeps them at his expense for the daughter. Does that fact, the fact of the payment of the price of the horses

* [1907] 2 I. R. 462, 467.

by the father and the keep of them by him, supply any evidence that the father held out the daughter, constituted the daughter, as his general agent to buy as many horses as she pleased – to buy, for instance, all the horses at the Dublin Horse Show! This, in my opinion, would be the very extravagance of absurdity; but let me assume – which is not the fact – that there was in this case clearly proved an antecedent authority to buy from time to time some particular horses. It has been decided in this Court that no multiplication of transactions, each of which depended upon particular special authorisation, can constitute general agency. However, it is argued that there are some additional circumstances in this case: there was a civil-bill decree obtained against the mother in relation to the price of another horse, and the fact that the Roscarberry hounds were kept in premises belonging to her. I do not think that the civil-bill decree was any evidence whatever of a general agency in the son. She had made a promise in the goodness of her heart in a particular transaction, and was decreed for the sum she promised to pay. As to the hounds, I cannot conceive how allowing a subscription pack to be kept in some out-offices is any evidence that she authorised the Master of the pack to act as her general agent in the purchase of horses.

No doubt a fond mother paid for a pink coat for her sporting son, and no doubt, paid also for a horse to carry him in the hunting-field – £25, was, I believe, the price. I hope this horse was not what is sometimes called 'a clever cripple'. In these country places good bargains are not infrequently picked up.

The defendant was referred to as if she kept a fashionable pack of hounds in elaborate kennels.

The Roscarberry pack was certainly interesting by reason of its diversified character. Variety has a charm of its own. What is unique is always attractive. The pack was composed of all sorts and conditions of hunting dogs – uniform neither in size nor pace nor breeding – and though it was styled the 'Roscarberry Foxhounds', it could boast of only one pure-bred foxhound – *lucus a non lucendo*. The proclivities of the pack were as diversified as its composition; it pursued with equal ardour every description of quadruped, whatever the nature of the scent. I am not sure that the feathered tribe was altogether without some measure of attention. However, though the menage at Roscarberry was not quite up to Leicestershire standard, I feel quite certain that the heart of the young Master was, so far as related to physical courage, in the right place, and that he often afforded good sport, and that the followers of the pack had not infrequently, to use an expression amongst hunting men, 'a clinking run'. The mother's heart was proud, and the field was at once gratified and grateful. This was all interesting and picturesque, but it did not at all involve that the mother held out the son as her general agent to buy horses. It has been also said that the defendant paid some of the expenses of her son in connection with racing matters, such as the cost of the entry of horses. This certainly in no way tends to establish the general agency that has been contended for. It has been further alleged that she attended some race meetings. No doubt she did. A sporting instinct, in my opinion, is not to be decried. It would be difficult indeed to eliminate it from our Irish nature. The defendant went to see her son ride, and, I dare say, the mother's heart beat a little loudly when she saw him clear some stiff regulation fence amid the plaudits of an admiring crowd; but surely it is fantastic to allege that this affords any evidence of a general agency in the son to buy horses at the mother's expense. Indeed, I think it is quite plain, from Mr Barrett's own evidence, that he sold Easter Boy, not to or for the mother, but to the son, on his assurance that he would get the mother to pay. This is plain from the evidence of the plaintiff himself, and of his witness, Mr Burns. He (Barrett) swore, in his cross-examination, that he said to the son, 'Are you quite sure that your mother won't object to pay for the horse?' and that he said this, as he wanted to make sure he would be paid.

The plaintiff's direct evidence is to the same effect. He swore that in reply to the son's statement that the horse was his (the son's) he said 'yes', and that he (the son) should pay for him. I think the answer of the jury to sub-question (b) of question 4 is not only not supported by the evidence, but is directly in the teeth of it.

It is argued, however, there was ratification on the part of the mother. There was, in my opinion, no contract by the mother to ratify. This is the part of the case I liked least. It was nothing more or less than an attempt to make the effort on the part of a worried mother to put an end to litigation evidence that she ratified a contract which, so far as she was concerned, never existed. Ratification implies the existence of something to ratify. I described the defendant as 'worried'. Indeed she was worried. Her letter of 22 April, from Ayr, is a pathetic description of the pitiful condition to which she was reduced by her inconsiderate son, and by the horse dealers who traded *with* him, but *on* her affection for him. I am of opinion that no twelve men, who fairly considered the evidence, could reasonably find a verdict for the plaintiff. This is indeed a curious case, and if Miss Somerville confers further lustre on literature and Roscarberry by bringing out another edition of her charming book,* perhaps that most interesting writer may be induced to add a new chapter.

* Somerville and Ross, *Some Experiences of an Irish Resident Magistrate.*

A Woman's Place . . .

Dissenting judgment in Wright & Cedzich†

. . . [501] DEFAMATION IMPUTING UNCHASTITY is now actionable *per se*. But if by any other means, however malicious, dishonest or immoral, a husband is by some person induced, reasonably it may be so far as the husband is concerned, to turn his wife out, thereby disgracing her in the eyes of the world, separating her from her children, and even reducing her to poverty, the contention on behalf of the respondent is that so far as these results are concerned she is without redress against the person maliciously, dishonestly, or immorally causing her the loss and misery. The thesis of this immunity from the ordinary liability of a wrongdoer to make reparation for the injury he occasions, is that the husband's acknowledged and . . . unquestionable right to obtain redress for wrongful deprivation of *consortium* was originally founded, and therefore theoretically still rests, on his right to physical possession of his wife, on which an action of trespass could be founded, and his property right in respect of her services in the quality of servant, and that consequently there can be no analogous right in her to redress in the converse and precisely similar case. Petruchio stated that argument so admirably as to leave nothing to be desired when he said:

> I will be master of what is mine own:
> She is my goods, my chattels; she is my house,

* Within a fortnight of delivering this judgment Sir Isaac Isaacs became Chief Justice of Australia, and subsequently the first native-born Governor-General of Australia.

† (1930) 43 C.L.R. 493, 500. The other four judges held that a wife has no cause of action against a woman who had induced her husband, against the will of his wife, to depart and remain absent from the matrimonial home whereby the wife loses the society, comfort, protection and support of her husband; even though, *mutatis mutandis*, a husband has a cause of action for the enticement of his wife.

My household stuff, my field, my barn,
My horse, my ox, my ass, my any thing:
And here she stands, touch her whoever dare;
I'll bring mine action on the proudest he
That stops my way in Padua.*

That was based ultimately on the mediæval doctrine that Bentham, about a hundred years ago, with his usual perspicacity called the 'nonsensical reason – that of the identity of the two persons thus connected. Baron and Feme are one person in law. On questions relative to the two matrimonial conditions, this quibble is the foundation of all reasoning' (*Works*, Vol. VII, chap. 5, p. 485). He was there dealing with the application of the doctrine to the law of evidence, but the absurdity is even more striking when carried to the length necessary for the present respondent's argument. It postulates that the 'one person' is the husband, and that his is the only legal *persona*, the wife being by reason of her status the working property of that *persona*. In the middle of the nineteenth century Mr Justice Maule pointed out that the unity was only 'a strong figurative expression', and that 'for many purposes, they are essentially distinct and different persons' as, for instance, to protect 'the honour and the feelings of the husband'.† Why not her own? And now, well into the twentieth century, amid legal and social surroundings so openly and utterly opposed to the theory relied on, that the argument cannot but shock the conscience, it devolves upon this Court to take up a position that, no matter how it may be shaded off with gentle phrases, necessarily means alignment either with Petruchio or Bentham. Either the status of a wife imposes upon her a dependent lifelong servitude as a menial in her husband's house, terminable only by legal separation or by death, or else it leaves her with the independent right, now unimpeded by obstacles of procedure, to protect herself from the wrongful deprivation of her honourable rights as a wife. For myself, I cannot hesitate an instant as to the proper choice. To a suggestion that modern circumstances, including enlightened legislation, have emancipated married women from their former subordinate position, the answer is made that

* *Taming of the Shrew*, Act III, sc. II, line 232.
† *Wenman* v. *Ash* (1853) 13 C.B. 836, 844–845; 138 E.R. 1432, 1435.

it is only an additional reason for denying them redress, since it also makes the husband's remedy out of date. That last view, however much I disagree with it, has at least this merit, that in effect it concedes to the two parties to the marriage status that they ought in this regard to stand in the same position, whatever that position may be. In truth, however, nothing more was needed in modern circumstances to effectuate the wife's remedy, and to place her in that respect on a level with her husband, than our improved procedural law, which has removed ancient disabilities standing in the way of asserting her rights. Those fundamental rights, so far as relevant in this case, have never changed, because they are basically entrenched in the very conception of marriage.

Before discussing the law independently it may be interesting, and it certainly is not unimportant, to observe the recent opinions of lawyers on the subject, so far as I have been able to ascertain them. The greater part are certainly not of the Petruchian order. ... Now, the simple ground on which the appellant's claim is, in my opinion, sustainable is one which has received very distinct enunciation in the modern law of torts. ... In reality, it lay for centuries at the basis of the husband's action for loss of *consortium*, and was judicially expressed and acknowledged nearly two hundred years ago. As it exists today it is applicable to husband and wife alike. There is no need of antiquated reasons springing from a primitive state of civilisation originally impressed into service to attain justice, later abandoned in favour of better reasons, and today utterly repugnant to the present conditions of society. Still less is there any justification for rummaging among the ruined and abandoned structures of the past to find materials for erecting a barrier against the wife's claim for redress, when a clearly recognised principle of law admits it. It may, however, be added, the exploration rendered necessary by the objections taken will demonstrate that the materials suggested are now seen to be imaginary. The ground on which the appellant's case, in my opinion, firmly rests may be thus sufficiently marked out: (a) the rights and obligations of persons are sometimes derived from the circumstances and from the relative positions of the parties; (b) a violation of legal right committed knowingly is a cause of action, and it is a violation of legal right to interfere with contractual relations or other legal relations without sufficient cause or justi-fication for such interference; (c) causing a violation of the hus-band's marital obligations in regard to society, comfort, protection and support, is a violation of the wife's legal right and is preju-dicial to her, and as on the allegations in the statement of claim, which must be taken as true, those obligations were consequently broken, the breach imports damage, and if actual pecuniary damage is necessary to be alleged, the required averment exists. In my opinion that is sufficient to end the matter. Had this been a husband's action, the principles stated would maintain his claim without controversy. But then it is said a husband has no legal obligations towards his wife but that of maintaining her, and as to that her only redress is to sue him for maintenance. True, it is said, if her obligations towards him are broken, he has various remedies, and may pursue the wrongdoer also. But she, according to the contention, is not permitted to pursue a wrongdoer; she has a right merely to sue her husband under special statutory pro-visions. The reasoning appears to me to fail at every point. The mutual relations of all persons in the community are regulated by the circumstances of today. To those circumstances the recognised principles of the common law apply – and assumed conditions of society that have in any case no existence now may and must be dismissed from consideration. When we see that women are admitted to the capacity of commercial and professional life in most of its branches, that they are received on equal terms with men as voters and legislators, that they act judicially, can hold property, may sue and be sued alone, may and frequently have to provide a home and maintain the family, when too, they are organised in time of national danger as virtual combatants in defence of the country, it is time, I think, to abandon the assertion that in the eye of the law they are merely the adjuncts or property or the servants of their husbands, that they have the legal duty of yielding and employing their body to their husband's will and bidding in all his domestic relations, and that all they are correlatively entitled to in return for obedience, subordination, child-bearing and domestic services is the right to receive such necessaries of life as are suitable to the husband's position in life – apparently, so as to keep them in physical condition for their duties – to be specially sued for against the husband alone, if he should fail to maintain her. If someone, a paramour of her husband perhaps, by scheming or any other illicit means, succeeds in causing her husband to deprive her of her home and of his society and companionship as a husband, of access to her children, of her husband's protective presence against danger and insult, of his physical comfort and assistance in health and sickness, his reasonable participation in the family life and burden that certainly in the twentieth century the marriage union, to my mind, connotes under what is shortly called *consortium*, the common law is, in my opinion, flexible enough, strong enough and just enough by means of the principles above stated to afford her direct redress against the wrongdoer.

As I view the matter it is no mere sentimental right that is given to each spouse by the marriage union. Sentiment there should be, sincere affection, and all the eager devotion it should prompt. But there are also, as I hold, legal obligations on both sides, implied by the circumstances, status and relations of the parties, the obligations not merely of mutual fidelity but also of society, comfort, aid and assistance in all the vicissitudes of the united life into which the man and the woman have entered – obligations that cannot be accurately measured in money, but are real and substantial and carry temporal benefits, and the deprivation of which by a wrongdoer are quite as open to be compensated for as physical suffering, deprivation of hospitality, personal insult by defamation, or many other injuries recognised every day as legitimate grounds for compensation. When the husband is the complaining party against a man or a woman who, it may be, has deprived him of his *consortium*, these considerations are acknowledged as sound and proper. Why not also when the wife is the injured party? This is quite consistent with the natural leadership, and in most cases the decisive voice of the husband as head of the family in the management of domestic affairs. But his leadership is not that of a despot or a slave-master; and it is accompanied with mutual and correlative rights and duties which the law will recognise and enforce. I utterly reject the view that *consortium* in point of law means, on the part of the woman, her society and services (using those terms in the most unmeasured sense), and, on the part of the man, the one duty of cash remuneration in maintaining her, for which she may sue her husband directly if he fails to provide it. Sitting here, I decline to declare judicially that Australian

wives occupy such a repellent position of legal and moral degradation. In *Yeatman* v. *Yeatman** Lord Penzance said: 'A wife is
entitled to her husband's society, and the protection of his name
and home, in cohabitation.' That this is a legal right is incontest-
able since its denial constitutes the matrimonial offence of deser-
tion. As to morality, what, when stripped of technical embroidery,
is the doctrine contended for in effect but legalised white slavery?
[506]

*

[509] The test of analogy to the husband's action depends
entirely on the meaning given to *consortium*. As to that, Lord
Wensleydale† thinks that, although in most respects dissimilar
from that of master and servant, yet *in one respect* the husband's
relation to the wife has a *similar* character. That respect is: 'The
assistance of the wife in the conduct of the household of the husband, and in the education of his children.' He says it *resembles*
'the services of a hired domestic, tutor or governess'. I must candidly admit I cannot understand it. What does 'resemble' mean?
The children are hers as well as his, a fact which appears to be
entirely ignored by those who hold the opposite view. Why is her
care for her own child to be considered that of his *servant*, rather
than that of *a wife and a mother*, and as the natural consequence
of the union into which both have entered, and of the responsibility to the child which both parents owe by every tie of nature
and justice? Does she tend and watch and care for her children
because she is ordered – actually or impliedly – by her husband,
and does he either actually or impliedly pay her wages as for
services rendered to him at his direction in so doing? I am utterly
incapable of understanding the mental attitude that leads to such
a conclusion. If the nature of the services expected of a wife
determines the character in which she renders it, then the husband's expected daily services to his wife are equally those of a
servant. To say that her services are of material value, capable of
being estimated in money, may be met by saying that his presence
in the house in protecting her as part of the consideration for
her duties resembles that of a hired watchman, or that the assist-

* (1868) L.R. 1 P. & D. 489, 491.
† *Lynch* v. *Knight* (1861) 9 H.L.C. 598; 5 L.T. (N.S.) 298; 11 E.R. 863.

ance and comfort he gives her in her daily life 'resembles' the conduct of a hired personal attendant performing the thousand acts of attention that contribute to her material wants and convenience, all being equally measureable in money. To drive her in his car, to assist her into it and out of it, to accompany her when she visits the theatre or friends, are facts 'resembling' those of a hired chauffeur or attendant; to feed and tend her when she is ill is to do acts 'resembling' those of a hired nurse; to bind a wound is to act as if he were a paid medical man. But the truth is, such analogies are entirely strained and misleading, and must be brushed aside. The marriage compact, as it is reasonably and indeed necessarily understood, is a natural standing by each other in all the vicissitudes of life, and, however much some of its incidents resemble isolated events in other relations, they are all referable to the one unique category – the marriage status – and must be adjudged of in that relation. A wife's services, if analogy is permissible, are those not of a hired employee, but of a *partner* in the common undertaking. The husband may be the managing partner in many respects, but the business of life in which both parties have embarked is a life partnership, whether viewed from the individual standpoint or that of the community. With deep respect, this is the true correction of Lord Wensleydale's dictum. The mass of indefinable duties and rights are conveniently gathered under the one word *consortium*, and that is a word of equality, subject only to natural, not legal, diversities, and betokens not a state of despotism on the one side and submission on the other, but of honourable intercourse which neither is rightfully entitled to abridge, and with which no third person may interfere without responsibility. If that be the correct connotation of '*consortium*', it follows as a necessary legal consequence that, the interference alleged here being without lawful excuse or justification, the appellant has a right of action. [510]

*

[512] So far I have approached the question, so to speak, from the *positive* side.

But now it is also necessary, as I have said, to examine the *negative* opinion in order to test the foundations on which it is said to rest. It is true that in some ancient texts there are found statements that lend some colour to the notion that a husband has dominion over his wife and a right to the possession of her person. For instance, *Bacon's Abridgment*, Baron and Feme (B), 7th edn., Vol. I, p. 693, says: 'The husband hath, by law, power and dominion over his wife, and may keep her by force within the bounds of duty, and may beat her, but not in a violent or cruel manner.' That is a type of the so-called authorities which underlie the demurrer in this case. Now in 1891 this doctrine was challenged and came up for examination before a Court of Appeal consisting of Lord Chancellor Halsbury, Lord Esher, M.R. and Lord Justice Fry.* Learned counsel for the husband, who claimed the right to take and hold possession of his wife against her will, certainly disclaimed reliance on the old authorities so far as castigation was concerned, but they still relied on the 'dominion' and 'possession' portions, just as those supporting the demurrer do today. To this Lord Halsbury, during the argument, offered the crushing observation which he amplified in his judgment: 'Where ancient dicta, which state that a husband is entitled to imprison his wife, also state that he has a right to beat her, can they be rejected as authorities for the latter proposition without being affected as authorities for the former?' Clearly not, one would think. The whole orientation is wrong. And so in the present case ... The Lord Chancellor in his judgment said: 'I confess that some of the propositions which have been referred to during the argument are such as I should be reluctant to suppose ever to have been the law of England. More than a century ago it was boldly contended that slavery existed in England; but, if anyone were to set up such a conclusion now, it would be regarded as ridiculous.' In view of the contention here Lord Halsbury must surely be regarded as unduly optimistic. He said also: 'The authorities cited for the husband were all tainted *with this sort of notion of the absolute dominion of the husband over the wife*.' Lord Halsbury refers to 'the conjugal *consortium*' clearly in the mutual sense. He says: 'I confess to regarding with something like indignation the statement of the facts of this case, and the absence of a due sense of the delicacy and respect due to a wife *whom the husband has sworn to cherish and protect*.' And yet it is gravely said

* *R. v. Jackson* [1891] 1 Q.B. 671.

the *consortium* is all *his*, that she has no rights except that of payment that he is bound in law to respect. Lord Esher is no less emphatic. He says, with perfect appositeness to the contentions in this present case: 'A series of propositions have been quoted which, if true, make an English wife the slave, the abject slave, of her husband.' One of those propositions he thus quotes: 'It was said that by the law of England the husband has the custody of his wife ... I do not believe that an English husband has by law any such rights over his wife's person, as have been suggested.' Lord Justice Fry was equally clear. If that case is good law – and it was a case where the husband had already obtained a decree for restitution of conjugal rights – it entirely undermines the contention with regard to the husband's rights in respect of the wife's person.

> The times have been,
> That, when the brains were out, the man would die,
> And there an end.*

But, like Banquo's ghost, the shadows of 'dominion', '*potestas*', 'possession' and 'servant' still stalk about as if they were living realities. For it has been argued with great fervour that the older supposed law as to dominion governs this case. I say 'supposed' law not only because it has been definitely negatived in 1891, but because for nearly two hundred years it has been virtually abandoned as an essential basis in favour of a broader and more reasonable principle, which is practically that I have above formulated. [513]

*

[518] I am at a loss to understand why she should be unable to obtain in the King's courts on ordinary principles, and in the ordinary way, redress for deprivation of rights which, if she is a normal wife and mother, are the most precious she possesses. For these reasons, it seems clear to me that the opinions above referred to in judicial decisions and text-books which are in favour of the wife's right of action preponderate not merely in number but also in adherence to principle and to the line of legal development. The respondent asks us to take a retrograde step into the dark ages of the law.

* Macbeth, Act III, sc. IV, line 78.

Wounded Feelings

Judgment in Potgieter v. Potgieter and another*

THE PLAINTIFF IS a serious-minded and industrious young man who works for the municipality and studies for the B.Comm. degree in his spare time. His wife, blonde and nineteen, swelled the joint income by working at a hairdressing establishment called Maison Charlotte.

This place was under the management of one Reginald O'Neill, who admired her so strongly that he, despite her youthfulness, soon placed her in a supervising position. After hours he managed to convince her that he owned the business and was rich. He opened vistas of a journey overseas. Fascinated, she yielded to his importunities with such abandon that she soon found herself carrying O'Neill's child. To her husband she admitted her adultery, and she informed him that she preferred O'Neill and was going to live with him in his flat.

The plaintiff, outraged by this assault on the sanctity of his home, went to have it out with his rival. O'Neill treated him with contempt and was so infuriating that the plaintiff fired a shot at him which penetrated the lung. Luck was with him because O'Neill recovered and, instead of facing a murder charge, the plaintiff was convicted merely of pointing a firearm. He was sentenced to a fine of only £25.

He instituted action against his wife for divorce and against O'Neill – as second defendant – for damages for the *injuria*. The divorce claim has been withdrawn, and he proceeds only with the claim for damages. The plaintiff's wife returned to him repentantly immediately after the shooting. Not only was her lover seriously wounded but his financial attractions had also vanished. She found that he was not the owner but merely the manager of Maison Charlotte and that his wealth had been grossly inflated.

* 1959 (1) S.A. 194.

She went to see a doctor and by some circumstance which was left unexplained, her pregnancy was terminated. The young couple are reunited and are striving to heal the breach completely. They have made excellent progress because already she is once more in expectation, and this time *pater est quem nuptiae demonstrant.*

The plaintiff's claim for damages must therefore be strictly confined to the *contumelia.* No claim for loss of *consortium* arises. This is however a serious *injuria* in view of the cunning misuse of his position by O'Neill and the subsequent contempt with which he treated the plaintiff. It is what *Voet* describes as

a wrongdoing committed in contempt of a free human being and by which his person or dignity or reputation is injured with evil intent.

In *Foulds* v. *Smith*, 1950 (1) S.A. 1, 11 (A.D.), van den Heever, J.A., explains that insult to the other need not be the object – in fact mostly the wrongdoer would prefer the husband to know nothing about his activities.

The plaintiff clearly has a claim. The amount to be awarded presents the only difficulty. There is a penal element in this form of damages and O'Neill certainly deserves to be penalised. On the other hand he has been seriously wounded by the plaintiff. (He put in a counter-claim of £2,000 for this, but did not appear in court to prosecute it.)

Must this assault on O'Neill affect the amount of damages? In my opinion it must have an important effect. The money is awarded to the claimant to assuage his injured feelings. He has, however, in a more robust way richly obtained balm for his wounded soul. The cry of pain, the writhing form of his adversary, must especially in view of the lenient view which the criminal law subsequently took of his action, have given the plaintiff intense satisfaction in some primitive manner. What is more, it profoundly impressed the woman. The punishment inherent in damages for *injuria*, and which O'Neill ought to get, has likewise already been richly inflicted on him.

A judgment in a matter like this must never even seem to overlook conduct like that of the plaintiff, however understandable it may have been. The law strives to eliminate private vengeance and dare not give it countenance in a civil judgment by shrugging it off as a matter for the criminal courts to deal with. The plaintiff's self-righteous action must bring about a massive reduction in the amount he should otherwise have recovered. This is not punishment to the plaintiff – it is adjustment of the amount in view of what he has already taken for himself. The amount must, however, not be so small as to represent purely 'contemptuous damages'.

The plaintiff's wife also erred. She must not reap advantage from her own wrong. This is, however, difficult to prevent and the most that can be done in that respect is to exclude the amount awarded from the community of property which exists between her and the plaintiff.

The order is:

(1) Second defendant must pay plaintiff £25 damages and costs. This amount does not form part of the joint estate of plaintiff and his wife, but belongs to plaintiff alone.

(2) Second defendant's counterclaim is dismissed with costs.

The Lay-About

*Dissenting judgment in Gollins v. Gollins**

I HAVE FELT constrained to reach a different conclusion from that just expressed, notwithstanding the fact that, as I understand, it has the assent of my brother Davies. I would dismiss the appeal. I am aware that it smacks of temerity to take a different path through a field of this kind, where the roads are so much better known to my brethren than to me, but I at least have the support of the Divisional Court. I do not propose even to attempt to follow that tribunal in the steps it took through the maze of authorities cited. It would, in my view, serve no useful purpose; for, as I remind myself once more, cruelty or no cruelty is a question of fact. The only too numerous cases reported on the subject, a number alas likely to be added to by the labours of this division of this Court during the present sittings, are in truth only illustrations of the way in which various judges have considered the almost infinitely varied circumstances of married life in an effort to answer the question which in the end is the only one for decision: Did the conduct of *this* husband amount to cruelty to this wife? Rightly did the preacher say: 'Of making many books there is no end'.† I stand on the last sentence of the judgment of the Divisional Court, which is in these words:

Above all, we do not consider that the husband's conduct, however reprehensible, can properly be stigmatised by the word 'cruelty' in its ordinary acceptation.

This seems to me to be the beginning and the end of the matter. The words of the Matrimonial Proceedings (Magistrates' Courts)

---

* [1964] P. 32, 54, reversing the decision of the Divisional Court of the Probate, Divorce and Admiralty Division, [1964] P. 35; the House of Lords, by a majority of 3–2, upheld the majority decision of the Court of Appeal: [1964] A. C. 644.

† Ecclesiastes, ch. 12, verse 12.

Act 1960, s. 1 (1), are: '. . . that the defendant . . . (b) has been
guilty of persistent cruelty *to* (i) – the complainant . . .'. The
words in the parallel Act applying in the High Court were 'has
treated the complainant with persistent cruelty'. These show that
there must be some wrong done *to* the complainant. If, whatever
the subject-matter of the complaint, it is not done *to* the complainant, that is not cruelty.

How do the facts stand with relation to that state of the law?
Shortly put, this man is bone idle. He may be described in a
modern slang phrase as a lay-about. He married a competent
active woman and has made no effort since. He was in debt when
he married, though he did not tell his wife so. He sold his farm
to pacify his creditors. With what was left out of the wreck a new
house was bought, which he either caused or allowed to be put
in his wife's name, she being thus saddled with the mortgage,
and all that he has done is to hang up his hat in the hall. He
started by keeping some poultry, but these seem to have been
sold off and the proceeds have gone into or through his pocket.
He does a little gardening and suggests that that is quite enough.
The wife has gone on from year to year shouldering the burdens
of the establishment, carrying on a business at the house, by
which she has succeeded in keeping down the mortgage, educat-
ing her daughters and maintaining the family. She has also from
time to time staved off his creditors. Her complaint is not that
she cannot carry on the business, nor that she is in want of money,
but that the continual irritation of his debts, though she is not
responsible for them, and the exasperation she feels at his continued refusal to help her and her sense of injustice that she
should do all the work and he none, have driven her to revolt and
have produced what her doctor calls a 'moderate anxiety state'.
As to the business, she says: 'I shall have to give it up as I am
getting so impatient.' She also says: 'I don't claim that I am
short of money. I have to work to raise money to pay for the
mortgage and keep myself. One expects the husband to pay.'

There was no direct evidence at all that the husband sought to
injure his wife, nor even that he knew that his conduct might be
injurious to her health. It is said, however, that she wrote him a
letter last year, threatening to take proceedings unless he mended
his ways, and that after receiving that he must have known that his

wife was likely to suffer in health. I do not think this follows from what we know. We have not seen this letter. What it did apparently was to say in effect: 'If you do not set-to and earn some money for your family, I shall take steps to make you', and that is precisely what she did by her first application to the magistrates' court. That is as far as the evidence goes. This order, however, was *brutum fulmen*. You cannot get blood out of a stone, nor money out of a lay-about. She therefore makes a further application, the object being to enable her to turn the husband out of the house. With this object I must say I sympathise. I see no reason why she should give him house room, if he defaults in all his obligations to her. Nor, so far as the statute is concerned, is there any reason why a non-cohabitation order should not be inserted into an order based on wilful neglect to maintain: see s. 2′(1) (a). As a matter of practice, however, magistrates' courts do not include such an order except in cases of cruelty. The Divisional Court treats that as a matter of course. . . . Counsel for the wife has argued that the true inquiry is: (a) was there injury to health? and (b) can the blame for it be attributed to the other spouse? If so, he says, that is cruelty. I cannot accept this. The cause of the spouse's ill-health may be entirely trivial, but to be cruelty the conduct must be something serious which can be properly so described. In this case there is an absence of conduct directed at the wife, and that is why the Divisional Court describes it as 'negative'. I am not enamoured of this word, nor indeed of other descriptive phrases. I think the answer is 'No'. As a husband, he was everything he should not be. Above all, he exasperated his wife, who feels a husband ought to bear his share of the burden. Many husbands have felt the same about their wives, but that has never been counted cruelty, unless it results in damage to the home or the family. These conditions do not exist here. Whatever opprobrious names one may give to this husband, I do not think that 'cruel' is one of them.

Slaves and Citizens

The Black Goes Free

*Dissenting judgment in Re John Anderson**

[The prisoner John Anderson, a negro, having been arrested in Brant County, Upper Canada, upon a charge of murder committed in the State of Missouri, U.S.A., a writ of habeas corpus was granted.

Anderson had been a slave in Missouri where he killed Seneca T. P. Diggs. The killing was admitted, but it was contended that since the deceased was at the time in pursuit of Anderson, who was endeavouring to escape from slavery and acted only in defence of his freedom, the evidence failed to show any ground for a charge of murder according to the law of the Province of Canada; and that Anderson's surrender could therefore not be claimed under the U.S.-Canadian extradition treaty of Ashburton of 1842.

The dissent of Mr Justice McLean was subsequently upheld, both first in the Court of Common Pleas for Upper Canada and then by the Court of Queen's Bench in England. Discussion arose in English legal circles as to the power of the courts at Westminster to issue writs of habeas corpus out of England into the colonies and foreign dominions of the Crown. As a result the Habeas Corpus Act 1862 was passed to prohibit applications for habeas corpus in England where the same remedy existed in the colonial territory.]

[185] THE FACTS TO which the evidence applies are, that Diggs was a farmer residing on land of his own, in Howard County, in the State of Missouri: that the prisoner was a slave, bound, himself and his children, to perpetual servitude to any person to whom they might be transferred, and in 1853 a slave of one McDonald, living in Saline County, in the State of Missouri: that he had been transferred to McDonald by his former master,

* (1860) 20 Upper Canada Queen's Bench Reports 124.

one Moses Burton, and compelled to remove from the immediate vicinity of his wife and child to a distance of 30 or 32 miles, where his new master resided: that he left McDonald's, and was seen at Samuel Brown's, where his wife was a slave, in September 1853; and that he was chased there by several persons, for the purpose of returning him again to McDonald as a slave, but succeeded at that time in making his escape from them: that soon after, while still engaged in trying to make his escape from the man who claimed him as his property, he was passing over Diggs' farm, when he was accosted by Diggs, and asked whether he had a pass, and was told that without a pass he would not be allowed to proceed: that the prisoner attempted to escape by running away, and was pursued by Diggs and four slaves under his orders: that Diggs encouraged his slaves in the pursuit by offering to them the premium of five dollars, to which under the law of the State he would be entitled for the arrest of a slave attempting to become free by escaping from his master; that, after pursuing the prisoner upwards of a mile from his own house, Diggs, with a stick in his hand, in order to intercept the prisoner, crossed a fence and approached him, and that, on their meeting, Diggs struck at the prisoner with his stick, as it is alleged, in self-defence, and the prisoner, with a knife which he had in his hand, inflicted a wound or wounds which caused the death of Diggs.

The law of England, or rather of the British Empire, not only does not recognise slavery within the dominions of the Crown, but imposes upon any British subject who shall have become the owner of slaves in a foreign state the severest penalties, and declares that all persons engaged in carrying on the slave trade, when captured at sea, shall be liable to be treated as pirates. In all the British possessions the institution of slavery, which at one time prevailed to a certain extent, was abolished at the enormous expense of twenty millions of pounds sterling in remunerating the holders of slaves. An immense amount has since been expended in efforts to suppress the African slave trade, and by every possible means the British Government has put down and discountenanced the traffic in human beings.

Even when slavery was tolerated in some of the British possessions, no person could be brought into England without becoming free the moment he touched the soil; and though other nations have not chosen to follow the noble example of the British nation, and some are even yet embarking in nefarious and unchristian attempts to import human beings from the coast of Africa to be held in perpetual bondage, for the purpose of this world's gain, even at the risk of being regarded as pirates, happily the traffic has become too uncertain and too hazardous to be carried on to so great an extent as formerly prevailed. In the adjoining republic the evils and the curse of slavery are every day becoming more manifest, and even now threaten to lead to a dissolution of the federal compact of the United States, under which the several states have enjoyed an unexampled degree of prosperity. The evil is not less revolting in a social point of view, for though the laws of some of the states of the Union may tolerate the dealing in human beings as if they were sheep or oxen, the best feelings of our nature must shudder at the thought of the severance of those endearing relations which usually form the solace and happiness of mankind. A father and mother, husband and wife, are liable, at the caprice of a master, or perhaps from his necessities, to be separated from each other and from their children; and they are bound to submit, or if they attempt to escape from bondage, and to consult their own happiness in preference to the gain of their masters, are liable to be hunted by any white or black man who chooses to engage in the pursuit, and when captured are liable to severe punishment and increased severity from their task-masters.

The prisoner, Anderson, as appears by the statement of Baker, who came to this province to identify him, has felt the horrors of such treatment. He was brought up to manhood by one Moses Burton, and married a slave on a neighbouring property, by whom he had one child. His master, for his own purposes, disregarding the relationship which had been formed, sold and transferred him to a person at a distance, to whose will he was forced to submit. The laws of Missouri, enacted by their white oppressors, while they perpetuate slavery, confer no rights on the slaves, unless it be the bare protection of their lives. Can it, then, be a matter of surprise that the prisoner should endeavour to escape from so degrading a position; or rather, would it not be a cause of surprise if the attempt were not made? Diggs, though he could have no other interest in it than that which binds slaveholders for

their common interest to prevent the escape of their slaves, interfered to prevent the prisoner getting beyond the bounds of his
bondage; and with his slaves pursued and hunted him, with a
spirit and determination which might well drive him to despera-
tion; and when at length the prisoner appeared within reach of
capture, he, with a stick in his hand, crossed over a fence and
advanced to intercept and seize him. The prisoner was anxious to
escape, and in order to do so made every effort to avoid his
pursuers. Diggs, as their leader, on the contrary, was most
anxious to overtake and come in contact with the prisoner for the
unholy purpose of riveting his chains more securely. Could it be
expected from any man indulging in the desire to be free, which
nature has implanted in his breast, that he should quietly submit
to be returned to bondage and to stripes, if by any effort of his
strength, or any means within his reach, he could emancipate
himself? Such an expectation, it appears to me, would be most
unreasonable, and I must say that, in my judgment, the prisoner
was justified in using any necessary degree of force to prevent
what to him must inevitably have proved a most fearful evil.

He was committing no crime in endeavouring to escape and to
better his own condition; and the fact of his being a slave cannot,
in my humble judgment, make that a crime which would not be
so if he were a white man. If in this country any number of persons were to pursue a coloured man with an avowed determination to return him into slavery, it cannot, I think, be doubted that
the man pursued would be justified in using, in the same circumstances as the prisoner, the same means of relieving himself from
so dreadful a result. Can, then, or must, the law of slavery in
Missouri be recognised by us to such an extent as to make it
murder in Missouri, while it is justifiable in this province to do
precisely the same act? I confess that I feel it too repugnant to
every sense of religion and every feeling of justice to recognise a
rule, designated as a law, passed by the strong for enslaving and
tyrannising over the weak—a law which would not be tolerated
for a moment, if those who are reduced to the condition of slaves,
and deprived of all human rights, were possessed of white instead
of black or dark complexions.

The Declaration of Independence of the present United States
proclaimed to the world that all men are born equal and possessed

of certain inalienable rights, amongst which are life, liberty, and the pursuit of happiness; but the first of these is the only one accorded to the unfortunate slaves; the others of these inalienable rights are denied, because the white population have found themselves strong enough to deprive the blacks of them. A love of liberty is inherent in the human breast, whatever may be the complexion of the skin. 'Its taste is grateful, and ever will be so, till nature herself shall change;' and, in administering the laws of a British province, I can never feel bound to recognise as law any enactment which can convert into chattels a very large number of the human race.

No Caste Here

*Dissenting opinion in Plessy v. Ferguson**

[In 1896 the Supreme Court of the United States for the first time upheld a state law that commanded the provision of special accommodation for negroes travelling on public transport. The Court refused to declare unconstitutional a Louisiana law requiring white and coloured railway passengers to be transported in separate carriages. The Court said that to keep groups of citizens apart was not objectionable so long as the facilities provided for each group were of the same quality. The 'separate but equal' doctrine survived until the schools desegregation decision of 1954, when the court unanimously repudiated by implication its opinion in *Plessy* v. *Ferguson*, and endorsed the famous dissent of Mr Justice Harlan a half-century before.]

BY THE LOUISIANA statute, the validity of which is here involved, all railway companies (other than street railroad companies) carrying passengers in that State are required to have separate but equal accommodations for white and coloured persons, 'by providing two or more passenger coaches for each passenger train, *or* by dividing the passenger coaches by a *partition* so as to secure separate accommodations'. Under this statute, no coloured person is permitted to occupy a seat in a coach assigned to white persons; nor any white person, to occupy a seat in a coach assigned to coloured persons. The managers of the railroad are not allowed to exercise any discretion in the premises, but are required to assign each passenger to some coach or compartment set apart for the exclusive use of his race. If a passenger insists upon going into a coach or compartment not set apart for persons of his race, he is subject to be fined, or to be imprisoned in the parish jail. Penalties are prescribed for the refusal or neglect of the officers, directors, conductors and

* 163 U.S. 537, 552 (1896).

employees of railroad companies to comply with the provisions of the act.

Only 'nurses attending children of the other race' are excepted from the operation of the statute. No exception is made of coloured attendants travelling with adults. A white man is not permitted to have his coloured servant with him in the same coach, even if his condition of health requires the constant, personal assistance of such servant. If a coloured maid insists upon riding in the same coach with a white woman whom she has been employed to serve, and who may need her personal attention while travelling, she is subject to be fined or imprisoned for such an exhibition of zeal in the discharge of duty.

While there may be in Louisiana persons of different races who are not citizens of the United States, the words in the act, 'white and coloured races', necessarily include all citizens of the United States of both races residing in that State. So that we have before us a State enactment that compels, under penalties, the separation of the two races in railroad passenger coaches, and makes it a crime for a citizen of either race to enter a coach that has been assigned to citizens of the other race.

Thus the State regulates the use of a public highway by citizens of the United States solely upon the basis of race.

However apparent the injustice of such legislation may be, we have only to consider whether it is consistent with the Constitution of the United States. . . . [553]

[554] In respect of civil rights, common to all citizens, the Constitution of the United States does not, I think, permit any public authority to know the race of those entitled to be protected in the enjoyment of such rights. Every true man has pride of race, and under appropriate circumstances when the rights of others, his equals before the law, are not to be affected, it is his privilege to express such pride and to take such action based upon it as to him seems proper. But I deny that any legislative body or judicial tribunal may have regard to the race of citizens when the civil rights of those citizens are involved. Indeed, such legislation, as that here in question, is inconsistent not only with that equality of rights which pertains to citizenship, national and state, but with the personal liberty enjoyed by everyone within the United States.

The Thirteenth Amendment does not permit the withholding or the deprivation of any right necessarily inhering in freedom. It not only struck down the institution of slavery as previously existing in the United States, but it prevents the imposition of any burdens or disabilities that constitute badges of slavery or servitude. It decreed universal civil freedom in this country. This court has so adjudged. But that amendment having been found inadequate to the protection of the rights of those who had been in slavery, it was followed by the Fourteenth Amendment, which added greatly to the dignity and glory of American citizenship, and to the security of personal liberty, by declaring that 'all persons born or naturalized in the United States, and subject to the jurisdiction thereof, are citizens of the United States and of the State wherein they reside,' and that 'no State shall make or enforce any law which shall abridge the privileges or immunities of citizens of the United States; nor shall any State deprive any person of life, liberty or property without due process of law, nor deny to any person within its jurisdiction the equal protection of the laws'. These two amendments, if enforced according to their true intent and meaning, will protect all the civil rights that pertain to freedom and citizenship. Finally, and to the end that no citizen should be denied, on account of his race, the privilege of participating in the political control of his country, it was declared by the Fifteenth Amendment that 'the right of citizens of the United States to vote shall not be denied or abridged by the United States or by any state on account of race, colour or previous condition of servitude'.

These notable additions to the fundamental law were welcomed by the friends of liberty throughout the world. They removed the race line from our governmental systems. They had, as this court has said, a common purpose, namely, to secure 'to a race recently emancipated, a race that through many generations have been held in slavery, all the civil rights that the superior race enjoy'. They declared, in legal effect, this court has further said, 'that the law in the states shall be the same for the black as for the white; that all persons, whether coloured or white, shall stand equal before the laws of the states, and, in regard to the coloured race, for whose protection the amendment was primarily designed, that no discrimination shall be made against them by law because of their colour' ... [556]

*

[557] It is one thing for railroad carriers to furnish, or to be required by law to furnish, equal accommodations for all whom they are under a legal duty to carry. It is quite another thing for government to forbid citizens of the white and black races from travelling in the same public conveyance, and to punish officers of railroad companies for permitting persons of the two races to occupy the same passenger coach. If a state can prescribe, as a rule of civil conduct, that whites and blacks shall not travel as passengers in the same railroad coach, why may it not so regulate the use of the streets of its cities and towns so as to compel white citizens to keep on one side of a street and black citizens to keep on the other? Why may it not, upon like grounds, punish whites and blacks who ride together in streetcars or in open vehicles on a public road or street? Why may it not require sheriffs to assign whites to one side of a court-room and blacks to the other? And why may it not also prohibit the commingling of the two races in the galleries of legislative halls or in public assemblages convened for the consideration of the political questions of the day? Further, if this statute of Louisiana is consistent with the personal liberty of citizens, why may not the state require the separation in railroad coaches of native and naturalized citizens of the United States, or of Protestants and Roman Catholics? ... [558]

[559] The white race deems itself to be the dominant race in this country. And so it is, in prestige, in achievements, in education, in wealth and in power. So, I doubt not, it will continue to be for all time, if it remains true to its great heritage and holds fast to the principles of constitutional liberty. But in view of the Constitution, in the eye of the law, there is in this country no superior, dominant, ruling class of citizens. There is no caste here. Our Constitution is colour-blind, and neither knows nor tolerates classes among citizens. In respect of civil rights, all citizens are equal before the law. The humblest is the peer of the most powerful. The law regards man as man, and takes no account of his surroundings or of his colour when his civil rights as guaranteed by the supreme law of the land are involved. It is,

therefore, to be regretted that this high tribunal, the final expositor of the fundamental law of the land, has reached the conclusion that it is competent for a State to regulate the enjoyment by citizens of their civil rights solely upon the basis of race.

In my opinion, the judgment this day rendered will, in time, prove to be quite as pernicious as the decision made by this tribunal in the *Dred Scott case*. It was adjudged in that case that the descendants of Africans who were imported into this country and sold as slaves were not included nor intended to be included under the word 'citizens' in the Constitution, and could not claim any of the rights and privileges which that instrument provided for and secured to citizens of the United States; that at the time of the adoption of the Constitution they were 'considered as a subordinate and inferior class of beings, who had been subjugated by the dominant race, and, whether emancipated or not, yet remained subject to their authority, and had no rights or privileges but such as those who held the power and the government might choose to grant them.' . . . The destinies of the two races, in this country, are indissolubly linked together, and the interests of both require that the common government of all shall not permit the seeds of race hate to be planted under the sanction of law. What can more certainly arouse race hate, what more certainly create and perpetuate a feeling of distrust between these races, than state enactments, which, in fact, proceed on the ground that coloured citizens are so inferior and degraded that they cannot be allowed to sit in public coaches occupied by white citizens? That, as all will admit, is the real meaning of such legislation as was enacted in Louisiana.

The sure guarantee of the peace and security of each race is the clear, distinct, unconditional recognition by our governments, national and state, of every right that inheres in civil freedom, and of the equality before the law of all citizens of the United States without regard to race. State enactments, regulating the enjoyment of civil rights, upon the basis of race, and cunningly devised to defeat legitimate results of the war, under the pretence of recognising equality of rights, can have no other result than to render permanent peace impossible, and to keep alive a conflict of races, the continuance of which must do harm to all concerned. This question is not met by the suggestion that social equality cannot exist between the white and black races in this country. That argument, if it can be properly regarded as one, is scarcely worthy of consideration; for social equality no more exists between two races when travelling in a passenger coach or a public highway than when members of the same races sit by each other in a street car or in the jury box, or stand or sit with each other in a political assembly, or when they use in common the streets of a city or town, or when they are in the same room for the purpose of having their names placed on the registry of voters, or when they approach the ballot-box in order to exercise the high privilege of voting. . . . [561]

[562] If evils will result from the commingling of the two races upon public highways established for the benefit of all, they will be infinitely less than those that will surely come from state legislation regulating the enjoyment of civil rights upon the basis of race. We boast of the freedom enjoyed by our people above all other peoples. But it is difficult to reconcile that boast with a state of the law which, practically, puts the brand of servitude and degradation upon a large class of our fellow-citizens, our equals before the law. The thin disguise of 'equal' accommodations for passengers in railroad coaches will not mislead anyone, nor atone for the wrong this day done.

*

[563] I am of opinion that the statute of Louisiana is inconsistent with the personal liberty of citizens, white and black, in that state, and hostile to both the spirit and letter of the Constitution of the United States. If laws of like character should be enacted in the several states of the Union, the effect would be in the highest degree mischievous. Slavery as an institution tolerated by law would, it is true, have disappeared from our country, but there would remain a power in the states, by sinister legislation, to interfere with the full enjoyment of the blessings of freedom; to regulate civil rights, common to all citizens, upon the basis of race; and to place in a condition of legal inferiority a large body of American citizens, now constituting a part of the political community called the People of the United States, for whom, and by whom through representatives, our government is administered. Such a system is inconsistent with the guarantee given by the

Constitution to each state of a republican form of government, and may be stricken down by Congressional action, or by the courts in the discharge of their solemn duty to maintain the supreme law of the land, anything in the constitution or laws of any state to the contrary notwithstanding.

Entrenched Clauses

*Judgment in Minister of the Interior v. Harris and others**

[When the Nationalists came to power in South Africa in 1948 and began to erect the edifice that is now apartheid they found one inheritance a serious stumbling block to their programme—the inclusion of the Cape Coloureds on the common electoral roll. The Act of Union had safeguarded the colour-blind franchise of the Cape by specifically guaranteeing that no one should be disqualified in that province 'by reason of his race or colour only' unless by a Bill passed by both Houses of Parliament sitting together, and by a two-thirds of their members at third reading. Out of this 'entrenched clause' was born the constitutional crisis of 1951–1956.

Since at that time the Nationalists had not a two-thirds majority, other devices had to be resorted to. Certain legal opinion contended that no Act of the South African Parliament could be declared unconstitutional by the courts. On 8 March 1951 Dr T. E. Dönges therefore introduced the Separate Representation of Voters Bill. Ultimately the Bill was passed, and then challenged in the courts. In *Harris* v. *Dönges*, 1952 (2) S.A. 428, the Appellate Division of the Supreme Court of South Africa unanimously declared that the entrenched clause was still in force, and thus invalidated the Act.

The next step in the constitutional struggle was calculated to exacerbate the Government's relations with the judiciary, even if it appeared to have a greater chance of survival. The Government introduced a Bill whereby a special committee of the Union Parliament—called the High Court of Parliament—had power to review any judgment of the courts which had invalidated a Parliamentary Act. Again the opponents of the Government invoked the assistance of the courts. Although the five judges were unanimous in striking down the Government's ploy, five separate

* 1952 (4) S.A. 769, 789.

opinions were delivered. All of them found that the High Court of Parliament did not possess the essential qualities of a court of law, and the composition of the tribunal violated the fundamental principle that no one should be a judge in his own cause. While four of the judges reaffirmed their strict interpretation of the Act of Union to demonstrate the continued binding force of the 'entrenched clause', Mr Justice van den Heever (whose judgment is reproduced) delivered his own very individualistic Afrikaner opinion. He saw the source of the authority of the 'entrenched clause' in the fact of its very existence, implying that the South African constitution derived its validity not from its enactment by the United Kingdom Parliament but from its local source within South Africa.

Twice rebuffed, the Government at last took to constitutional action by seeking to remove the 'entrenched clause' by legislation. In September 1953, the day before the third reading of this new Bill, the Nationalists made it known that if the Bill failed they proposed to make special provision for the composition of the Appellate Division in constitutional cases, a device faintly reminiscent of the Roosevelt threat to the United States Supreme Court in 1936. The Bill failed to get the required two-thirds majority. A second attempt to secure the necessary majority likewise failed, but the device of packing the Appellate Division with pliant judges went through. The Appellate Division Quorum Act raised the number of judges to eleven whenever the Court was considering the validity of a statute. At the same time the Government increased the size of the Senate so as to secure enough votes to pass a constitutional amendment, finally to take the Coloureds off the common roll.

The trilogy of legislation to establish political apartheid was completed by the South Africa Act Amendment Act re-enacting the Separate Representation of Voters Act 1951, which had been judicially invalidated. Yet again the Cape Coloureds appealed to the courts. In November 1956 the Government won the last round, the Court upholding the legislation by a majority of ten to one. The lone dissent came from one of South Africa's great judges, Mr Justice Schreiner, whose ancestor Olive Schreiner, the writer, had prophetically written: 'It is ordered by the laws of human life that a nemesis should follow the subjection and use, purely for purposes of their own, of one race by another which lives among them. Spain fell before it in America; Rome felt it; it has dogged the feet of all conquering races. In the end the subjected people write their features on the face of the conquerors ... The continual association with creatures who are not free will ultimately take from us our strength and our own freedom, and men will see in our faces the reflection of that on which we are always treading and looking down. If we raise the dark man we shall rise with him; if we kick him under our feet, he will hold us fast by them.'

The political history of South Africa during this period is best told in *The Politics of Inequality* by Gwendolen M. Carter (Thames & Hudson, 1958).]

IT IS ADVISABLE briefly to summarise the rights with which we are concerned. Sec. 35 of the South Africa Act provides that Parliament may by law prescribe the qualifications which shall be necessary to entitle persons to vote at the election of members of the House of Assembly but that

no such law shall disqualify any person ... in the Province of the Cape of Good Hope who, under the laws existing in the Colony of the Cape of Good Hope at the establishment of the Union, is or may become capable of being registered in the Province of the Cape of Good Hope by reason of his race or colour only.

unless the bill be passed by a two-thirds majority at a joint session of both Houses of Parliament. Sec. 137 provides that the two official languages shall be treated on a footing of equality.

Sec. 152 in so far as it is relevant provides:

Parliament may by law repeal or alter any provision of this Act ... Provided further that no repeal or alteration of the provisions contained in this section, or in secs. 35 and 137 shall be valid unless the Bill embodying such repeal or alteration shall be passed by both Houses of Parliament sitting together, and at the third reading be agreed to by not less than two-thirds of the total number of members of both Houses ...

For convenience I use the expression 'Cape franchise' to denote the principle that Parliament functioning as ordinarily constituted, that is the Queen (or her representative) and the two

Houses acting separately and successively, has not the power to pass laws which disqualify on the grounds of race or colour only any person who according to the laws existing in the Cape Province at Union was or could become capable of being registered as a voter in that Province.

The Cape franchise is doubly entrenched. First it is entrenched in sec. 35 of the South Africa Act, the very section which authorises Parliament to make laws regulating the franchise. Then it was again entrenched in sec. 152. The object is plain. Since the widest powers of constitutional amendment were given in sec. 152, a brake was put upon their exercise in so far as they could affect the Cape franchise. Subject to Imperial checks which then existed, Parliament could write and rewrite its own mandate. As ordinarily constituted, however, Parliament cannot expand its mandate by deleting the inhibition of its powers in relation to the Cape franchise. It stands to reason that it cannot empower another to do what it cannot do itself. One must keep in mind that this inhibition is in restraint of power and not a regulation of method. No legislative organ can perform an act of levitation and lift itself above its own powers by the bootstraps of method.

Mr *Beyers* based certain arguments upon the different constitutional relations which existed between the Union and Great Britain before and after the enactment of the Statute of Westminster. He suggested that sec. 152 contemplated a situation in which Great Britain could by executive action as well as by legislation prevent our Parliament from putting on the statute book a measure of which it did not approve; that since Great Britain has by legislation and constitutional convention abdicated from its Imperial position in relation to the Union, the inhibiting force of the provisions of sec. 152 has in some manner ceased to operate or been weakened. If that be true sec. 152 was at the time of its enactment mere surplusage, entirely unnecessary and meaningless. Putting aside nomenclature, the Act of Union in substance created a Kingdom, the Kingdom of South Africa, and had far-reaching constitutional and political implications. The product was a constitutional Kingdom with the checks and safeguards which one expects in a body politic so organised, but since our Constitution is a modern creation they are not necessarily fashioned on British models. One of these checks is contained in sec. 152 read with sec. 35. It says that 'no person' shall be deprived of his Cape franchise by ordinary legislation; in other words, a check was put upon legislative power in favour of the individual.

How it can be contended that since the Imperial abdication of Great Britain that check has become weakened, I cannot grasp. That contention assumes that as soon as the policeman is round the corner there is no law. In this connection the fact that our constitution is the creature of the British Parliament seems to me a fortuitous circumstance which is quite irrelevant; so too is the fact that we have a written constitution. I would have been of the same opinion if it had been framed by a constituent assembly of the people, made by Solon or extracted from the laws of Hammurabi. It seems to me immaterial whether one adheres to the mandatory theory of legislative power or any other. The fact remains that the South Africa Act is our Constitution and apart from that constitution there are no organs of state and no powers. If you will, call the cohesive force what Jellinek used to term '*die normirende Kraft des Factischen*'.* Neither the people nor any other constituent authority has conferred upon Parliament as ordinarily constituted the power to alter the Cape franchise. In fact such power has been expressly withheld. Parliament as ordinarily constituted has not as yet effectively and finally assumed such power in a revolution, nor has Parliament functioning unicamerally with the requisite majority conferred such power. There is no other conceivable source of such power; consequently it does not exist. If nevertheless Parliament as ordinarily constituted assumes the power to alter the Cape franchise, its act would have no greater validity than if the City Council of Bloemfontein had presumed to do so. Only British bias could prompt the thought that since such a power resides in the legislature in Britain our Parliament as ordinarily constituted must necessarily have it too.

In the Act under consideration, Mr *Beyers* and Mr *van Wyk* strenuously contended, Parliament as ordinarily constituted has not attempted to exercise powers in disregard of the provisions of sec. 152; on the contrary, it has left that section intact. Parlia-

* The power of facts to create standards.

ment in that form has full power to reorganise the judiciary; exercising those undoubted powers, it has created a court superior to the Appellate Division. Substantive rights are guaranteed in the Constitution; they still 'stand', counsel contended, although by the amendment of adjective law their enforcement may have become impossible. How rights so prostrate can be said to remain 'standing' I cannot grasp—but these are words.

I go part of the way with counsel for respondents. As ordinarily constituted Parliament has unlimited powers to reorganise the judiciary. It can create a court or courts superior to the Appellate Division and confer upon them such jurisdiction as it thinks fit. From the second preamble to the South Africa Act it is clear that the authors of our constitution had in mind the doctrine of the *trias politica* and the existence of some judicial power to enforce the constitutional guarantees. That seems to follow by necessary intendment. But I do not think the further inference is justified that they had in contemplation that the judicial power had for ever to be exercised by courts constituted in a manner which satisfies certain criteria to the end that the independence, competence and justness of these tribunals be manifest and secured. I do not think they intended that courts should always be of the kind to which they were accustomed. We have had many kinds of courts; we have had trial by battle, by fire and by flood. We have heard of modern 'people's courts', in which the standard of justice was perhaps no higher than in the *iudicium ferri candentis* of the Lombards (Gengler, *Germanische R-Denkmäler*, p. 759). In Holland today there is *cassatie in belang der wet* which the *Attorney-General* may set in motion although the parties to the dispute have acquiesced in the judgment taken on review (Art. 89, Wet op de Regterlijke Organisatie). In this respect the legislature has absolute freedom of action and it is not for the existing courts to criticise the wisdom or equity of a measure passed in the exercise of that power by a comparison of the court established with courts answering to some preconceived standard.

All this, however, is subject to one limitation which follows by necessary implication and has no relation to the character or competence of the new creation: it must be a court. Since it was conceived as being the arbiter between Parliament as ordinarily constituted or even in joint session and subjects who complain that they have unconstitutionally been deprived of their rights, it must necessarily be a body other than Parliament and capable of passing judgment on that issue.

In the light of these considerations I now examine the High Court of Parliament Act, 35 of 1952. Sec. 3 (1) provides that every senator and every member of the House of Assembly shall be a member of the Court. Sub-sec. (6) of that section excludes certain members, but that is only in order to avoid the absurdity of their passing judgment in a matter which was already part heard when they became members. Fifty members shall form a quorum. The Governor-General may determine the venue of the Court (sec. 4). The decision of the majority of the members present shall be the decision of the Court (sec. 8 (2)).

If we winnow out the chaff of nomenclature and regard the substance, what have we here? Parliament as ordinarily constituted enacts that Parliament in joint session may change its venue and its name and by a bare majority of those present (the Constitution requires a two-thirds majority of the total number of members of both Houses) and at one reading (the Constitution requires three) pass a declaratory act as to the meaning of secs. 35, 137 and 152 of the South Africa Act. That the meaning so given is in direct conflict with the judgment of what was hitherto the highest court in the land, is to my mind interesting but irrelevant. If a statutory provision is capable of two constructions and a law is passed that henceforth it shall bear only one construction, that law *pro tanto* repeals and certainly alters the provision.

How is this affected by the provision that the High Court may do so on legal grounds? Save as an evasion I can see no virtue in these words. If an Act is beyond the competence of a legislative body, its motives are irrelevant, whether they be ethical, legal or political. Where courts of law have in two instances been exercised by the question whether or not a legislature has exceeded its powers and deprived subjects of their rights and the constituent individuals of that legislative body functioning in a different manner are appointed as a final court of appeal to determine whether they had acted lawfully or otherwise, their newly-acquired capacity and functions cannot by any standard be said to be judicial.

I have come to the conclusion therefore that in Act 35 of 1952 Parliament as ordinarily constituted purports to empower Parliament in joint session to ignore the checks limiting the powers of both. The measure is therefore invalid.

Freedom for Thought

Dissenting opinion in United States v. Schwimmer*

THE APPLICANT SEEMS to be a woman of superior character and intelligence, obviously more than ordinarily desirable as a citizen of the United States. It is agreed that she is qualified for citizenship except so far as the views set forth in a statement of facts 'may show that the applicant is not attached to the principles of the Constitution of the United States and well disposed to the good order and happiness of the same, and except in so far as the same may show that she cannot take the oath of allegiance without a mental reservation'. The views referred to are an extreme opinion in favour of pacifism and a statement that she would not bear arms to defend the Constitution. So far as the adequacy of her oath is concerned I hardly can see how that is affected by the statement, inasmuch as she is a woman over fifty years of age, and would not be allowed to bear arms if she wanted to. And as to the opinion, the whole examination of the applicant shows that she holds none of the now-dreaded creeds but thoroughly believes in organised government and prefers that of the United States to any other in the world. Surely it cannot show lack of attachment to the principles of the Constitution that she thinks that it can be improved. I suppose that most intelligent people think that it might be. Her particular improvement looking to the abolition of war seems to me not materially different in its bearing on this case from a wish to establish cabinet government as in England, or a single house, or one term of seven years for the President. To touch a more burning question, only a judge mad with partisanship would exclude because the applicant thought that the Eighteenth Amendment† should be repealed.

Of course the fear is that if a war came the applicant would exert activities such as were dealt with in *Schenck* v. *United*

---

* 279 U.S. 644, 653 (1929).

† The law relating to prohibition, which Mr Justice Holmes detested.

States, 249 U.S. 47. But that seems to me unfounded. Her position and motives are wholly different from those of Schenck. She is an optimist and states in strong and, I do not doubt, sincere words her belief that war will disappear and that the impending destiny of mankind is to unite in peaceful leagues. I do not share that optimism nor do I think that a philosophic view of the world would regard war as absurd. But most people who have known it regard it with horror, as a last resort, and even if not yet ready for cosmopolitan efforts, would welcome any practicable combinations that would increase the power on the side of peace. The notion that the applicant's optimistic anticipations would make her a worse citizen is sufficiently answered by her examination, which seems to me a better argument for her admission than any that I can offer. Some of her answers might excite popular prejudice, but if there is any principle of the Constitution that more imperatively calls for attachment than any other it is the principle of free thought—not free thought for those who agree with us but freedom for the thought that we hate. I think that we should adhere to that principle with regard to admission into, as well as to life within, this country. And recurring to the opinion that bars this applicant's way, I would suggest that the Quakers have done their share to make the country what it is, that many citizens agree with the applicant's belief and that I had not supposed hitherto that we regretted our inability to expel them because they believe more than some of us do in the teachings of the Sermon on the Mount.

P.P.E.

Laissez-Faire

Judgment in Mogul Steamship Co. v. *McGregor, Gow & Co.*†

WE ARE PRESENTED in this case with an apparent conflict or antinomy between two rights that are equally regarded by the law – the right of the plaintiffs to be protected in the legitimate exercise of their trade, and the right of the defendants to carry on their business as seems best to them, provided they commit no wrong to others. The plaintiffs complain that the defendants have crossed the line which the common law permits; and inasmuch as, for the purposes of the present case, we are to assume some possible damage to the plaintiffs, the real question to be decided is whether, on such an assumption, the defendants in the conduct of their commercial affairs have done anything that is unjustifiable in law.

The defendants are a number of shipowners who formed themselves into a league or conference for the purpose of ultimately keeping in their own hands the control of the tea carriage from certain Chinese ports, and for the purpose of driving the plaintiffs and other competitors from the field. In order to succeed in this object, and to discourage the plaintiffs' vessels from resorting to those ports, the defendants during the 'tea harvest' of 1885 combined to offer to the local shippers very low freights, with a view of generally reducing or 'smashing' rates, and thus rendering it unprofitable for the plaintiffs to send their ships thither. They offered, moreover, a rebate of 5 per cent. to all local shippers and agents who would deal exclusively with vessels belonging to the conference, and any agent who broke the condition was to forfeit the entire rebate on all shipments made on behalf of any and every one of his principals during the whole year – a forfeiture of rebate or allowance which was denominated as 'penal' by the plaintiffs' counsel. It must, however, be taken as

* Then Lord Justice Bowen.
† (1889) 23 Q.B.D. 598, 611.

established that the rebate was one which the defendants need never have allowed at all to their customers. It must also be taken that the defendants had no personal ill-will to the plaintiffs, nor any desire to harm them except such as is involved in the wish and intention to discourage by such measures the plaintiffs from sending rival vessels to such ports. The acts of which the plaintiffs particularly complained were as follows: – First, a circular of 10 May 1885, by which the defendants offered to the local shippers and their agents a benefit by way of rebate if they would not deal with the plaintiffs, which was to be lost if this condition was not fulfilled. Secondly, the sending of special ships to Hankow in order by competition to deprive the plaintiffs' vessels of profitable freight. Thirdly, the offer at Hankow of freights at a level which would not repay a shipowner for his adventure, in order to 'smash' freights and frighten the plaintiffs from the field. Fourthly, pressure put on the defendants' own agents to induce them to ship only by the defendants' vessels, and not by those of the plaintiffs. It is to be observed with regard to all these acts of which complaint is made that they were acts that in themselves could not be said to be illegal unless made so by the object with which, or the combination in the course of which, they were done; and that in reality what is complained of is the pursuing of trade competition to a length which the plaintiffs consider oppressive and prejudicial to themselves. We were invited by the plaintiffs' counsel to accept the position from which their argument started – that an action will lie if a man maliciously and wrongfully conducts himself so as to injure another in that other's trade. Obscurity resides in the language used to state this proposition. The terms 'maliciously', 'wrongfully', and 'injure' are words all of which have accurate meanings, well known to the law, but which also have a popular and less precise signification, into which it is necessary to see that the argument does not imperceptibly slide. An intent to 'injure' in strictness means more than an intent to harm. It connotes an intent to do wrongful harm. 'Maliciously', in like manner, means and implies an intention to do an act which is wrongful, to the detriment of another. The term 'wrongful' imports in its turn the infringement of some right. The ambiguous proposition to which we were invited by the plaintiffs' counsel still, therefore, leaves unsolved the question of what, as between the plaintiffs and defendants, are the rights of trade. For the purpose of clearness, I desire, as far as possible, to avoid terms in their popular use so slippery, and to translate them into less fallacious language wherever possible.

The English law, which in its earlier stages began with but an imperfect line of demarcation between torts and breaches of contract, presents us with no scientific analysis of the degree to which the intent to do harm, or, in the language of the civil law, the *animus vicino nocendi*, may enter into or affect the conception of a personal wrong. All personal wrong means the infringement of some personal right. ... What, then, were the rights of the plaintiffs as traders as against the defendants? The plaintiffs had a right to be protected against certain kind of conduct; and we have to consider what conduct would pass this legal line or boundary. Now, intentionally to do that which is calculated in the ordinary course of events to damage, and which does, in fact, damage another in that other person's property or trade, is actionable if done without just cause or excuse. Such intentional action when done without just cause or excuse is what the law calls a malicious wrong. The acts of the defendants which are complained of here were intentional, and were also calculated, no doubt, to do the plaintiffs damage in their trade. But in order to see whether they were wrongful we have still to discuss the question whether they were done without any just cause or excuse. Such just cause or excuse the defendants on their side assert to be found in their own positive right (subject to certain limitations) to carry on their own trade freely in the mode and manner that best suits them, and which they think best calculated to secure their own advantage.

What, then, are the limitations which the law imposes on a trader in the conduct of his business as between himself and other traders? There seem to be no burdens or restrictions in law upon a trader which arise merely from the fact that he is a trader, and which are not equally laid on all other subjects of the Crown. His right to trade freely is a right which the law recognises and encourages, but it is one which places him at no special disadvantage as compared with others. No man, whether trader or not, can, however, justify damaging another in his commercial business by fraud or misrepresentation. Intimidation, obstruction, and molestation are forbidden; so is the intentional procurement of a violation of individual rights, contractual or other, assuming always that there is no just cause for it. The intentional driving away of customers by shew of violence: the obstruction of actors on the stage by preconcerted hissing: the disturbance of wild fowl in decoys by the firing of guns: the impeding or threatening servants or workmen: the inducing persons under personal contracts to break their contracts: all are instances of such forbidden acts. But the defendants have been guilty of none of these acts. They have done nothing more against the plaintiffs than pursue to the bitter end a war of competition waged in the interest of their own trade. To the argument that a competition so pursued ceases to have a just cause or excuse when there is ill-will or a personal intention to harm, it is sufficient to reply (as I have already pointed out) that there was here no personal intention to do any other or greater harm to the plaintiffs than such as was necessarily involved in the desire to attract to the defendants' ships the entire tea freights of the ports, a portion of which would otherwise have fallen to the plaintiffs' share. I can find no authority for the doctrine that such a commercial motive deprives of 'just cause or excuse' acts done in the course of trade which would but for such a motive be justifiable. So to hold would be to convert into an illegal motive the instinct of self-advancement and self-protection, which is the very incentive to all trade. To say that a man is to trade freely, but that he is to stop short at any act which is calculated to harm other tradesmen, and which is designed to attract business to his own shop, would be a strange and impossible counsel of perfection. But we were told that competition ceases to be the lawful exercise of trade, and so to be a lawful excuse for what will harm another, if carried to a length which is not fair or reasonable. The offering of reduced rates by the defendants in the present case is said to have been 'unfair'. This seems to assume that, apart from fraud, intimidation, molestation, or obstruction, of some other personal right *in rem* or *in personam*, there is some natural standard of 'fairness' or 'reasonableness' (to be determined by the internal consciousness of judges and juries) beyond which competition ought not in law to go. There seems to be no authority, and I think, with submission, that there is no sufficient reason for such a proposition. It would impose a novel fetter upon trade. The defendants, we are told by the plaintiffs' counsel, might lawfully lower rates provided they did not lower them beyond a 'fair freight', whatever that may mean. But where is it established that there is any such restriction upon commerce? And what is to be the definition of a 'fair freight'? It is said that it ought to be a normal rate of freight, such as is reasonably remunerative to the shipowner. But over what period of time is the average of this reasonable remunerativeness to be calculated? All commercial men with capital are acquainted with the ordinary expedient of sowing one year a crop of apparently unfruitful prices, in order by driving competition away to reap a fuller harvest of profit in the future; and until the present argument at the bar it may be doubted whether shipowners or merchants were ever deemed to be bound by law to conform to some imaginary 'normal' standard of freights or prices, or that law courts had a right to say to them in respect of their competitive tariffs, 'Thus far shalt thou go and no further.' To attempt to limit English competition in this way would probably be as hopeless an endeavour as the experiment of King Canute. But on ordinary principles of law no such fetter on freedom of trade can in my opinion be warranted. A man is bound not to use his property so as to infringe upon another's right. *Sic utere tuo ut alienum non laedas.* If engaged in actions which may involve danger to others, he ought, speaking generally, to take reasonable care to avoid endangering them. But there is surely no doctrine of law which compels him to use his property in a way that judges and juries may consider reasonable. If there is no such fetter upon the use of property known to the English law, why should there be any such a fetter upon trade?

It is urged, however, on the part of the plaintiffs, that even if the acts complained of would not be wrongful had they been committed by a single individual, they become actionable when they are the result of concerted action among several. In other words, the plaintiffs, it is contended, have been injured by an illegal conspiracy. Of the general proposition, that certain kinds of conduct not criminal in any one individual may become criminal if done by combination among several, there can be no doubt. The distinction is based on sound reason, for a combination may make oppressive or dangerous that which if it proceeded only from a single person would be otherwise, and the very fact of the combination may shew that the object is simply to do harm, and not to exercise one's own just rights. In the application of this undoubted principle it is necessary to be very careful not to press the doctrine of illegal conspiracy beyond that which is necessary for the protection of individuals or of the public; and it may be observed in passing that as a rule it is the damage wrongfully done, and not the conspiracy, that is the gist of actions on the case for conspiracy. But what is the definition of an illegal combination? It is an agreement by one or more to do an unlawful act, or to do a lawful act by unlawful means; and the question to be solved is whether there has been any such agreement here. Have the defendants combined to do an unlawful act? Have they combined to do a lawful act by unlawful means? A moment's consideration will be sufficient to shew that this new inquiry only drives us back to the circle of definitions and legal propositions which I have already traversed in the previous part of this judgment. The unlawful act agreed to, if any, between the defendants must have been the intentional doing of some act to the detriment of the plaintiff's business without just cause or excuse. Whether there was any such justification or excuse for the defendants is the old question over again, which, so far as regards an individual trader, has been already solved. The only differentia that can exist must arise, if at all, out of the fact that the acts done are the joint acts of several capitalists, and not of one capitalist only.

The next point is whether the means adopted were unlawful. The means adopted were competition carried to a bitter end. Whether such means were unlawful is in like manner nothing but the old discussion which I have gone through, and which is now revived under a second head of inquiry, except so far as a combination of capitalists differentiates the case of acts jointly done by them from similar acts done by a single man of capital. But I find it impossible myself to acquiesce in the view that the English law places any such restriction on the combination of capital as would be involved in the recognition of such a distinction. If so, one rich capitalist may innocently carry competition to a length which would become unlawful in the case of a syndicate with a joint capital no larger than his own, and one individual merchant may lawfully do that which a firm or a partnership may not.

What limits, on such a theory, would be imposed by law on the competitive action of a joint-stock company limited, is a problem which might well puzzle a casuist. The truth is, that the combination of capital for purposes of trade and competition is a very different thing from such a combination of several persons against one, with a view to harm him, as falls under the head of an indictable conspiracy. There is no just cause or excuse in the latter class of cases. There is such a just cause or excuse in the former. There are cases in which the very fact of a combination is evidence of a design to do that which is hurtful without just cause – is evidence – to use a technical expression – of malice. But it is perfectly legitimate, as it seems to me, to combine capital for all the mere purposes of trade for which capital may, apart from combination, be legitimately used in trade. To limit combinations of capital, when used for purposes of competition, in the manner proposed by the argument of the plaintiffs, would, in the present day, be impossible – would be only another method of attempting to set boundaries to the tides. Legal puzzles which might well distract a theorist may easily be conceived of imaginary conflicts between the selfishness of a group of individuals and the obvious well-being of other members of the community. Would it be an indictable conspiracy to agree to drink up all the water from a common spring in a time of drought; to buy up by preconcerted action all the provisions in a market or district in times of scarcity; to combine to purchase all the shares of a company against a coming settling-day; or to agree to give away articles of trade gratis in order to withdraw custom from a trader? May two itinerant match-vendors combine to sell matches below their value in order by competition to drive a third match-vendor from the street? In cases like these, where the elements of intimidation, molestation, or the other kinds of illegality to which I have alluded are not present, the question must be decided by the application of the test I have indicated. Assume that what is done is intentional, and that it is calculated to do harm to others. Then comes the question, Was it done with or without 'just cause or excuse'? If it was bona fide done in the use of a man's own property, in the exercise of a man's own trade, such legal justification would, I think, exist not the less because what was done might seem to others to be selfish or unreasonable. But such legal justification would not exist when the act was merely done with the intention of causing temporal harm, without reference to one's own lawful gain, or the lawful enjoyment of one's own rights. The good sense of the tribunal which had to decide would have to analyse the circumstances and to discover on which side of the line each case fell. But if the real object were to enjoy what was one's own, or to acquire for one's self some advantage in one's property or trade, and what was done was done honestly, peaceably, and without any of the illegal acts above referred to, it could not, in my opinion, properly be said that it was done without just cause or excuse. . . .

Lastly, we are asked to hold the defendants' conference or association illegal, as being in restraint of trade. The term 'illegal' here is a misleading one. Contracts, as they are called, in restraint of trade, are not, in my opinion, illegal in any sense, except that the law will not enforce them. It does not prohibit the making of such contracts; it merely declines, after they have been made, to recognise their validity. The law considers the disadvantage so imposed upon the contract a sufficient shelter to the public. No action at common law will lie or ever has lain against any individual or individuals for entering into a contract merely because it is in restraint of trade. Lord Eldon's equity decision in *Cousins* v. *Smith** is not very intelligible, even if it be not open to the somewhat personal criticism passed on it by Lord Campbell in his Lives of the Chancellors. If indeed it could be plainly proved that the mere formation of 'conferences', 'trusts', or 'associations' such as these were always necessarily injurious to the public – a view which involves, perhaps, the disputable assumption that, in a country of free trade, and one which is not under the iron regime of statutory monopolies, such confederations can ever be really successful – and if the evil of them were not sufficiently dealt with by the common law rule, which held such agreements to be void as distinct from holding them to be criminal, there might be some reason for thinking that the common law ought to discover within its arsenal of sound commonsense principles some further remedy commensurate with the mischief. Neither of these assumptions are, to my mind, at all evident, nor is it the province of judges to mould and stretch the

* 13 Ves. 542.

law of conspiracy in order to keep pace with the calculations of political economy. If peaceable and honest combinations of capital for purposes of trade competition are to be struck at, it must, I think, be by legislation, for I do not see that they are under the ban of the common law.

The substance of my view is this, that competition, however severe and egotistical, if unattended by circumstances of dishonesty, intimidation, molestation, or such illegalities as I have above referred to, gives rise to no cause of action at common law. I myself should deem it to be a misfortune if we were to attempt to prescribe to the business world how honest and peaceable trade was to be carried on in a case where no such illegal elements as I have mentioned exist, or were to adopt some standard of judicial 'reasonableness', or of 'normal' prices, or 'fair freights', to which commercial adventurers, otherwise innocent, were bound to conform.

Free Trade

*Judgment in James v. Cowan**

[A fruit grower in South Australia, who sold dried fruit throughout Australia, had a consignment seized by the Ministry of Agriculture for South Australia in accordance with powers conferred by the South Australian legislature in the Dried Fruits Acts 1924–1927. The question before the High Court of Australia was whether the acquisition and seizure in any way contravened section 92 of the Australian Constitution which declares that inter-State trade is to be 'absolutely free'. The court unanimously held that there had been no violation of the Constitution.]

IN THIS CASE the inferences drawn by the learned primary judge [Mr Justice Starke] as to the purpose, intention or motive of the Minister were attacked, but I see no reason to disagree with them. But in substance I think they do attribute to the Minister an intention or desire to prevent the appellant's fruit being sold by him for consumption in Australia, and it may be conceded that this necessarily involves the purpose or desire that the fruit should not be sold in any of the five States which with South Australia make up the Commonwealth. This fact gives the appellant a basis for an argument which, apart from authority, would appear formidable – that the freedom of trade, commerce and intercourse between the States, which sec. 92 of the Constitution guarantees, had been impinged upon by the Minister's orders of compulsory acquisition.

The rhetorical affirmation of sec. 92 that trade, commerce and intercourse between the States shall be absolutely free has a terseness and elevation of style which doubtless befits the expression of a sentiment so inspiring. But inspiring sentiments are often vague, and grandiloquence is sometimes obscure. If this declaration of liberty had not stopped short at the high-sounding

* (1930) 43 C.L.R. 386, 422.

words 'absolutely free', the pith and force of its diction might have been sadly diminished. But even if it was impossible to define precisely what it was from which inter-State trade was to be free, either because a commonplace definition forms such a pedestrian conclusion or because it needs an exactness of conception seldom achieved where constitutions are projected, yet obmutescence was both unnecessary and unsafe. Some hint at least might have been dropped, some distant allusion made, from which the nature of the immunity intended could afterwards have been deduced by those whose lot it is to explain the elliptical and expound the unexpressed. As soon as the section was brought down from the lofty clouds whence constitutional precepts are fulminated and came to be applied to the everyday practice of trade and commerce and the sordid intercourse of human affairs, the necessity of knowing and so determining precisely what impediments and hindrances were no longer to obstruct inter-State trade obliged this Court to attempt the impossible task of supplying an exclusive and inclusive definition of a conception to be discovered only in the silences of the Constitution. The evils from which sec. 92 meant to free inter-State trade were evidently particular. Universal freedom from all laws both natural and human was not in contemplation. It was plain that the Constitution was not dealing with the physical restraints which nature still inflicts on travellers who journey across this Continent. It was almost as clear that the Constitution was not conferring upon those engaged in inter-State commerce and intercourse a private right to immunity from hindrance at the hands of their fellow-citizens. No one could suppose that the consignee of goods shipped from another State could claim a constitutional right to damages from a shipowner who failed to deliver them, or that a larcenous inter-State carrier committed not only a felony but an outrage upon the Constitution. Still less possible was it to believe that sec. 92 meant to free inter-State trade of all legal regulation whatever. The operation of the criminal law which is supposed to preserve property could scarcely have been excluded from inter-State trade. However much reliance in and before 1900* may have been placed upon the eighth commandment, sec. 92 can scarcely have been framed to put an absconding

* The year of the Australian Federal Constitution.

thief at his legal ease so long as his destination was over the boundary. Indeed this Court* was so appalled by the contention that sec. 92 guaranteed freedom of inter-State movement to the criminal classes that it refused to hold that sec. 92 forbade one State in any circumstances to refuse admittance to another's convicted citizens. But, if inter-State trade is not to be free of all legal regulation, what kind of regulation is forbidden? At an early stage of the long controversy as to the true meaning of what sec. 92 omits to say, I joined with my brother *Gavan Duffy* in thinking that the immunity was confined to legal restrictions imposed upon trade and commerce in virtue of its inter-State character. The justification for this view, if any there be, is set out at length in *Duncan* v. *State of Queensland.*† One demerit was found in this view which was sufficient to make it untenable, namely, a majority of the Court steadfastly refused to adhere to it. It must be confessed that it supplied a criterion which was difficult of application, but it may also be claimed that no criterion which is easier of application has hitherto been revealed. But with the progress of time and in spite of the fluctuations of mind and matter the Court has arrived at definite decisions which declare that some things are and some things are not impairments of the freedom guaranteed by sec. 92. . . . After many years of exploration into the dark recesses of this subject I am content to take the decided cases as sailing directions upon which I may set some course, however unexpected may be the destination to which it brings me, and await with a patience not entirely hopeless the powerful beacon light of complete authoritative exposition from those who can speak with finality. In the meantime I can only express my opinion that these decisions do suggest a working principle, and a principle which is all the more satisfactory because it accommodates itself to the decision of this Court in the *Wheat Case*,‡ the application of which was so much canvassed in this case . . . What is forbidden by sec. 92 is State legislation in respect of trade and commerce when it operates to restrict, regulate, fetter or control it, and to do this immediately or directly as distinct from giving rise to some consequential impediment. The *Wheat Case*

* In *R.* v. *Smithers*; *ex parte Brown*, (1912) 16 C.L.R. 99.
† (1916) 22 C.L.R. 556, 640, 641.
‡ (1915) 20 C.L.R. 54.

decided that a general law expropriating wheat in New South Wales effectually operated to transfer the property in wheat which was in course of inter-State transportation and wheat which was devoted to inter-State transactions. The reasoning was that a transfer, compulsory or otherwise, of the ownership in a chattel was not an impairment of the liberty to transact business inter-State. Apart from the nature of the inquiry which would be involved, it could scarcely be in doubt in the *Wheat Case* that the New South Wales Legislature was impelled to resort to compulsory acquisition as a means of controlling the wheat market because of the difficulty of applying other methods in view of sec. 92. It appears to me at bottom that the decision of the Court rested on the principle that legislation authorising compulsory acquisition did not immediately or directly affect inter-State trade but did so only consequentially. If this view is right it goes a long distance to decide the present case. The State of South Australia undertook the control of the marketing of dried fruit and authorised the compulsory acquisition of parcels of such fruit in order that the entire crop should be disposed of according to its scheme. The exercise of the power by the acquisition of a particular parcel of fruit may operate consequentially to disable the owner from embarking upon or carrying out some contemplated or actual inter-State transaction, but it is not a law which operates directly upon inter-State commerce. The fact that the Minister by the exercise of the power prevents the sale of the fruit inter-State is therefore unimportant. The investigation into his motive or design is immaterial. It would, indeed, be strange if a power reposed in a person who forms part of the Executive were allowed or disallowed by the Federal Constitution according to the motive which actuated its exercise.

Pyrrhic Victory

Dissenting opinion in Beauharnais v. Illinois*

THIS CASE IS here because Illinois inflicted criminal punishment on Beauharnais for causing the distribution of leaflets in the city of Chicago. The conviction rests on the leaflet's contents, not on the time, manner or place of distribution. Beauharnais is head of an organisation that opposes amalgamation and favours segregation of white and coloured people. After discussion, an assembly of his group decided to petition the mayor and council of Chicago to pass laws for segregation. Volunteer members of the group agreed to stand on street corners, solicit signers to petitions addressed to the city authorities, and distribute leaflets giving information about the group, its beliefs and its plans. In carrying out this programme a solicitor handed out a leaflet which was the basis of this prosecution. . . .

I

That Beauharnais and his group were making a genuine effort to petition their elected representatives is not disputed. Even as far back as 1689, the Bill of Rights exacted of William & Mary said: 'It is the Right of the Subjects to petition the King, and all Commitments and Prosecutions for such petitioning are illegal.' And 178 years ago the Declaration of Rights of the Continental Congress proclaimed to the monarch of that day that his American subjects had 'a right peaceably to assemble, consider of their grievances, and petition the King; and that all prosecutions, prohibitory proclamations, and commitments for the same, are illegal.' After independence was won, Americans stated as the first unequivocal command of their Bill of Rights: 'Congress shall make no law . . . abridging the freedom of speech, or of the press; or the right of the people peaceably to assemble, and to petition the Government for a redress of grievances.' Without distortion,

* 343 U.S. 250, 267 (1952).

this First Amendment could not possibly be read so as to hold that Congress has power to punish Beauharnais and others for petitioning Congress as they have sought here to petition the Chicago authorities. And we have held in a number of prior cases that the Fourteenth Amendment makes the specific prohibitions of the First Amendment equally applicable to the states.

In view of these prior holdings, how does the Court justify its holding today that states can punish people for exercising the vital freedoms intended to be safeguarded from suppression by the First Amendment? The prior holdings are not referred to; the Court simply acts on the bland assumption that the First Amendment is wholly irrelevant. It is not even accorded the respect of a passing mention. This follows logically, I suppose, from recent constitutional doctrine which appears to measure state laws solely by this Court's notions of civilised 'canons of decency', reasonableness, etc. Under this 'reasonableness' test, state laws abridging First Amendment freedoms are sustained if found to have a 'rational basis'. Today's case degrades First Amendment freedoms to the 'rational basis' level. It is now a certainty that the new 'due process' coverall offers far less protection to liberty than would adherence to our former cases compelling states to abide by the unequivocal First Amendment command that its defined freedoms shall not be abridged.

The Court's holding here and the constitutional doctrine behind it leave the rights of assembly, petition, speech and press almost completely at the mercy of state legislative, executive, and judicial agencies. I say 'almost' because state curtailment of these freedoms may still be invalidated if a majority of this Court conclude that a particular infringement is 'without reason', or is 'a wilful and purposeless restriction unrelated to the peace and well-being of the State'. But lest this encouragement should give too much hope as to how and when this Court might protect these basic freedoms from state invasion, we are cautioned that state legislatures must be left free to 'experiment' and to make 'legislative' judgments. We are told that mistakes may be made during the legislative process of curbing public opinion. In such event the Court fortunately does not leave those mistakenly curbed, or any of us for that matter, unadvised. Consolation can be sought and must be found in the philosophical reflection that State legislative error in stifling speech and press 'is the price to be paid for the trial-and-error inherent in legislative efforts to deal with obstinate social issues'. My own belief is that no legislature is charged with the duty or vested with the power to decide what public issues Americans can discuss. In a free country this is the individual's choice, not the State's. State experimentation in curbing freedom of expression is a startling and frightening doctrine in a country dedicated to self-government by its people. I reject the holding that either State or nation can punish people for having their say in matters of public concern.

II

The Illinois statute imposes state censorship over the theatre, moving pictures, radio, television, leaflets, magazines, books and newspapers. No doubt the statute is broad enough to make criminal the 'publication, sale, presentation or exhibition' of many of the world's great classics, both secular and religious.

The Court condones this expansive state censorship by painstakingly analogising it to the law of criminal libel. As a result of this refined analysis, the Illinois statute emerges labelled a 'group libel law'. This label may make the Court's holding more palatable for those who sustain it, but the sugar-coating does not make the censorship less deadly. However tagged, the Illinois law is not that criminal libel which has been 'defined, limited and constitutionally recognised time out of mind'.* For as 'consti-

---

* The Court's finding of a close kinship between 'criminal libel' and 'group libel' because both contain the word 'libel' and have some factors in common is reminiscent of what Earl Stanhope said in 1792 in discussing Mr Fox's Libel Bill. He was arguing that a jury of laymen might more likely protect liberty than judges, because judges were prone to rely too heavily on word books. 'He put the case, that an action for a libel was brought for using a modern word, not to be found in any grammar or glossary, viz. for saying that a man was "a great bore"; a jury would laugh at such a ground of prosecution, but the judges would turn to their grammars and glossaries, and not being able to meet with it, would say they could not find such a phrase as "a great bore", but they had found a wild boar, which no doubt it meant; and yet it could not be, as a wild boar had four legs, and a man was a two-legged animal; then it must mean, that the plaintiff was like a wild boar in disposition, which was a wicked libel, and therefore let the defendant be hanged.' 29 Hansard, *Parliamentary History of England*, p. 1412.

tutionally recognised' that crime has provided for punishment of false, malicious, scurrilous charges against individuals, not against huge groups. This limited scope of the law of criminal libel is of no small importance. It has confined state punishment of speech and expression to the narrowest of areas involving nothing more than purely private feuds. Every expansion of the law of criminal libel so as to punish discussions of matters of public concern means a corresponding invasion of the area dedicated to free expression by the First Amendment.

Prior efforts to expand the scope of criminal libel beyond its traditional boundaries have not usually met with widespread popular acclaim. 'Seditious libel' was such an expansion and it did have its day, particularly in the English Court of Star Chamber. But the First Amendment repudiated seditious libel for this country. And one need only glance through the parliamentary discussion of Fox's Libel Law passed in England in 1792, to sense the bad odour of criminal libel in that country even when confined to charges against individuals only.

*

Unless I misread history the majority is giving libel a more expansive scope and more respectable status than it was ever accorded even in the Star Chamber. For here it is held to be punishable to give publicity to any picture, moving picture, play, drama or sketch, or any printed matter which a judge may find unduly offensive to any race, colour, creed or religion. In other words, in arguing for or against the enactment of laws that may differently affect huge groups, it is now very dangerous indeed to say something critical of one of the groups. And any 'person, firm or corporation' can be tried for this crime. 'Person, firm or corporation' certainly includes a book publisher, newspaper, radio or television station, candidate or even a preacher.

It is easy enough to say that none of this latter group have been proceeded against under the Illinois Act. And they have not – yet. But emotions bubble and tempers flare in racial and religious controversies, the kind here involved. It would not be easy for any court, in good conscience, to narrow this Act so as to exclude from it any of those I have mentioned. Furthermore, persons tried under the Act could not even get a jury trial except as to the bare fact of publication. Here, the court simply charged the jury that Beauharnais was guilty if he had caused distribution of the leaflet. Such trial by judge rather than by jury was outlawed in England in 1792 by Fox's Libel Law.

This Act sets up a system of state censorship which is at war with the kind of free government envisioned by those who forced adoption of our Bill of Rights. The motives behind the state law may have been to do good. But the same can be said about most laws making opinions punishable as crimes. History indicates that urges to do good have led to the burning of books and even to the burning of 'witches'.

No rationalisation on a purely legal level can conceal the fact that state laws like this one present a constant overhanging threat to freedom of speech, press and religion. Today Beauharnais is punished for publicly expressing strong views in favour of segregation. Ironically enough, Beauharnais, convicted of a crime in Chicago, would probably be given a hero's reception in many other localities, if not in some parts of Chicago itself. Moreover, the same kind of state law that makes Beauharnais a criminal for advocating segregation in Illinois can be utilised to send people to jail in other states for advocating equality and non-segregation. What Beauharnais said in his leaflet is mild compared with usual arguments on both sides of racial controversies.

We are told that freedom of petition and discussion are in no danger 'while this Court sits'. This case raises considerable doubt. Since those who peacefully petition for changes in the law are not to be protected 'while this Court sits', who is? I do not agree that the Constitution leaves freedom of petition, assembly, speech, press or worship at the mercy of a case-by-case, day-by-day majority of this Court. I had supposed that our people could rely for their freedom on the Constitution's commands, rather than on the grace of this Court on an individual case basis. To say that a legislative body can, with this Court's approval, make it a crime to petition for and publicly discuss proposed legislation seems as far-fetched to me as it would be to say that a valid law could be enacted to punish a candidate for President for telling the people his views. I think the First Amendment, with the Fourteenth, 'absolutely' forbids such laws without any 'ifs' or 'buts' or 'whereases'. Whatever the danger, if any, in such public discussions, it is a danger the Founders deemed outweighed by the danger incident to the stifling of thought and speech. The Court does not act on this view of the Founders. It calculates what it deems to be the danger of public discussion, holds the scales are tipped on the side of state suppression, and upholds state censorship. This method of decision offers little protection to First Amendment liberties 'while this Court sits'.

If there be minority groups who hail this holding as their victory, they might consider the possible relevancy of this ancient remark:

Another such victory and I am undone.*

* Bacon, Apophthegms, 193.

The Authorised Voice

Dissenting opinion in Tyson & Brother v. *Banton**

[A New York statute forbade the resale of theatre tickets at a price of 50 cents more than the printed price. The Supreme Court, by 5 to 4, declared the law unconstitutional as being an infringement upon the property rights of the individual. The Court negatived the argument that the granting of a licence to theatres puts the proprietor under any duty to furnish entertainment to the public and admit all who apply; a theatre remained a private enterprise. The statutory fixing of prices at which theatre tickets might be resold could not be sustained as a measure for preventing fraud, extortion and collusive arrangements between theatre managers and ticket brokers. Mr Justice Holmes, in a characteristically incisive opinion, reverted to his old theme of where political power in a democratic state resides.]

WE FEAR TO grant power and are unwilling to recognise it when it exists. The States very generally have stripped jury trials of one of their most important characteristics by forbidding the judges to advise the jury upon the facts, and when legislatures are held to be authorised to do anything considerably affecting public welfare it is covered by apologetic phrases like the police power, or the statement that the business concerned has been dedicated to a public use. The former expression is convenient, to be sure, to conciliate the mind to something that needs explanation: the fact that the constitutional requirement of compensation when property is taken cannot be pressed to its grammatical extreme; that property rights may be taken for public purposes without pay if you do not take too much; that some play must be allowed to the joints if the machine is to work. But police power often is used in a wide sense to cover and, as I said, to apologise for the

* 273 U.S. 418, 445 (1926).

general power of the legislature to make a part of the community uncomfortable by a change.

I do not believe in such apologies. I think the proper course is to recognise that a state legislature can do whatever it sees fit to do unless it is restrained by some express prohibition in the Constitution of the United States or of the State, and that courts should be careful not to extend such prohibitions beyond their obvious meaning by reading into them conceptions of public policy that the particular court may happen to entertain. Coming down to the case before us I think that the notion that a business is clothed with a public interest and has been devoted to the public use is little more than a fiction intended to beautify what is disagreeable to the sufferers. The truth seems to me to be that, subject to compensation when compensation is due, the legislature may forbid or restrict any business when it has a sufficient force of public opinion behind it. Lotteries were thought useful adjuncts of the State a century or so ago; now they are believed to be immoral and they have been stopped. Wine has been thought good for man from the time of the Apostles until recent years. But when public opinion changed it did not need the Eighteenth Amendment, notwithstanding the Fourteenth, to enable a State to say that the business should end. What has happened to lotteries and wine might happen to theatres in some moral storm of the future, not because theatres were devoted to a public use, but because people had come to think that way.

But if we are to yield to fashionable conventions, it seems to me that theatres are as much devoted to public use as anything well can be. We have not that respect for art that is one of the glories of France. But to many people the superfluous is necessary, and it seems to me that Government does not go beyond its sphere in attempting to make life livable for them. I am far from saying that I think this particular law a wise and rational provision. That is not my affair. But if the people of the State of New York speaking by their authorised voice say that they want it, I see nothing in the Constitution of the United States to prevent their having their will.

Marxism at Law

*Judgment in The King v. Hush; ex parte Devanny**

THE APPELLANT WAS convicted before a stipendiary magistrate of the offence specified in sec. 30D (2) of the Commonwealth Crimes Act. That sub-section provides, in substance, that the printer and publisher of any newspaper which contains any solicitation of subscriptions 'for an unlawful association' shall be guilty of the offence defined in sec. 30D (1), i.e., soliciting subscriptions for an unlawful association.

Part IIA of the Crimes Act contains a number of sections dealing with the 'Protection of the Constitution'. Their general aim is the suppression of associations which advocate or encourage doctrines considered as dangerous to 'constitutional' government, including the form and frame of government which is expressed in the Commonwealth Constitution.

*

[His Lordship considered the evidence and concluded that the only reasonable inference from the terms of the printed matter admitted in evidence was that contributions were being invited by the appellants not for the Communist Party, but for the special organisation set up by a large number of working-class bodies, including the Communist Party. He continued:]

[516] Upon this footing, the appeal necessarily succeeds, and the prosecution must fail.

It becomes unnecessary therefore to determine the question whether enough matter was averred or proved in order to show that the Communist Party was advocating the overthrow by force or violence of the established government of the Commonwealth of Australia. In order to determine this question, the courts will necessarily have to pay proper attention to the distinction between

* (1932) 48 C.L.R. 487, 510.

advocacy of a complete and radical social, political and economic change, and advocacy of the use of actual physical violence in securing that change.

There is much in the matters averred and printed to suggest that the Communist Party advocates that the whole parliamentary machine must be completely changed – transformed – revolutionised, in order that a monopoly of political power shall be given to the working class, and that owners of private industries, property and wealth shall be dispossessed without compensation; further, that it is highly probable that so great a change, whether or not it is approved by the majority or ordained by law, will not be acquiesced in without resort to force on the part of those dispossessed; that, in this sense, a violent civil upheaval will, almost certainly, accompany the proposed transformation of society and that actual civil violence and disturbance will accompany the attempted socialisation of industry.

In order to determine the bearing of all these matters, reference would have to be made to the leading exponents of more modern socialist thought, from Marx and Engels onwards. It is a subject upon which every student of history, political science, sociology and philosophy should be tolerably well informed. Even the averments in the present case include an historical reference to the three Internationals. In the ultimate ideal of a classless society, the communist movement has much in common with the socialist and working-class movement throughout the world. They all profess to welcome a revolutionary change from the present economic system, which, conveniently enough, is called capitalism, and the more violent protagonists of which are now called fascists. The doctrine of the class struggle raises a dispute as to fact, rather than opinion. It is not a question whether it is desirable to have a struggle between a property-less class and a property-owning class, but whether such struggle exists in fact. The communists claim that democratic institutions conceal, but do not mitigate, the concentration of political and economic power in the property-owning class, and that, for such dictatorship, there should be substituted the open, undisguised dictatorship of the property-less classes. They say that it is extremely probable that a violent upheaval will ensue when the time comes to effect such substitution (*Encyclopædia Britannica*, 12th edn., vol. 30,

p. 732 (R. P. Dutt); cf. Laski's *Democracy in Crisis*, pp. 194, 226, 227, 241).

It is, it would seem from the writings in evidence, the element of time which must be closely examined in determining whether at the present, or in the near, or very far distant, future there is to be any employment of violence and force on the part of the classes for which the Communist Party claims to speak. 'The inevitability of gradualness', as a socialist and labour doctrine, the communists reject. But they believe and advocate that a socialist state must inevitably emerge from the very nature of capitalist economy. But when? So far as the evidence placed before us goes, there is no answer to this question. So that one possible argument, which may be open to the Communist Party in explaining their references to physical force, is that force and the threat of force are far distant from the present or the near future. The history of the attempts and failures of communism to gain control of other political movements of the working classes may tend, upon close analysis, to show that, to turn the phrase, communism illustrates the gradualness, the extreme gradualness, of inevitability.

Point of Danger

*Judgment in United States v. Dennis**

[205] THE DEFENDANTS Dennis and others appeal from a judgment of conviction upon an indictment for violation of Section 3 of the 'Smith Act', that is, for 'wilfully and knowingly' conspiring to organise the Communist Party of the United States as a group to 'teach and advocate the overthrow and destruction' of the government 'by force and violence', and 'knowingly and wilfully to advocate and teach the duty and necessity of overthrowing and destroying' the government by 'force and violence'. All the defendants were at one time or another officials of the Party during the period laid in the indictment – 1 April 1945 to 20 July 1948. The case was tried at great length. The defendants challenged the array, and the trial of that issue extended from 20 January 1949 to 1 March 1949; the trial of the issues began the following week and went on continuously until 23 September 1949. The jury brought in a verdict against all the defendants on 14 October 1949, and they were sentenced on 21 October 1949. The trial of the challenge to the array took 23 days; the Government's case on the issues took 40 days, and the appellants, 75 days.

Logically the first issue, and incidentally the most important, is whether the evidence was sufficient to support the jury's verdict that the defendants were guilty of the crime charged in the indictment. There was abundant evidence, if believed, to show that they were all engaged in an extensive concerted action to teach what indeed they do not disavow – the doctrines of Marxism-Leninism. These doctrines were set forth in many pamphlets put in evidence at the trial, the upshot of which is – indeed an honest jury could scarcely have found otherwise – that capitalism inescapably rests upon, and must perpetuate, the oppression of those who do not own the means of production; that to it in

* 183 F. 2d 201 (1950), upheld by the U.S. Supreme Court: 341 U.S. 494 (1951).

time there must and will succeed a 'classless' society, which will finally make unnecessary most of the paraphernalia of government; but that there must be an intermediate and transitional period of the 'dictatorship of the proletariat', which can be established only by the violent overthrow of any existing government, if that be capitalistic. No entrenched bourgeoisie, having everything to lose and nothing to gain by the abolition of capitalism, by which alone it can continue to enjoy its privileged position, will ever permit itself to be superseded by the means which it may have itself provided for constitutional change: e.g., by the ballot. No matter how solemnly it may profess its readiness to abide the result, and no matter how honestly and literally the accredited processes of amendment may in fact be followed, it is absurd to expect that a bourgeoisie will yield; and indeed to rely upon such a possibility is to range oneself among the enemies of Marxist–Leninist principles. Therefore the transition period involves the use of 'force and violence', temporary it is true, but inescapable; and, although it is impossible to predict when a propitious occasion will arise, one certainly will arise: as, for example, by financial crisis or other internal division. When the time comes the proletariat will find it necessary to establish its 'dictatorship' by violence.

The defendants protest against this interpretation of their teaching and advocacy. They say that the use of 'force and violence' is no part of their programme, except as it may become necessary after the proletariat has succeeded in securing power by constitutional processes. Thereafter, being itself the lawful government, it will of course resist any attempt of the ousted bourgeoisie to regain its position; it will meet force with force as all governments may, and must. If the defendants had in fact so confined their teaching and advocacy, the First Amendment would indubitably protect them, for it protects all utterances, individual or concerted, seeking constitutional changes, however revolutionary, by the processes which the Constitution provides. Any amendment to the Constitution passed in conformity with Article V is as valid as though it had been originally incorporated in it; the only exception being that no state shall be denied 'its equal Suffrage in the Senate'. It is unnecessary to quote in detail the many passages in the pamphlets and books, published and disseminated by the defendants, which flatly contradict their declarations that they mean to confine the use of 'force or violence' to the protection of political power, once lawfully obtained. The prosecution proved this part of its case quite independently of the testimony of its witnesses, though the jury might have relied upon that, had it stood alone. The sufficiency of the evidence therefore comes down to whether it is a crime to form a conspiracy to advocate or teach the duty and necessity of overthrowing the government by violence, and to organise the Communist Party as a group so to teach and to advocate.

This being true, three questions arise: (1) whether the Act is constitutional as the judge construed it, (2) whether his construction was right, and (3) whether the evidence was admissible under the indictment. To the last of these we shall devote no time, for it is patent on the merest inspection that the indictment is sufficient; even had it not been, any variances would have been harmless error. Coming then to the first point, although the interest which the Amendment was designed to protect – especially as regards matters political – does not presuppose that utterances, divergent from current official opinion, are more likely to be true than that opinion, it does presuppose that official opinion may be wrong, and that one way – and perhaps the best way – to correct or supplement it is complete freedom of criticism and protest. This may convince the officials themselves, and in any event it may rouse up a body of contrary opinion to which they will yield, or which will displace them. Thus, the interest rests upon a scepticism as to all political orthodoxy, upon a belief that there are no impregnable political absolutes, and that a flux of tentative doctrines is preferable to any authoritative creed. It rests upon a premise as yet unproved, and perhaps incompatible with men's impatience of a suspended judgment when the stakes are high. However, it concerns beliefs alone, not actions, except in so far as a change of belief is a condition upon action.

Nobody doubts that, when the leader of a mob already ripe for riot gives the word to start, his utterance is not protected by the Amendment. It is not difficult to deal with such situations; doubt arises only when the utterance is at once an effort to affect the hearers' beliefs and a call upon them to act when they have been convinced. As a new question it might have been held that the

Amendment did not protect utterances, when they had this double aspect: i.e., when persuasion and instigation were inseparably confused. In that view the Amendment would give protection to all utterances designed to convince, but its protection would be conditional upon their not being part of, or coupled with, provocation to unlawful conduct, whether that was remote or immediate. True, one does not become an accessory to a crime who 'counsels, commands, induces . . . its commission' unless the crime is committed; but he will be guilty of conspiracy by the mere agreement; and it will not protect him that the objective of the conspiracy is lawful, and only the means contemplated are illegal. Had this view of the Amendment been taken, although the utterances of these defendants so far as they attempted to persuade others of the aims of Communism would have been protected, they would have lost that protection, coupled as they were with the advocacy of the unlawful means. And that is probably in fact true of utterances not political or religious; for it is at least doubtful whether other kinds of utterance, however lawful in so far as they were persuasive only, would retain their privilege if coupled with appeals to unlawful means. One can hardly believe that one would be protected in seeking funds for a school, if he suggested that they should be obtained by fraud. His privilege would be conditional upon separating the means from the end. However that may be, it is not true of political agitation and the question is what limits, if any, the advocacy of illegal means imposes upon the privilege which the aims or purposes of the utterer would otherwise enjoy. [207]

[212] From this wearisome analysis of the decisions of the Supreme Court* it has appeared, as we indicated at the outset, that to deprive an utterance of the protection of the Amendment it is not always enough that the purpose of the utterer may include stirring up his hearers to illegal conduct – at least, when the utterance is political. The same utterance may be unprotected, if it be a bare appeal to action, which the Amendment will cover, if it be accompanied by, or incorporated into, utterances addressed to the understanding and seeking to persuade. The phrase, 'clear

---

* This is an allusion to the series of decisions, starting with *Schenck* v. *United States*, 249 U.S. 47 (1919), which since the first World War have shown a certain tenderness towards political utterances.

and present danger', has come to be used as a shorthand statement of those among such mixed or compounded utterances which the Amendment does not protect. Yet it is not a *vade mecum*; indeed, from its very words it could not be. It is a way to describe a penumbra of occasions, even the outskirts of which are indefinable, but within which, as is so often the case, the courts must find their way as they can. In each case they must ask whether the gravity of the 'evil', discounted by its improbability, justifies such invasion of free speech as is necessary to avoid the danger. We have purposely substituted 'improbability' for 'remoteness', because that must be the right interpretation. Given the same probability, it would be wholly irrational to condone future evils which we should prevent if they were immediate; that could be reconciled only by an indifference to those who come after us. It is only because a substantial intervening period between the utterance and its realisation may check its effect and change its importance, that its immediacy is important. We can never forecast with certainty; all prophecy is a guess, but the reliability of a guess decreases with the length of the future which it seeks to penetrate. In application of such a standard courts may strike a wrong balance; they may tolerate 'incitements' which they should forbid; they may repress utterances they should allow; but that is a responsibility that they cannot avoid. Abdication is as much a failure of duty, as indifference is a failure to protect primal rights.

In the case at bar the defence seems to us to kick the beam. One may reasonably think it wiser in the long run to let an unhappy, bitter outcast vent his venom before any crowds he can muster and in any terms that he wishes, be they as ferocious as he will; one may trust that his patent impotence will be a foil to anything he may propose. Indeed, it is a measure of the confidence of a society in its own stability that it suffers such fustian to go unchecked. Here we are faced with something very different. The American Communist Party, of which the defendants are the controlling spirits, is a highly articulated, well-contrived, far-spread organisation, numbering thousands of adherents, rigidly and ruthlessly disciplined, many of whom are infused with a passionate Utopian faith that is to redeem mankind. It has its Founder, its apostles, its sacred texts – perhaps even its martyrs.

It seeks converts far and wide by an extensive system of schooling, demanding of all an inflexible doctrinal orthodoxy. The violent capture of all existing governments is one article of the creed of that faith, which abjures the possibility of success by lawful means. That article, which is a common-place among initiates, is a part of the homiletics for novitiates, although, so far as conveniently it can be, it is covered by an innocent terminology, designed to prevent its disclosure. Our democracy, like any other, must meet that faith and that creed on the merits, or it will perish; and we must not flinch at the challenge. Nevertheless, we may insist that the rules of the game be observed, and the rules confine the conflict to weapons drawn from the universe of discourse. The advocacy of violence may, or may not, fail; but in neither case can there be any 'right' to use it. Revolutions are often 'right', but a 'right of revolution' is a contradiction in terms, for a society which acknowledged it could not stop at tolerating conspiracies to overthrow it, but must include their execution. The question before us, and the only one, is how long a government, having discovered such a conspiracy, must wait. When does the conspiracy become a 'present danger'? The jury has found that the conspirators will strike as soon as success seems possible, and obviously, no one in his senses would strike sooner. Meanwhile they claim the constitutional privilege of going on indoctrinating their pupils, preparing increasing numbers to pledge themselves to the crusade, and awaiting the moment when we may be so far extended by foreign engagements, so far divided in counsel, or so far in industrial or financial straits, that the chance seems worth trying. That position presupposes that the Amendment assures them freedom for all preparatory steps and in the end the choice of initiative, dependent upon that moment when they believe us, who must await the blow, to be worst prepared to receive it.

We need not say that even so thoroughly planned and so extensive a confederation would be a 'present danger' at all times and in all circumstances; the question is how imminent – that is, how probable of execution – it was in the summer of 1948, when the indictment was found. We must not close our eyes to our position in the world at that time. By far the most powerful of all the European nations had been a convert to communism for over thirty years; its leaders were the most devoted and potent proponents of the faith; no such movement in Europe of East to West had arisen since Islam. Moreover in most of West Europe there were important political communist factions, always agitating to increase their power; and the defendants were acting in close concert with the movement. The *status quo*, hastily contrived in 1945, was showing strains and tensions, not originally expected. Save for the unexpected success of the airlift, Britain, France and ourselves would have been forced out of Berlin, contrary to our understanding of the convention by which we were there. We had become the object of invective upon invective; we were continuously charged with aggressive designs against other nations; our efforts to reestablish their economic stability were repeatedly set down as a scheme to enslave them; we had been singled out as the chief enemy of the faith; we were the eventually doomed, but the still formidable, protagonist of that decadent system which it was to supplant. Any border fray, any diplomatic incident, any difference in construction of the *modus vivendi* – such as the Berlin blockade we have just mentioned – might prove a spark in the tinder-box, and lead to war. We do not understand how one could ask for a more probable danger, unless we must wait till the actual eve of hostilities. The only justification which can be suggested is that in spite of their efforts to mask their purposes, so far as they can do so consistently with the spread of the gospel, discussion and publicity may so weaken their power that it will have ceased to be dangerous when the moment may come. That may be a proper enough antidote in ordinary times and for less redoubtable combinations; but certainly it does not apply to this one. *Corruptio optimi pessima*. True, we must not forget our own faith; we must be sensitive to the dangers that lurk in any choice; but choose we must, and we shall be silly dupes if we forget that again and again in the past thirty years, just such preparations in other countries have aided to supplant existing governments, when the time was ripe. Nothing short of a revived doctrine of *laissez faire*, which would have amazed even the Manchester School at its apogee, can fail to realise that such a conspiracy creates a danger of the utmost gravity and of enough probability to justify its suppression. We hold that it is a danger 'clear and present'.

McCarthy Redivivus?

Dissenting opinion in Scales v. United States*

WHEN WE ALLOW petitioner to be sentenced to prison for six years for being a 'member' of the Communist Party, we make a sharp break with traditional concepts of First Amendment rights and make serious Mark Twain's lighthearted comment that 'It is by the goodness of God that in our country we have those three unspeakably precious things: freedom of speech, freedom of conscience, and the prudence never to practise either of them.'†

Even the Alien and Sedition Laws – shameful reminders of an early chapter in intolerance – never went so far as we go today. They were aimed at conspiracy and advocacy of insurrection and at the publication of 'false, scandalous, and malicious' writing against the Government, 1 Stat. 596. The Government then sought control over the press 'in order to strike at one of the chief sources of disaffection and sedition'. Miller, *Crisis in Freedom* (1951), p. 56. There is here no charge of conspiracy, no charge of any overt act to overthrow the Government by force and violence, no charge of any other criminal act. The charge is being a 'member' of the Communist Party, 'well knowing' that it advocated the overthrow of the Government by force and violence, 'said defendant intending to bring about such overthrow by force and violence as speedily as circumstances would permit'. That falls far short of a charge of conspiracy. Conspiracy rests not in intention alone but in an agreement with one or more others to promote an unlawful project. No charge of any kind or sort of agreement hitherto embraced in the concept of a conspiracy is made here.

We legalise today guilt by association, sending a man to prison when he committed no unlawful act. . . . The case is not saved by showing that petitioner was an active member. None of the

* 367 U.S. 203, 262 (1961).
† *Following the Equator* (1903), Vol. I, p. 198.

activity constitutes a crime. . . . Not one single illegal act is charged to petitioner. That is why the essence of the crime covered by the indictment is merely belief* – belief in the proletarian revolution, belief in communist creed.

Spinoza summed up in a sentence much of the history of the struggle of man to think and speak what he believes: 'Laws which decree what everyone must believe, and forbid utterance against this or that opinion, have too often been enacted to confirm or enlarge the power of those who dared not suffer free inquiry to be made, and have by a perversion of authority turned the superstition of the mob into violence against opponents.' [*Tractatus Theologico-Politicus* (London, 1862), p. 349.] 'The thought of man shall not be tried, for the devil himself knoweth not the thought of man', said Chief Justice Brian in Year Book Pasch, 17 Edw. IV, j. 2, pl. 2. The crime of belief – presently prosecuted – is a carryback to the old law of treason where men were punished for Compassing the Death of the King . . . sedition or treason in the realm of politics and heresy in the ecclesiastical field had long centred on *beliefs* as the abhorrent criminal act. The struggle on this side of the Atlantic was to get rid of the concept and to punish men not for what they thought but for overt acts against the peace of the nation.

*

[270] Of course, government can move against those who take up arms against it. Of course, the constituted authority has the right of self-preservation. But we deal in this prosecution of Scales

---

* The prototype of the present prosecution in found in communist lands. The Communist Government in Czechoslavakia on 6 October 1948 promulgated a law, § 3 of which provided:

'(1) Whoever publicly or before several people instigates against the Republic, against its independence, constitutional unity, territorial integrity or its people's democratic system [of government], its social or economic order, or against its national character as guaranteed by the Constitution, shall be punished for a minor crime by rigorous confinement for from three months to three years.

'(2) The following shall be punished in like manner: Whoever intentionally or through gross negligence makes the dissemination of the instigative statement specified in subsection 1 possible or easy.'

only with the legality of ideas and beliefs, not with overt acts. The Court speaks of the prevention of 'dangerous behaviour' by punishing those 'who work to bring about that behaviour'. That formula returns man to the dark days when government determined what behaviour was 'dangerous' and then policed the dissidents for tell-tale signs of advocacy. What is 'dangerous behaviour' that must be suppressed in its talk-stage has had a vivid history even on this continent.

*

[275] 'The most indifferent arguments', Bismarck said, 'are good when one has a majority of bayonets.' That is also true when one has the votes.

What we lose by majority vote today may be reclaimed at a future time when the fear of advocacy, dissent, and nonconformity no longer casts a shadow over us.

Limits of Tolerance

Dissenting opinion in Abrams v. *United States**

THIS INDICTMENT IS founded wholly upon the publication of two leaflets which I shall describe in a moment. The first count charges a conspiracy pending the war with Germany to publish abusive language about the form of government of the United States, laying the preparation and publishing of the first leaflet as overt acts. The second count charges a conspiracy pending the war to publish language intended to bring the form of government into contempt, laying the preparation and publishing of the two leaflets as overt acts. The third count alleges a conspiracy to encourage resistance to the United States in the same war and to attempt to effectuate the purpose by publishing the same leaflets. The fourth count lays a conspiracy to incite curtailment of production of things necessary to the prosecution of the war and to attempt to accomplish it by publishing the second leaflet to which I have referred.

The first of these leaflets says that the President's cowardly silence about the intervention in Russia reveals the hypocrisy of the plutocratic gang in Washington. It intimates that 'German militarism combined with allied capitalism to crush the Russian revolution' – goes on that the tyrants of the world fight each other until they see a common enemy – working-class enlightenment – when they combine to crush it; and that now militarism and capitalism combined, though not openly, to crush the Russian revolution. It says that there is only one enemy of the workers of the world and that is capitalism; that it is a crime for workers of America, &c., to fight the workers' republic of Russia, and ends 'Awake! Awake, you Workers of the World! Revolutionists.' A note adds 'It is absurd to call us pro-German. We hate and despise German militarism more than do you hypocritical

* 250 U.S. 616, 624 (1919).

tyrants. We have more reasons for denouncing German militarism than has the coward of the White House.'

The other leaflet, headed 'Workers – Wake Up', with abusive language says that America together with the Allies will march for Russia to help the Czecho-Slovaks in their struggle against the Bolsheviki, and that this time the hypocrites shall not fool the Russian emigrants and friends of Russia in America. It tells the Russian emigrants that they now must spit in the face of the false military propaganda by which their sympathy and help to the prosecution of the war have been called forth and says that with the money they have lent or are going to lend 'they will make bullets not only for the Germans but also for the Workers Soviets of Russia', and further, 'Workers in the ammunition factories, you are producing bullets, bayonets, cannon, to murder not only the Germans, but also your dearest, best, who are in Russia and are fighting for freedom.' It then appeals to the same Russian emigrants at some length not to consent to the 'inquisitionary expedition to Russia', and says that the destruction of the Russian revolution is 'the politics of the march to Russia'. The leaflet winds up by saying 'Workers, our reply to this barbaric intervention has to be a general strike!' and after a few words on the spirit of revolution, exhortations not to be afraid, and some usual tall talk ends 'Woe unto those who will be in the way of progress. Let solidarity live! The Rebels.'

No argument seems to me necessary to show that these pronunciamentos in no way attack the form of government of the United States, or that they do not support either of the first two counts. What little I have to say about the third count may be postponed until I have considered the fourth. With regard to that it seems too plain to be denied that the suggestion to workers in the ammunition factories that they are producing bullets to murder their dearest, and the further advocacy of a general strike, both in the second leaflet, do urge curtailment of production of things necessary to the prosecution of the war. . . . But to make the conduct criminal that statute requires that it should be 'with intent by such curtailment to cripple or hinder the United States in the prosecution of the war'. It seems to me that no such intent is proved.

I am aware of course that the word intent as vaguely used in ordinary legal discussion means no more than knowledge at the time of the act that the consequences said to be intended will ensue. Even less than that will satisfy the general principle of civil and criminal liability. A man may have to pay damages, may be sent to prison, at common law might be hanged, if at the time of his act he knew facts from which common experience showed that the consequences would follow, whether he individually could foresee them or not. But, when words are used exactly, a deed is not done with intent to produce a consequence unless that consequence is the aim of the deed. It may be obvious, and obvious to the actor, that the consequence will follow, and he may be liable for it even if he regrets it, but he does not do the act with intent to produce it unless the aim to produce it is the proximate motive of the specific act, although there may be some deeper motive behind.

It seems to me that this statute must be taken to use its words in a strict and accurate sense. They would be absurd in any other. A patriot might think that we were wasting money on aeroplanes, or making more cannon of a certain kind than we needed, and might advocate curtailment with success, yet even if it turned out that the curtailment hindered and was thought by other minds to have been obviously likely to hinder the United States in the prosecution of the war, no one would hold such conduct a crime. I admit that my illustration does not answer all that might be said but it is enough to show what I think and to let me pass to a more important aspect of the case. I refer to the First Amendment to the Constitution that Congress shall make no law abridging the freedom of speech.

I do not doubt for a moment that by the same reasoning [in cases like *Schenck*] that would justify punishing persuasion to murder, the United States constitutionally may punish speech that produces or is intended to produce a clear and imminent danger that it will bring about forthwith certain substantive evils that the United States constitutionally may seek to prevent. The power undoubtedly is greater in time of war than in time of peace because war opens dangers that do not exist at other times.

But as against dangers peculiar to war, as against others, the principle of the right to free speech is always the same. It is only the present danger of immediate evil or an intent to bring it about that warrants Congress in setting a limit to the expression of opinion where private rights are not concerned. Congress certainly cannot forbid all effort to change the mind of the country. Now nobody can suppose that the surreptitious publishing of a silly leaflet by an unknown man, without more, would present any immediate danger that its opinions would hinder the success of the government arms or have any appreciable tendency to do so. Publishing those opinions for the very purpose of obstructing, however, might indicate a greater danger and at any rate would have the quality of an attempt. So I assume that the second leaflet if published for the purposes alleged in the fourth count might be punishable. But it seems pretty clear to me that nothing less than that would bring these papers within the scope of this law. [628]

*

[629] In this case sentences of twenty years imprisonment have been imposed for the publishing of two leaflets that I believe the defendants had as much right to publish as the Government has to publish the Constitution of the United States now vainly invoked by them. Even if I am technically wrong and enough can be squeezed from these poor and puny anonymities to turn the colour of legal litmus paper; I will add, even if what I think the necessary intent were shown; the most nominal punishment seems to me all that possibly could be inflicted, unless the defendants are to be made to suffer not for what the indictment alleges but for the creed that they avow – a creed that I believe to be the creed of ignorance and immaturity when honestly held, as I see no reason to doubt that it was held here, but which, although made the subject of examination at the trial, no one has a right even to consider in dealing with the charges before the court.

Persecution for the expression of opinions seems to me perfectly logical. If you have no doubt of your premises or your power and want a certain result with all your heart you naturally express your wishes in law and sweep away all opposition. To allow opposition by speech seems to indicate that you think the speech impotent, as when a man says that he has squared the circle, or that you do not care whole-heartedly for the result, or that you doubt either your power or your premises. But when men have realised that time has upset many fighting faiths, they may come to believe even more than they believe the very foundations of their own conduct that the ultimate good desired is better reached by free trade in ideas – that the best test of truth is the power of the thought to get itself accepted in the competition of the market, and that truth is the only ground upon which their wishes safely can be carried out. That at any rate is the theory of our Constitution. It is an experiment, as all life is an experiment. Every year, if not every day, we have to wager our salvation upon some prophecy based upon imperfect knowledge. While that experiment is part of our system I think that we should be eternally vigilant against attempts to check the expression of opinions that we loathe and believe to be fraught with death, unless they so imminently threaten immediate interference with the lawful and pressing purposes of the law that an immediate check is required to save the country. I wholly disagree with the argument of the Government that the First Amendment left the common law as to seditious libel in force. History seems to me against the notion. I had conceived that the United States through many years had shown its repentance for the Sedition Act of 1798, by repaying fines that it imposed. Only the emergency that makes it immediately dangerous to leave the correction of evil counsels to time warrants making any exception to the sweeping command, 'Congress shall make no law . . . . abridging the freedom of speech.' Of course I am speaking only of expressions of opinion and exhortations, which were all that were uttered here, but I regret that I cannot put into more impressive words my belief that in their conviction upon this indictment the defendants were deprived of their rights under the Constitution of the United States.

Incitement

Dissenting opinion in Gitlow v. *New York**

MR JUSTICE BRANDEIS and I are of opinion that this judgment should be reversed. The general principle of free speech, it seems to me, must be taken to be included in the Fourteenth Amendment, in view of the scope that has been given to the word 'liberty' as there used, although perhaps it may be accepted with a somewhat larger latitude of interpretation than is allowed to Congress by the sweeping language that governs or ought to govern the laws of the United States. If I am right, then I think that the criterion sanctioned by the full Court in *Schenck* v. *United States*, 249 U.S. 47, 52, applies. 'The question in every case is whether the words used are used in such circumstances and are of such a nature as to create a clear and present danger that they will bring about the substantive evils that [the State] has a right to prevent.' It is true that in my opinion this criterion was departed from in *Abrams* v. *United States*, 250 U.S. 616, but the convictions that I expressed in that case are too deep for it to be possible for me as yet to believe that it and *Schaefer* v. *United States*, 251 U.S. 466, have settled the law. If what I think the correct test is applied, it is manifest that there was no present danger of an attempt to overthrow the government by force on the part of the admittedly small minority who shared the defendant's views. It is said that this manifesto was more than a theory, that it was an incitement. Every idea is an incitement. It offers itself for belief and if believed it is acted on unless some other belief outweighs it or some failure of energy stifles the movement at its birth. The only difference between the expression of an opinion and an incitement in the narrower sense is the speaker's enthusiasm for the result. Eloquence may set fire to reason. But whatever may be thought of the redundant discourse before us it had no

* 268 U.S. 652, 672 (1924).

224

chance of starting a present conflagration.* If in the long run the beliefs expressed in proletarian dictatorship are destined to be accepted by the dominant forces of the community, the only meaning of free speech is that they should be given their chance and have their way.

If the publication of this document had been laid as an attempt to induce an uprising against government at once and not at some indefinite time in the future it would have presented a different question. The object would have been one with which the law might deal, subject to the doubt whether there was any danger that the publication could produce any result, or in other words, whether it was not futile and too remote from possible consequences. But the indictment alleges the publication and nothing more.

* 'Redundant discourse' is an allusion to a passage in the court's opinion delivered by Mr Justice Sandford at p. 669: 'That utterances inciting to the overthrow of organised government by unlawful means present a sufficient danger of substantive evil to bring their punishment within the range of legislative discretion is clear. Such utterances, by their very nature, involve danger to the public peace and to the security of the State. They threaten breaches of the peace and ultimate revolution. And the immediate danger is none the less real and substantial, because the effect of a given utterance cannot be accurately foreseen. The State cannot reasonably be required to measure the danger from every such utterance in the nice balance of a jeweller's scale. A single revolutionary spark may kindle a fire that, smouldering for a time, may burst into a sweeping and destructive conflagration. It cannot be said that the State is acting arbitrarily or unreasonably when in the exercise of its judgment as to the measures necessary to protect the public peace and safety, it seeks to extinguish the spark without waiting until it has enkindled the flame or blazed into the conflagration.'

Words, Words, Words . . .

Art for Art's Sake

*A judgment and a dissent in United States v. Ulysses**

[Judge Woolsey's decision, on appeal from which these judgments are given, is more often cited in the anthologies. But widely praised as it is, there is a better reflection of the diametrically opposed views on obscene libel to be found in the judgments of Augustus Hand and Manton.

James Joyce's *Ulysses* was seized by the immigration authorities of the United States in 1933 on the ground that the book was obscene, and hence not importable into the United States, but was subject to seizure, forfeiture, confiscation and destruction (the case is reported at 5 F. Supp. 182). Judge Augustus Hand's judgment was concurred in by his brother, Judge Learned Hand (the two were known as 'left hand, right hand'). Sad to relate, the career of Judge Manton, a part of whose dissent follows, came to an end in 1939 when, after some years of shameless canvassing for a seat on the Supreme Court, he was convicted of accepting bribes for premature sight of his judgments: see Joseph Borki, *The Corrupt Judge* (1962).]

THIS APPEAL RAISES sharply the question of the proper interpretation of section 305 (a) of the Tariff Act of 1930 (19 USCA § 1305 (a)). That section provides that 'all persons are prohibited from importing into the United States from any foreign country ... any obscene book, pamphlet, paper, writing, advertisement, circular, print, picture, drawing, or other representation, figure, or image on or of paper or other material, ...' and directs that, upon the appearance of any such book or matter at any customs office, the collector shall seize it and inform the district attorney, who shall institute proceedings for forfeiture. In accordance with the statute, the collector seized *Ulysses*, a book written by James

* 72 F. 2d 705 (1934).

Joyce, and the United States filed a libel for forfeiture. The claimant, Random House, Inc., the publisher of the American edition, intervened in the cause and filed its answer denying that the book was obscene and was subject to confiscation, and praying that it be admitted into the United States. The case came on for trial before Judge Woolsey, who found that the book, taken as a whole, 'did not tend to excite sexual impulses or lustful thoughts but that its net effect . . . was only that of a somewhat tragic and very powerful commentary on the inner lives of men and women.' He accordingly granted a decree adjudging that the book was 'not of the character the entry of which is prohibited under the provision of section 305 of the Tariff Act of 1930 . . . and . . . dismissing the libel', from which this appeal has been taken.

James Joyce, the author of *Ulysses*, may be regarded as a pioneer among those writers who have adopted the 'stream of consciousness' method of presenting fiction, which has attracted considerable attention in academic and literary circles. In this field *Ulysses* is rated as a book of considerable power by persons whose opinions are entitled to weight. Indeed it has become a sort of contemporary classic, dealing with a new subject-matter. It attempts to depict the thoughts and lay bare the souls of a number of people, some of them intellectuals and some social outcasts and nothing more, with a literalism that leaves nothing unsaid. Certain of its passages are of beauty and undoubted distinction, while others are of a vulgarity that is extreme and the book as a whole has a realism characteristic of the present age. It is supposed to portray the thoughts of the principal characters during a period of about eighteen hours.

We may discount the laudation of *Ulysses* by some of its admirers and reject the view that it will permanently stand among the great works of literature, but it is fair to say that it is a sincere portrayal with skilful artistry of the 'streams of consciousness' of its characters. Though the depiction happily is not of the 'stream of consciousness' of all men and perhaps of only those of a morbid type, it seems to be sincere, truthful, relevant to the subject, and executed with real art. Joyce, in the words of *Paradise Lost*, has dealt with 'things unattempted yet in prose or rime'* – with things that very likely might better have remained 'unattempted'

* Book I, line 16.

– but his book shows originality and is a work of symmetry and excellent craftsmanship of a sort. The question before us is whether such a book of artistic merit and scientific insight should be regarded as 'obscene' within section 305 (a) of the Tariff Act.

That numerous long passages in *Ulysses* contain matter that is obscene under any fair definition of the word cannot be gainsaid; yet they are relevant to the purpose of depicting the thoughts of the characters and are introduced to give meaning to the whole, rather than to promote lust or portray filth for its own sake. The net effect even of portions most open to attack, such as the closing monologue of the wife of Leopold Bloom, is pitiful and tragic, rather than lustful. The book depicts the souls of men and women that are by turns bewildered and keenly apprehensive, sordid and aspiring, ugly and beautiful, hateful and loving. In the end one feels, more than anything else, pity and sorrow for the confusion, misery, and degradation of humanity. Page after page of the book is, or seems to be, incomprehensible. But many passages show the trained hand of an artist, who can at one moment adapt to perfection the style of an ancient chronicler, and at another become a veritable personification of Thomas Carlyle. In numerous places there are found originality, beauty, and distinction. The book as a whole is not pornographic, and, while in not a few spots it is coarse, blasphemous, and obscene, it does not, in our opinion, tend to promote lust. The erotic passages are submerged in the book as a whole and have little resultant effect. If these are to make the book subject to confiscation, by the same test *Venus and Adonis, Hamlet, Romeo and Juliet,* and the story told in the Eighth Book of the *Odyssey* by the bard Demodocus of how Ares and Aphrodite were entrapped in a net spread by the outraged Hephaestus amid the laughter of the immortal gods, as well as many other classics, would have to be suppressed. Indeed, it may be questioned whether the obscene passages in *Romeo and Juliet* were as necessary to the development of the play as those in the monologue of Mrs Bloom are to the depiction of the latter's tortured soul.

It is unnecessary to add illustrations to show that, in the administration of statutes aimed at the suppression of immoral books, standard works of literature have not been barred merely because they contained *some* obscene passages, and that confiscation for such a reason would destroy much that is precious in order to benefit a few.

It is settled, at least so far as this court is concerned, that works of physiology, medicine, science, and sex instruction are not within the statute, though to some extent and among some persons they may tend to promote lustful thoughts. We think the same immunity should apply to literature as to science, where the presentation, when viewed objectively, is sincere, and the erotic matter is not introduced to promote lust and does not furnish the dominant note of the publication. The question in each case is whether a publication taken as a whole has a libidinous effect. The book before us has such portentous length, is written with such evident truthfulness in its depiction of certain types of humanity, and is so little erotic in its result, that it does not fall within the forbidden class.

In *Halsey* v. *New York Society for Suppression of Vice*,* the New York Court of Appeals dealt with *Mademoiselle de Maupin*, by Théophile Gautier, for the sale of which the plaintiff had been prosecuted under a New York statute forbidding the sale of obscene books, upon the complaint of the defendant. After acquittal, the plaintiff sued for malicious prosecution, and a jury rendered a verdict in his favour. The Court of Appeals refused to disturb the judgment because the book had become a recognised French classic and its merits on the whole outweighed its objectionable qualities, though, as Judge Andrews said, it contained many paragraphs which, 'taken by themselves', were 'undoubtedly vulgar and indecent'. In referring to the obscene passages, he remarked that: 'No work may be judged from a selection of such paragraphs alone. Printed by themselves they might, as a matter of law, come within the prohibition of the statute. So might a similar selection from Aristophanes or Chaucer or Boccaccio, or even from the Bible. The book, however, must be considered broadly, as a whole.' We think Judge Andrews was clearly right, and that the effect of the book as a whole is the test.

In the New York Supreme Court, Judge Morgan J. O'Brien declined to prohibit a receiver from selling *Arabian Nights*,

* 234 N.Y. 1.

Rabelais, Ovid's *Art of Love*, the *Decameron* of Boccaccio, the *Heptameron* of Queen Margaret of Navarre, or the *Confessions* of Rousseau. He remarked that a rule which would exclude them would bar 'a very large proportion of the works of fiction of the most famous writers of the English language'. The main difference between many standard works and *Ulysses* is its far more abundant use of coarse and colloquial words and presentation of dirty scenes, rather than in any excess of prurient suggestion. We do not think that *Ulysses*, taken as a whole, tends to promote lust, and its criticised passages do this no more than scores of standard books that are constantly bought and sold. Indeed a book of physiology in the hands of adolescents may be more objectionable on this ground than almost anything else.

It is true that the motive of an author to promote good morals is not the test of whether a book is obscene, and it may also be true that the applicability of the statute does not depend on the persons to whom a publication is likely to be distributed. The importation of obscene books is prohibited generally, and no provision is made permitting such importation because of the character of those to whom they are sold. While any construction of the statute that will fit all cases is difficult, we believe that the proper test of whether a given book is obscene is its dominant effect. In applying this test, relevancy of the objectionable parts to the theme, the established reputation of the work in the estimation of approved critics, if the book is modern, and the verdict of the past, if it is ancient, are persuasive pieces of evidence; for works of art are not likely to sustain a high position with no better warrant for their existence than their obscene content.

It may be that *Ulysses* will not last as a substantial contribution to literature, and it is certainly easy to believe that, in spite of the opinion of Joyce's laudators, the immortals will still reign, but the same thing may be said of current works of art and music and of many other serious efforts of the mind. Art certainly cannot advance under compulsion to traditional forms, and nothing in such a field is more stifling to progress than limitation of the right to experiment with a new technique. The foolish judgments of Lord Eldon about one hundred years ago, proscribing the works of Byron and Southey, and the finding by the jury under a charge by Lord Denman that the publication of Shelley's 'Queen

Mab' was an indictable offence, are a warning to all who have to determine the limits of the field within which authors may exercise themselves.

*

Judge Manton concluded his dissenting opinion in these words:
[711] Congress passed this statute against obscenity for the protection of the great mass of our people; the unusual literator can, or thinks he can, protect himself. The people do not exist for the sake of literature, to give the author fame, the publisher wealth, and the book a market. On the contrary, literature exists for the sake of the people, to refresh the weary, to console the sad, to hearten the dull and downcast, to increase man's interest in the world, his joy of living, and his sympathy in all sorts and conditions of men. Art for art's sake is heartless and soon grows artless; art for the public market is not art at all, but commerce; art for the people's service is a noble, vital, and permanent element of human life.

The public is content with the standard of saleability; the prigs with the standard of preciosity. The people need and deserve a moral standard; it should be a point of honour with men of letters to maintain it. Masterpieces have never been produced by men given to obscenity or lustful thoughts – men who have no Master. Reverence for good work is the foundation of literary character. A refusal to imitate obscenity or to load a book with it is an author's professional chastity.

Good work in literature has its permanent mark; it is like all good work, noble and lasting. It requires a human aim – to cheer, console, purify, or ennoble the life of people. Without this aim, literature has never sent an arrow close to the mark. It is by good work only that men of letters can justify their right to a place in the world.

Speaking Up for Hitler

*Judgment in Verwoerd v. Paver and others**

[The present Prime Minister of the Republic of South Africa is a man whose dedication to the cause of Afrikanerism and white supremacy borders on fanaticism. He has always been violently anti-British and anti-Semitic, as well as a fervent supporter of the philosophy of apartheid, the doctrine of the separation of the races.

He had an outstanding academic career – at the age of 28 he was Stellenbosch's first professor of applied psychology. Three years later he became professor of sociology when he came face to face with the plight of the poor whites of South Africa, most of whom were Afrikaners.

In 1936 Verwoerd gave up his academic life and turned to journalism, as the first editor of *Die Transvaler*. It was as a result of its identification with the Nazi philosophy that Verwoerd was caught up in 1941 in a libel action. Attacked by his English-speaking rival, *The Star* of Johannesburg, Verwoerd was stung into defending his position. He was accused of supporting Nazi propaganda and of making his newspaper a tool of Nazis in South Africa. Frederic Paver, the *Star*'s editor, the paper's proprietor and its publisher all pleaded justification of the libels, and succeeded.

The judge who tried the case was Mr Justice Millin, the husband of the authoress, Sarah Gertrude Millin. Apart from being an able lawyer, Millin was by early training a journalist.]

[155] THESE ACTIONS OF damages for defamation arise out of a leading article which appeared in *The Star* newspaper, Johannesburg, on 31 October 1941. The article is entitled 'Speaking up for Hitler' and the material part of it runs as follows:

---

* 1943 W.L.D. 153.

(1) *Die Transvaler*, which is published in Johannesburg, though its spiritual home lies somewhere between Keerom Street and the Munich beer hall, has this week given a rather better example than usual of the process of falsification which it applies to current news in its support of Nazi propaganda.

(2) On Saturday the Bureau of Information supplied the Union newspapers with a sample of the broadcasts dealing with South African affairs which have been coming from Berlin. Like many previous ones, it reiterated the assurance to South Africa that Germany does not wish to force its system of government upon other countries – 'a statement', the information Bureau's script remarked, 'which is belied by what is happening in Europe.' *Die Transvaler* not only omitted this passage in reproducing the message, but made Zeesen's profession of benevolent intentions towards this country the occasion for a full-dress article on the theme that Germany 'would not deny the Afrikaners their republic' and the unwisdom of criticising National Socialism as practised within Germany.

(3) This manner of using the opportunity to give the Zeesen statement as a substantive publication by the Government's information authority was 'slim', but not really clever. Its dishonesty is too easy to expose, and it identified *Die Transvaler* so closely with Nazi propaganda that it must assist in opening the eyes of those who read the paper in question, as to the extent to which it is a tool of malignant forces from which this country has everything to fear.

The plaintiff, Hendrik Frensch Verwoerd, is the editor of the newspaper to which the article refers. It is a daily newspaper in the Afrikaans language conducted at Johannesburg to promote the policy of the Herenigde Nasionale Party. The plaintiff alleges that the article in *The Star* was published of and concerning him and means that in his capacity as editor, responsible for all articles and news reports appearing in *Die Transvaler*, he is unscrupulous and dishonest, regularly (*gereeld*) and intentionally falsifies news in order to further Nazi propaganda, makes *Die Transvaler* the tool of malignant forces which threaten South Africa, and (in particular) by the omission of words from the statement of the Bureau of Information, as alleged in the article, wilfully falsified current news in order to further Nazi propaganda.

The defendants denied that the article was published of and concerning the plaintiff, but he (the plaintiff) had no difficulty in showing, by appropriate evidence, that the article would be read as meaning that he as editor was responsible for the conduct imputed to *Die Transvaler*. Whatever the exact meaning of these imputations may be it is evident that the article contains a specific and a general charge of wilfully falsifying current news; and it was said by the plaintiff's witnesses, most of whom were fellow-journalists, that because they regarded it as impossible that falsification of news could go on without the knowledge of the responsible editor they took the article as pointing to the plaintiff. There was nothing to contradict this. [156]

*

[158] The first paragraph in the article contains both the specific charge and the general charge. The third paragraph relates mainly to the specific charge but brings in also the general charge. The general charge (leaving aside for the moment the reference to Nazi propaganda) is that *Die Transvaler* applies a process of falsification to current news. . . . It is clear that the specific charge is one of falsification by altering the contents of a document sent to *Die Transvaler* for publication. Mr *de Villiers* argues that as this is said to be a better example than usual of the process the process must in all cases be a process of falsifying documents, e.g. news messages coming into *Die Transvaler* office from outside sources. 'Current news', he says, is news circulating in a defined form and the process of falsification alleged is a process of falsifying it in the same way as a forger is said to falsify a cheque by fraudulently altering it. I cannot agree that it follows from the example that the writer means the falsification is always done in one way. To falsify in the sense of fraudulently altering a document is not the only, or the whole, meaning of the word. In the large *Oxford Dictionary* it is stated to mean 'to give a false account of, to misrepresent'; as when Emerson in his 'Representative Men' described Napoleon sitting in his lonely island 'coldly falsifying facts and dates'. So also one speaks of the falsification of history when the meaning is that that which is false is represented to be historical fact. If a person were said to apply a process of falsification to history I do not think the remark would be restricted to a particular kind of falsification because an example was given of falsification by altering a document. In my opinion the writer here intended to convey that current news was falsified in *Die Transvaler* in the broad sense that matter which was false was dishonestly put forward as part of the current news. By

saying that the instance given was a better example than usual of the application of the process of falsification to current news, he meant no more, I think, than that it was an instance in which the process was more readily discernible than in most instances; for he proposed to show that matter was designedly omitted from a communication from the Bureau of Information so as to give a false impression of what the Bureau intended to convey to the public.

Then as to the words relating to Nazi propaganda. The reference is admittedly to the messages in the Afrikaans language which are sent daily to the Union by wireless telephony from the German transmitting station at Zeesen.... Any reader of the article would realise that the person or persons meant could not well be ignorant of the effect of what they were said to be doing; and in any event there are the title 'Speaking up for Hitler' and the statement that the 'spiritual home' of *Die Transvaler* is somewhere between Keerom Street (which was explained to be the address in Cape Town of *Die Burger*, a newspaper associated with *Die Transvaler*) and the Munich beer hall, a place generally thought to have witnessed the origin of the Nazi party. I consider that the words at the end of the first paragraph, 'in its support of Nazi propaganda', are meant to indicate that the falsification of news is carried out in the course of making propaganda not necessarily designed to assist the Germans but propaganda known by those making it – that is to say, by the plaintiff and his assistants – to have the effect of confirming, and aiding the acceptance of, propaganda made in the Union by the Germans. Similarly, the statement in the third paragraph about *Die Transvaler* being a tool of malignant forces (clearly the German enemy) cannot be looked upon as meaning that those responsible for the policy of *Die Transvaler*, and particularly the plaintiff, are unconscious of the fact that the paper is being so used. The meaning is that the Germans find *Die Transvaler* of assistance in what they are trying to do by their Afrikaans broadcasts to the Union and that the plaintiff and his associates know that perfectly well. These then are the things which it is incumbent on the defendants to prove of the plaintiff: a particular instance of wilful falsification of current news as alleged in the article: a sufficient number of other instances of any kind to justify the general charge that current news was falsified; and that these things were done in the course of carrying on a propaganda known by the plaintiff to have the effect of confirming, or rendering more acceptable, the enemy propaganda coming by wireless telephony to the Union. [160]

*

[206] In the circumstances of this case, I find that the instances which the defendants have proved are sufficient to sustain the general charge.

It must now be inquired how the evidence stands in the matter of the charge that these things were done in the course of a propaganda carried on by the plaintiff which had the effect, and was known by him to have the effect, of supporting the propaganda transmitted by the Germans to the Union. It is not the defendants' case that the plaintiff and his staff listened to the Zeesen radio and then simply reproduced the content in their paper. It was conceded from the beginning that the propaganda carried on by the plaintiff is propaganda of his own, or rather of the party for which his paper speaks; and the plaintiff's objects are distinct from the objects the Germans may be presumed to have in view of sending their radio messages to the Union. The plaintiff's objects, as he himself says, are to achieve the complete separation of the Union from Great Britain and, more immediately, the withdrawal of the Union from participation in the war. The defendants' case is that, in striving for these objects, the plaintiff to a large extent makes use of similar arguments and adopts similar methods to the arguments and methods which are characteristic of the Zeesen radio and that the effect of what the plaintiff does is on the one hand to confirm what Zeesen says and on the other to provide material for it to use. The plaintiff said he had no personal knowledge of the Zeesen themes but was ready to admit what the leading themes would necessarily be. The Germans would, he said, encourage discontented minorities in Allied countries to oppose the war, actively or passively, and, so far as South Africa was concerned, would obviously try to stimulate dislike for Great Britain. It was proved that during the period of the war up to October 1941 Zeesen did these things in a number of ways, which included the revival of ancient wrongs Great Britain is said to have committed against the Afrikaner people, of memories of the Boer War and the concentration camps; a harping on the hypocrisy of the British Government and the British people in claiming to be fighting for the freedom of small nations and the maintenance of international law; allegations that Great Britain is, and always has been, the enemy of small nations and the arch-violator of international law; predictions that England would have to sue for peace, having no allies left in Europe and nothing to hope from Russia or the United States; and so on. It was also proved that exactly the same themes constantly ran through the editorial pages of *Die Transvaler*.

The keynote of *Die Transvaler*'s policy on the war is to be found in the first paragraph of the leading article of 27 October 1941. ... 'The Herenigde Nasionale Party has always proclaimed that South Africa throughout its history has had only one enemy of its freedom, namely, Great Britain, and that Germany has never yet attacked South Africa. That is why the declaration of war against Germany was so bitterly opposed and why the party has always, with all its might, both in Parliament and outside, contested it (i.e. the declaration of war). The party has declared that when it gains office it will immediately seek an honourable peace.' [207]

*

[213] It is unnecessary to go on multiplying instances of matter in *Die Transvaler* which it was quite easy for the defendants to parallel with similar matter in the transcripts of the Zeesen broadcasts which were proved. One constant theme, already mentioned, which runs through both is the alleged mendacity of the Ministry of Information particularly when under the control of Mr Duff Cooper. In one instance of falsification, the news about the effect of the air attacks on London in September 1940, as issued by Mr Duff Cooper, is said to insult the intelligence of any reader looking for the truth; the inference drawn is that the British Government is afraid to come out with the truth. After discussing the enormous damage to strategic objects which he is sure the Germans must be inflicting in England, the writer goes on to say that in the last war the civil population of London showed that air attacks were shocking to its morale and that in the long run

it would not be proof against such attacks. Yet Mr Duff Cooper in this war talks about the morale of the London people when he tells the world about their determination. 'The English propagandists have by enchantment changed every Englishman into a being who is frightened by nothing and faces German bombs as if they were snowdrops falling from the skies. It is a strange world if you look at it through the English propaganda service. The days when giants walked the earth have come again. These giants have all thought fit to make their home in England where they now carry on a giants' war and offer giants' resistance for a giants' cause. But these giants differ in one point from the giants of old. The modern giants can also tell gigantic lies.'

It is not disputed that all these and kindred themes are to be found in the Zeesen broadcasts; but they were said to have occurred spontaneously to the plaintiff and his assistant in their desire, as neutral-minded observers of events, to bring out the truth and to protect their readers from the influence of pro-British and pro-Allied propaganda. It is immaterial whether *Die Transvaler* copied Zeesen, whether Zeesen copied *Die Transvaler* or whether the same ideas occurred independently in both organisations. The point is that, in fact, Zeesen propaganda and *Transvaler* propaganda had much in common and each may be said to have supported the other. It is insisted, however, on behalf of the plaintiff that *Die Transvaler* does not go all the way with Zeesen. The articles complained of as supporting Nazi propaganda were, it is said, written at a time when in fact the war seemed to be going entirely in favour of the Germans; but, even so, *Die Transvaler* always gave adequate prominence to pronouncements in England, America and the Union which told against the ultimate prospects of the Germans, and never committed itself to the definite statement that England had lost, or was certain to lose, the war. Moreover, it is said that since the course of the war has turned against the Axis Powers, Allied victories are reflected in the pages of *Die Transvaler* as strongly as formerly the German victories were. This may be so, but the fact remains that during the period which is relevant in this case the plaintiff saw fit to print matter, by way of editorial comment, which it is hardly possible to distinguish in tone or spirit from what the Germans were trying at this time to say to the people of the Union. . . . It is not necessary for the defendants to establish that *Die Transvaler* propaganda agreed in every respect with that of Zeesen. What they have proved is that the plaintiff caused to be published a large body of matter which was on the same general lines as matter coming to the Union in the Afrikaans transmissions from Zeesen and which was calculated to make the Germans look on *Die Transvaler* as a most useful adjunct to this propaganda service. The plaintiff cannot really deny this. He says it is not his fault. He appeals to the principles of free speech and a free press in a democratic country as justifying him in writing as he did in support of his policy of neutrality and a separate peace between the Union and Germany as a means towards a republic in South Africa. He argues that if he had to consider whether what he said would be useful to the Germans the effect would be to silence him; and the law does not compel him to be silent. But the question in this case is not whether the plaintiff should be silenced. His legal right to publish what he did is not in question. The question is, whether when he exercises his legal right in the way he does, he is entitled to complain if it is said of him that what he writes supports Nazi propaganda and makes his paper a tool of the Nazis. On the evidence he is not entitled to complain. He did support Nazi propaganda, he did make his paper a tool of the Nazis in South Africa, and he knew it.

Anglo-Indian Privilege

*Judgment in Mayr v. Rivaz**

[The defendant in this action wrote a letter to the Calcutta Commissioner of Police, in the course of which there were admittedly defamatory remarks of the plaintiff. The letter contained grievances of the defendant which, if genuine, were properly brought to the attention of the police commissioner. The libellous language is not recorded in the report of the case; the only issue before the Court at this stage of the case was whether the defendant, even if he honestly thought that the allegations he was making were true – and that he had a legal, as well as a moral, duty to inform the police authorities – could plead absolute privilege for his letter: or whether the defendant had merely a qualified privilege, which could be destroyed by proof that he was malicious towards the plaintiff.

Apart from its intrinsic merit as a piece of clear exposition and a nice turn of phrase, the judgment illustrates some of the problems of an 'imperial' jurisprudence.]

[254] IT IS NOT disputed that the occasion of publishing this letter was privileged. The defendant has pleaded publication without malice on a privileged occasion, but he takes the point (which I have to decide) that his denial of malice was, not strictly, necessary, the privilege in question being, as a matter of law, absolute: that is to say that, no matter how improper the motive of the publication, it is still not actionable.

The question whether he is right is extremely interesting and has been very ably argued on both sides. . . . English history is largely that of a struggle, both in domestic and foreign affairs, against any form of despotism. English common law is a reflection of English history, and most citizens of the country take it

* I.L.R. [1943] 1 Cal. 250.

for granted that every man in a civilised country is equal before the law.

Actually the idea is almost peculiar, in origin, to Great Britain, where it has been established by bloodless battles in the courts. It survives today principally in that country and in those countries to which it has been exported and which are still free from enemy domination.

One consequence of this fundamental principle of the common law is that it has been most reluctant to make the words or actions of any man wholly immune from question in courts of law. It has been readily admitted that there are numerous occasions when a man can and should, for proper reasons, speak what he believes to be the truth, even though it may be damaging to the reputation of another. He (for example) who discharges his butler for theft and thereafter tells an enquirer as to his character that he is an admirable servant is guilty of a heinous moral offence not only against the enquirer but also (which is worse) against the whole class of honest butlers. If he replies at all – which he is not bound to do – it is his clear duty – and the law recognises and respects that duty – to say in plain language what he believes to be the truth, namely, 'I dismissed him because he was a thief'. But if the employer says this not because he really believes that the butler stole, but because he dislikes the butler, he is doing a cruel wrong to the butler, for which he can, and should, be made to atone in heavy damages irrespective of the parties' position in society. Consequently, English law, while not ungenerous to qualified privilege, has been reluctant to extend the categories of occasions absolutely privileged. Wherever it has done so, it has, I believe, been actuated, always and exclusively, by consideration for the public interest. ... It is necessary to consider in some detail how far absolute privilege in this connection has been extended.

Even before the end of the seventeenth century (when the Judicature was, in theory at all events, freed from any possibility of pressure by the Executive) the Common Law recognised that a judge as such could speak as he liked without any fear or favour whatsoever. One reason for this is clearly stated as early as 1676 by Chief Justice North in *Barnardiston* v. *Soame** as follows:

* (1676) How. St. Tr. 1063, 1096.

They who are entrusted to judge ought to be free from vexation, that they may determine without fear; the law requires courage in a judge, and there provides security for the support of that courage.

This passage was cited with approval in *More* v. *Weaver** by Lord Justice Scrutton, who himself, through a long career on the Bench, was plain-spoken to, and sometimes beyond, the limits of good manners, utterly fearless, and conspicuously impartial between the Government and the governed. These qualities earned him the hatred of bureaucrats, but the memory of this great judge will long be revered by many who practised before him and could be sure of a fair hearing for their clients, however poor or disreputable, so long as they themselves talked sense boldly and distinctly.

It is important to observe that even a judge is not (in Lord Justice Scrutton's words) 'privileged to be malicious or careless' but, as was said by Mr Justice Channell in *Bottomley* v. *Brougham*,† 'is privileged from enquiry as to whether he is malicious or not'. Nor is even that privilege the privilege of the individual holder of the office or even that of the high office he holds. If a man says 'I should like to be a judge because then I could say exactly what I like about everybody' he is demonstrating his own unfitness for that office. We are but bare trustees of our privilege, which is, really, the privilege of the public to have their disputes decided by persons who shall be free from favour and from fear.

It is, theoretically, unfortunate that no one can prevent an abuse of this privilege by judges, but in a court of law someone must be supreme if business is to proceed, and that someone must be the judge. In this, democracy forbids, but necessity compels.

How early the extension of the same absolute privilege to counsel engaged in a case was recognised I do not know, but the reasons for it are equally obvious, and it is long settled law that it does extend to them. Equally, it must extend to a litigant in person who is acting as his own counsel, since fairness demands that the amateur and professional advocate should at least bat on the same wicket. Here, again, the privilege is that of the public. A man has no right to say just what he likes about someone else

* [1928] 2 K.B. 520, 522.
† [1908] 1 K.B. 584, 587.

because he is a party to a law suit or a member of the Bar, but the public have a right, if involved in litigation, to say, personally or by counsel, exactly what they wish to say to the judge who has to decide their dispute. It is for him to prevent or check any abuse of their privilege by them or by their advocates. The privilege is applicable, equally clearly, to pleadings, affidavits and other similar documents used or intended to be used in the course of judicial proceedings.

I do not know that the absolute or any privilege extends to officers of a court subordinate and assistant to the judge, when not acting judicially. If, for example, the officer whose duty it is to call on cases should, when the case next to be called on was *Brown* v. *Jones*, cry out 'Burglar Brown against Honest Jones', I doubt if he would have any defence to an action of slander by Brown except upon proof that the word 'burglar' was a truthful description of the plaintiff, and he certainly could, and I hope would, be summarily dealt with by the court for contempt. It certainly was, however, long ago and clearly extended (in England) to the utterances of witnesses and jurors in the course of judicial proceedings. . . . Apart from interruptions of and interpolations in judicial proceedings (such as the Usher's charge in Gilbert and Sullivan's *Trial by Jury*, which was a clear contempt and a quite unprivileged slander*) the foregoing cover the case of every person, who in the course of proceedings in court is entitled to make a statement and makes one.

If the foregoing people were not absolutely protected, most ordinary suits would no sooner be decided than they would each beget a number of others, since the losing party would promptly

---

* The Usher's charge was:

> Oh, listen to the plaintiff's case;
> Observe the features of her face—
> The broken-hearted bride!
> Condole with her distress of mind!
> And when, amid the plaintiff's shrieks,
> The ruffianly defendant speaks
> Upon the other side,
> What he may say you need not mind.
> From bias free of every kind
> This trial must be tried.

sue the judge, the successful counsel, and the witnesses whom the latter called. The courts would be snowed under with work and justice thereby delayed, impeded, and finally frustrated.

Only, apparently, in the last forty years has the question arisen whether there are any more instances of absolute privilege of this class, mainly through the ingenuity of a Scotch lady and/or her advisers. It would be useless and hazardous for a litigant to call a witness if he had no idea at all what the latter would say even in chief: consequently, it is an almost invariable practice for both parties to a suit involving question of fact to obtain proofs, if they can, from those whose evidence will, they think, assist their case. Jessie Prentice M'Ewan hit on the happy idea of suing a witness (whose evidence imputed to her an addiction to drugs and a criminal intention) not for what he said in the box but for what he said to the solicitor for the party who called him, and to that party himself, when he was asked what he was prepared to say in the box. The result was *Watson* v. *M'Ewan*.† It is the most important British authority which affects the present case. The House of Lords there clearly recognised as settled law the absolute privilege of a witness in respect of what he says in giving evidence: that to uphold the contention of Jessie Prentice M'Ewan would virtually destroy that privilege: and that, therefore, the reasons on which that undoubted privilege was founded were fatal to the ingenious device of the plaintiff-respondent for getting round the privilege. It is not now disputed that a witness who gives evidence is as fully protected as regards his proof as he is as regards his actual testimony, whether he volunteers his statement or whether it is made in response to a request, and whether he makes it to a litigant or to his agent.

But the Lord Chancellor carefully left open the question of the donor of a proof who is not in fact called. He admitted that this case might be one of hardship to a person defamed, and clearly pointed out that his opinion (with which the other noble and learned Lords agreed) was confined to the case of a witness – that is, a person who actually gives evidence. To the question of the statement of a person who did not do so Lord Halsbury gave only what he thought 'practically, would be the answer', namely that 'nobody knows anything about it – it slumbers, I suppose,

† [1905] A.C. 48c.

in the office of the solicitor, and nobody hears or cares anything about it'. Doubtless in the overwhelming majority of cases that is what would happen. But that means, not that the person defamed has not been injured, but only that he does not know of his injury. Actually the solicitor, and probably his managing and articled clerks, have seen what was said: at any rate if litigation ensues, so have his typists who typed out the briefs to counsel, and who love to use their tongues in a good gossip. So have learned counsel, senior or junior, and so have their 'clients' and the latter's pupils. So, finally, has the taxing master. In all, even if the maker of the statement is not called, thirty people may easily have seen the statement or a copy of it: some of them will doubtless be female, and others male. It is therefore quite impossible, whatever their obligations to secrecy, if any, to say how far the statement may not spread and that its nature might not come to the knowledge of the person defamed. It would be an odd case if it did, but it is odd cases which provide interesting and instructive legal problems.

To deny a cause of action to the person defamed in such a case, when he has had no opportunity to test by cross-examination, still less to disprove, that which is imputed to him, or to prosecute his defamer for perjury, would, as Lord Halsbury indicates, be to create a hardship. But to allow him one might easily create a very paradoxical and puzzling situation, best illustrated by a hypothetical case. Mr and Mrs A attempt to cross a street, Mr A escapes uninjured, but Mrs A is knocked down and injured by a motor car driven by X, who drives on. Obeying the impulses of his head rather than his heart, Mr A at once notes the number of the car and begins to collect statements from the onlookers, of whom one M says that he saw the whole incident and that the driver was obviously drunk – thereby imputing to X the serious crime of being drunk in charge of a motor car. At the very next moment X either has or has not a good cause of action against M. Mrs A later commences a suit for damages against X. But meanwhile someone has told X what M said about him, and X has commenced a suit for slander against M, which comes on for hearing before suit A *v.* X. In the suit X *v.* M the defendant does not allege that what he said was true, but pleads only privilege. It is found in that suit that in fact he spoke maliciously. If his privilege be not absolute (unless he becomes a witness) what conceivable right has M to have the suit against him stayed pending that of A *v*. X in order to see whether he will be called in that suit? I know of none. Suppose M fails to get a stay and suffers judgment, what is the effect on that judgment, if, as a result of what happened at the trial of A *v*. X, it transpires that M's privilege was really absolute? . . . I know of no precedent for holding that, if judgment in such a suit has actually been pronounced it can be, in effect, satisfied merely by something that happens in another suit between different parties. To such most perplexing problems the decision in *Watson* v. *M'Ewan* affords no answer. . . . I do think that the English Court of Appeal carried the matter a long stage further in *Beresford* v. *White*,* which seems to show that the answer to the problem of Mr and Mrs A, M and X is that M's statement is in any event absolutely privileged. The plaintiff in that case had for over eight years been intermittently putting forward a claim to an Irish peerage, but had never actually commenced proceedings. Learning that the defendant was likely to have some knowledge of the matters in question, his solicitor sought and obtained an interview with her. Her statement to him, imputing to his client bastardy and imposture, was held by the Court of Appeal to have been made on an absolutely privileged occasion, though in fact she never gave evidence. . . . Whether the absolute privilege, which thus attaches to a statement to an actual or potential litigant or to his agent with the idea that the person making it may give evidence, extends to a statement made by such a litigant in preparation for his law suit (for example, instructions to his solicitor), or to statements by a solicitor to his own client, is very doubtful.

What is the test of 'relevancy' for the purpose of a claim to absolute privilege was considered by Lord Justice Scrutton in *More* v. *Weaver*.† The question, he thought, is one of fact for the jury. This seems to indicate that what is meant is not that the statement should, as a matter of law, be material for the purpose of obtaining or giving advice (for of that only a lawyer could judge) but that it should be one which the maker of the statement genuinely (or, perhaps, reasonably) thinks material for that

* (1914) 30 T.L.R. 591.
† [1928] 2 K.B. 520.

purpose. His Lordship gives an excellent instance of a statement which might on the face of it be irrelevant and which a jury would probably so find, *viz.*, that of a building owner, who, when consulting his solicitor about a dispute with his builder, adds to his instructions the statement that Jones has run away with another man's wife. I will venture to give a case nearer the border line: an intending purchaser of immoveable property obtains an abstract of title, which he sends to his solicitor with a covering letter, asking his opinion as to the soundness of the title. He adds the observation that the vendor is a bigamist. His object may be merely to brighten the solicitor's grey life with a bit of interesting gossip or it may be that he genuinely believes that the felonious character of the vendor may affect his capacity to own or give a good title to property, for which belief there would have been considerable reason seventy-two years ago. Which it is is a question of fact.

From the foregoing and earlier authorities it seems to me that by the law of England the occasion of making each of the following statements is absolutely privileged:

(1) Any statement by a judge as such.

(2) Any statement made by a subordinate officer of a court, when acting either judicially or in the course of his duty on judicial proceedings, but not otherwise.

(3) Any statement by an advocate as such (advocate including counsel, a solicitor or Official Receiver where he has a right of audience in judicial proceedings, and a litigant in person).

(4) Any statement in a pleading, affidavit, notice, summons, report, bill of indictment, information, or other similar document used or prepared with a view to use in litigation, actual or contemplated.

(5) Any statement by a juror or assessor as such.

(6) Any statement by a witness as such.

(7) Any statement as to the subject-matter of litigation, actual or potential, by a person not a party thereto to a party or his adviser made at the request of, or with a view to assisting, that party.

(8) Any statement, supposed or, perhaps, reasonably supposed to be material for the purpose, made by a person seeking legal

advice or assistance to a legal practitioner, or by such practitioner to such person in the course and/or for the purpose
of advising him. . . .

On the authorities as they stand I do not think there are any
more categories of the absolute privilege which attaches to
judicial proceedings. In particular, a statement to an officer of the
police with a view to his setting the criminal law in motion is
certainly not, as such, privileged absolutely in England. [264]

*

. . . If the complainant is worth powder and shot, and the person
complained against so elects, I know of no principle on which he
should be restricted to the meagre remedy offered him by the
criminal law, even if no prosecution takes place. Learned counsel
for the defendant has most persuasively suggested that if a false
and defamatory statement can innocuously 'slumber in a solicitor's office' it can do so even better in a *thânâ*,* but I cannot
see any reason to suppose that its rest, in either dormitory, will
necessarily be harmless. True, fewer women are likely to see it in
the police station than in the solicitor's office; but even male
police officers, both in England and in the East, not infrequently
fail to appreciate the nice distinction between proved crimes and
alleged crimes – at least, that has been my own experience – and
their lawful powers of annoyance are greater than those of solicitors. . . . Nothing in the letter suggests that these ends, and
especially the preservation of the peace, could be achieved only
by the Commissioner's assuming to exercise judicial powers. In
fact it leaves it to his discretion what steps he should take if he
decides to act on it, though it contains several alternative suggestions. In substance, it invites the Commissioner of Police to
take action as such, that is as an administrative and executive
officer, and some of the powers whose exercise is expressly suggested are purely administrative. Even the Commissioner's
powers are inquisitorial rather than judicial. Their exercise leads
him not to make a decision affecting the rights of others but gives
him information to assist him in deciding whether he will or will
not take other steps to obtain such a decision. To my mind, it

* *Thânâ* in Urdu means police-station.

imports into the case a complete air of unreality to suggest that the letter on the face of it is written to a judicial officer. That is why I have alluded to its distinguished recipient as 'a policeman', for such he is, although a very senior and responsible policeman. In so doing, I have not intended to cause the gentleman who now occupies the office any offence, though I recognise that, today, the use of accurate language often does do so. . . . [267]

[269] One difference between English and Indian law there certainly is, and it arises out of a difference in criminal procedure. Where a Magistrate directs the police to enquire into and report on a complaint he is exercising a power which does not exist in England, and a statement to the police when they are acting in pursuance of his orders is absolutely privileged. They are, for the time being, the delegates of a judicial authority and their investigation is to be considered as part of a judicial proceeding.

Mr Justice King in *Bapalal and Co.* v. *A. R. Krishnaswami Iyer** held that a complaint to a policeman alleging theft by the plaintiff was absolutely privileged in a suit for defamation. The final ground given by the learned Judge, as reported, is very curious. He reached the conclusion 'that the weight of authority is in favour of the view that a complaint to a police officer from its very nature as a statement which the complainant is prepared later, if called upon to do so, to substantiate upon oath is absolutely privileged'.

If this reasoning is correct, the gates are thrown open to the editor of every newspaper to libel anybody to any extent he pleases with impunity, He has only to say—

A. B. is a murderer. 'I' am (or rather 'we' are) prepared later, if called upon to do so, to substantiate this upon oath. We challenge A. B. to take proceedings, in which we will prove that he is a murderer.

Should A. B. take the proceedings invited, the editor need not bother with the hazardous defence of justification, if Mr Justice King's reasoning is correct; he can plead, and plead only, privilege, and no evidence of malice which A.B. may be able to adduce will assist him in the least. This seems to me a completely untenable proposition.

The result is paradoxical for another reason. If there appears, to the police, to be some substance in the complaint and an

* I.L.R. [1941] Mad. 332, 335-6.

unsuccessful prosecution ensues, the person charged clearly has open to him a suit for malicious prosecution, to succeed in which he will have to prove (*inter alia*) malice. But if the charge appears to the police utterly groundless, and no prosecution follows, then according to Mr Justice King he would have no civil remedy at all. It is true that the injury he has suffered may in the latter case be less than in the former. But it is at least odd if the more reckless the complaint the safer is the complainant. . . . In *Majju* v. *Lachman Prasad** a Bench of the Allahabad High Court held that the privilege now in question is only qualified privilege. The value of the decision is not great. The presiding Judge on the Bench was Acting Chief Justice Walsh, and it was an appeal from Mr Justice Walsh. His two brethren on the Bench agreed with the judgment of the trial Judge in judgments of seventeen and two words respectively, while the learned Acting Chief Justice, though he referred kindly to the merits of learned counsel for the appellants, said nothing whatsoever about the merits of the appeal, described as 'indefinite' the very definite and, in my opinion, most proper protest made by counsel against his sitting on appeal from himself, and did not seriously attempt to justify his position. In fact, the judgment appealed against contained statements to the effect that on a defence of qualified privilege the onus is on the defendant to prove absence of malice and that the defence of qualified privilege is 'illogical and impossible' where the defendant also pleads that the words complained of are to his knowledge true. The latter error arises from the former, which itself would be serious if made by a candidate in a Bar examination and is truly astonishing in three High Court Judges. *Ignorantia juris non excusat* – but one ought not to assume, because three Judges display crass ignorance on one point, that they are necessarily wrong in their decision on another. . . . In that state, as far as I know, Indian authority rests. It does not compel me to hold that there is anything in the conditions of life in Calcutta (including the conditions created by the legislature) which prevents the application of English common law. On the contrary it supports me, on the whole, in thinking that English common law is applicable to the present question. By that law the writer of the letter is not, in my opinion, protected by absolute privilege.

* (1924) I.L.R. 46 All. 471.

The Meaning of Money

*Speech in Perrin v. Morgan**

THE SUBSTANCE OF the matter seems to be that the word 'money' at the present time has a diversity of meanings, and that when it is found in a will there is no presumption that it bears one meaning rather than another. The testator obviously meant to dispose of, at any rate, some part of his property by the phrase, and the construing court has to ascertain what was meant, being guided by the other provisions of the will and the other relevant circumstances, including the age and education of the testator, his relations to the beneficiary chosen, whether of kinship or friendship, the provision for other beneficiaries, and other admissible circumstances. Weighing all these, the court must adopt what appears the most probable meaning. To decide on proven probabilities is not to guess but to adjudicate. If this is to decide according to the 'context' I am content but I cannot agree that the court is precluded from looking outside the terms of the will. No will can be analysed *in vacuo*. There are material surroundings such as I have suggested in every case, and they have to be taken into account. The sole object is, of course, to ascertain from the will the testator's intentions.

The result of your Lordships' decision will be to relieve judges in the future from the thraldom, often I think self-imposed, of judgments in other cases believed to constrain them to give a meaning to wills which they know to be contrary to the testator's intention. In the competition for bad pre-eminence in departure from the true meaning I think I should place first the decision of Lords Justices Turner and Knight Bruce in *Lowe* v. *Thomas* where the testator being possessed of stocks and some cash had left his 'money' to his brother for life and on his death to the brother's two daughters with ultimate remainder to the survivor. The testator left £50 cash, and it was held that, despite the series of

* [1943] A.C. 399, 414.

life interests, the bequest only passed the cash. The poorest mind would know that this was absurd, and so plainly, did the lords justices, but they were held in thrall. A high place, however, in the competition could be given *In Re Hodgson* where a nurse asked to make her will within two days of her death and having in her case by the side of her bed some £800 in cash and £600 in savings certificates left all her 'money' to a named beneficiary. She left no next of kin and the Crown claimed and was awarded the savings certificates as *bona vacantia*. In the future the resources of the Crown will receive no such flagitious increment. I anticipate with satisfaction that henceforth the group of ghosts of dissatisfied testators who, according to a late Chancery judge, wait on the other bank of the Styx to receive the judicial personages who have misconstrued their wills, may be considerably diminished. It will be a relief to the whole legal profession that at last what the Master of the Rolls rightly called a blot on our jurisprudence has been removed. . . .

Cows and Bitches

*Judgment in Wood, N. O. and another v. Branson**

TWO PLAINTIFFS SUED the same defendant for damages for alleged defamation. The plaintiff in the one case is Mrs A. E. Wood, represented by her husband, W. M. Wood, to whom she is married in community of property. The plaintiff in the other case is Mrs S. C. Wood, a widow and the mother of Mrs A. E. Wood. The complaint was that the defendant, who is a deputy-messenger of the magistrates' court, Johannesburg, while serving a summons on Mrs A. E. Wood for her husband, Mr W. M. Wood, referred to both the plaintiffs as 'cheap South Hills cows'. This remark was addressed to both of them, and in each case the only publication was to the other of them. The summonses were issued on 29 August 1951. On 16 October 1951 a further alleged defamation was added by amendment, to the effect that at the same time the defendant in speaking to a certain Mrs Momen (a neighbour of the two plaintiffs, who live in the same house) referred to the plaintiffs as 'bloody bitches'.

The magistrate held that the defamation had not been proved and gave a judgment of absolution from the instance. Against this judgment the present appeal is brought. The two cases were consolidated by consent of parties and were conducted together as if a single summons had been issued under the provisions of sec. 41 of the Magistrates' Courts Act. The appeal is against the decision on the facts. One judgment was given and there is one notice of appeal. After the cases were consolidated, they were treated as one action, and for convenience I shall refer to the two cases in the singular.

The setting in which the defamation is alleged to have occurred is the following: The defendant called at the plaintiff's house with a summons for Mr W. M. Wood. An altercation took place between the defendant and Mr Wood's wife, Mrs A. E. Wood,

* 1952 (3) S.A. 369.

who it is said refused to accept the summons, with the result that
the defendant proceeded to pin it to the front door. Mrs Wood,
senior, interfered at some stage, precisely when it is not clear.
There was an interchange of vulgar and somewhat obscene abuse,
the defendant charging one of the plaintiffs with abuse, and the
plaintiffs charging the defendant with abuse. I think that there
is very little doubt that the parties abused each other. While this
interchange was proceeding, it is alleged that the defendant made
use of the first defamatory words, in which he referred to the
plaintiffs as 'South Hills cows'. I should have mentioned that
all these events took place in the suburb of South Hills. At a later
stage when the defendant was serving a summons on Mrs Momen
next door, Mrs Momen says he referred to the plaintiffs as 'old
bitches'.

My impression, after reading the record and hearing argument,
is that the defendant did use the words complained of.

(The learned Judge, after dealing with certain evidence not
material to this report, continued.)

The innuendo alleged in relation to the words 'you are a cheap
South Hills cow' is that they meant that the plaintiffs were
women of 'low moral standing, not fit to associate with respectable people'. No innuendo is alleged in regards to the words
'leave the bloody bitches alone'. According to Mrs Momen, for
the word 'bloody' there must be substituted the word 'old'. In
the magistrate's judgment occurs the following:

Meaning of the words. The summonses allege that both expressions
which the defendant is alleged to have used have defamatory meanings.
Defendant admits in cross-examination that to call a woman a cow
usually means a prostitute. Defendant's counsel during argument admitted the defamatory meaning of the expression complained of.

In an action for damages for alleged defamation the words must
be given their ordinary meaning – unless they are alleged and are
proved to have some other meaning. *Prima facie* it seems to me
that neither the word 'cow' nor the word 'bitch' when applied
to a person is defamatory. Such words are, in my opinion, words
of meaningless abuse. If it is sought to prove that the words have
a defamatory meaning, that meaning must be alleged and proved.
An innuendo is not proved by asking a witness what he understood the words to mean. To prove that a word of meaningless

abuse has a defamatory meaning requires evidence. The context in which a word is used, the circumstances in which it is used, the tone in which it is uttered, are all facts which may render meaningless abuse defamatory. Words which have an innocent meaning in one locality may by local usage in another locality be defamatory. But all this is a matter for proof, and it must be proved in the proper way.

Certain characteristics are by common consent associated with certain animals. It would not be difficult, for instance, to prove that if a certain person was referred to as a donkey or an ass, the innuendo was that he was stupid. If a person was referred to as a mule, it would be easy to prove that what was meant was that he was obstinately stupid. The characteristics suggested are often associated with the animals named. Nevertheless, there would have to be some evidence to prove how the words would have been understood. A cow has no particular characteristic which would tend to make such a word applied to a person defamatory. After all, a cow is a harmless, docile and useful animal. If a woman is called a cow it is necessary to prove that the word would have been understood in a defamatory sense. The word bitch is a somewhat less pleasant appellation than the word cow; but what is a bitch? It is a female dog. When a woman is referred to as a bitch it may mean that she is an unladylike, coarse and ill-mannered person – and it may have some sexual connotation – but all this must be proved in a proper legal way according to the rules of evidence, for to say of a woman that she is a bitch in its primary sense is mere meaningless abuse. One thing that cannot be done is to ask a witness who heard the words what he understood them to mean, for this is totally irrelevant. If such evidence were allowed, it would result in a Gilbertian situation, for, owing to some personal idiosyncrasy, a particular hearer of the words may assign to them an altogether unusual meaning, which is entirely different from how the words are usually understood, and a person who had made a perfectly innocent remark would find himself liable to pay damages for defamation. It is necessary to show how the words would be ordinarily understood in the circumstances and in the place and context in which they were spoken by the ordinary person. There is no evidence in this case to prove how the words complained of would have been understood. To go to a dictionary to find the meaning of the words is to introduce an unreal and fictitious element into the enquiry, for it is not the learned bookish meaning that the words must be given, but the meaning they convey to the man in the street. The ordinary man does not carry about with him a pocket dictionary which he consults to see whether or not he has been defamed. The exchange of epithet is usually much too rapid for any such distraction. The *Oxford Dictionary*, which has been quoted, gives the meaning of the word cow when applied to a person as it is understood in certain parts of educated England; but what has this to do with how the word is usually understood in the suburb of South Hills, Johannesburg? Nothing whatever. In some grades of society Smith may say: 'Mrs Jones is a pleasant old cow; I rather like her', or 'She is a decent old cow.' These remarks in a different grade of society would be regarded as uncouth and coarse, but hardly as defamatory. Everything depends on the context, the tone, the circumstances, the setting and the locality. The words cannot be regarded *in abstracto*.

Apart from this, I am also of opinion that the evidence shows plainly that the words were spoken *in rixa** without *animus injuriandi*. Mrs Momen's evidence – indeed, all the evidence – shows that the words were uttered in the course of a violent quarrel, which came very near an assault. The parties were shouting at each other, and there was a running flow of abuse. The truth lies obviously between the two stories. I have no doubt that each side abused the other. Mr *Miller* says that a defendant who relies upon the defence that the words were spoken in the heat of anger must necessarily admit that he used the words. There is, however, no such logical necessity. A defendant may have been so angry that he does not know what he said. Why can he not put the *onus* of proving the use of the words on the plaintiff, and at the same time plead that if he did use the words he did so *in rixa* without *animus injuriandi*? The defence that the words complained of were spoken in anger without *animus injuriandi* (if the court finds that they were uttered) is an altogether different defence from the defences of privilege or fair comment. In both

---

* Rixa is the Roman-Dutch legal defence to an action for defamation where the defamor has uttered the words in anger in the heat of the moment.

of these defences the defendant relies upon the fact that he consciously realised the character of the occasion or of the publication or statement and considered that it was his duty, or that he was at least entitled, to say what he did say. He must use the occasion consciously. In the defence that the words were spoken *in rixa*, the very opposite is the case. The defendant must have been unconscious of any intention to defame. Indeed, he need not be conscious of what he was saying. Carried away by anger, he makes statements wildly and without *animus injuriandi*. This last defence is perfectly consistent with a denial that the words were spoken. There is no logical inconsistency.

A town councillor sitting to consider an application for an appointment as town clerk would say to himself: 'I know this applicant; he has been convicted of theft. I must state this, for it is relevant and it is my duty to say it.' This would provide a defence of privilege. A person who was going to plead that he used the words *in rixa* would not say to himself: 'I am now so angry that I do not intend any *injuria*; I can therefore say what I like about X.' This illustration shows how completely different are the two defences. The defendant himself says that he did not lose his temper and was not angry. This is obviously false. He did lose his temper and was exceedingly angry. All the evidence shows that. The court is no more bound by his statement that he was not angry than it is by his statement that he did not use the words. If he is disbelieved in one respect, why must he necessarily be believed in the other respect? The duty of the court is to find the truth, and in the search for the truth the court cannot be frustrated by artificialities. If the evidence shows overwhelmingly that the defendant was in a violent temper, why must the court find that he was not in any temper merely because he says so?

In my opinion all the circumstances prove that the words were spoken *in rixa* without *animus injuriandi* – even if they had the defamatory meaning ascribed to them – (which I am satisfied they did not have), and consequently the magistrate's conclusion, albeit for different reasons, is correct in the result.

SIR KENNETH GRESSON*

Nymphet on Trial

Dissenting judgment in Re Lolita†

THE WHOLE THEME of *Lolita* is the obsession a man of mature years has for a young girl even before she has reached her teens. The purpose of the author is, it seems to me, to show how the man's mind became completely dominated by his yearning for the child; that it led him to marry the child's mother as a means of facilitating his approach to the child, and subsequently even seriously to entertain the idea of murdering the mother. This theme permeates the book; it must in order to portray the character as he really is. *Lolita* does not 'unduly emphasise' matters of sex. It is wholly devoted to a sexual theme; except for some well-written passages descriptive of the countryside, there is little else.

It sets out to describe the infatuation of the middle-aged Humbert for the child and the ecstatic pleasure he derived from intimacy with her (which any healthy-minded person would condemn as a perverted taste); it is therefore a study in sex, but I do not think it can be said 'unduly' to emphasise matters of sex any more than a book which was a study of the game of cricket, in the form of a novel, could be said 'unduly' to emphasise cricket. The theme may be, indeed in my opinion it is, a revolting one, but nevertheless the book is sincere, well written, and not without considerable literary merit. The author's sincerity of purpose is an important consideration in judging whether there is an undue – i.e. an excessive or unjustified – emphasis on sex [but] I think such emphasis as there is on sex was essential. Moreover the author in his treatment of this dominant theme has avoided crude or vulgar expressions and has treated the subject with skill and artistry. In my opinion, therefore, the work being devoted to the portrayal of a sexual aberration, matters of sex must

* Then President of the New Zealand Court of Appeal.
† [1961] N.Z.L.R. 542, 548.

261

necessarily pervade the whole book and it does not in my view 'unduly emphasise matters of sex'.

I am not unaware that some Australian judges have held that 'unduly emphasising matters of sex' should be construed as dealing with matters of sex in a manner which offends against the standards of the community in which the book or article is published. I find it difficult to adopt so very free an interpretation. That is not what the Legislature has said and it is surely a primary principle of construction that plain words must be given their plain meaning. This I have tried to do. Moreover I should find myself in some difficulty if I adopted the 'standard of the community' test for I just don't know what the standard of the community is, nor how to ascertain it. I can decide for myself (and so can anyone else) whether in my, or his, opinion there is an 'undue', i.e., an excessive emphasis on matters of sex. But if I am called upon to determine whether sex matters have been treated in a manner which offends against the standard of the community I am at a loss to know what is the standard of the community. It is certainly not a high one if the novels current today are any criterion; many show no reticence at all in describing – often quite unnecessarily – the sexual behaviour of the characters. This seems to be acceptable to the community. No doubt any individual exercising his own judgment as to whether there is an 'undue' emphasis on matters of sex would be influenced, consciously or subconsciously, by what seemed to him to be the standard of the community in which he lived, but how is a tribunal to ascertain that standard in a society the members of which have such diverse tastes, standards of education, attitudes and outlook? Accordingly I prefer to adopt the plain language of the statute and to exercise my own judgment as to whether the work 'unduly emphasises matters of sex' – obviously a matter upon which opinion may differ. With respect to those who might think otherwise I do not think the book in question does.

However, lest I be wrong in holding as I do that there is no 'undue' emphasis on matters of sex, I turn to consider the terms of section 5 to which section 6 is subordinated. The matters which [the Act] directs shall be taken into consideration in determining whether any document or other matter is indecent are:

(a) *The nature of the document or matter.*

The book is a work of fiction depicting the life of a pervert – his obsession for a young girl; his pursuit of her, the subordination of his whole life to the advancement of his purpose, and the deterioration in the lives of both of them which resulted, until in the end both are brought to disaster. There is a narration of the hopes and ecstasies, the emotions and the suffering of this middle-aged man, and to a lesser extent the emotions and reactions of the child. It is not presented as having brought any permanent happiness to either. It is a work of art, written with considerable skill, and though it describes in great detail the sexual relations of the man with the child whom he terms a 'nymphet' there is no crudeness or coarseness of expression nor any descent to the pornographic. That, in my opinion, is a fair assessment of the 'nature of the document or matter'.

(b) *The nature and circumstances of the act done by the defendant with respect thereto and the purpose for which the act was done.*

This is sufficiently comprehended in the assessment of the book I have set out above. There does not appear to have been any particular purpose other than that which normally motivates any writer of fiction.

(c) *The literary or artistic merit or medical, legal, political, or scientific character or importance of the document or matter.*

It was common ground that the book has some literary merit. Evidence was given by persons of standing in the academic world who all, in various terms, assessed the book as evidencing literary skill and possessing merit. The opinions so expressed were not challenged.

(d) *The persons, classes of persons, or age groups to or amongst whom the document or matter was or was intended or was likely to be published, distributed, sold, exhibited, given, sent, or delivered; and the tendency of the matter or thing to deprave or corrupt any such persons, class of persons, or age group (notwithstanding that persons in other classes or age groups may not be similarly affected thereby).*

It was upon this statutory requirement that argument largely centred. I do not understand why the court should have the assistance of persons who from their calling or eminence may be regarded as competent to assess literary merit but not be permitted to have the assistance of persons of similar standing as to the effect upon the mind of a perusal of the book, though I would concede readily that evidence upon both questions will be of little assistance to the court which must necessarily make its own evaluation. One can readily imagine a parade of witnesses, leading figures in the literary world, ecclesiastics, sociologists, psychiatrists and the like all contending for no tendency to deprave being matched by a similar parade taking exactly the opposite view. Even if evidence could be produced of a person who asserted that his or her mind previously unsullied had become depraved as a result of reading the book, that would not be conclusive since it would be open to doubt whether in fact there had been such a deterioration in character as was claimed.

Evidence that no ill-effects had resulted from a reading would of course be of negative value only. Accordingly, it seems to me the judge or magistrate must form his opinion unassisted and untrammelled by the opinions of others. This I accordingly proceed to do, and my conclusion is that revolting as the theme of the book is, it is a sincere and well-written portrayal of the lives of two persons, the reading of which will not tend to deprave. With great respect, I find myself in disagreement with the view expressed in the judgment appealed from that the book is 'aphrodisiac', that it should be condemned because of 'a likelihood of introducing lustful thoughts, and exciting sexual impulses to a point at which normal restraints might fail'. I do not think that would be its effect at all. Though well written this book is so boring and tedious that I do not think many young readers, or for that matter many adults, would do more than 'skim' it. Nothing but the necessity of judging it would have induced me to read it to the end.

The book must be considered as a whole as a presentation of an abnormal life. The subject is an unpleasant one, but the mere fact that the book deals with a sexual aberration does not warrant attributing to it a tendency to deprave. There was an outburst against *The Well of Loneliness* when it was first published and indeed a prosecution, but I venture to think that today nobody but a bigot would condemn it as tending to deprave. I do not think that *Lolita* has a libidinous effect. There are descriptions of the intimate relations of Humbert and his nymphet with a wealth of detail but in more restrained terms than many of today's novels employ; nor should the book be judged from a selection of passages. I do not think a reading of the book is likely to lead to any other result than disgust; that is something very different from tending to deprave. Liberty of expression is too precious a thing to be lightly interfered with, though of course freedom of speech must not be carried to such lengths as to lead to a lowering of standards or a debasing of minds. I do not think *Lolita* does so.

Freedom of expression should, in my opinion, extend to every field of human conduct, including sexual behaviour. It is a feature of present-day literature to describe frankly and realistically sexual episodes not only between married couples but also between those not married and between teenagers. Provided crudity of expression and coarseness of language is avoided, in my opinion this does not contravene the statute. I see no reason why the generation growing up should not be permitted to learn from their reading something of the vagaries of sexual behaviour. If accounts of seduction or detailed descriptions of sexual episodes are to be held to have a tendency to deprave, a considerable portion of today's output of novels would have to be condemned. At any rate, unless loose or perverted sexual conduct is held up as something to be emulated or is invested with an atmosphere of glamour, there is not, in my opinion, any 'tendency to deprave'. Since perversion in sexual relationships does exist, I do not see why it should be a forbidden topic. The effect of the portrayal of such conduct will I think be to repel or to disgust and not to deprave. There is no cogent scientific evidence to support a view that the description of perverted behaviour debases or depraves, and I am not satisfied that it is so. . . . The work must be judged in an age in which sexual relations are treated with very great candour and my view is that *Lolita* does not qualify for condemnation as having a tendency to deprave. The problem of course involves a conflict between the right of free expression and the necessity of maintaining proper standards in the community. Publication of anything of which it can fairly be held that it exalts vice, viciousness or cruelty or is an incentive to immoral behaviour must of course be restrained in the public interest. In my opinion *Lolita* is not in that category.

English Idioms from the Penal Law*

IT IS THE common people who, by taking a phrase into current usage, determine what is to be idiomatic speech. Since punishment is apt to make most impression on those at the receiving end, it is small wonder that PENAL LAW has made a generous contribution to English phraseology. The idioms in this section bear dire testimony to man's agelong and enduring inhumanity.

First, for the legacy of the gallows:

Hang me! (*or* you *or* him)	as well be hanged for a sheep
You be hanged!	as a lamb
Be hanged to you! (*or* him)	give one rope (enough) (and
Go hang yourself!	he'll hang himself)
Hang it all!	have (*or* give) plenty of rope
I'll see you (*or* him) hanged first!	come (*or* run) to the end of
I'll be hanged if I . . .	one's rope
a hanging matter	one's rope is out
born to be hanged	put (*or* ? run) one's head into
hanging's too good for him	a noose
hang together or hang separately	save one's own neck

The exclamatory phrases first noted hardly need explanation or illustration. Most are to be found in Shakespeare or before. They occur constantly in Swift's *Polite Conversation*, that repository of then current idiom. They again became popular round the turn of last century, to judge by their frequency in the pages of such diverse authors as Henry James and Jerome K. Jerome. Mrs Wix, the governess in *What Maisie Knew*, 'had never been so profane' as when she was goaded into saying 'Yes, hang him!' But the taste for stronger expletives was already apparent: 'You damned

* Reprinted with permission from the January 1965 issue of *The Law Quarterly Review* where it formed the fourth instalment of a general study, *English Idioms from the Law*. The author has revised and slightly shortened the original text: in particular the references and authorities for the statements in the text have been omitted in this reprint.

old b . . . . .!' – Maisie could not quite hear all, and reported, 'He
has called her a damned old brute.' Compare the modern child
who flushed on hearing a distinguished visitor refer to the mother
of her pups as a bitch, but explained that it was only that she had
never heard the word applied to a dog. The phrases with *hang*
have thus a primly old-fashioned sound to the contemporary ear.

A hanging matter is idiomatic in that it only facetiously connotes
mortal consequences, and certainly not necessarily on the gallows.
'It was a hanging matter to laugh unseasonably,' wrote Dryden
of the dramatic ventures of the tyrants Dionysius and Nero in a
passage cited by Pearsall Smith as an outstanding instance of how
idiom can give life to prose, exemplifying those 'enchanting qualities, the rhythm, the phrasing, the timbre and accent of the living
voice.' Mr Partridge, in his *Dictionary of Slang and Unconven-
tional English*, cites *It isn't a hanging matter* as a catchphrase of
the late nineteenth/twentieth centuries, meaning 'Well, after all,
it's not so very serious, is it?' *Born to be hanged* is probably an
echo of a proverb common to most European languages, 'He that
is born to be hanged shall never be drowned.' 'He hath no drown-
ing marke vpon him, his complexion is perfect Gallowes . . .' says
Gonzalo of the Boatswain in *The Tempest*. *Hanging's too good for
him* is a frequent contribution to the popular discussion of capital
punishment; but those who use the phrase can hardly be conscious that it comes from the mouth of Mr Cruelty in *The
Pilgrim's Progress* – indeed, it is his sole observation. But the
phrase may already have been proverbial. In *I Henry VI* her
shepherd father, disowned by Joan of Arc, cries, 'O burne her,
burne her, hanging is too good.' *Hang together or hang separately*
was a blend of homely wisdom and verbal wit characteristic of
Benjamin Franklin. *As well be hanged for a sheep as a lamb* goes
back to the days when the theft of anything of greater value than
one shilling was a capital offence and sheepstealing one of the more
frequent forms of such larceny. *Come to the end of one's rope* and
one's rope is out are, I think, to be listed with *give one rope (and
he'll hang himself*, express or implied) rather than with 'come to
the end of one's tether', which is, of course, an idiom from graz-
ing. *Run one's head into a noose* could come from trapping rather
than the law, though *put one's head in a noose* seems more appropriate to penal strangulation.

From some of the former incidents of capital punishment come:

get it in the neck	make short shrift of
stick one's neck out	die hard, diehard
Halifax law*	in the cart
go to the stake for	? go west
?? send to Coventry	hung, drawn and quartered
give short shrift to	

Get it in the neck is equally consistent with death by hanging and by the axe, though *stick one's neck out* seems clearly more apt to the latter. In France of the *ancien régime* decapitation was the privilege of the nobility, whereas the commonalty had to suffer the agony and ignominy of hanging. It was as much egalitarianism as humanity which led to the introduction of the guillotine. On 1 December 1789 Dr Guillotin presented six resolutions to the *Tiers Etats*. The first, and the only one carried that day, reads: 'Offences of the same kind will be punished by the same kind of penalty, whatever the rank and station of the guilty parties.' Oddly enough, the second, providing that the sole method of capital punishment should be decapitation by a simple mechanism, seems never to have been formally adopted at all. Our own peerage had no such privilege as the French, and the sentence of beheading is, strictly, unknown to English law. 'In felony,' wrote Bacon, 'the corporal punishment is by hanging, and it is doubtful whether the king may turn it into beheading in the case of a peer or other person of dignity.' But in treason beheading was part of the sentence (following the drawing, hanging, emasculation and disembowelling, and preceding the quartering), so that the sovereign, in the exercise of his prerogative, could, and sometimes did, respite all except that part; and in practice felons, too, of high birth were sometimes beheaded instead of being hanged.

Burning was the common law punishment of women found guilty of high or petty treason. The latter generally consisted either of husband-murder or of assisting in or instigating it; and a lover would no doubt often be the other principal or at least the

* This idiom had been discussed in a previous instalment. It means punishment first, trial afterwards.

motive. Nevertheless I should guess that the idiom *go to the stake for* comes rather from the burning of heretics who refused to recant.* They were tried before an ecclesiastical court, and on conviction handed over to the lay power for punishment. The crime seems to have been a rare one in mediæval England: the first English statute enacting death for heretics was not until 1401. Tudor times, however, made up for the slow start, and the writ de haeretico comburendo, once invented, was in frequent issue.

There has been no convincing explanation of *send to Coventry*. I list it here, though with considerable scepticism, in view of two of the theories put forward to account for its origin.† The first is that the phrase derives from a practice in the late Middle Ages of sending traitors from their place of condemnation to Coventry for their execution. This certainly occurred on occasion:‡ but it was only an infinitesimal minority of capital sentences, even for treason, which were executed at Coventry; and certainly no more than in any other comparable town. Moreover, this derivation entirely fails to account for the connotation of ostracism which is of the essence of the phrase. The second theory, a refinement of the first, seems to me to have even less to commend it. It is that

* Cf. *Much Ado About Nothing* (I, i, 225).
    Benedick . . . the opinion that fire cannot melt out of me; I will die in it at the stake.
    Don Pedro. Thou wast euer an obstinate heretique.
† Both by 'Spectator in Warwickshire' (Walter Carson).
‡ Walter Carson cited the clerk who attempted the life of Henry III at Woodstock [1238]; Hereford and Norfolk for their wager of battle [1398]; Lord Rivers and his son [Sir John Woodville] (1468); the leader of the Kentish insurgents (1471); Thomas Harrington, who claimed to be son of the Duke of Clarence (1487); Sir Henry Mumford and Sir Robert Mallerie (1495); Laurence Saunders [1555]. I have not been able to trace all of these: but it was not for execution that Hereford and Norfolk were sent to Coventry; Rivers and Woodville were, according to the D.N.B., executed at Kenilworth, outside Coventry, on 12 August 1469; and the Bastard of Fauconberg (who else could be described as 'the leader of the Kentish insurgents, 1471'?) was beheaded at Middleham, Yorkshire.
|| *e.g.*, Saunders was sent to Coventry to be burnt, but Hooper and Ferrar to their own respective sees of Gloucester and St David's, and Ridley and Latimer to Oxford.

'Coventry is derived from "covin-tree" – the tree of punishment ... feudal lords made short shrift of their enemies by hanging them on the covin-tree. "Send him to the covin-tree" would be their command ... By this reasoning Coventry was the town of punishment.' (A covin-tree was explained by Sir Walter Scott in a note to *Quentin Durward*, as being 'the large tree in front of a Scottish castle ... [where] the laird received guests of rank, and thither he conveyed them on their departure.') As against this theory, first, modern place-name authorities concur in deriving Coventry from 'Cofa's tree' not 'covin-tree'; secondly, there is no evidence that Cofa's tree became a covin-tree or, for that matter, that there ever was a covin-tree in the town at all; thirdly, although no doubt high-handed actions took place in disturbed times, the occasions when English feudal lords hanged their enemies must have been very infrequent – indeed, their power to hang even criminals was closely restricted; fourthly, the only instance I know of anyone being hanged on a covin-tree occurs in a work of fiction, *Quentin Durward*, and then in a French setting, and nothing I have come across suggests that the covin-tree was considered as 'the tree of punishment'; fifthly, in none of the cited instances of persons being sent to Coventry for execution was death by hanging;* and, lastly, this theory, too, fails to allow for the sense of boycotting in the idiom. I need not enlarge on other suggested derivations of the phrase, since they have no connection with any legal theme; and none seems convincing.

Shrift comes ultimately from a teutonic word meaning a prescribed penalty. In the *Laws of Cnut* it signified the penance imposed by a priest after absolution. The word was gradually extended to include the confession and absolution which preceded the penance.

> Come, come, dispatch, the Duke would be at dinner:
> Make a short Shrift, he longs to see your Head.

says Ratcliffe to the condemned Hastings in *Richard III*. So *short shrift* means the brief space of time allowed for a criminal

---

* The clerk who tried to kill Henry III, 1238, was torn apart by horses; Rivers and Woodville were beheaded, as also (according to Carson) were Harrington, Mumford and Mallerie; Saunders was burnt.

to make his confession and to receive his absolution before execution. Thence it came to mean any brief respite, so that to *give short shrift to* is to make short work of. Indeed, the idiom can now actually take the form *make short shrift of*, as when *The Times* newspaper not long ago had, 'It would have been asking too much for the M.C.C. to make short shrift of their opponents a second time.'

But it was not every convict who demanded even the shortest shrift: to many it was an article of self-respect to *die hard*, which was their cant phrase for dying obdurate and impenitent, in particular showing no sign of fear or contrition at the gallows. It got its sense of physical resistance to the last from Colonel Inglis' exhortation to the 57th Regiment of Foot at the Battle of Albuhera, using no doubt language which they well understood: 'Fifty-seventh, die hard!' This usage survives. But the phrase came to be applied to those peers and their supporters in the constitutional crisis of 1910–11 who were prepared to oppose the Parliament Bill even to the point where the Liberal Government would have advised the creation of sufficient new peerages to carry the measure. In consequence, *diehard* now refers to any person or group of extremely tenacious conservatism; and to say that a belief, idea or custom *dies hard* means that it is resistant to the controversion of argument or evidence or to the movement of opinion.

But for those criminals who were not resolved to *die hard* means of grace were available. 'Like Theef and Parson in a *Tyburn*-cart,' wrote Dryden: he is referring to the melancholy two-hour journey by cart from Newgate Jail to the place of execution at Tyburn, now Marble Arch. Once there, the rope from the gallows was knotted round the victim's neck, and the cart was drawn forward from under his feet, leaving him dangling in the air. (But he was not the only one at risk: the chaplain was on one occasion himself nearly hanged in error by a drunken hangman.) Eighteenth-century literature abounds in references to criminals being *in the cart*. For example, in *The Beggar's Opera* Polly says of Macheath, 'Methinks I see him already in the cart, sweeter and more lovely than the nosegay in his hand.' And in 1774 Boswell wrote anonymously to *The London Chronicle* as part of his campaign to respite the capital sentence on John Reed:

'His case is very much similar to that of Madan, who was lately in the cart at Tyburn just going to be turned off. ...' Small wonder that *in the cart* came to mean in disastrous trouble.

I believe that two other current phrases derive from the Tyburn cart. First, *go west*, meaning disappear or perish. Although the dictionaries tend to ascribe its origin to the setting of the sun, it seems to me far more likely to have come from the fatal passage from Newgate to Tyburn. Not only does the flavour of the phrase appear more consonant with such a source, but one finds Greene writing in *The Art of Coney-Catching*, '. . . so long the foists [i.e., pickpockets] put their villanie in practice that Westward they goe, and solemnly make a rehearsall sermon at tiborne.' Secondly, to *cart* someone, meaning to get him into trouble by an act of disloyalty, or, sometimes, ineptitude – 'the carter carted', wrote Mr Bernard Levin of a contemporary politician not renowned for his steadfastness towards colleagues. This, I believe, derives its peculiar sense from the betrayals of the eighteenth-century thief-catchers. '"Tom Tipple" – a guzzling, soaking sot, who is always too drunk to stand himself, or to make others stand. A cart is absolutely necessary for him,' says Peachum (note the name) in *The Beggar's Opera*. When this work came to be plagiarised and burlesqued in *The Bow Street Opera*, the passage ran, 'He drinks so confoundedly that he is seldom able to *stand* to his business – He shall therefore be *carted*.' Mr Partridge, in his *Dictionary of the Underworld*, gives '*cart*, To convict (a person) of a crime . . . Obs. by 1889 if not, indeed, by 1840.' This undoubtedly represents the intermediate stage in the development of the expression, and led naturally to its contemporary sense.

It was, however, not only Newgate convicts who were put *in the cart*. In *Auberry* v. *Barton* the defendant had complained in the ecclesiastical court that the plaintiff had said to her, 'You are a brandy-nos'd whore, you stink of brandy.' The plaintiff moved in the King's Bench for an order prohibiting the ecclesiastical court from proceeding in the case, on the ground that 'they were words of heat, and did rather charge the defendant with intemperance than incontinency' – only the latter being the concern of the ecclesiastical court. Whether prohibition would lie in such circumstances had apparently been 'a brangled question'. Powell, J., explained that cases where the words were spoken in London had exceptionally been the subject of prohibition 'because an action [i.e., at common law] will lie for them in *London*, upon account, that a woman that is a whore in *London* may by the custom of *London* be carted'.* But in fact the custom was by no means confined to London. William Harrison in his *Description of England* (1574) says quite ubiquitously, '. . . harlots and their mates, by carting, ducking, and dooing of open penance in sheets, . . . are often put to rebuke'.† Moreover, the ancient name for the cucking stool, the instrument used in all parts of England for ducking offenders, was the *tumbrel*, in origin a dung-cart: and in some places the cucking stool seems to the end to have been a cart which finished the parade by being lowered into the water. As such it was peculiarly the punishment for scolds. Hence the passage in *The Taming of the Shrew*:

> *Baptista*   Leaue shall you haue to court her at your pleasure.
> *Gremio*   To cart her rather. She's too rough for mee.‡

Juries which delayed their verdicts were also liable to be carted round the circuit, as appears from a characteristically entertaining passage in Mr Megarry's *Miscellany at Law*; but this can hardly have occurred frequently enough to have contributed to the

---

* *E.g.*, 'Item the last day of July (and) the furst of August [1552] . . . a tayler of Fletstret and hys syster rydde in a carte abowte London, and bothe ther heddes shavynne, for avouttre, that he had ij. childerne by harre': *Chronicle of the Grey Friars*. There are frequent references in this work and in the contemporary *Diary of Henry Machyn* to both men and women being carted.

† See also the Court-book of Fyebridge, Norwich, for 1562, quoted by Francis Blomefield, *An Essay towards a Topographical History of Norfolk*: 'A Woman for Whoredom to ryde on a Cart . . . '; Picton, *Liverpool Municipal Records* for 1708, 'That Marg^t Justice be whipt the next day . . . att a cart's arse, and Ann Blevin and Jane Justice be carried in the cart at the same time from the Exchange to Jane Justice's house . . . ' and a similar entry relating to 1712.

‡ *Cf.* also *As You Like It* (III, ii, 107):
> They that reap must sheafe and binde
> Then to cart with Rosalinde.

development of the idiom *in the cart*, which rests adequately on the fate of whores, bawds, scolds and Newgate convicts.

Nevertheless, not every criminal making his way to death at Tyburn had the privilege of riding in a cart: in cases of high treason the offender was dragged to the gallows. In early times he was stripped and drawn at a horse's tail; later, 'by connivance at length ripened into law,' says Blackstone, 'a sledge or hurdle is allowed, to preserve the offender from the extreme torment of being dragged on the ground or pavement'. (But one may take leave to doubt whether the change was not due less to humanity than to a desire to deliver a living victim to the hangman.) This is the meaning of *drawn* when it precedes *hanged* in the formula 'drawn, hanged and quartered', as it generally does in legal and historical use. But where, as in the popular *hung, drawn and quartered* (meaning, facetiously, of a person, completely disposed of), *drawn* follows *hanged* or *hung*, it is to be referred to the disembowelling of the traitor; for it was part of the hideous ritual that his entrails had to be removed and burnt before his eyes while he was still living. This was specifically enjoined in the sentence, and its omission actually rendered the judgment a nullity. Thus, in *R. v. Walcott*, the accused had been attainted of treason and executed. His son sought to have the attainder reversed on the ground that the injunction as to the burning of the entrails had been omitted from the formal judgment: though success could not bring the father to life, it should at least secure the return of his estate, which would have been forfeited on attainder. The Crown argued that '*drawing, hanging*, and *quartering*, are the substantial parts of the judgment, and the other words are only *in terrorem*, and may therefore be omitted'. The court would have none of this. 'The giving of judgment against *malefactors* is part of the constitution of the government, therefore it was something extraordinary to affirm at THE BAR, that judgments in high treason were *discretionary*, which indeed is only a softer word for *arbitrary*. If that doctrine should once pass for law, then the courts which give judgments might make new punishments as they should think more suitable to the crimes; they might pronounce a *Jewish judgment*, "that the offender should be stoned to death"; or a *Turkish judgment*, "that he should be strangled"; or a *Roman judgment*, "that he should be murdered"; or a *French judgment*, "that he should be broken on the wheel"; all of which are contrary to the known laws of this realm.'

Such outlandish methods of capital execution have, however, made a significant contribution to English idiom:

bear one's cross
break a butterfly on a wheel
cast the first stone
die (*or* kill) by inches

throw one to the lions
wild horses wouldn't drag it
from (*or* out of) one

'This is simply breaking a butterfly on a wheel,' says Mr Valentine in *You Never Can Tell*, dazed after the verbal onslaught of the formidable Q.C., Mr Bohun. The direct source of the idiom is the opening passage of the direst piece of invective in the English language, the portrait of Lord Hervey in Pope's *Epistle to Arbuthnot*:

> Let *Sporus* tremble – 'What? that Thing of silk,
> *Sporus*, that mere white Curd of Ass's milk?
> Satire or Sense alas! can *Sporus* feel?
> Who breaks a Butterfly upon a wheel?'*

Its ultimate source evoked one of the most extraordinary *tours de force* in political philosophy – Joseph de Maistre's fantasy of the hangman as the pivot of society. After an appalling description of a criminal being broken on the wheel, he proceeds: 'The executioner comes down, blood-drenched. . . . The crowd parts in horror to let him through. . . . And yet on him depend all majesty, all power, all subordination. He is at once the abomination and the bond of human association. Take away from the world this incomprehensible agent, in that very moment order gives place to chaos, thrones fall into the abyss, society dissolves. God, who is the author of sovereignty, is author also of punishment.' Strange and morbid though this is, it is the very heart of de Maistre's political argument. Indeed, I have often felt that if I had to single out of all others one touchstone to assay the conservative temper in any social group, it would be this concept of

---

* Execution by breaking on the wheel has given the French an idiom which we have adopted untranslated – *coup de grâce*: this was the mercy-stroke over the victim's heart which ended his sufferings.

punishment as not primarily deterrent or even therapeutic, but as retributive – society's vindication of its code; though, curiously, its most convincing modern justification is from a figure generally claimed by the Left, the late Archbishop Temple.

Wild horses wouldn't drag it from one could refer to the original method of drawing a condemned traitor unclothed over the rough ground at the tail of a horse or of horses or, as I think more likely, to the actual tearing apart of the victim by horses urged in different directions. 'Reynawde . . . made Hernyer to be bound hys foure membres, that is to wyte feete and handes, to foure horses taylles And soo he was drawnen all quyck, and quartered in foure peces as a traytoure oughte to be doon unto', wrote Caxton. However, this was a translation from the French; and I have been able to trace only one sure instance in this country – that of the man who attempted the life of King Henry III in 1238. His punishment was clearly regarded as extraordinary and exemplary: Matthew Paris wrote, 'The King ordered him . . . to be torn limb from limb by horses at Coventry, a terrible example and lamentable sight to all who dared to plot such crimes.' But in France it was an eighteenth century of filigree and minuet which not only knew the wheel as an accepted instrument of capital sentence but actually witnessed the last execution of a criminal torn to pieces by wild horses. This was Damiens in 1757 for his attempt on the life of Louis XV. It is understandable that Dr Guillotin was greeted as a major contributor to human felicity.

So much for capital punishment. In his *Eirenarcha* William Lambarde wrote: 'Corporale punishment, . . . *not capital*, is of divers sorts allso, as cutting off the hand, eare, burning (or marking) the hand or face, boaring through the eare, whipping, imprisoning, stocking, setting on the Pillorie, or *Cucking* stoole, . . .' Most of these have yielded English idioms, which I list in an order following Lambarde's catalogue of punishments:

be willing to give one's ears for	throw off the shackles
as much as one's ears are worth	the iron enters (into) one's
whip (*or* lash) of scorpions	soul
kiss the rod	fast (*or* safe) as a thief in a
(make) a rod for one's own back	mill
a rod in pickle	? in durance vile

? rule with a rod of iron   lay (*or* have *or* clap) by the
hug one's chains   heels
fetters of gold   ? from pillar to post

A *whip of scorpions* comes from I Kings xii, 11, and II Chronicles x, 11, where it probably denotes a whip made of knotted cords or armed with plummets. When *Wycliffe's Bible* came to be revised in 1388 such an explanation was added: 'My fader beet 3ou with scourgis, Y schal bete 3ou with scorpiouns, that is, hard knottid roopis.' But the exegesis dropped out of subsequent translations; and a *whip* (or *lash*) *of scorpions* is used idiomatically, without consciousness of what is described, to denote specially sharp chastisement. It was Milton's use of the phrase which particularly gave currency to the expression:

> . . . to thy speed add wings,
> Least with a whip of Scorpions I pursue
> Thy lingring.

Rule with a rod of iron is another hebraism, coming from Revelation ii, 27: 'And he shall rule them [the nations] with a rod of yron.' But the allusion is to Psalm II, 9: 'Thou shalt break them with a rod of iron',* where it may refer metaphorically to the breaking of pottery jars with an iron bar.

The iron entered into his soul refers to the iron fetters with which prisoners were formerly loaded. It has an odd genesis. Verse 18 of Psalm 105 reads in the Authorised Version of 1611: '[Joseph] . . . Whose feete they hurt with fetters: he was layd in iron.' A translation of the Hebrew original runs literally 'his person entered into the iron'. The Vulgate mistakenly rendered this as '*ferrum pertransiit animam ejus*'. The *Great Bible* of 1539, following earlier English versions, translated this as 'the yron entred in to hys soule'. Though the error was corrected in the Authorised Version, it was the *Great Bible* version of the Psalms which was used for the Psalter of *The Book of Common Prayer* (1552), where it has remained unaffected by subsequent recensions. The phrase passed into figurative use to denote the impression made by affliction upon the very soul or inner being of the sufferer; so that Lloyd George could say of Sir John Simon, 'He has sat on the fence so long that the iron has entered his soul.'

* Similarly Rev. xix, 15.

As safe as a thief in a mill is first recorded in 1606; Ray included it amongst his proverbial similes; and it was sufficiently current in ordinary speech to have been gathered by Swift into his *Polite Conversation*. But Mr Eric Partridge in his recent edition of this last work states that in the nineteenth and twentieth centuries the phrase had become mostly rural. My own impression is that today, at any rate in the north country, it generally takes the form *fast as a thief in a mill*. It cannot refer to the treadmill, which was not invented and named until 1822. It must be derived from the curious mediæval use of mills as prisons, not a few millers actually holding by the serjeanty of guarding prisoners committed to their charge.

I have included *in durance vile*, now a humorous archaism meaning forced confinement, somewhat speculatively. It is apparent from the *Dialogus de Scaccario* that there were two types of imprisonment, one suitable for lords or knights and the other for baser men. The former was *libera custodia*, free custody, within the prison house but away from the common prisoners – a privilege which was reflected in the *Knights' Ward* of Newgate Jail. The other involved fettering or incarceration in a dungeon: but though Pollock and Maitland call it *durance vile*, I do not know that it was ever technically distinguished as such. On the other hand, the order of words suggests that the phrase goes back to an Anglo-Norman origin.*

The whipping-post and the pillory together influenced the development at least of *from pillar to post*, since in both Howell's and Ray's collections of proverbs the saying takes the form *from post to pillory*. Instances certainly occurred of offenders being both whipped and pilloried, were it necessary, which I doubt, to postulate such an actuality to engender the idiom. Alternatively, I suggest, the *post* could have been the one set up outside the sheriff's house, at which the offender might be handed over to the beadle or other executioner. But whether common law punishments were really the origin of the phrase is in dispute. It is first recorded in Lydgate's *The Assembly of the Gods*, written about 1420. Freewill, having enlisted in the army of Vice and been

---

* *Cf.* court-martial, attorney-general, malice prepense or aforethought, proof positive, etc. But the earliest usages noted in the *Oxford English Dictionary* are 1663 (*durance base*) and 1794 (*durance vile*). See p. 351 *infra*.

captured on its defeat by Virtue, is passed successively to Con-science, Humylyte, Confessyon, Contrycion and Satysfaccion:

> Thus fro poost to pylo*ur* was he made to daunce.
> And at the last he went forthe to Penaunce.

The idiom thus emerges fully-fledged in its modern connotation of harassment from one person or place to another, but disclosing no clear indication of its origin. Sir James Murray wrote that he had before him twenty-two quotations with the phrase from before 1700: seventeen had the idiom in what was clearly its original form, *from post to pillar*; and in all except one of the quotations before 1600 the governing verb was *toss*: these early uses suggested to him that the expression referred to some game of ball in which posts and pillars were used or came in the way. When the article in the *Oxford English Dictionary* came to be written under Murray's editorship, the origin of the phrase was ascribed to the tennis court. It is true that in many of the old tennis courts what correspond to the modern gallery posts were unquestionably pillars. But I have not been able to find that for the purpose of the game they were in English ever called pillars or indeed anything except posts. *Toss* could have been used as a term in tennis either as a translation of the French *balloter* or *peloter*, the knocking-up without following any of the rules of the game, or perhaps as equivalent to lobbing in contrast to 'forcing'. But in that the configuration of the court was not used, the former sense makes the concept of 'tossing' the ball from, say, gallery 'pillar' to dedans post seem inappropriate; and, as for the latter, the idea represented by the idiom would surely have been more significantly expressed by *forcing* than by *tossing* from *pillar to post*, if its origin is to be sought in this field.* Nor do I know of any other game which fits the bill. My own tentative surmise would be that *pillar* and *post* were both used originally in their common

---

* The coincidence that the *chase* plays a crucial part in the scoring at tennis and that the idiom often takes the form *chase from pillar to post* is a red herring. *Chase* in tennis is always a noun, and this form of the idiom is a late usage. But *Liberality and Prodigality* (published 1602), though standing alone, may be significant:

> Ech day, ech houre, yea, every minute tost,
> Like to a tennis ball, from piller to post.

sense of whipping-post. In their having thus no separate connotation the idiom would approximate in this regard not only to
its nearest English equivalent, 'from smoke to smother', but also
to its nearest French and German ones, since 'renvoyer de Ponce
à Pilate' is a not infrequent variant of the more usual 'renvoyer
de Caïphe à Pilate', while in German 'von Pontius zu Pilatus
schicken' is actually the primary phrase.

Except in the form of the *peine forte et dure*, by which a person
accused of felony who refused to plead on arraignment was
pressed ultimately to death, the common law of England did not
countenance the use of torture. It was, however, used in the prerogative and statutory courts, such as Star Chamber and High
Commission, once a prima facie case had been established against
an accused in order to elicit further and clinching evidence, or
even otherwise when urgent reasons of State seemed to justify
it. Hence –

be (*or* put *or* set, *etc*.) on the rack	put the screw on one
be racked with (*pain, etc.*)	put one under the screw
rack rent	screw something out of one
put on (*or* apply *or* turn) the	screw up (*rents, etc.*)
screw	an old screw†
a turn of the screw	

These refer, of course, to the *rack* and *thumbscrew*. A beautiful
prayer composed for landlords by Thomas Becon went: '. . . that
they remembrying them selues to be the tenauntes, may not racke
and stretch out the rentes of their houses and landes. . . .' Even
allowing that idioms are evolved by tenants rather than by landlords, it is an interesting sidelight on our social history that both
tortures should have given an idiomatic expression for what is on
the face of it no more than the exaction of the full economic rent
of a tenement. But there has rarely been a true market in real
property: in general, social pressures (caste on the side of the
landlord, family responsibilities against the tenant) and the
tardy response of supply to demand in this field have inevitably
produced distortions. These constitute the justification for the

† In the sense of a mean, miserly person, such as screws up rents. The
same expression for a broken-down horse cannot be from this source.

intervention of the State: though this is not to deny that some of its manifestations have accentuated the distortions by further inhibiting supply, or that wise statecraft would not limit itself to counterbalancing uneconomic pressures and thus and by other means seek to galvanise the market.

Corporal punishments from other penal systems have given us:

relegate to	? no room (*or* space) to swing a cat
in retaliation (for)	run the gauntlet
an eye for an eye	? haul (? *or* call *or* bring) over the
work like a galley slave	coals
chained to one's oar	

'A whole chapter might be written on the numerous English words whose meanings can be traced back to the usages of Roman law,' stated Owen Barfield. Two from the Roman penal codes have given rise to English idioms. *Relegatio* was a form of banishment, milder than *deportatio*. Unlike the latter it did not involve loss of citizenship or property, nor was the exile under military surveillance. Often, moreover, it did not mean confinement to a specific place (such as the dreaded Sardinia or, worse, the oasis in the Libyan desert – *quasi in insulam* – of the *deportatio*), but merely exclusion from a particular area; it could, for example, take the form of exile to a prescribed distance from Rome, leaving the offender otherwise free to choose his abode: nor was it necessarily for life. Originally in English *relegate* and *relegation* were used in this sense of banishment or exile.

In retaliation (for) derives from a more archaic stage in the development of Roman penal law, the *lex talionis* – the provision of the XII Tables that the criminal was to suffer the same hurt as he had done his victim. Such a concept is a feature of many primitive systems of law. Its presence in the ancient Jewish code has given rise to the idiom *an eye for an eye*,* though the actual wording comes from the reference in the Authorised Version of the Gospel according to St Matthew: 'Yee haue heard that it hath beene said, An eie for an eie, and a tooth for a tooth. . . .'

The labour of a *galley slave chained to his oar* was apparently

---

* ' . . . life *shall goe* for life, eye for eye, tooth for tooth, hand for hand, foot for foot' (Deut. xix, 21); see also Ex. xxi, 23–25; Lev. xxiv, 17–20.

already proverbial when Jean Marteilhe wrote his *Memoirs of a Protestant* (translated so vividly by Oliver Goldsmith), describing the hardships and cruelties of the galleys, to which he had been condemned in 1700 merely for trying as a Huguenot to escape from persecution in France after the Revocation of the Edict of Nantes. Service in the galleys was never an English punishment – indeed, the galley was not used in the British navy or marine after the Middle Ages, ships propelled solely by sailpower having a clear tactical advantage except in flat calm and operating close to base. But other powers continued to employ galleys, especially in the Mediterranean, where the conditions for their use were more favourable; and it became the practice to sentence condemned criminals to row in them. In France, even after the galleys ceased to operate as war vesssels, they were still, as hulks moored in the harbour of Toulon, used for the reception of convicts; and the name *galérien* continued to be given to all convicts. So terrible were the associations of the term in folk memory that it was a characteristic reform of the French Revolution to alter it to *forçat* – yet another tribute to the almost magical power ascribed to words, so that a change of terminology is somehow held to effect a change in the character of the object described or at least, hopefully, in the general public attitude towards it.*

Nautical discipline is also invoked as the source of the idiom *no room to swing a cat*, which is popularly ascribed to the use of the *cat-o'-nine-tails* on board ship, and this explanation has received the distinguished stamp of Mr Partridge's approval. But it presents difficulties. Although the use of the term *cat-o'-nine-tails* can be traced back to 1665, *cat* is not found as its abbreviation earlier than 1788 (although it is, of course, the sort of usage likely to have been circulating in popular speech for some time before it became recorded). But *not space enough to swing a cat in* was noted as 'a vulgar saying' as early as 1665; and it must, moreover, be linked with the contemporary proverbial phrase 'a

---

* *Cf.* the replacement of *Whig* and *Tory* by *Liberal* and *Conservative*; the 18th century *madman* by *lunatic* and then in our own time by *of unsound mind* and *mentally ill*; and *negro* by *coloured*; or the entitling of a measure 'The Strengthening of Marriage Bill' which permits the spouse solely responsible for the break-up of a marriage to divorce the innocent partner.

conscience wide enough to swing a cat in', where the *cat-o'-nine-tails*, even if it were already known as a *cat*, would seem quite inappropriate. An alternative origin has been suggested in the barbarous sport of suspending a cat in a bag or leather bottle for arrows to be shot at ('. . . hang me in a bottle like a Cat, & shoot at me,' says Benedick in *Much Ado About Nothing*): but the pastime does not appear ever to have been called 'swinging' a cat. To my mind the most likely origin of the phrase was simply an ordinary domestic cat being swung round by its tail: from time immemorial boys have, alas, done no less.

There is no doubt, on the other hand, that *run the gauntlet* originated in a military (also, occasionally, naval) punishment, in which the culprit, stripped to the waist, ran between two rows of men who struck at him with sticks or knotted cords. *Gauntlet* here has nothing to do with the term for a glove: it was originally *gantlope*, corrupted from the Swedish *gatlopp*, literally a course down a lane, being a compound of *gata*, lane, and *lopp*, running. The adoption of the punishment by many European forces was no doubt a reflection of the prestige of the Swedish army in the Thirty Years' War. *Run the gauntlet* became a proverbial phrase for passing through any critical ordeal. Probably the fact that the punishment is still practised and so called by schoolboys has kept alive in the idiom the sense of being hounded from all sides.

The *Oxford English Dictionary* (1893) considered the idioms *bring* and *fetch over the coals* as obsolete, but *call over the coals* as still current. Dixon (1891) cited the idioms with both *call* and *bring* as still current. I would myself have said that none of these is in use today, *haul over the coals* being the exclusive usage – meaning to call to account and convict, or to reprimand. The *Oxford English Dictionary* states that the phrase was originally in reference to the treatment of heretics. Brewer is more explicit; he says that it was a very common punishment to haul Jews over the coals of a slow fire if they resisted a call for money from king or baron. In *Ivanhoe* Front-de-Boeuf threatens such a punishment to Isaac of York, and Cardinal Allen wrote: '*S. Augustine* that knewe best how to fetche an heretike ouer the coles.' But the punishment does not appear to have been countenanced by any law. The Jews were virtually villeins if not serfs of the king, and it would have been an interference with royal rights for any subject to extort from or ill-treat them. (But of course Jews were ill-treated and pillaged whenever subjects got out of hand.) The Exchequer of the Jews has no record of *hauling over the coals*. Nor have our tribunals of exclusive jurisdiction over heretics, the Church courts.

For side by side with the penal codes administered in this country in the local, common law and prerogative courts was a wholly separate system enforced for the salvation of souls in the ecclesiastical courts. This was as much a part of the law of England as was the matrimonial or testamentary jurisprudence of these courts; though, having passed more completely into history, it is not always recognised as such – hence such assertions as that bigamy was not a crime until 1603 or incest until 1908 or adultery at all except for a few years under the Commonwealth. On the contrary, it was the constant interference of the Court Christian with these and similar pleasures that caused its official, the summoner, to be so execrated a figure in mediæval England,* and its most active judge, the archdeacon, to be the subject of anxious speculation as to whether it was possible for him to be saved. The extent and nature of the latter's jurisdiction can be gauged from the opening of Chaucer's *The Freres Tale*:

> Whilom ther was dwellinge in my contree
> An erchedeken, a man of heigh degree,
> That boldely dide execucioun
> In punisshinge of fornicacioun,
> Of wicchecraft, and eek of bauderye,
> Of diffamacioun, and avoutrye,
> Of chirche-reves, and of testaments,
> Of contractes, and lakke of sacraments,
> And eek of many another maner cryme
> Which nedeth nat rehercen at this tyme;
> Of usure, and of symonye also.
> But certes, lechours dide he grettest wo.

As for the punishments for such offences, some, such as

---

* Also, of course, for his venality. In Chaucer, *The Frères Tale*, a summoner disavows his calling –

> He dorste nat, for verray filthe and shame,
> Saye that he was a somnour, for the name.

fining, whipping and imprisonment (but this last only for clerics, not laymen), were similar to those for crimes at common law. The penalties peculiar to the ecclesiastical law have given us by way of idiom—

do penance for	(stand in *or* wear) sackcloth and
give short shrift to*	ashes
make short shrift of*	(sit on the *or* a) stool of repentance
wear (*or* stand in) a white sheet	curse with (*or* by) bell, book and candle

Of the ecclesiastical penalties the commonest was that the offender should parade publicly clad *in a white sheet.*

> With taper burning, shrouded in a sheet,
> Three days a row, to passe the open streete,
> Bare leg'd and barefoote . . .

was the fate of Dame Eleanor Cobham, Duchess of Gloucester, in 1441. Though this is sometimes spoken of as peculiarly the punishment for adultery or fornication, that is only because those offences were of such frequent cognisance in the ecclesiastical courts. The Duchess's offences were witchcraft, necromancy and heresy (not the treason with which she was also charged, since she had 'submitted her only to the correction of the bishops'). Machyn described the white sheet penances of 'a temporall man that had ij wyeffes' and of a bigamous priest. Incest, too, was held to be thus sufficiently punished – but then the canonists had so multiplied the prohibited degrees of relationship that incest can hardly have carried the horror which it has had for most peoples at most times. Working on the sabbath or a holiday was a *white sheet* offence; and a breach of sanctuary was so punished in 1313 (though accompanied by a beating). The *white sheet* was also the appropriate penalty for defamation: Machyn himself thus did penance for retailing gossip that the French Protestant Minister, Veron, 'was taken with a wenche'; and in Durham it seems that it would have been a *white sheet* offence to say that a person was a Scot. As late as 1797 a man *did penance in a white sheet* in Lambeth Parish Church for calling 'the domestic female of a neighbouring Baker, by an improper name'; and apparently

* Already discussed, pp. 270, 271 above.

the custom subsisted well into the nineteenth century in the Isle of Man. *Stand in a white sheet* therefore naturally signifies the expression of contrition for an acknowledged fault.*

> When *Israel's* Daughters mourn'd their past Offences,
> They dealt in *Sackcloth*, and turn'd *Cynder-Wenches* . . .

wrote Pope. *Sackcloth*, as the penitential (or mourning) garb of the ancient Jews was a fabric of rough camels' or goats' hair. (This was, presumably, what St John the Baptist wore.) Sprinkling or daubing with *ashes* has been a widespread sign of mourning or contrition† – holy men in the East are still to be seen so embellished. *Ashes* have possessed magical properties for many peoples: as a penitential mode possibly they were, and are, also intended as a reminder of mortality, the body being whitened so that it resembles a corpse; or they may symbolise the subduing of earthly passions ('pallid ashes follow fire'); or they may merely constitute self-mortification by discomfort or disfiguring – or, of course, something of each of these concepts. Mortification of the penitent with *sackcloth and ashes* was enjoined by the canon law as part of the rite of solemn penance; and Ayliffe (1726) cites it as if it were not only part of the ecclesiastical law of England, but actually practised here. However, I have not come across any historical instance. As a modern idiom *sackcloth and ashes* is virtually interchangeable with *a white sheet*.

In Scotland the penitent was required to make his public profession of repentance while sitting on a special stool or pew placed in a prominent position in the kirk. This was called the *stool of repentance*.‡ That there was a similar custom at one time in England appears from 'a mery tale' told by Sir Thomas More: '[A] pore man . . . had founde ye priest ouer famylier with his

---

* Although the test of idiom is usage only, I cannot but think that Mr Harold Wilson made a verbal slip when he said, 'Lord Carrington comes out . . . in a white sheet,' meaning he had been completely exculpated by the investigations of the tribunal inquiring into the Vassall case.

† *Cf.* Ash Wednesday, especially the Roman Catholic ritual of blessing the ashes.

‡ Also *cutty-stool* (cutty meaning short) or, in Burns, who himself sat on it, *creepie-chair* (creepie meaning low stool); see 'The Rantin Dog the Daddie O't'.

wife, and bycause he spake it a brode and coulde not proue it, the priest sued him before ye bishoppes offyciall for dyffamatyon, where the pore man vpon paine of cursynge was commaunded that in his paryshe chyrch, he should vpon ye sondaye, at high masse time stande up & sai, mouth thou lyest. Whereupon for fulfillinge of his penance, vp was the pore soule set in a pew, that ye people might wonder on him and hyre what he sayd. And there all allowed (when he had rehersyd what he had reportyd by the prieste) that he sett his handys on his mouth, & said, mouth mouth thou lyest. And by and by therevpon he set his hand vpon both his eyen & sayd, but eyen, eyen quod he, by ye masse ye lye not a whitte.' Though I cannot find that in England the penitential pew was ever called a *stool of repentance*, by Sheridan's time this had already become an English idiom.*

The poor man in More's story was compelled to obedience 'vpon paine of cursynge'. The same expression is used in this connection in *The Freres Tale* –

'Up peyne of cursing, loke that thou be
To-morn bifore the erchedeknes knee,
Tanswere to the court of certeyn thinges,'

says the Sompnour to the poor widow. For the *curse* meant excommunication, and was the primary sanction for the enforcement of the judgments of the Church and her courts. There were two degrees. The minor was a comparatively mild affair, excluding the offender from the sacraments until he had repented and been absolved by the imposer of the curse. But the major excommunication – the *curse with bell, book and candle* – was a much more serious matter, from which, unless the excommunicate was on the point of death, he could only be absolved by the bishop. This major excommunication could be pronounced against a particular named offender or against the unknown perpetrator of an ascertained crime. The Durham courts provide characteristic examples. On the one hand excommunication was pronounced on two separate occasions against Ranulph de Nevill,

* *The School for Scandal*, 1777 (II, iii):
    Rowley . . . he has been married only seven months.
    Sir Oliver Surface. Then he has been just half a year on the stool of repentance!

first for making away with a suit of armour part of the estate of an intestate, and later for incestuous adultery with his own daughter. On the other hand it was promulgated against whoever had stolen some merlins which had disappeared from the bishop's woodland and against persons unknown for cutting down an ash-tree in a churchyard. (It was, of course, this latter type of curse which proved the downfall of the Jackdaw of Rheims.) Moreover, three or four times a year anathema was proclaimed generally against all who had committed a long list of offences against Church or State – the Commination Service of *The Book of Common Prayer* is a pale reflection of the awful rite. Every effort was made that it should inspire terror. In the presence of the full congregation at high mass the book was brought to the celebrant, and the cross was elevated before his eyes as he read out the terrible sentence: '. . . that thei ben acursed of God and holy cherche, fro the sole of the foot unto the crowne of the head, slepinge and wakynge, sythynge and standinge, and in all their wordes and werkes, . . . for to dwelle in the peynes of hell for ever withouten end: fiat, fiat. Amen.' The bell, wont to proclaim the Saviour present in bread and wine, now tolls to pronounce eternal exile from His grace; and the priests extinguish the flames of their uplifted candles as the soul of the offender is given over to the powers of darkness. He was thenceforward a spiritual leper, to be avoided by all humans upon pain of being themselves excommunicated. No one could trade with him, or eat with him, or pray with him, or even speak privately with him. He could perform no legal act; so that although he could be sued, he could himself bring no action to vindicate his own interests. If all this still failed to compel his submission, after forty days the Bishop could so signify to the Chancery (though in practice far longer was usually allowed to lapse); and a writ would then issue to the sheriff to take the excommunicate into custody, where he remained until he was finally ready to show proper contrition and compliance.

The following idioms come from various past terms for punishments –

on (*or* upon *or* under) pain of	take (the) forfeit (of)
pains and penalties	in forfeit of

pay the penalty (of)   make amends
on (*or* upon *or* under) penalty of   go (*or* bring *or* run *or* come) to
pay (the) forfeit   rack (*or* wrack) and ruin

The earliest recorded use of the word *pain* in English was in the sense (now obsolete except in the idioms listed above) of a punishment, penalty or fine. In Boswell's time 'the pains of law' was still used in Scottish indictments in this sense: John Reed's for sheepstealing ended '. . . you ought to be punished with the pains of law, to deter others from committing the like in time coming.' *Under pain of* is a translation of the French *sous peine de*, itself from the Latin *sub poena*; *on pain of* from *sur peine de*. Similarly, the earliest use of *penalty* was as a punishment imposed for breach of the criminal law. It is tempting to relate the phrase *pay the penalty* to the Anglo-Saxon system of *wergild*, the legal tariff of money values according to a man's rank; but *penalty* is not recorded before 1500, and probably has an Anglo-French origin.

Forfeit comes via old French from the mediæval Latin *foris factum*, something done outside (the law), therefore a trespass or, thence, a fine for such. In its earliest use in English it meant a crime, transgression, misdeed or wilful injury. But it was from the secondary meaning, fine, that the idioms listed above and all the modern connotations of the word have derived. *Make amends* is from the Old French *amendes*, the plural of *amende*, reparation.*
In English it was from the first a collective singular, meaning originally money paid or things given to make reparation for any injury or offence. (It was used as a translation of the Latin *poenae*, a fine.) Thence it came to mean reparation, restitution, compensation or satisfaction. Originally the primary sense of *wrack* was retributive punishment; and no doubt it was the severity of the penal code which brought the word to its modern meaning, destruction – though the phrase *rack* (or *wrack*) *and ruin* is typically idiomatic in that no separate significance is really attached to the first word in either usage, which indeed are now hardly to be found in this sense apart from the idioms.

Finally some miscellaneous idioms relating to the penal law

---

* Note also our adoption of the French idiom *amende honorable*, from the same legal source.

which do not fall within any of the categories so far considered –

let (or make) the punishment fit   let off with a caution
    the crime   (without) benefit of clergy
on probation

The expression *let the punishment fit the crime* has been given an ineffaceably comic colour by its use in *The Mikado*. But it represents a long-held and widespread view of the proper approach to punishment: *noxiae poena par esto* (let the punishment fit the offence). The concept inspired not only the *lex talionis* but also the 'characteristic' punishments – castration for rape or adultery, cutting off the tongue for false accusation or the hand for forgery, and so on – which more sophisticated times preferred. The retributive theory of punishment long held exclusive sway. 'In cases which outrage the normal feelings of the community to a great degree,' wrote Fitzjames Stephen in 1883, 'the feeling of moral indignation and desire for revenge which is excited in the minds of decent people is, I think, deserving of legitimate satisfaction.'

On probation is not given in the *Oxford English Dictionary*. But it is unquestionably a current idiom. Its legal origin differentiates its meaning from 'on approval' (an idiom from commerce), since it is exclusively used with reference to living subjects and bears the sense that the subject has got actively to prove himself, making good for previous unsatisfactory or doubtful performance.

Benefit of clergy was originally the right of immunity from punishment for felony by a secular court enjoyed by those in holy orders.* It was modified and extended to allow any barely literate person who could read his 'neck-verse' to escape with a burnt hand (or, later, transportation) on a first conviction for felony, and in the end even the 'neck-verse' was dispensed with: as such the rule was a valuable if crude mitigation of the savagery of the penal code before the nineteenth-century abolition of capital punishment for most felonies. In the seventeenth and eighteenth centuries, however, certain statutory offences were declared to be *without benefit of clergy*. Today that phrase is used with reference to the marriage service. It is the title of one of

* The immunity was claimed on the strength of I Chron. xvi, 22, and Ps. cv, 15: 'Touch not mine anointed . . . '

Kipling's most attractive short stories, where it means cohabitation without being married. The priest who married the Duke of Windsor and Mrs Simpson wrote, 'It was God's will that I give benefit of clergy to the Duke and Duchess of Windsor': here it refers to the wedding service in an Anglican church, since they could of course have been validly married in a register office or nonconformist chapel.

Judicial Restraint

Name and Dignity

[The Resolution, delivered by Chief Justice Crewe in Parliament, concerning the Earldom of Oxford: Chief Baron Walter, Justices Dodridge and Yelverton, and Baron Trevor 'advising with him together therein'.*

These judges were called in to advise the House of Lords in a peerage claim when the Earl of Oxford died without issue. The answer given was contained in the following memorable speech.]

My Lords,

This great and weighty cause, incomparable to any other that hath happened in any time, requires great deliberation, and solid and mature judgment to determine it; and therefore I wish all the judges of England had heard it (being a case fit for all) to the end we all together might have given our humble advice to your Lordships herein.

Here is represented unto your Lordships *certamen honoris*, and as I may well say, *illustris honoris*, illustrious honour.

I heard a great peer of this realm and a learned say, when he lived, there was no King in Christendom had such a subject as Oxford.

He came in with the Conqueror Earl of Gwynes; shortly after the Conquest made Great Chamberlain of England, above five hundred years ago, by Henry the First the Conquerour's son, brother to Rufus; by Mawd the Empress, Earl of Oxford, confirmed and approved by Henry Fitz Empress, Henry II *Alberico Comiti*, so earl before.

This great honour, this high and noble dignity hath continued ever since in the remarkable sirname of De Vere, by so many ages, descents and generations as no other kingdom can produce such a peer in one and the self same name and title.

I find in all this length of time but two attainders of this noble

* (1626) 82 E.R. 50, 53.

family, and those in stormy and tempestuous times, when the Government was unsettled, and the kingdom in competition.

I have laboured to make a covenant with my self, that affection may not press upon judgment; for I suppose there is no man that hath any apprehension of gentry or nobleness, but his affection stands to the continuance of so noble a name and house and would take hold of a twig or twine-thread to uphold it; and yet time hath his revolution, there must be a period and an end of all temporal things, *finis rerum*, an end of names and dignities, and whatsoever is terrene, and why not of De Vere?

For where is Bohun? where's Mowbray? where's Mortimer? &c, Nay, which is more, and most of all, where is Plantagenet? they are intombed in the urnes and sepulchres of mortality.

And yet let the name and dignity of De Vere stand so long as it pleaseth God. This case stands upon many parts. Subtile disputants may perturb the best judgments; there have been many thick and dark fogs and mists raised in the face of this cause.

But *magna est veritas et prevalet*, truth lets in the sun to scatter and disperse them.*

* These last two paragraphs are omitted from the version in the English Reports, but appear in Collins's *Baronies by Writ*.

Right to be Heard

*Judgments in The King v. The Chancellor, Masters
and Scholars of the University of Cambridge**

[The principle that every person has a right to be heard in his
defence, even before domestic tribunals, was established in
the case of Richard Bentley who in 1718 had been deprived
of his degrees of B.A., B.D. and D.D. by the University of
Cambridge.

A member of the University, Conyers Middleton, D.D., had
claimed before the University Court a debt owed by Bentley of
£4 6s od, which was the fee exacted by Bentley for the D.D.
degree. The beadle was thereupon ordered to compel Bentley
to appear before the Court. When served with the summons,
Bentley contemptuously said that the process was 'illegal and
unstatutable', and that he would not obey it. He took the summons
out of the Beadle's hand, saying that the Vice-Chancellor of the
University was not his judge, *et quod praed' procancellarius
stulte egit.*

At the next hearing, and without notice that he was also being
charged with contempt of court, Bentley was suspended. According to custom, the Vice-Chancellor summoned a congregation of those members of the University who had the sole right
to take away degrees for 'contumacy or reasonable cause'.
At that meeting the Vice-Chancellor related the whole case,
whereupon Bentley was deprived of his degrees. Bentley challenged the University's decision in the courts of law, and his
degrees were restored.

Richard Bentley (1662-1742) was a great scholar and a friend
of Wren, Locke and Newton. In 1700 he was appointed
Master of Trinity College. He ruled the College and the Fellows

* (1723) 1 Str. 557.

despotically, and several attempts were made to remove him. In 1714 he was about to be dismissed by Bishop Moore of Ely for 'petty encroachments' of the Fellows' rights. But the Bishop died before giving the judgment, which was later found among his papers, Queen Anne's death helping to divert attention. There were further disputes with a Dr Colbatch in 1728, concerning Bentley's despotic rule. In 1734 there was a new trial by the Bishop of Ely, and Bentley was sentenced to be removed. This could only be done by the Vice-Master of the College who refused to so act. Actions in the years 1734–38 for a writ of mandamus failed

    (i) to compel the Vice-Master to act;
    (ii) to compel the Bishop of Ely to compel the Vice-Master to act; and
    (iii) to compel the Bishop of Ely to act.

Bentley died in 1742, still Master of Trinity. He is buried in the Chapel, but his tombstone does not record the fact that he was Master. While Master, he had built an observatory and a chemical laboratory; he was responsible for much of the interior of the Master's Lodge as it exists today.]

THIS IS A case of great consequence, not only as to the gentleman who is deprived, but likewise as it will affect all the members of the university in general. . . . It is the glory and happiness of our excellent constitution, that to prevent any injustice no man is to be concluded by the first judgment; but that if he apprehends himself to be aggrieved, he has another court to which he can resort for relief; for this purpose the law furnishes him with appeals, with writs of error and false judgment: and lest in this particular case the party should be remediless, it was become absolutely necessary for this court to require the university to lay the state of their proceedings before us; that if they have erred, the party may have right done him, or if they have acted according to the rules of law, that their acts may be confirmed.

The university ought not to think it any diminution of their honour, that their proceedings are examinable in a superior court. I am sure this Court, which is superior to the university, thinks it none; for my own part I can say, it is a consideration of great comfort to me, that if I do err my judgment is not conclusive to the party, but my mistake will be rectified, and so injustice not be done.

As to the proceeding against Dr Bentley, it must be agreed that the Vice-Chancellor had conusance of the cause, and so the suit was well instituted against him. I must likewise take the process to compel an appearance to be regular, being averred to be according to the course of that court.

As to Dr Bentley's behaviour upon being served with the process, I must say it was very indecent, and I can tell him if he had said as much of our process we would have laid him by the heels for it: he is not to arraign the justice of the proceedings out of court before an officer, who has no power to examine it.

When he said the Vice-Chancellor *stulte egit*, it was what he might have been bound over for to his good behaviour; but I believe it is also established, that such behaviour will not warrant a suspension or deprivation.

He said he would not obey, but *non constat* but he thought better of it afterwards, and did appear.

I cannot think the evidence of this contempt was sufficient: it does not appear to have been upon oath, as it should have been.

But be these matters how they will, yet surely he could never be deprived without notice. I do not observe but it is a total deprivation, and not temporary only, as was said at the bar.

As to the proceedings before the congregation, it does not appear they reheard the matter any otherwise than by the relation of the Vice-Chancellor. They should have adjudged all the facts again, and have averred, that the deprivation was for them; whereas *his de causis* they deprived him, amounts to no more than that the Vice-Chancellor told them so.

The Vice-Chancellor's authority ought to be supported for the sake of keeping peace within the university; but then he must act according to law, which I do not think he has done in this case.

MR JUSTICE FORTESCUE: A deprivation can never be the proper punishment for a contempt, because it cannot hold in the case of undergraduates. I think the behaviour of Dr Bentley was a contempt, for which he might be bound to his good behaviour, as it was out of court.

There is another thing considerable in this case, whether upon any account the university can deprive a man of his degrees; because he is in from the Crown, whence the power originally flows.

Besides, the objection for want of notice can never be got over. The laws of God and man both give the party an opportunity to make his defence, if he has any. I remember to have heard it observed by a very learned man upon such an occasion, that even God himself did not pass sentence upon Adam, before he was called upon to make his defence. Adam (says God) where art thou? Hast thou not eaten of the tree, whereof I commanded thee that thou shouldest not eat? And the same question was put to Eve also.

Common Law

Dissenting opinion in Southern Pacific Co. v. Jensen*

[American lawyers have long wrestled with the problem of the parallel existence within each State of both State Courts and Federal Courts. Does this mean that the Common Law, which varies widely from State to State, also varies between the two sets of courts within each State?

Historically, the leading opinion on this question was delivered in 1842 by that great American lawyer, Mr Justice Story, who held that in case of conflict 'the general principles of commercial jurisprudence' applied, and that the Federal Courts were better qualified to determine 'the general law' (or the common law) than the Courts of New York. What was this 'general law'? It could not be the command of a sovereign power: that, presumably, was the State of New York, the Federal Government having no power to make laws about ordinary intra-state commerce. Rather it was a law to be derived from reason, from general principles available to all judges.

Mr Justice Holmes' dissent from this view of twin sovereignty was vindicated twenty years later when his regular co-dissenter, Mr Justice Brandeis, handed down the opinion of the Supreme Court in *Erie R. R.* v. *Tompkins*, 304 U.S. 64 (1938).]

THE SOUTHERN Pacific Company has been held liable under the statutes of New York for an accidental injury happening upon a gang-plank between a pier and the company's vessel and causing the death of one of its employees. The company not having insured as permitted, the statute may be taken as if it simply imposed a limited but absolute liability in such a case. The short question is whether the power of the State to regulate the liability in that place and to enforce it in the State's own courts

---

* 244 U.S. 205, 218 (1917).

is taken away by the conferring of exclusive jurisdiction of all civil causes of admiralty and maritime jurisdiction upon the courts of the United States.

There is no doubt that the saving to suitors of the right of a common-law remedy leaves open the common-law jurisdiction of the state courts, and leaves some power of legislation at least, to the States. The liability created by the New York act ends in a money judgment, and the mode in which the amount is ascertained, or is to be paid, being one that the State constitutionally might adopt, cannot matter to the question before us if any liability can be imposed that was not known to the maritime law. And as such a liability can be imposed where it was unknown not only to the maritime but to the common law, I can see no difference between one otherwise constitutionally created for death caused by accident and one for death due to fault. Neither can the statutes limiting the liability of owners affect the case. Those statutes extend to non-maritime torts, which of course are the creation of state law. They are paramount to but not inconsistent with the new cause of action. However, as my opinion stands on grounds that equally would support a judgment for a maritime tort not ending in death, with which admiralty courts have begun to deal, I will state the reasons that satisfy my mind.

No doubt there sometimes has been an air of benevolent gratuity in the admiralty's attitude about enforcing state laws. But of course there is no gratuity about it. Courts cannot give or withhold at pleasure. If the claim is enforced or recognized it is because the claim is a right, and if a claim depending upon a state statute is enforced it is because the State had constitutional power to pass the law. Taking it as established that a State has constitutional power to pass laws giving rights and imposing liabilities for acts done upon the high seas when there were no such rights or liabilities before, what is there to hinder its doing so in the case of a maritime tort? Not the existence of an inconsistent law emanating from a superior source, that is, from the United States. There is no such law. The maritime law is not a *corpus juris* – it is a very limited body of customs and ordinances of the sea. The nearest to anything of the sort in question was the rule that a seaman was entitled to recover the expenses necessary for his cure when the master's negligence caused his hurt. The maritime law gave him no more. *The Osceola*, 189 U.S. 158, 175. One may affirm with the sanction of that case that it is an innovation to allow suits in the admiralty by seamen to recover damages for personal injuries caused by the negligence of the master and to apply the common-law principles of tort.

Now, however, common-law principles have been applied to sustain a libel by a stevedore *in personam* against the master for personal injuries suffered while loading a ship. From what source do these new rights come? The earliest case relies upon 'the analogies of the municipal law'—sufficient evidence of the obvious pattern, but inadequate for the specific origin. I recognise without hesitation that judges do and must legislate, but they can do so only interstitially; they are confined from molar to molecular motions. A common-law judge could not say I think the doctrine of consideration a bit of historical nonsense and shall not enforce it in my court. No more could a judge exercising the limited jurisdiction of admiralty say I think well of the common-law rules of master and servant and propose to introduce them here *en bloc*. Certainly he could not in that way enlarge the exclusive jurisdiction of the District Courts and cut down the power of the States. If admiralty adopts common-law rules without an act of Congress it cannot extend the maritime law as understood by the Constitution. It must take the rights of the parties from a different authority, just as it does when it enforces a lien created by a State. The only authority available is the common law or statutes of a State. For from the often repeated statement that there is no common law of the United States, and from the principles recognised in *Atlantic Transport Co.* v. *Imbrovekt* having been unknown to the maritime law, the natural inference is that in the silence of Congress this court has believed the very limited law of the sea to be supplemented here as in England by the common law, and that here that means, by the common law of the State. So far as I know, the state courts have made this assumption without criticism or attempt at revision from the beginning to this day. Even where the admiralty has unquestioned jurisdiction the common law may have concurrent authority and the state courts concurrent power. The invalidity of state attempts to create a remedy for maritime contracts or torts, parallel to that in the admiralty, is immaterial to the present point.

The common law is not a brooding omnipresence in the sky but the articulate voice of some sovereign or quasi-sovereign that can be identified; although some decisions with which I have disagreed seem to me to have forgotten the fact. It always is the law of some State, and if the District Courts adopt the common law of torts, as they have shown a tendency to do, they thereby assume that a law not of maritime origin and deriving its authority in that territory only from some particular State of this Union also governs maritime torts in that territory—and if the common law, the statute law has at least equal force, as the discussion in *The Osceola* assumes. On the other hand the refusal of the District Courts to give remedies coextensive with the common law would prove no more than that they regarded their jurisdiction as limited by the ancient lines—not that they doubted that the common law might and would be enforced in the courts of the States as it always has been. This Court has recognised that in some cases different principles of liability would be applied as the suit should happen to be brought in a common-law or admiralty court. But hitherto it has not been doubted authoritatively, so far as I know, that even when the admiralty had a rule of its own to which it adhered, the state law, common or statute, would prevail in the courts of the State. Happily such conflicts are few.

It might be asked why, if the grant of jurisdiction to the courts of the United States imports a power in Congress to legislate, the saving of a common-law remedy, i.e., in the state courts, did not import a like if subordinate power in the States. But leaving that question on one side . . . it is too late to say that the mere silence of Congress excludes the statute or common law of a State from supplementing the wholly inadequate maritime law of the time of the Constitution, in the regulation of personal rights, and I venture to say that it never has been supposed to do so, or had any such effect.

Lawyers as Judges

Judgment in Rex v. *Chondi and another**

[Mr Justice Krause must be unique among the judiciary of the English-speaking world in having served a prison sentence in his early days. While in England on parole, having been taken prisoner during the Boer War, Krause was convicted of an attempt to incite someone to commit murder. Krause had been incensed by something written in the *Pall Mall Gazette* by a Mr Douglas Forster who had strongly advocated that the war in South Africa should in future be conducted on the lines that all members of the Republican forces in the field should no longer be treated as belligerents but as bandits and robbers; and should, if captured, be taken out and shot. Krause wrote to a fellow Afrikaner telling him that his duty was to deal with Forster, who besides being a correspondent was on the staff of the General Officer Commanding the Imperial forces at Johannesburg. Krause was sentenced to two years' imprisonment. When he had served his sentence he was disbarred from practice at the English Bar, which he had been doing at the time of his offence. The Benchers of his Inn of Court decreed that he was unworthy to continue as a member of the English Bar.

After the war all those who had been advocates of the High Court of the former South African Republic had to reapply for admission to the Bar. The judges in the Transvaal Supreme Court and in the courts of the Orange Free Colony, who exercised the disciplinary powers of the profession, permitted Krause's readmission. As Sir James Rose-Innes, the Chief Justice of the Transvaal, put it, war had blunted the moral sense, and Krause's motives were entirely political; he had committed his offence with no idea of personal gain or revenge. [1905 T.S. 221.]

Krause became the greatest advocate of his day in the criminal courts in South Africa. Never a great lawyer himself, he believed

* 1933 O.P.D. 267.

passionately in justice, a passion he took with him on to the Bench. He was first a Judge in the Transvaal, and then in the Orange Free State, of which division of the South African Supreme Court he became Judge President.

The precedent of Krause's case was relied upon to prevent Nelson Mandela being struck off the roll of attorneys in 1954 after he had been convicted under the Suppression of Communism Act 1950 for having advocated the repeal of the pass laws and having encouraged disobedience of certain laws. Likewise the court [1954 (3) S.A. 102] held that the offence being political in its nature did not of itself disqualify a person from practice of the law.]

THE ACCUSED WERE jointly charged with stealing two sheep, both were found guilty and sentenced to six months' imprisonment with hard labour, and were fined £1 each.

The proceedings now come before the Court on review. The magistrate has forwarded a detailed statement of what transpired at the trial, and, in answer thereto, the attorney for the accused submitted his version of what took place. It is needless to add that there is not only a very serious conflict in the two reports, but it is also alleged that evidence has not been recorded, which, if recorded, would undoubtedly demonstrate that the version given on behalf of the accused was the correct one. I do not consider it necessary that this question should be further investigated, or to direct that an amendment of the record should be applied for, as it appears to me, solely on the report itself of the magistrate, the irregularities are of such a grave nature that the accused must have been prejudiced in their trial. The magistrate says that, at the close of the case for the Crown, the attorney for the accused, after cross-examining Sergt. Victor, applied for a further remand and asked for bail to be fixed. There had already been one remand. The public prosecutor objected to a further remand and replied that the case had already been remanded to meet Mr Allant and that he had 'good reasons'; unfortunately the prosecutor then qualified those reasons by adding that one of the accused had a previous conviction. The application for a further remand was refused; whereupon Mr Allant closed his case for the defence, and applied for the discharge of the accused on the grounds: (1) that the policemen had contradicted each other (*re* searching the accused's hut), (2) that it was out of order for the prosecutor to inform the Court about a previous conviction.

The magistrate then deals in his report with ground (1). It is not necessary to labour this point, as the representations made on behalf of the accused are, as stated, in direct conflict with what the magistrate says, and, in order to settle this difference, the question of an amendment to the record would have to be considered.

In dealing with ground (2), however, the magistrate says: 'As the Court was fully satisfied about the guilt of the accused, before the irregularity on the part of the prosecutor, it was not influenced or prejudiced in the slightest degree by the irregularity and did not make use of the previous conviction against accused No. 2, but passed the same sentence upon each accused.'

It should be observed that the prosecutor stated 'generally' that there was a previous conviction against 'one of the accused' and did not specify against which one – whereas the magistrate, in his *ex post facto* report, says that the previous conviction was against No. 2. I may add that the record shows that accused No. 2 was convicted of a similar offence (stock theft) on 15 July 1931, at Koffiefontein, and was sentenced to nine months' imprisonment.

In all cases where inadmissible evidence has been brought to the notice of the trial court or jury, whether inadvertently or intentionally, either due to a misapprehension or a wrong conception of the law, the main question which has to be considered is whether or not such evidence either prejudiced or was calculated to prejudice the accused. In many cases, where the guilt or innocence of the accused has to be judged of by a jury, it would be almost impossible to ascertain to what extent the accused may or may not have been prejudiced. One has to deal with nine jurors – temperamentally, as well as in other respects, entirely different ... Where the accused is tried by a magistrate or by a Judge, sitting as a jury, the danger of inadmissible evidence is, in my view, accentuated; because, human nature being what it is, there is no certainty as to how the individual will react to information illegally disclosed and detrimental to the accused. Individual idiosyncrasies then play a great part, and these vary as the colours of a kaleidoscope.

In many decided cases the courts, in dealing with convictions from magistrates' courts, have quashed the convictions, notwithstanding the fact that the magistrates in their reasons have most emphatically stated that they were not influenced by the inadmissible evidence. Generally speaking, one cannot honestly say after the event, and especially after a conviction where there is other evidence to justify a conviction, to what extent one was influenced. The operation of the unconscious or sub-conscious mind cannot be gauged. To say that a judge or a magistrate, by reason of his training, would overcome the disability, is the height of folly and shows an utter ignorance of what human nature is. It is not so much a question of legal training, or one's ability to weigh evidence, as of temperament, education, and particularly experience of one's fellow creatures. It is solely a question of fact, which in each case will have to be decided on its merits, and no definite rule, which has to be followed, can be laid down by any court. There is unfortunately a large scope for difference of opinion. The only reasonably safe guide one can adopt is to view all the circumstances from every point of view, and then to decide whether the accused did have that fairness of trial which he was entitled to expect.

Some judges, by reason of their self-imposed isolation, are less calculated to appreciate the weakness of human nature than the intelligent man of the world. It is not the free intercourse with one's fellow citizens that detracts from the dignity of the position that one may hold, but one's behaviour during such intercourse. The oyster is sufficiently protected by its natural shell, but the canned variety needs a many-coloured tin.

A man learned in the law alone generally makes a bad judge, and such a person is often a greater danger to the liberty of the subject than the commonsense juryman. In the fair and impartial administration of justice more than a knowledge of the law is required. Often political expediency, especially during times of war and great social upheaval, dictates the quality of justice that has to be and is dispensed, and it is of no use blinking the fact that in England, as well as elsewhere, the courts have succumbed to such influences during our generation.

It is, therefore, essential, if one desires to maintain that high standard, which is the only haven of safety and strength to which the citizen can steer his threatened barque of liberty, that no unnecessary risks should be taken, and rather that a guilty man should be released than that one innocent person should suffer.

It is a matter of the gravest public policy that the impartiality of the courts of justice should not be doubted, or that the fairness of a trial should be questioned; otherwise, the only bulwark of the liberty of the subject, in these times of revolutionary tendencies, would be undermined.

Let us now consider what happened in the present case and what was the mental attitude of the magistrate as it appears from his own report.

It is the duty of a judicial officer to keep an open mind until all the evidence against an accused person has been disclosed – in fact it often happens that the evidence given by or on behalf of the accused is the determining factor in securing a conviction against him. The magistrate here gives, as his reason why he was 'not influenced or prejudiced in the slightest degree by this irregularity', the fact that he had made up his mind, before the irregularity occurred, that the accused were guilty – in other words, before he knew, or could have known, what evidence the accused would or could lead in rebuttal; and then, to make matters worse, he gives a further reason (which is no reason at all, but shows an entire disregard of his plain duty, only after and not before conviction, to award such punishment as the previous conduct of the accused might warrant) – and that is that he passed the same sentence on each of the accused, thereby proving conclusively to the world that 'he did not make use of the previous conviction against accused No. 2' before he was convicted.

This laboured and extraordinary attempt at self-justification, couched in the superlative degree, is decidedly not convincing, and can lead only to one conclusion, and that is that the accused were and must have been prejudiced by the premature disclosal of 'a previous conviction against one of the accused'. The convictions, therefore, will be quashed, and the sentences set aside.

The Unbranded Order

Speech in Smith v. *East Elloe Rural District Council and others*

[On 26 August 1948 the Council made a compulsory purchase order authorising its officers to acquire the appellant's house and land. After the usual public local inquiry had been duly held, the Minister confirmed the order on 29 November 1948. The house was demolished, and a number of other houses were built: the issue of compensation was decided by the Lands Tribunal, which awarded £3,000.

By paragraph 15 (1) of Part IV of the 1st Schedule to the Acquisition of Land (Authorisation Procedure) Act 1946: 'If any person aggrieved by a compulsory purchase order desires to question the validity thereof . . . on the ground that the authorisation . . . is not empowered to be granted under this Act . . . he may, within 6 weeks from the date on which notice of the confirmation . . . is first published . . . make an application to the High Court'.

By paragraph 16: 'Subject to the provisions of the last foregoing paragraph, a compulsory purchase order . . . shall not . . . be questioned in any legal proceedings whatsoever . . . '.

On 6 July 1954 the appellant issued a writ impugning the said order on the ground that it had been made and confirmed wrongfully, and in bad faith. The lower courts set aside the writ as against all the defendants. The House of Lords, however, allowed the action to proceed against the clerk to the Council, while dismissing the appeal as to all the other defendants: in reference to whom Lord Radcliffe's speech was as follows:]

THE RELIEF THAT the appellant seeks against them in her action depends wholly on her ability to establish that a compulsory purchase order dated August [26], 1948 made by the rural district council and confirmed by the Minister was invalid. I do not wish

* [1956] A.C. 736, 766.

to beg any question by using the word 'invalid'. I mean that she has to show that in the eyes of the law this compulsory purchase order was not effective to confer upon the rural district council the authority to enter upon her land, which they certainly would not have possessed without the making of the order. It follows, therefore, that her action must stand or fall by her ability to question this compulsory purchase order in the legal proceedings.

But the act of questioning a compulsory purchase order in legal proceedings is what is dealt with under those very words in paragraphs 15 and 16 of Part IV of Schedule I of the Acquisition of Land (Authorisation Procedure) Act 1946: and the defendants say that having regard to the provisions of those paragraphs it is not open to the appellant by a writ issued in July 1954, to question a compulsory purchase order made in August 1948. . . . If, as is obvious, her proceedings are not within the brief measure of time allowed by paragraph 15, I am bound to say that I think that she faces a very great difficulty in showing that what appears to be the absolute prohibition, 'shall not . . . be questioned in any legal proceedings whatsoever', is to be understood in a court of law as amounting to something much less than such a prohibition. It is quite true, as is said, that these are merely general words: but then, unless there is some compelling reason to the contrary, I should be inclined to regard general words as the most apt to produce a corresponding general result.

Now, the appellant says that the reason for an exception being made in her case lies in the fact that, as her writ shows, she intends to establish that the compulsory purchase order in question was made and confirmed 'in bad faith'; and that, when such a plea is raised, it is the duty of a court of law so to interpret the apparently general words used by Parliament as not to apply them to legal proceedings that are designed to determine that issue. It is because I do not think that the law either requires or entitles us to adopt such a method of construing an Act of Parliament that, in my opinion, the appellant's action must be stopped.

Of course, it is well known that courts of law have always exercised a certain authority to restrain the abuse of statutory powers. Such powers are not conferred for the private advantage of their holders. They are given for certain limited purposes, which the holders are not entitled to depart from: and if the authority that confers them prescribes, explicitly or by implication, certain conditions as to their exercise, those conditions ought to be adhered to. It is, or may be, an abuse of power not to observe the conditions. It is certainly an abuse of power to seek to exercise it when the statute relied upon does not truly confer it, and the invalidity of the act does not depend in any way upon the question whether the person concerned knows or does not know that he is acting *ultra vires*. It is an abuse of power to exercise it for a purpose different from that for which it is entrusted to the holder, not the less because he may be acting ostensibly for the authorised purpose. Probably most of the recognised grounds of invalidity could be brought under this head: the introduction of illegitimate considerations, the rejection of legitimate ones, manifest unreasonableness, arbitrary or capricious conduct, the motive of personal advantage or the gratification of personal ill-will. However that may be, an exercise of power in bad faith does not seem to me to have any special pre-eminence of its own among the causes that make for invalidity. It is one of several instances of abuse of power, and it may or may not be involved in several of the recognised grounds that I have mentioned. Indeed, I think it plain that the courts have often been content to allow such circumstances, if established, to speak for themselves rather than to press the issue to a finding that the group of persons responsible for the exercise of the power have actually proceeded in bad faith.

It must be assumed that the legislature which enacted the Acquisition of Land (Authorisation Procedure) Act, 1946 was aware that the law protected persons disturbed by an exercise of statutory powers in that it allowed them to come to the courts to challenge the validity of the exercise on any of such grounds. But, if so, I do not see how it is possible to treat the provisions of paragraphs 15 and 16 of Part IV of Schedule I of the Act as enacting anything less than a complete statutory code for regulating the extent to which, and the conditions under which, courts of law might be resorted to for the purpose of questioning the validity of a compulsory purchase order within the protection of the Act. . . . I should regard a challenge to the order on the ground that it had not been made in good faith as within the purview of paragraph 15. After all, the point which concerns the aggrieved person is the same in all cases: an order has been made constituting an ostensible exercise of statutory power and his purpose in resorting to the courts is to show that there is no statutory authority behind the order. I do not see any need to pick and choose among the different reasons which may support the plea that the authorisation ostensibly granted does not carry the powers of the Act. But, even if I did not think that an order could be questioned under paragraph 15 on the ground that it had been exercised in bad faith, and I thought, therefore, that the statutory code did not allow for an order being questioned on this ground at all, I should still think that paragraph 16 concluded the matter, and that it did not leave to the courts any surviving jurisdiction.

The appellant's argument for an exception rests on certain general reflections which do not seem to me to make up into any legal principle of construction as applied to an Act of Parliament. It is said that the six weeks which are all the grace that, on any view, paragraph 15 allows an aggrieved person for his taking action, are pitifully inadequate as an allowance of time when bad faith, which may involve concealment or deception, is thought to be present. And indeed they are. Further, it is said that it would be an outrageous thing if a person who by ordinary legal principles would have a right to upset an order affecting him were to be precluded from coming to the courts for his right, either absolutely or after six weeks, when the order is claimed by him to have been tainted by bad faith. And perhaps it is. But these reflections seem to me to be such as must or should have occurred to Parliament when it enacted paragraph 16. They are not reflections which are capable of determining the construction of the Act once it has been passed, unless there is something that one can lay hold of in the context of the Act which justifies the introduction of the exception sought for. Merely to say that Parliament cannot be presumed to have intended to bring about a consequence which many people might think to be unjust is not, in my opinion, a principle of construction for this purpose. In point of fact, whatever innocence of view may have been allowable to the lawyers of the eighteenth and nineteenth centuries, the twentieth-century lawyer is entitled to few assumptions in this field. It is not open to him to ignore the fact that the legislature has often shown indifference to the assertion of rights which courts of law have been accustomed to recognise and enforce, and that it has often excluded the authority of courts of law in favour of other preferred tribunals.

At one time the argument was shaped into the form of saying that an order made in bad faith was in law a nullity and that, consequently, all references to compulsory purchase orders in paragraphs 15 and 16 must be treated as references to such orders only as had been made in good faith. But this argument is in reality a play on the meaning of the word nullity. An order, even if not made in good faith, is still an act capable of legal consequences. It bears no brand of invalidity upon its forehead. Unless the necessary proceedings are taken at law to establish the cause of invalidity and to get it quashed or otherwise upset, it will remain as effective for its ostensible purpose as the most impeccable of orders. And that brings us back to the question that determines this case: Has Parliament allowed the necessary proceedings to be taken?

I am afraid that I have searched in vain for a principle of construction as applied to Acts of Parliament which would enable the appellant to succeed. On the other hand, it is difficult not to recall in the respondents' favour the dictum of Bacon:

> Non est interpretatio, sed divinatio, quae recedit a litera.

No Well-tuned Cymbal

Judgment in Jones v. National Coal Board†

MR GARDINER‡ TOOK a further ground of appeal which is stated in the notice of appeal to be 'that the nature and extent of the judge's interruptions during the hearing of the evidence called on behalf of the defendants made it virtually impossible for counsel for the plaintiff to put the plaintiff's case properly or adequately or to cross-examine the witnesses called on behalf of the defendants adequately or effectively'. . . We much regret that it has fallen to our lot to consider such a complaint against one of Her Majesty's judges: but consider it we must, because we can only do justice between these parties if we are satisfied that the primary facts have been properly found by the judge on a fair trial between the parties. Once we have the primary facts fairly found, we are in as good a position as the judge to draw inferences or conclusions from those facts, but we cannot embark on this task unless the foundation of primary facts is secure. [61]

*

[63] No one can doubt that the judge, in intervening as he did, was actuated by the best motives. He was anxious to understand the details of this complicated case, and asked questions to get them clear in his mind. He was anxious that the witnesses should not be harassed unduly in cross-examination, and intervened to protect them when he thought necessary. He was anxious to investigate all the various criticisms that had been made against the Board, and to see whether they were well founded or not. Hence, he took them up

* Then Lord Justice Denning.
† [1957] 2 Q.B. 55, 61.
‡ Now Lord Gardiner, the Lord Chancellor.

himself with the witnesses from time to time. He was anxious that the case should not be dragged on too long, and intimated clearly when he thought that a point had been sufficiently explored. All those are worthy motives on which judges daily intervene in the conduct of cases, and have done for centuries.

Nevertheless, we are quite clear that the interventions, taken together, were far more than they should have been. In the system of trial which we have evolved in this country, the judge sits to hear and determine the issues raised by the parties, not to conduct an investigation or examination on behalf of society at large, as happens, we believe, in some foreign countries. Even in England, however, a judge is not a mere umpire to answer the question 'How's that?' His object, above all, is to find out the truth, and to do justice according to law; and in the daily pursuit of it the advocate plays an honourable and necessary role. Was it not Lord Chancellor Eldon who said in a notable passage that 'truth is best discovered by powerful statements on both sides of the question'? And Lord Greene, M.R., who explained that justice is best done by a judge who holds the balance between the contending parties without himself taking part in their disputations? If a judge, said Lord Greene, should himself conduct the examination of witnesses, 'he, so to speak, descends into the arena and is liable to have his vision clouded by the dust of conflict'.*

Yes, he must keep his vision unclouded. It is all very well to paint justice blind, but she does better without a bandage round her eyes. She should be blind indeed to favour or prejudice, but clear to see which way lies the truth: and the less dust there is about the better. Let the advocates one after the other put the weights into the scales – the 'nicely calculated less or more' – but the judge at the end decides which way the balance tilts, be it ever so slightly. So firmly is all this established in our law that the judge is not allowed in a civil dispute to call a witness who he thinks might throw some light on the facts. He must rest content with the witnesses called by the parties. So also it is for the advocates, each in his turn, to examine the witnesses, and not

* *Yuill* v. *Yuill* [1945] P. 15, 20.

for the judge to take it on himself lest by so doing he appear to favour one side or the other: see especially the judgment of Lord Justice Birkett in *Harris* v. *Harris*.* And it is for the advocate to state his case as fairly and strongly as he can, without undue interruption, lest the sequence of his argument be lost. The judge's part in all this is to hearken to the evidence, only himself asking questions of witnesses when it is necessary to clear up any point that has been overlooked or left obscure; to see that the advocates behave themselves seemly and keep to the rules laid down by law; to exclude irrelevancies and discourage repetition; to make sure by wise intervention that he follows the points that the advocates are making and can assess their worth; and at the end to make up his mind where the truth lies. If he goes beyond this, he drops the mantle of a Judge and assumes the robe of an advocate; and the change does not become him well. Lord Chancellor Bacon spoke right when he said that†: 'Patience and gravity of hearing is an essential part of justice; and an over-speaking judge is no well-tuned cymbal.'

Such are our standards. They are set so high that we cannot hope to attain them all the time. In the very pursuit of justice, our keenness may outrun our sureness, and we may trip and fall. That is what has happened here. A judge of acute perception, acknowledged learning, and actuated by the best of motives, has

* Judgments of the Court of Appeal, 8 April 1952, No. 148. Lord Justice Birkett said:
'The task of eliciting the truth is assigned to counsel by the method of examination-in-chief and perhaps particularly in cross-examination. In performing this task counsel may be gentle or stern, hostile or friendly, as the occasion and the circumstances warrant; but the judge best serves the administration of justice by preserving the judicial calm and the judicial demeanour, aloof and detached from the arena of contention. . . . People are unaccustomed to the procedure of the courts; and they are likely to be overawed or frightened, or confused, or distressed when under the ordeal of prolonged questioning from the presiding judge. Moreover when the questioning takes on a sarcastic or ironic note, as it is apt to do, or when it takes on a hostile note, as is sometimes inevitable, the danger is not only that witnesses are unable to present the evidence that they would wish but the parties may begin to think – quite wrongly it may be – that the judge is not holding the scales of justice quite evenly.'

† see *supra*, p. 4.

nevertheless himself intervened so much in the conduct of the case that one of the parties – nay, each of them – has come away complaining that he was not able properly to put his case; and these complaints are, we think, justified. [65]

Non-conformity No Disgrace

*Judgment in Hughes v. Architects' Registration Council
of the United Kingdom*†

THE ARCHITECTS (REGISTRATION) ACT 1931, Section 7, gives the council power to strike the name of an architect from the register if he has been 'guilty of conduct disgraceful to him in his capacity as an architect'. I cannot accept the argument that the term 'disgraceful' is in any sense a term of art. In accordance with the usual rule it is to be given its natural and popular meaning. But it is qualified by the phrase 'in his capacity as an architect'. The effect of that qualification is twofold. First, the conduct must not only be what would ordinarily be considered disgraceful, but it must also be a disgrace which affects him professionally: to that extent the qualification diminishes the term. Secondly, conduct which is not disgraceful for an ordinary man may be disgraceful for a professional man: to that extent the qualification amplifies the term. The amplification does not, however, require that 'disgraceful' is to be given any technical meaning: it requires only that the ordinary meaning of the word should be applied in relation to the special obligations and duties of a professional man. It must not be forgotten that, if the finding of the committee stands, anyone may hereafter say of the appellant with impunity that he was struck off the register for disgraceful conduct and may add that that means what it says.

What, then, is the disgraceful conduct with which the appellant is charged? It is not simply that he combined the activities of architect and house agent. There is nothing inherently disgraceful in that.

The council make no such allegation and could not without exposing themselves to the charge that they had for the last twenty years at least condoned disgraceful behaviour. What they

* Then Mr Justice Devlin.

† [1957] 2 Q.B. 550, 559.

say about it is that it is a 'wrong practice' to which the profession
as a whole is opposed, as witnessed by its condemnation in the
code. I accept that this condemnation is reasonable and that the
code, while it has no statutory or contractual force, does, at this
point at least, express the best opinion in the profession. But the
pursuit of a wrong practice is not of itself disgraceful; and the
council's allegation does not rest solely on that.

I do not say that the pursuit of an undesirable practice can
never be disgraceful. Every profession has practices which it bars.
Among the commonest of these are advertising, poaching and
undercutting. These activities which are considered in the business
world to be laudable examples of enterprise – so much so that
their restraint is prima facie contrary to public policy – have
always been considered offensive professionally. If a man joins a
profession in which the use of trade weapons is barred, and then
proceeds to employ them, he is taking an unfair advantage over
his fellows. They restrain themselves, believing, rightly or wrongly,
that such restraint is essential to the good health of the profession
as a whole; he gets the benefit of their restraint and fills his purse
at their expense. He is defaulting on the obligation, by which
explicitly or impliedly he undertook to be bound when they made
him of their company. Such conduct could be thought disgraceful not merely by those of the profession but by outsiders who
were not themselves bound by the same standards. This is in fact
the basis of the finding against the appellant, which is expressed
in the following terms:

the [appellant] was deliberately and knowingly flouting, because of his
own private interests, the standard which the profession as a whole has
set itself and which has been set out in the code of conduct.

In reaching their conclusion, expressed in these terms, that the
appellant's conduct is disgraceful, the committee have overlooked the absence from it of an essential element. It is not of
itself disgraceful to disagree with a majority view and to act
accordingly. It is only if a man has bound himself in honour
to accept that view and to act according to the code that a
deliberate breach of the code for his own profit can be called
disgraceful. The appellant has never bound himself in that way.
He was in practice as an architect and estate agent long before the

code was first formulated or the Act of 1931 passed. His case differs, not merely in degree but *toto coelo*, from that of the new entrant who is admitted on terms, written or unwritten.

I sympathise with the efforts of the council to eradicate undesirable practices from the profession. In a time of transition and when standards are being changed, it is hoped, for the better, it must always be difficult to decide how fast it is fair and reasonable to go. Some might say that the older members, who had established themselves in accordance with the standards then current, ought not to be asked to change their ways at cost to themselves, even though their lagging behind put off the day of complete purification. Others might say that some sacrifice from the older members could fairly be demanded and that the seven years' grace given to them was generous enough. I am bound to say that, having regard to the assurances given in 1937, I should have thought the former course to be the fairer. It is submitted that the one adopted by the council is reasonable. Perhaps it is: and then, if the council had power derived from statute or contract to decide the point, that would settle it. But it has not. I do not understand how it can be said that anyone who takes a different view on such a point and acts accordingly is behaving disgracefully.

In truth and in fact, and however plausibly the argument may seek to disguise it, what the council is trying to do is to enforce a code which has no legislative sanction and to coerce a minority, which is free and unpledged, into submission to an arbitrary decision. I do not mean that it is arbitrary in the sense of unreasonable; it is arbitrary because the force that lies behind it is simply that it is an edict of the council – nothing more. It is idle to say that the appellant's offence is that he is flouting the common opinion of the profession. That opinion has existed, so the council say, at least since 1936. The appellant has been flouting it for the last twenty years and for the last seven of them – the period of grace – with the express approval of the council. His offence is, not that he is flouting it but that he is continuing to flout it far longer than the council consider it reasonable that it should be flouted. They might have said eight years, in which case they would have postponed the appellant's disgrace by a year; but they picked on seven. So the appellant had until 31 December

1955 to conform. If in December 1955 anyone had suggested that the appellant was behaving disgracefully, he could have recovered heavy damages for defamation; but, it is said, when the clock struck midnight he began to sin. So high a degree of punctuality brings the point near to absurdity. Disgrace is not something that gets brought in with the New Year.

It is said that this is an important case. So it is. But there is something more important than the standing of a profession about which the council is naturally and properly concerned. There is the right of every man to earn his living in whatever way he chooses unless by the law or by his own voluntary submission his way is taken from him; and in the exercise of that right he must not be punished by a professional majority under the pretext – for that is all it is, though I am sure it was not consciously adopted as such – that nonconformity is of itself disgraceful.

THE SUPREME COURT OF ISRAEL

*(The President, Justice Olshan; the Deputy-President,
Justice Agranat; Justice Silberg, Justice Sussman and
Justice Witkon)**

A Judge's Duty

---

*Part of the judgment in Adolf, the son of Adolf Karl Eichmann
v. The Attorney General of the Government of Israel*

WE SHALL REPLY briefly to the contention of counsel for the
appellant that the judges of the District Court† – and he advanced the same contention with reference to the judges of this
Court – were psychologically incapable of judging the case of his
client objectively.

Like the District Court, we too reject this contention, and the
reply it gave in so doing is also our reply:

As to the fears of the accused on the score of the background to the
hearing of this case, we can do no more than reiterate the views that
hold good with respect to every system of law worthy of its name:
that the judge, when dispensing justice in a court of law, does not
cease to be a human being, with human passions and human emotions.
Yet he is enjoined by the law to restrain and control such passions and
emotions, else there will never be a judge qualified to try a criminal
case which evokes deep feelings and revulsion, such as a case of treason
or murder or any other grave crime. It is true that the memory of the
Nazi holocaust stirs every Jew to the depths of his being, but once this
case has been brought before us it becomes our duty to control even
these emotions when we sit in judgment, and this duty we shall honour.

The learned judges did abide by their duty – fully, and to the
end.

---

* Decision of 29 May 1962; Eichmann was hanged on 31 May 1962 and his
ashes scattered in the Mediterranean Sea outside the territory of Israel.
† Justice Landau, Justice Halevi and Justice Raveh delivered their judgment
on 11 December 1961.

MR JUSTICE FRANKFURTER and
MR JUSTICE DOUGLAS

Judicial Silence – Public Noise

A statement and a dissent in Public Utilities Commission
v. Pollak*

[The majority of the United States Supreme Court in 1952 held that there was no violation of the freedom of speech – guaranteed in the First Amendment – in the Public Utilities Commission permitting the Washington transport company to play music and broadcast propaganda in its street cars and buses. Mr Justice Frankfurter was an inveterate traveller on the city's street cars, and felt so strongly about the practice that he declined to sit and hear the case, the reasons for which he announced publicly:]

THE JUDICIAL PROCESS demands that a judge move within the framework of relevant legal rules and the covenanted modes of thought for ascertaining them. He must think dispassionately and submerge private feeling on every aspect of a case. There is a good deal of shallow talk that the judicial robe does not change the man within it. It does. The fact is that on the whole judges do lay aside private views in discharging their judicial functions. This is achieved through training, professional habits, self-discipline and that fortunate alchemy by which men are loyal to the obligation with which they are entrusted. But it is also true that reason cannot control the subconscious influence of feelings of which it is unaware. When there is ground for believing that such unconscious feelings may operate in the ultimate judgment, or may not unfairly lead others to believe they are operating, judges recuse themselves. They do not sit in judgment. They do this for a variety of reasons. The guiding consideration is that the administration of justice should reasonably appear to be disinterested as well as be so in fact.

This case for me presents such a situation. My feelings are so

* 343 U.S. 451, 466, 467 (1952).

strongly engaged as a victim of the practice in controversy that I had better not participate in judicial judgment upon it. I am explicit as to the reason for my non-participation in this case because I have for some time been of the view that it is desirable to state why one takes oneself out of a case.

MR JUSTICE DOUGLAS, dissenting:

This is a case of first impression. There are no precedents to construe; no principles previously expounded to apply. We write on a clean slate.

The case comes down to the meaning of 'liberty' as used in the Fifth Amendment. Liberty in the constitutional sense must mean more than freedom from unlawful governmental restraint; it must include privacy as well, if it is to be a repository of freedom. The right to be let alone is indeed the beginning of all freedom. Part of our claim to privacy is in the prohibition of the Fourth Amendment against unreasonable searches and seizures. It gives the guarantee that a man's home is his castle beyond invasion either by inquisitive or by officious people. A man loses that privacy of course when he goes upon the streets or enters public places. But even in his activities outside the home he has immunities from controls bearing on privacy. He may not be compelled against his will to attend a religious service; he may not be forced to make an affirmation or observe a ritual that violates his scruples; he may not be made to accept one religious, political, or philosophical creed as against another. Freedom of religion and freedom of speech guaranteed by the First Amendment give more than the privilege to worship, to write, to speak as one chooses; they give freedom not to do nor to act as the government chooses. The First Amendment in its respect for the conscience of the individual honours the sanctity of thought and belief. To think as one chooses, to believe what one wishes, are important aspects of the constitutional right to be let alone.

If we remembered this lesson taught by the First Amendment, I do not believe we would construe 'liberty' within the meaning of the Fifth Amendment as narrowly as the Court does. The present case involves a form of coercion to make people listen. The listeners are of course in a public place; they are on street cars travelling to and from home. In one sense it can be said that those who ride the street cars do so voluntarily. Yet in a practical sense they are forced to ride, since this mode of transportation is today essential for many thousands. Compulsion which comes from circumstances can be as real as compulsion which comes from a command.

The street car audience is a captive audience. It is there as a matter of necessity, not of choice. One who is in a public vehicle may not of course complain of the noise of the crowd and the babble of tongues. One who enters any public place sacrifices some of his privacy. My protest is against the invasion of his privacy over and beyond the risks of travel.

The government may use the radio (or television) on public vehicles for many purposes. Today it may use it for a cultural end. Tomorrow it may use it for political purposes. So far as the right of privacy is concerned the purpose makes no difference. The music selected by one bureaucrat may be as offensive to some as it is soothing to others. The news commentator chosen to report on the events of the day may give overtones to the news that please the bureau head but which rile the street car captive audience. The political philosophy which one radio speaker exudes may be thought by the official who makes up the street car programmes to be best for the welfare of the people. But the man who listens to it on his way to work in the morning and on his way home at night may think it marks the destruction of the Republic.

One who tunes in on an offensive programme at home can turn it off or tune in another station, as he wishes. One who hears disquieting or unpleasant programmes in public places, such as restaurants, can get up and leave. But the man on the street car has no choice but to sit and listen, or perhaps to sit and to try *not* to listen.

When we force people to listen to another's ideas, we give the propagandist a powerful weapon. Today it is a business enterprise working out a radio programme under the auspices of government. Tomorrow it may be a dominant political or religious group. Today the purpose is benign; there is no invidious cast to the programmes. But the vice is inherent in the system. Once privacy is invaded, privacy is gone. Once a man is forced to submit to one type of radio programme, he can be forced to submit to another.

It may be but a short step from a cultural programme to a political programme.

If liberty is to flourish, government should never be allowed to force people to listen to any radio programme. The right of privacy should include the right to pick and choose from competing entertainments, competing propaganda, competing political philosophies. If people are let alone in those choices, the right of privacy will pay dividends in character and integrity. The strength of our system is in the dignity, the resourcefulness, and the independence of our people. Our confidence is in their ability as individuals to make the wisest choice. That system cannot flourish if regimentation takes hold. The right of privacy, today violated, is a powerful deterrent to anyone who would control men's minds.

Judicial Felicities

Mrs Bunch's Baggage

Speech in Great Western Railway Co. v. *Bunch**

[57] YOUR LORDSHIPS ARE FAMILIAR with the evidence in the case, and I do not propose to repeat it. It is enough to say that on 24 December 1884 at 4.20 p.m. Mrs Bunch came to Paddington with a Gladstone bag and some other luggage, meaning to travel with her husband by the 5 p.m. train to Bath, that on her arrival at the station the luggage was received by a porter in the employment of the company, and taken by him to the platform for the purpose of the journey, and that the Gladstone bag was last seen on the platform with the same porter a few minutes afterwards. From that time all trace of the bag is lost. The porter and the bag both vanish from the scene. It was suggested by the learned counsel for the appellants, by way of explanation, that the porter was possibly one of a number of men picked up by the company for the day to meet the pressure of Christmas traffic. But I may observe, in passing, that so far as the public was concerned, there was apparently nothing to distinguish the casual helper, of whom little if anything was known, from the regular and trusted servants of the company.

On these bare facts standing alone it seems to me that there would be evidence upon which the county court judge might reasonably find for the plaintiff, even if the company were not under the liability of common carriers as regards the lost bag.

But then it was contended with much earnestness that it ought to have been inferred from the circumstances of the case and from Mrs Bunch's conduct that at the time of the loss the bag was not in the custody of the company for the purpose of the journey. It was said that Mrs Bunch came to the station too soon – that she came before the train was drawn up – that she broke the journey, if the journey is to be taken as having begun – and left the bag in the charge of a porter who was then not acting as the servant

* (1888) 13 App. Cas. 31, 55.

of the company within the scope of his authority as such, but acting as her agent in his individual capacity, and that if this was not what she meant, it was an attempt on her part to saddle the company with a liability which they were not bound to undertake.

It seems to me that there is no substance in any of these objections. Mrs Bunch, no doubt, came to the station somewhat early. But the one thing railway companies try to impress on the public is to come in good time. And considering the crowd likely to be attracted by cheap fares during the Christmas holidays and the special bustle and throng on Christmas eve, it does not seem to me that Mrs Bunch came so unreasonably early as to relieve the company who received the luggage from the ordinary obligations flowing from that receipt. It is impossible to define within the extreme limits on both sides the proper time for arrival. Everything must depend upon the circumstances of the particular case. But among those circumstances, the least important, as it seems to me, is the time when the train is drawn up at the departure platform. That is, as everybody knows, a very variable time. And it is a matter over which the passenger has no control, and of which he can have no notice before he comes to the station.

Then I think there is nothing in the conversation which took place between Mrs Bunch and the porter. Mrs Bunch's question was a very natural one. The answer she received was just what might have been expected.* Nine women out of ten parting with a travelling bag on which they set any store would ask the same question. In ninety-nine times out of a hundred the same answer would be returned. I do not think that this conversation altered the relation between the parties in the least degree. It seems to me almost absurd to treat it as a solemn negotiation by which the lady abdicated such rights as she possessed against the Great Western Railway Company, and constituted this ephemeral and evanescent porter in his individual capacity the sole custodian of her Gladstone bag.

Nor can it, I think, be said that Mrs Bunch broke the journey by

* The porter who came forward to put the luggage on a trolley was asked by Mrs Bunch to put the travelling bag into the carriage with her; and she asked him if it was safe to leave it with him. The porter replied that it would be quite safe, and that he would take care of the luggage and put it into the train.

leaving the platform to meet her husband and get her ticket. To take a ticket is a necessary incident of a railway journey. It is, at least, a very common incident in railway travelling for persons, who intend to travel in company, whether they be members of the same family or not, to meet by appointment in the railway station from which they mean to start, and it is certainly not unusual in such a case for the purchase of tickets to be deferred until the meeting takes place.

It may be that a passenger who has delivered his luggage to a porter at the entrance of the station, though the delivery is in proper time for the intended journey, is not entitled as of right and under all circumstances to consider the company responsible for the safe keeping of his luggage before it is put into the train. A passenger knows that he is not the only person to be attended to, and it might not be unreasonable to hold that there is an implied agreement on his part that he will be ready to resume possession of his luggage if the exigencies of the traffic require that it should be handed back to him in the interval before the time comes to put it into the train. No such question, however, arises here. The lost bag was not left unguarded owing to the exigencies of traffic, or neglected by the porter who took it in consequence of the pressure of conflicting duties. But I desire to say that, for my part, I am not satisfied that a passenger's luggage which has been received by the company's servants, and taken to the platform, lies there at the risk of the passenger, if he is not ready forthwith, or the moment he has got his ticket, to step into the train.

It was said that if everybody acted as Mrs Bunch acted in this case, railway companies would require an army of porters, and that it would be almost impossible for them to carry on their business. I quite agree; but I am not much impressed by that observation. I apprehend that if all travellers acted precisely alike, if everybody arrived at a station for a particular journey at precisely the same moment, though the time of arrival were the fittest that could be imagined, there would be no little confusion, and perhaps some consternation, among the railway officials. Whatever may be the result of your Lordships' judgment, there is no fear that it will have the effect of making everybody act alike. Some passengers will still give more trouble at the stations than others, but no one will give any more trouble for it. Things will go on just as usual. The fidgety and the nervous will still come too soon; the unready and the unpunctual will still put off their chance of arrival till the last moment, and the prudent may have their calculations upset by the many accidents and hindrances that may be met with on the way to the station. And it is just because of the irregularity of individuals that the stream of traffic is regular and easily managed.

In the result, therefore, I am of opinion that the majority of the Court of Appeal were right in the view they took. The nature of the case requires that a broad view should be taken. The contract between the company and the passenger is not a contract in writing, defining with mathematical accuracy the precise limits of the incidental services which the company are prepared to render, and punishing every transgression, every attempt on the part of the passenger to exact more than his just measure of attention, with the loss of that security which belongs to a contract by common carriers. Railway companies do their best to adapt the conduct of their business to the habits of the travelling public, who resent nothing so much as petty and vexatious regulations; and so the contract becomes moulded in matters incidental to its main purpose by that which is, and is known to be, the ordinary and everyday practice of railway companies. A narrow, technical and jealous view of the rights of individual passengers might, perhaps, enable railway companies to escape liability in some cases: I much doubt whether it would tend to their advantage in the long run.

Common Carrier

*Judgment in Walker v. Great Northern Railway
Company of Ireland†*

A WOMAN WHO is with child is in a railway accident, and the infant when born is found to be deformed. Can the infant maintain an action against the company for negligence? It is admitted that such a thing was never heard of before. And yet the circumstances which would give rise to such a claim at one time or another have existed. But as there was a germ of life *in esse* at the time of the occurrence, so it is thought there are to be found, in the principles and propositions of the law, the germs of the legal creation which for the first time professional ingenuity has produced. The pity of it is as novel as the case – that an innocent infant comes into the world with the cruel seal upon it of another's fault, and has to bear a burthen of infirmity and ignominy throughout the whole passage of life. It is no wonder, therefore, that sympathy for helpless and undeserved misfortune has led to what is literally a kind of creative boldness in litigation. I would not myself see any injustice in the abstract in such an action being held to lie, or in the risks of a carrier being extended to the necessary incidents of nature. And possibly the consideration from the mother could be construed to include the child also, with but a slight further stretch in the analogy of the case of a servant and others that have been cited. But there are instances in the law where rules of right are founded upon the inherent and inevitable difficulty or impossibility of proof. And it is easy to see on what a boundless sea of speculation in evidence this new idea would launch us. What a field would be opened to extravagance of testimony, already great enough – if science could carry her lamp, not over-certain in its light where people have their

---

* Not to be confused with Sir Peter (later Lord) O'Brien who was Chief Justice at the time.

† (1891) 28 L.R. Ir. 69, 81.

eyes, into the unseen laboratory of nature – could profess to reveal the causes and things that are hidden there – could trace a hare-lip to nervous shock, or a bunch of grapes on the face to the fright – could, in fact, make *lusus naturæ* the same thing as *lusus scientiæ*. There may be a question of evidence, Mr Gerrard modestly put it; but the law may see such danger in that evidence, may have such a suspicion of human ignorance and presumption, that it will not allow any question of evidence to be entered into at all. However, we have to see whether the right claimed exists in the English legal system, or flows out of any admitted principles in that system. The law is in some respects a stream that gathers accretions with time from new relations and conditions. But it is also a landmark that forbids advance on defined rights and engagements; and if these are to be altered, if new rights and engagements are to be created, that is the province of legislation and not of decision.

Now, let us see whether the law has decided the point at which this action can be maintained, or contains any principle out of which the right can be developed by any authority short of the legislature. The criminal law has been referred to for the purpose of showing that an unborn infant is a person in law, because murder may be committed if the infant be afterwards born and die from the effect of violence. But the criminal law is conversant with wrongs and not with rights. It regards not the person but society. It results not in a benefit to the party injured, but in a satisfaction to the community. Crimes are invasions of natural rights and relations, among which life and personal safety are the highest. In the instance put the violence is a continuing act, which takes away the life after birth, and therefore the legal consequence of murder is unavoidable. It would come nearer to the exigency of the case for the plaintiff, as was put in the argument, if it could be shown that a prosecution for an assault or an action for an assault had ever been maintained in the case of an unborn infant. As to the cases cited in reference to property, even those put by Mr Justice Buller, as to what this kind of entity, a child in the womb, could do – that he could take a gift by will – could be named executor – could be vouched in a recovery – could have waste restrained; these and others are all cases of relations cast upon the infant by law or by the act of others, and which relations must be fulfilled in some way. The rule of the civil law that made the infant a distinct person, when it was for his benefit, is supposed to include, in the extent of the principle, compensation for negligence. That rule has been adopted with English law in reference to property, of which we have the latest and perhaps the most extreme instance in a case to which the Chief Justice has referred us where it was held that a gift to children born and living vested in those who were unborn, and were not living, except in the sense that they were not dead; while in the same case it was necessary to hold that the period of division – twenty-one years of age – though applied to all the children alike, must still exclude the unborn children who were included in the gift. The rule quoted from the Digest says: '*Qui in utero sunt in toto poene jure civili intelliguntur in rerum naturâ esse.*' Yet the examples given in the Digest, in which unborn children were severed from the mother by fiction, except as to inheritance, relate wholly to personal status, and to the right of return, captivity in war, and patronage – relations and institutions unknown except to the civil law. That law did not include personal compensation for negligence – railway shock was not as yet. But the question remains, What has the carrier to say to this invisible person of the civil law? Railway liability is a branch of the general law of carriers. The stage-coach was the predecessor of the railway. The contract of carriage is founded on consideration. To the company as to the stage-coach manager a person is someone who can pay the fare. The carrier saw the person he was going to carry. His duty was to that person. The carrier would be surprised to hear, while he was paid for one, that he was carrying two, or even three, for it might be a case of twins, as Mr Walker suggested. He carries for hire. That is the fundamental account of his position and liability. The case put, of a child born and hurt during the journey, whether the liability could be enlarged to comprehend a case of that kind, in which there was no contract and no consideration, may involve much difficulty. There one element would be wanting – the consideration. Here the two are wanting – the right and the consideration. There is no person and no duty. In law, in reason, in the common language of mankind, in the dispensation of nature, in the bond of physical union, and the instinct of duty and solicitude, on which the continuance of the world depends, a woman is the common carrier of her unborn child, and not a railway company.*

* The right of a child to recover damages in respect of injuries inflicted pre-natally has been upheld in Canada, *Montreal Tramways Co.* v. *Léveillé* [1933] 4 D.L.R. 337, in South Africa, *Pinchin and another, N.O.* v. *Santain Insurance Co. Ltd.* 1963 (2) S.A. 254, and in some American jurisdictions. This case does not necessarily deny such a legal right. It merely decided that the railway company had contracted only to carry the mother, to whom it alone owed a duty to take care.

The Reasonable Rescuer

Judgment in Wagner v. *International Railway Co.*†

THE ACTION IS for personal injuries. The defendant operates an electric railway between Buffalo and Niagara Falls. There is a point on its line where an overhead crossing carries its tracks above those of the New York Central and the Erie. A gradual incline upwards over a trestle raises the tracks to a height of 25 feet. A turn is then made to the left at an angle of from 64 to 84 degrees. After making this turn, the line passes over a bridge, which is about 158 feet long from one abutment to the other. Then comes a turn to the right at about the same angle down the same kind of an incline to grade. Above the trestle, the tracks are laid on ties, unguarded at the ends. There is thus an overhang of the cars, which is accentuated at curves. On the bridge, a narrow footpath runs between the tracks, and beyond the line of overhang there are tie rods and a protecting rail.

Plaintiff, Arthur Wagner, and his cousin Herbert boarded a car at a station near the bottom of one of the trestles. Other passengers, entering at the same time, filled the platform, and blocked admission to the aisle. The platform was provided with doors, but the conductor did not close them. Moving at from 6 to 8 miles an hour, the car, without slackening, turned the curve. There was a violent lurch, and Herbert Wagner was thrown out, near the point where the trestle changes to a bridge. The cry was raised, 'Man overboard'. The car went on across the bridge, and stopped near the foot of the incline. Night and darkness had come on. Plaintiff walked along the trestle, a distance of 445 feet, until he arrived at the bridge, where he thought to find his cousin's body. He says that he was asked to go there by the

---

* Mr Justice Cardozo was at this time a judge of the New York Court of Appeals (the highest Court in the State) of which he was Chief Judge from 1927 until he was elevated in 1932 to the Supreme Court of the United States.
† 232 N. Y. 176 (1921).

conductor. He says, too, that the conductor followed with a lantern. Both these statements the conductor denies. Several other persons, instead of ascending the trestle, went beneath it, and discovered under the bridge the body they were seeking. As they stood there, the plaintiff's body struck the ground beside them. Reaching the bridge, he had found upon a beam his cousin's hat, but nothing else. About him there was darkness. He missed his footing, and fell.

The trial judge held that negligence toward Herbert Wagner would not charge the defendant with liability for injuries suffered by the plaintiff unless two other facts were found: First, that the plaintiff had been invited by the conductor to go upon the bridge; and, second, that the conductor had followed with a light. Thus limited, the jury found in favour of the defendant. Whether the limitation may be upheld is the question to be answered.

Danger invites rescue. The cry of distress is the summons to relief. The law does not ignore these reactions of the mind in tracing conduct to its consequences. It recognises them as normal. It places their effects within the range of the natural and probable. The wrong that imperils life is a wrong to the imperilled victim; it is a wrong also to his rescuer. The State that leaves an opening in a bridge is liable to the child that falls into the stream, but liable also to the parent who plunges to its aid. The railroad company whose train approaches without signal is a wrongdoer toward the traveller surprised between the rails, but a wrongdoer also to the bystander who drags him from the path. The risk of rescue, if only it be not wanton, is born of the occasion. The emergency begets the man. The wrongdoer may not have foreseen the coming of a deliverer. He is accountable as if he had.

The defendant says that we must stop, in following the chain of causes, when action ceases to be 'instinctive'. By this is meant, it seems, that rescue is at the peril of the rescuer, unless spontaneous and immediate. If there has been time to deliberate, if impulse has given way to judgment, one cause, it is said, has spent its force, and another has intervened. In this case the plaintiff walked more than 400 feet in going to Herbert's aid. He had time to reflect and weigh; impulse had been followed by choice; and choice, in the defendant's view, intercepts and breaks the sequence. We find no warrant for thus shortening the chain of jural causes. We may assume, though we are not required to decide, that peril and rescue must be in substance one transaction; that the sight of the one must have aroused the impulse to the other; in short, that there must be unbroken continuity between the commission of the wrong and the effort to avert its consequences. If all this be assumed, the defendant is not aided. Continuity in such circumstances is not broken by the exercise of volition. So sweeping an exception, if recognised, would leave little of the rule. 'The human mind', as we have said 'acts with celerity which it is sometimes impossible to measure'. The law does not discriminate between the rescuer oblivious of peril and the one who counts the cost. It is enough that the act, whether impulsive or deliberate, is the child of the occasion.

The defendant finds another obstacle, however, in the futility of the plaintiff's sacrifice. He should have gone, it is said, below the trestle with the others; he should have known, in view of the overhang of the cars, that the body would not be found above; his conduct was not responsive to the call of the emergency; it was a wanton exposure to a danger that was useless. We think the quality of his acts in the situation that confronted him was to be determined by the jury. Certainly he believed that good would come of his search upon the bridge. He was not going there to view the landscape. The law cannot say of his belief that a reasonable man would have been unable to share it. He could not know the precise point at which his cousin had fallen from the car. If the fall was from the bridge, there was no reason why the body, caught by some projection, might not be hanging on high, athwart the tie rods or the beams. Certainly no such reason was then apparent to the plaintiff, or so a jury might have found. Indeed, his judgment was confirmed by the finding of the hat. There was little time for delay, if the facts were as he states them. Another car was due, and the body, if not removed, might be ground beneath the wheels. The plaintiff had to choose at once, in agitation and with imperfect knowledge. He had seen his kinsman and companion thrown out into the darkness. Rescue could not charge the company with liability if rescue was condemned by reason. 'Errors of judgment', however, would not count against him if they resulted 'from the excitement and confusion of the moment'. The reason that was exacted of him was not the reason of the morrow. It was reason fitted and proportioned to the time and the event.*

* Whether the plaintiff in going to his cousin's rescue was foolhardy or reasonable in the light of the emergency confronting him was a question for the jury. The Court therefore ordered a new trial.

LORD THOMSON

Round in Bogey

*Judgment in Blaikie & others v. British
Transport Commission**

[On 1 October 1957 the deceased was driving an engine on the
line to Edinburgh: at Inverkeithing, water was taken on and, just
afterwards, the mud door at the foot of the front of the engine's
boiler blew out and water began to escape. The deceased backed
the engine, then left it and manœuvred its water bag up to the
fireman who was at the cab door. This required considerable
physical effort on his part. He then turned on the water for which
he had again to exert considerable force while the fireman
extinguished the fire. The deceased then ran to a signal box 150
yards away to report the accident, collapsed and died of a coronary
thrombosis.

This was an appeal from the dismissal by the trial judge of an
action brought by the deceased's dependent relatives on the
grounds of the negligence of the railways. Lord Thomson, Lord
Justice-Clerk of Scotland from 1954 to 1962, presided over the
hearing at which the appeal was dismissed.]

[191] THE PROBLEM IS the familiar one of the ambit of reasonable anticipation. If we are satisfied that the case as averred puts
itself clearly beyond that ambit it is our duty to say that it is
irrelevant. The problem has often been referred to as a sort of
jury point for judges, and that is a good enough description, in so
far as it emphasises that the decision as to where the axe is to fall
must be taken on broad lines. But it equally falls to be emphasised
that, if there is doubt as to where the axe is to fall, the decision
should be postponed till the facts have been ascertained . . .

The law has always had to come to some sort of compromise
with the doctrine of causation. The problem is always rather a
practical than an intellectual one. It is easy and usual to bedevil it

* 1961 S.L.T. 190.

343

with subtleties, but the attitude of the law is that expediency and good sense dictate that for practical purposes a line has to be drawn somewhere, and that in drawing it one must be guided by the practical experience of the reasonable man rather than by the theoretical speculations of the philosopher.

Stripped of its subtleties, the present case depends on the circumstances that the unfortunate deceased was a sick man. But for that, it is difficult to see how the various consequences which flowed from the faulty fixing of the mud door would have resulted in his death. The question therefore becomes whether in this branch of the law a reasonable man weighing the probable consequences of some activity is entitled to proceed on the footing that the human participator in the chain of consequences will be normal or abnormal in health. In my view in the absence of special knowledge or of circumstances under which special knowledge would be reasonably inferred, the reasonable man is entitled to proceed on the basis of what normally happens to normal people. The whole virtue of the reasonable man is that he functions normally in a normal world. It is the normal which is calculable; in face of the abnormal one can only guess. The reasonable man goes round in bogey because he plays the orthodox shots, is never in trouble and is not called on to do the unexpected. However that may be, it is enough for the decision of the present case to say that, looked at broadly, the death of this man would not have been anticipated by a reasonable man as a probable consequence of the initial act of negligence.

[Scots judges seem to have a penchant for the golfing analogy. In *Gollins* v. *Gollins* [1964] A.C. 644, Lord Reid used the golf course more appositely in applying the test of foreseeability to the acts of a husband towards his wife in a case of cruelty. He said ' . . . if I say I intend to reach the green people will believe me, although we all know that the odds are ten to one against my succeeding; and no one but a lawyer would say that I must be presumed to have intended to put my ball in the bunker because that was the natural and probable result of my shot'.]

Wicklow Picnic

Judgment in The Queen v. *Drury*†

AN APPLICATION IN this matter has been made for writs of *certiorari* and *mandamus* to compel Mr Drury, a Local Government Board auditor, to bring into court certain orders of allowance and disallowance made by him in his audit of the [Dublin] Corporation accounts. . . . The items in the account which are the subject-matter of controversy are six in all: (1) an allowance of a sum of £880 expended in the construction of a new supper-room at the Mansion House [this the Court confirmed]; (2) a disallowance of a fee of £120 to Mr Ashlin, an architect, who supervised the work in connection with the erection of the supper-room [this fee the Court allowed]; (3) a disallowance in respect of a sum of £5 5s paid by the Finance and Leases Committee for the illumination of a certificate of the Freedom of the City bestowed on the Provost of Trinity College, Dublin [also allowed]; (4) an allowance of the sum of £96 17s, expenses of floral decorations on the occasions of balls and dinner parties; (5) disallowances of certain sums of £51 16s 8d and £3 3s, which were charges made in respect of expenditure for lunch taken by the members of the Corporation on the occasion of a visit to the Vartry Waterworks; (6) an allowance of a sum of £27 in respect of the travelling expenses of the members of the Corporation on the same occasion. [493]

*

[494] The fourth item is the sum allowed for floral decorations on the occasion of balls and dinner parties. It appears to us that there is no sanction whatever for this expenditure. Mr Drury in his report says that it is difficult to believe that this is a necessary expenditure, and that he was decidedly of opinion that the expense

* Then Sir Peter O'Brien.

† [1894] 2 I.R. 489, 492.

of floral decorations on occasions of balls, dinner parties, &c., should not be paid out of the public funds. However, following the bad example of his predecessors, he allowed this sum, contrary to his own opinion, in deference to precedent. How can this allowance be justified? Expenditure on flowers does not benefit the corporate property. The Lord Mayor is allowed a substantial salary, which is supposed to cover the expense of entertainment, and as well might it be sought to justify the cost of the viands as the cost of the decoration of the civic banquets. The case of *Reg. (M'Evoy)* v. *Corporation of Dublin** has been referred to; but that case, so far as it goes, is an authority to show that the expenditure is not justified. Among the many questions in that case was one with reference to a certain item for gas used in the Mansion House. Mr Justice FitzGerald's opinion has been referred to. He is reported to have said: 'It appears to me that the Corporation have full power over that item, and that they are entitled in maintaining the Mansion House, if they choose, to consider it an item of maintenance.' But, in the same case, Chief Justice May said: 'I must confess that I do not see on what principle gas consumed at the residence of the Lord Mayor can be chargeable against the borough fund.' The late Mr Justice O'Brien is reported to have concurred in the judgment of Chief Justice May, so that the majority of the Court seem to have decided that a charge for gas as against the borough fund could not be maintained. About gas-fittings there might, perhaps, be some question, for these might become part and parcel of the corporate property; but I cannot understand how expenditure incurred in respect of the aeriform fluid called gas could be charged as against the borough fund; as well might the cost of candles be sought to be charged.

I now come to deal with the expenditure in respect of the lunch. This is the most interesting item with which we have to deal. How can it be maintained? I shall read from the report of Mr Drury what his views are. Mr Drury says:

In my last report I directed attention to the expense incurred in connection with what is called the 'Annual Inspection' of the Vartry Waterworks, and I intimated my opinion that a portion of it, at least, was not lawful, and gave the Committee the opportunity of considering

* 2 L.R. Ir. 371.

their position before again incurring a similar expenditure in 1892. The Committee referred my observations to the Law Agent for report, limiting their inquiry, however, to the point 'as to the legality of members of the Corporation, not being members of the Waterworks Committee, being permitted to join the inspection, and have their expenses paid'. Mr MacSheehy gave it as his opinion that: 'There is no question of the right of every member of the Corporation, without any permission, to attend any and every inspection of any portion of the corporate property; but I am of opinion that it is not legal that his expenses and entertainment while doing so should be paid out of the rates.' In spite of this clear and deliberate opinion from their legal adviser, the Committee appointed a day for the inspection; left the arrangements in the chairman's hands; directed that the Council should be informed of the date, and arranged the price to be charged to members of the Council for guests. It would be hard to imagine a more deliberate challenge than this.

Now I think it is relevant to refer to the character of this luncheon. I have before me the items in the bill. Amongst the list of wines are two dozen champagne, Ayala, 1885 – a very good brand – at 84s a dozen; one dozen Marcobrunn hock – a very nice hock; one dozen Château Margaux – an excellent claret; one dozen fine old Dublin whiskey – the best whiskey that can be got; one case of Ayala; six bottles of Amontillado sherry – a stimulating sherry; and the ninth item is some more fine Dublin whiskey! Then Mr Lovell supplies the '*dinner*' (this was a dinner, not a mere luncheon!) including all attendance, at 10s per head. There is an allowance for brakes; one box of cigars, 100; coachmen's dinner; beer, stout, minerals in syphons, and ice for wine. There is dessert, and there are sandwiches, and an allowance for four glasses broken – a very small number broken under the circumstances.

In sober earnestness, what was this luncheon and outing? It seems to me to have been a picnic on an expensive scale. What authority is there for it? No statutable authority exists. By what principle of our common law is it sustainable? By none that I can see. In *M'Evoy's Case*,* to which I have already referred, there was a question of maintaining the Mansion House, being the property of the Corporation. But this is a question of providing a sumptuous repast for the members of the Corporation on the Wicklow hills. It is not certainly for the benefit of the

* 2 L.R. Ir. 371.

property of the Corporation, or of the rate-paying citizens of Dublin, that the members of the Corporation should lunch sumptuously. I asked for statute or for case, but neither was cited. The Solicitor-General in his most able argument – I have always to guard myself against his plausibility – appealed pathetically to common sense; he asked, really with tears in his voice, whether the members of the Corporation should starve; he drew a most gruesome picture; he represented that the members of the Corporation would really traverse the Wicklow hills in a spectral condition, unless they were sustained by lunch. I do not know, whether he went so far as Ayala, Marcobrunn, Château Margaux, old Dublin whiskey, and cigars. In answer to the pathetic appeal of the Solicitor-General, we do not say that the members of the Corporation are not to lunch. But we do say that they are not to do so at the expense of the citizens of Dublin. They cannot banquet at their expense in the Mansion House, and, in our opinion, they cannot lunch at their expense in Wicklow. We agree with the opinion of the Law Adviser of the Corporation – an excellent opinion of a most admirable officer – when he expressed himself to the effect that the payment of the expenses and entertainment of the general body of the Corporation, when inspecting the Vartry Works, could not be legally justified.... Having regard to the duties imposed on this Committee, we think their travelling expenses – that is to say, the travelling expenses of so many of the persons who went to the Waterworks on the day in question as were members of the Waterworks Committee – should be allowed. But we cannot find any statutable authority or any decided case or any principle of law which would justify us in sanctioning the expenses of luncheon or entertainment so far even as relates to them. They should support themselves whilst in Dublin. This was in any case necessary. We can find no legal sanction for lunch of even a moderate character on such an occasion, but certainly the particular luncheon was infected in every part of it with excess.

Night Thoughts

Judgment in Mitchell v. *Martin and Rose**

[Two officials – a chief of police and a police magistrate – appealed against the refusal by a taxing officer to give them separate costs for their defence to an action brought by a citizen. The claim was for damages for the arrest, detention in custody and imprisonment, but had been discontinued by the plaintiff. The Court in Manitoba held that the two officials, who had employed the same solicitor to represent them, were not disentitled to separate costs of a discontinued action where their legal interests diverged.]

[262] INASMUCH AS THIS appeal follows upon the refusal of the taxing officer to tax costs of separate defences, we will have to glance for a few moments at the background of facts out of which the action arises.

The defendant Rose is the Chief of Police for St Vital, a flourishing suburb of Winnipeg, and is apparently a man of discriminating vigilance in enforcing a due and wholesome regard for the decencies of life within his bailiwick. The defendant Martin is a police magistrate for the same suburb, a well-intentioned man willing upon occasion to stretch his magisterial authority far enough to embrace and to bring back to the straight and narrow path an erring maiden whose venturesome feet have carried her out upon the wide and easy way.

The plaintiff on her part is described as an infant – being of the tender age of 20 years. Intermittently, she was employed in Winnipeg, but at the time of which we speak, August 1923, she had managed to 'cull her out a holiday' and to pay a visit of some days' duration to a friend of hers, in his summer tent on the east bank of the Red River, within the domain of the defendants' jurisdiction.

Upon that occasion and in and about that tent 'there were

* [1925] 1 D.L.R. 260 (Manitoba).

349

sounds of revelry by night'.* From the reports which reached the
attentive ear of Chief Rose, and which by him have been transmitted to us, we are led to understand that the revelries were
indulged in by several persons, male and female; that these
bacchanalian revellers frequently burst forth into nocturnal song
that filled the great spaces of the night with sounds that echoed
far and wide; and that they interspersed their choral offerings by
shouts and shrieks that 'nightly rent the midnight air'.

To the watchful sleepers on the opposite bank of the Red, the
nights grew hideous. They were annoyed and angered by what
they saw and heard, and shocked by what they had neither seen
nor heard, but suspected. They arose, and called upon Chief
Rose to rid them of these troublesome neighbours.

Prompt at the call of duty, the defendant Rose set out to find
the offenders, and at 4 o'clock on a summer's afternoon he found
the tent, and in it, the plaintiff, recumbent on a bed, in extreme
dishabille. On an adjoining bed lay her host, renewing his
energy by 'tired nature's sweet restorer – balmy sleep'.† To the
indulgent eye of the law this scene was not offensive, but to the
virtuous eye of Chief Rose it was highly reprehensible. He sought
information from the couple, but information was not given
him – at least not the sort calculated to satisfy his then inquiring
turn of mind. In the circumstances, being in doubt as to what he
ought to do, he of course arrested the plaintiff, and led her off
in captive bonds to the police station. There he detained her for
more than one weary hour till magistrate Martin could be
notified and brought upon the scene. With the magistrate's ready
assistance he laid an information charging the plaintiff for that
she 'was found in a tent . . . undressed on a bed . . . without employment . . .' for all of which – with other acts of commission or
omission – he termed her a 'vagrant'. She was immediately put
upon her trial. There was no defence, nor attempt at defence.
The magistrate wavered. He dimly saw his legal duty to acquit
her; but he strongly felt a fatherly desire 'to save her' from
something or other. He ended by expressing the view that she
ought to be confined with hard labour, and in order that she might
be so confined, he convicted her. Upon the same night before the

* Byron, *Childe Harold's Pilgrimage*, Canto III, Stanza 21.
† Edward Young, *Night Thoughts*, Night I, line 1.

sun went down, she was carried off to the place appointed for her confinement, and was there delivered into the safe-keeping of the Salvation Army Home, for a period of 6 months.

By zeal and a bail bond she was, in a few days, released from durance vile;* and in due course, as soon as the appeal could be reached, the conviction was quashed, and the proceedings declared to have been wholly illegal and unwarranted. . . .

> * In durance vile here must I wake and weep,
>   And all my frowsy couch in sorrow sleep.
>   – ROBERT BURNS, Epistle from Esopus
>   to Maria (1794)

Sir Jocelyn Simon alludes to this 'humorous archaism' in his 'English Idioms from the Penal Law,' p. 278 *supra*.

Ambidextrous Sheriff

Judgment in Dreyer v. *Naidoo**

THIS IS A whimsical case about a deputy sheriff who served a summons upon himself as defendant. As far as counsel are aware, this is the first time that it has happened in South Africa. The matter now comes before the Court as an application by the defendant for an order setting the service aside as irregular. The plaintiff issued a summons against the deputy sheriff at Estcourt, claiming £2,000 as damages for wrongful attachment. When the plaintiff's attorneys forwarded the summons to the deputy sheriff for service, he raised the question whether it would be regular for him to serve it on himself, and their reply was that this course would not be irregular, and indeed that if the summons were not served without further delay, the plaintiff would regard this as an irregularity! Thereupon the deputy sheriff served the summons on himself. He does not say how he accomplished this dexterous feat, save to aver modestly that he 'went through the motions' thereby no doubt letting his left hand know what his right hand was doing. For this nimble service he charged the plaintiff a fee of 10s 7d, which included cost of living allowance – an ambidextrous sheriff must live. The return of service indicates that he explained to himself the 'nature and exigency of the summons'. Doubtless this involved a little auto-suggestion. Thereafter he was prudent enough to enter appearance to defend. But the arrival of the declaration apparently caused him to have some misgivings, and he now applies, as defendant, for the service to be set aside as irregular. His right hand, however, has not lost its cunning, for he seeks to turn the irregularity to his advantage with a tactical prayer that the plaintiff be ordered to pay the costs of this application before reserving the summons, upon the ground that the plaintiff is a man of straw – a prayer which, if

* 1958 (2) S.A. 628.

granted, might have the effect of preventing him from bringing his case before the Court.

Well now, what is the Court to do about this drollery? ... In the present case, looking at the facts on the ground, the position is that the defendant did receive the summons and understand the nature and exigency thereof and enter appearance, and he has suffered no prejudice, and he can plead to the declaration; while to set aside the service now would involve the plaintiff in needless expense and repetition of procedural steps. In all these circumstances it seems to me that plain justice between man and man requires that the irregularity be condoned and the application dismissed. There will be no order as to costs because both sides were partly responsible for the irregularity of which the applicant complains.

Time and Space

Dissenting judgment in Rex v. *X**

THE APPELLANT WAS convicted of a contravention of the Reitz† traffic regulations in that he exceeded the speed limit of 15 miles per hour. It is alleged that he drove a motor-car, though carefully, at the rate of 25 miles per hour.

The only evidence for the prosecution is that of two constables, who got into a car belonging to neither of them, but to a garage, and trailed the car driven by the accused in a street across the Market Square, therefore for no considerable distance. They baldly state that he travelled at 25 m.p.h. without explaining how they gained this information. From the nature of the proceedings and the cross-examination, however, I infer that they trailed the accused, keeping the distance between the two cars more or less constant and read the speedometer of their car. Subsequently, at the request of the accused, both cars were driven simultaneously and it was found that each registered 20 miles per hour. Both constables admitted that they did not know whether the speedometer of the car they used registered correctly.

At the close of the Crown case the accused applied for his discharge. Upon this application failing, he closed his case and was convicted.

In his reasons for judgment the magistrate says: It is probable that the speedometers of motor vehicles are not absolutely accurate; but if the speedometers of two vehicles, when tested, register identically, the court cannot in circumstances such as this arrive at the improbable conclusion that both are inaccurate on the ground that one meter had not been tested before the speed was determined. In the light of this consideration and in view of the mere denial by the accused he could come to no other conclusion than that the prosecution had proved the charge.

* 1938 O.P.D. 155, 156.
† A small town in the province of the Orange Free State.

Now this is not a case in which it could be said that prima facie evidence if unanswered becomes conclusive. In all such cases the issue is something within the knowledge of the accused person and relating to his own conduct or intentions. Here we have a different situation; the matter at issue is the testimony of a scientific instrument, which cannot be cross-examined without any evidence as to its reliability. There is no evidence on record which would justify one in coming to the conclusion that the accused had special knowledge of the accuracy of the instrument of the car he was driving, and we have proof that the police have no notion as to the accuracy of theirs. Obviously the accused must have been unaware of the fact that he was trailed, so that it cannot be expected from him that he should be in possession of peculiar knowledge in regard to speed. What is clear is that, when stopped, he bona fide disbelieved the accusation, for the offer to compare the two instruments in action came from him. . . . Taylor on *Evidence* (section 183) says a jury would be advised, in the absence of evidence to the contrary, to rely on the general correctness of a watch or a clock, which had been consulted for the purpose of fixing the time when a certain event happened. He proceeds to announce his credo also in respect to thermometers, anemometers, pedometers and a variety of other ingenious contrivances.

It is significant that the admissibility of the readings of instruments is usually justified as cognate to that of maps in the ordinary course of business – in other words, the notoriety of their trustworthiness. If that is so, I am entitled to take judicial cognisance of their fallibility. I have seen thermometers registering blatant falsehoods. I have seen aneroids and clocks not functioning at all, or faultily. To my mind the reaction of an individual instrument at any particular time, when itself directly in issue, does not carry conviction. We are not here dealing with an instrument of direct registration, such as a clock or an aneroid; the speedometer gives the quotient of the measurements of two concepts, time and space. It is obvious, therefore, that a slight underestimate of one factor may gravely exaggerate the rate. It is notorious that a change of tyres may affect the registration of mileage by as much as five per cent. Take into consideration, further, that when two objects are moving relatively fast in the same direction, a considerable difference in rate is required before a change in the relative position becomes easily perceptible, especially if the distance over which the observation is made is short. Granted that these margins of error exist, what latitude then must the prosecution be given? Can one let it pass at, say 5 per cent. but jib at 20?

I think the rule was stated much too widely by *Taylor*. Wigmore on *Evidence*, sec. 795, states what appeals to me as the more logical rule. He says:

Our impression is not received by the unaided senses, but depends for its verity upon the correctness of the intermediate instrument or process. It would seem plain, however, that the situation is the same as if our senses had been abnormally enlarged in scope or capacity, and that we may here also claim to have knowledge, in the ordinary sense *provided only that the instrument or process is known to be a trustworthy one*. That trustworthiness may be based upon general experience as to the class of instrument in question, together with a knowledge of the mechanism of the particular instrument as one constructed according to a trustworthy type.

What is needed, then, in order to justify testimony based on such instruments, is merely preliminary professional testimony to the trustworthiness of the process or instrument in general (when not otherwise settled by judicial notice) and to the correctness of the particular instrument.

I cannot appreciate the value of the comparison of two untested instruments; it is like Anatole France's angels, just fallen from heaven, consulting Lucretius and the Fathers in a Paris library in search of proofs of what is directly ascertainable by them. The police should have furnished the best evidence. They could have driven the car over a measured distance in a checked space of time, or adopted any one of the many ways which suggest themselves of testing the instrument in question, or obtaining testimony as to its reliability.

Most legislators have taken elaborate precautions in regard to standards of weights and measures to protect the citizens' pocket. I do not think it was intended to jeopardise his liberty by such slap-dash methods as these. To my mind there was no trustworthy prima facie evidence that the accused has committed an offence.

Advice to a Young Man interested in going into Law

[In May 1954 a boy aged twelve, living in Alexandria, Virginia, sent a letter to Mr Justice Frankfurter. The boy wrote that he was 'interested in going into law as a career' and requested advice as to 'some ways to start preparing myself while still in junior high school'. That distinguished judge and scholar replied as follows:]

MY DEAR PAUL:

No one can be a truly competent lawyer unless he is a cultivated man. If I were you, I would forget all about any technical preparation for the law. The best way to prepare for the law is to come to the study of the law as a well-read person. Thus alone can one acquire the capacity to use the English language on paper and in speech and with the habits of clear thinking which only a truly liberal education can give. No less important for a lawyer is the cultivation of the imaginative faculties by reading poetry, seeing great paintings, in the original or in easily available reproductions, and listening to great music. Stock your mind with the deposit of much good reading, and widen and deepen your feelings by experiencing vicariously as much as possible the wonderful mysteries of the universe, and forget all about your future career.

With good wishes,
Sincerely yours,
[*Signed*] Felix Frankfurter

Master M. Paul Claussen, Jr.

D. F. WILSON*

This Charm of Endearment†

Facilis descensus Averni! The Virgilian epigram, which might, for present purposes, be translated 'How small the fall from destitution to prostitution!' epitomises the case for the prosecution against the defendant, who is charged, first, with having accosted or solicited a person for the purpose of prostitution in a public place, namely, the Windsor Ballroom; and, secondly, with having loitered for the same purpose in a public place, namely the Rio Grande Café.

The defendant, who is a female said to be 21 years of age, has already been married for four years and separated for the past few months from her husband, from whom she received no money. She is unemployed, except for some domestic help which she gives her landlady in exchange for her board and lodging; and her sole income is £3 5s per week unemployment benefit.

On the evening of Tuesday, 9 May 1961, she was literally penniless, and her next unemployment benefit was not due for some days. According to the evidence, there is in Pirie Street an establishment which combines the functions of boarding-house, café and fun parlour, and is known as the Rio Grande; it is also known as a haunt of thieves and prostitutes. To this establishment the defendant repaired on the date, and in the circumstances which I have mentioned. When Constables Quinn and Hobba visited the café they saw the defendant entwined with a youth who kissed her on the cheek and she returned what is referred to by Constable Hobba (apparently a connoisseur of Thomas Moore) as 'this charm of endearment'. Constable Quinn, sacrificing gallantry to duty, interrupted the love-duet, and, when the defendant admitted that she had made the acquaintance of the youth only that evening, she was taken away for further questioning in the presence of a woman police officer. According to

* The Chief Magistrate of Adelaide, Australia.
† Reported in *New Truth*, Melbourne, Australia, 24 June 1961.
‡ *Aeneid*, Book VI, line 126.

Constable Quinn, she at first denied having loitered at the Rio
Grande for the purpose of prostitution; she admitted having
kissed and made advances to the youth there, but said that this
was because she felt lonely and wanted someone to care for her.

When it was suggested that she had done this sort of thing
before, she admitted that this was so; asked for details, she said
that on one occasion a fortnight before, she had met a man at the
Windsor Ballroom (which is a public place) and had intercourse
with him for ten shillings. . . . Finally, she admitted that she had
gone to the Rio Grande that evening for the purpose of meeting
potential customers. The defendant has given evidence on oath
denying the charges, and denying also that anything took place
between her and the youth except that they had an arm around
each other as they listened to a juke box. (This I take to be a
mechanical device for the reproduction of what passes for
music.) . . . The defence has even gone to the length of calling the
defendant's husband to testify to her sexual coolness; whether
for that or other reasons, he fled to Woomera, and I am bound to
say that the relevance of his evidence is as remote as the region to
which he retreated.

This summarises the evidence. So far as the charge relating to
9 May is concerned, it is to be observed that the only person,
whom the evidence suggests may have been approached by the
defendant for the purpose of prostitution, has not been called to
confirm this. That being so it should not be inferred that he was
approached for this purpose unless there is no other reasonable
hypothesis open on the evidence. Not even the jealous Capulets
suspected Juliet of soliciting for the purposes of prostitution,
although she and Romeo were exchanging kisses on the lips within
a dozen lines of meeting for the first time. True, the meeting
place and the lady's circumstances were somewhat different;
nevertheless, if the case rested on this evidence alone and the
charge was denied, a court might well feel bound to hold that,
although highly suspicious, the evidence did not amount to
proof beyond doubt that the defendant was not merely seeking
sexuality but seeking to sell it.

I see not the slightest reason for entertaining any suspicion that
her confession may not represent the truth; indeed, my observation of her in the witness-box convinced me that, although all too

prone to lie, she did not have the intelligence to invent on the spur of the moment the details she gave to the police about her nocturnal activities.

I find both charges proved. It is but fair to the defendant to add that I have little doubt she is a mere beginner at the business. Who but a tyro at this of all trades would allow customers credit, or charge as little as ten shillings – even for cash on delivery? I record a conviction on each count.

JOHN WATSON

In the Lands Tribunal

[Some subjects are popularly believed to be too dry or esoteric to be capable of yielding any literary joy: and the Law of Rating may be such a subject. Yet it has a curious and special charm, and some of the best lawyers have managed to find themselves completely at home in it. Quite the most important character on its stage is a shadowy creature called 'The Hypothetical Tenant' – a name coined by the judiciary – who is conclusively deemed, for the purpose of arriving at the rateable value of every single hereditament in the United Kingdom, to have ventured on a yearly tenancy of it.

Nothing can deter this genial spectre from playing his leading role. Is the property expressly required, by statute, never to be let? Or is it in fact to be demolished tomorrow? Is it a large modern factory which will take some years fully to equip? Is it a coal-mine making a heavy loss, with no prospect whatever of trade improving within the coming year? No matter: in every instance this irrepressible optimist will be prepared to take a yearly tenancy and to pay a substantial (but of course hypothetical) rent.

Enough has perhaps been said already to explain why the subject is one where the uninitiate or the brash can go horribly astray. Even the highest courts are not always beyond reproach: in the edition of *Ryde on Rating*, for example, which followed the circular and muffled bombinations of the Earl of Halsbury in *Kirby* v. *Hunslet* [1906] A.C. at page 49, one may read reproach which borders on abuse. More recently a 4 – 1 decision (Lord Denning dissenting admirably) in a tricky little case involving an advertising sign was swiftly followed by legislation and the Irishism that 'The House of Lords cannot err: but, thank God, their mistakes can be put right by Parliament!'

Rating disputes come first before 'lay gents' sitting as local valuation courts, usually assisted by trained (and sometimes extremely able) clerks. Here no costs are awarded, and the atmosphere is sometimes disarmingly informal – for example, one of the editors was once willy-nilly subjected at the conclusion of his final speech to cross-examination by the opposing advocate! The next court to which appeal can be made is the Lands Tribunal – a body set up in 1949 to decide in addition a number of other disputes, including applications to discharge covenants restricting the use of land. Its members are two distinguished lawyers and five eminent chartered surveyors. In the following pages we print selections from five decisions of one of the surveyor members – Mr John Arthur Fergus Watson.

Mr Watson is not only a Fellow and Past President of the Royal Institution of Chartered Surveyors: he has for many years been actively interested in the treatment of juvenile delinquents, on which he has written three books, and is an experienced Metropolitan Juvenile Court Magistrate.]

Forshaw v. *Turner (Valuation Officer)**

[A successful appeal by the occupier of a semi-detached house in Stockport from a local valuation court which confirmed an assessment of £28 Gross Value. In reducing the assessment to £27 Watson said:]

The appellant gave evidence in support of his stated grounds of appeal. Beside the property is an open space and he complained of its constant misuse for the parking of cars, the tipping of refuse, and the sanitary convenience of dogs. Behind it is a railway goods yard and he complained of noise, smoke and dirt from railway engines and rolling stock engaged in shunting – by night as well as by day . . .

[As to] the plot of vacant land. There was a car parked on it when I made my visit, but no rubbish and no dogs. To the appellant, who has a tidy mind, its misuse must be a source of annoyance; but there is a great deal of vacant land in the neighbourhood and someone less meticulous than he might prefer to have a piece of grass alongside his house to being overlooked by a

* Decided, 5 June 1957.

neighbour. I have decided that there is no ground for reducing the assessment on this score.

[As to] the railway. This is no ordinary railway running behind a street of houses; it is a shunting yard of mammoth proportions. I believe the appellant when he complains of noise and smoke and dirt, and I am satisfied from my own observations that the noises are less penetrating when heard from the other side of the road. The back garden of the appeal property is only about 25 ft. long and the yard is immediately below. I find it difficult to believe that the appellant does not suffer more from smoke and dirt than the occupants of the houses opposite. Questioned by the tribunal, the valuation officer said that if he personally had to choose between one side of the road and the other he would take a house on the west side so that he could see the trains. I intend no disrespect to an experienced valuer when I say that every small boy in the country would wholeheartedly agree with him. But the hypothetical tenant, if I correctly interpret the authorities, is no longer a small boy; he is to be considered as an adult person who like the Apostle Paul has put away childish things. I have little doubt, if he were invited to select a house in Lloyd Street, that in defiance of the younger members of his family he would see that this shunting yard was as far away from him as possible. In short, I consider that the houses on the west side of Lloyd Street overlooking the railway are worth less than those on the east side, and I think that the disparity in rental value is sufficient to be reflected by a small difference in the assessments.

Lacon & Co. Ltd. v. Great Yarmouth and Vaughan (Valuation Officer)*

[One of five successful appeals by brewers, with the assistance of the Valuation Officer, against public-house assessments supported by the rating authority.]

The Fishwharf [assessed at £330 Gross Value] is a long grim Victorian building abutting a wide open space paved with cobbles

* Decided, 1 June 1959.

and intersected by railway lines. On the ground floor are four bars and a refreshment room about 60 ft long and 18 ft wide. On the first floor is a club room nearly as large as the refreshment room. One of the bars, no longer in regular use, is named The Captains' Room, and I can well believe that in the old days, before the tragic recession of our herring industry, The Fishwharf was often a scene of revelry. But today the captains and their crews have departed, and the evidence is conflicting about the extent to which their custom has been replaced by that of landlubbers employed in newly-established and possibly less thirsty industries . . .

[The brewers called as their expert Mr Gibbs; the valuation officer, Mr Darby; the rating authority, Mr King.]

All three valuers are agreed upon a common method of approach: namely, the 'direct method' . . . The assumptions upon which it is founded are as follows:

The brewer is conceived as the hypothetical tenant. In most cases he sub-lets the house to a licensee; alternatively the licensee may be a manager in the brewer's employment. The licensee is restricted to selling the brewer's draught and bottled beer, and such other beers, wines, and spirits as may be supplied to him through the brewer's agency. A licensee, when he is the brewer's tenant, normally pays the brewer a rent, called the 'tied rent', based upon his expectations of retail profit. Valuers split the tied rent theoretically into two parts: the 'wet' part, which is based upon the expected profit from the sale of liquor; and the 'dry' part, based upon any additional profit the licensee hopes to make by letting ancillary accommodation – e.g. rooms for letting and catering – but not deriving from the sale of drink . . .

. . . No one appears to know the actual profit on a barrel of beer. It is suggested for the brewers that the calculation is so complicated that no brewer has yet been able to work it out, the counter-suggestion is that the brewers know, but will not tell. I favour the second explanation, but there is no obligation upon a brewer or any other class of ratepayer to disclose his profit unless he wants to; this being so, the valuers of licensed property have to make estimates . . .

Mr Gibbs said that in a town like Great Yarmouth, for a house where there is no ancillary accommodation, he would expect the tied rent to work out at something between 5s and 10s a barrel. His rate would tend to increase if any exceptional quantity of beers were sold or if there was a high consumption of the more expensive beer or of wines and spirits. The tied rent would also be higher where there was a regular as opposed to a seasonal trade, where the house was particularly economical to run, or where there was exceptionally good accommodation for the licensee. Mr Darby, who supported Mr Gibbs, tendered a schedule of tied rents fixed in Yarmouth between 1950 and 1956. The range per barrel is admittedly a wide one, but most of the rents for houses without ancillary accommodation are between 4s 6d and 9s 6d ... Mr King, on the other hand, uses for this purpose a table of his own devising. The table enables the valuer, once he has learned or estimated the barrelage, at once to determine what the tied rent should be. He said that in general his table was not susceptible to adjustment, except possibly where the licensee's accommodation was unusually good or bad. He was definite, for example, that he would not vary the tied rent on his table because of the exceptionally high cost of running a house: 'If', he said, 'the trade is there the rent is there'. Mr King attached no value to Mr Darby's schedule of tied rents paid in Great Yarmouth. Actual tied rents, he said, were inconsistent and misleading; if I understood him correctly, he would pay little attention to the actual tied rents paid in any town. With respect to Mr King, it seems to me that this is like spurning a raft in a sea of hypothetical considerations. We have here a hypothetical landlord, a hypothetical tenant, a hypothetical licensee, and hypothetical profits on hypothetical barrels of beer. To reject the actual evidence of rents would be the apotheosis of hypothesis, and I will not be party to it.

[Finally, the Lands Tribunal decided in favour of Mr King's method – in estimating 'the brewer's bid' – of taking a percentage of the wholesale profit *plus* the 'wet' part of the tied rent, and dealing differently with the 'dry' part: and, having explained on what principle that 'dry' part should be split between licensee and brewer, added:]

I do not for one moment believe that the average brewer undertakes the mental gymnastics with which his advisers seem to credit him. But we are concerned here with the theory of valuation and, having studied the evidence, that is how I think this kind of valuation ought to be made. . . .

The appeal will be allowed and the assessment determined at Gross Value £220 . . .

Wand (*Valuation Officer*) v. *Bell**

[An unsuccessful appeal against a local valuation court reduction of the assessment of a bungalow known as 'Four Bells' in Hamble, Hampshire from £55 to £50 Gross Value.]

This is a new bungalow and the respondent, Mr Bell, is its owner and first occupier. It is built of brick with cavity walls and has a tiled pitched roof . . . The floor area, measured externally, is 1,137 square feet. It forms part of the Crowsport Estate, which is a private estate occupying a sloping site between Satchell Lane and the river. All the dwellings on the estate are bungalows, of which 25 were built before the war and four, including 'Four Bells', since the war ended. The pre-war bungalows have flat roofs and, because their external walls are of 9-inch brickwork, tend to be affected by condensation. For these reasons, in the opinion of the valuation officer, they are structurally inferior to the bungalow I am concerned with. . . . Mr Bell, the respondent ratepayer, advanced a number of reasons why 'Four Bells' should be assessed on a lower basis than the other bungalows, as determined by the local valuation court. It was, he said, on the extreme edge of the Crowsport Estate and its only frontage was to Satchell Lane; he was thus denied the quietude and privacy afforded to the other houses which had frontages to the private estate roads. Satchell Lane, moreover, was narrow at this point and had no pavement or street lighting; opposite to him was a concrete wall, and beyond the wall on a higher level a terrace of artisan houses whose occupants could see into his windows. He complained, further, that there was an ugly building used for sail-making immediately next door to him. He admitted in cross-examination that a cavity wall was better than a 9-inch wall, but said he thought the flat roofs of the pre-war bungalows were an

* Decided, 2 November 1959.

advantage. Most of them had a view over the river and their occupants could sit on the roof to enjoy it. Mr Bell agreed that there were workshops and boat-building sheds close to some of the other bungalows; but denied that they caused any nuisance to the occupants, or that their view of the river was impaired by the spectacle of workmen walking along the water's edge. The matter is one of valuation, and what I have to decide is whether 'Four Bells' should be assessed like the other bungalows or whether some reduction is warranted because of peculiar disadvantages.

I have inspected 'Four Bells'. I have also viewed externally all the other bungalows on the Crowsport Estate; the river; the sail-making factory; the other workshops and boat sheds; the concrete wall; the artisan houses. In the result, I have arrived at the following conclusions.

The Crowsport Estate is inhabited by a small community who, if they do not all claim to be yachtsmen, share an enthusiasm for messing about with boats. The view of the Hamble River is charming, with small craft of all shapes and sizes riding at their moorings. It is not a very tidy estate and the surface of some of the roads, although made up, is poor. Yet undoubtedly it has character. There is salt in the air, and a smell of tar, and one suspects that most of the residents are busy at week-ends building boats in their back gardens. And if the noise from the nearby workshops is not in fact caused by someone stepping a mast or splicing a mainbrace, it sounds just like it – which is nearly as good. Within this setting the cream-washed flat-roofed houses are not unattractive. Some of them have a distinctly nautical appearance. They are ornamented with ships' lanterns; life-belts do duty as name boards; manifestly the occupiers go *aloft* to see the view, not *upstairs*; some of the roofs are bounded by taffrails to prevent them falling overboard in a storm. Such is the character of the Crowsport Estate and character creates value.

'Four Bells' is different. Structurally it may be a better house, but it is an ordinary conventional bungalow close to and overlooking a main road. With respect to Mr Bell, who owns a dinghy, any ordinary conventional landlubber might live there. There is nothing nautical about it, except perhaps its name; and that illusion was dispelled when the respondent mentioned that his family comprised himself, his wife and two children. In summer at all events 'Four Bells' has no view of the river. It does not enjoy the character of the rest of the estate and the knowledge that a sail-maker works in the rather ugly building next door can be little consolation. The respondent said that by comparison with the other properties on the Crowsport Estate his bungalow was 'odd man out'. The local valuation court said the same thing in more technical language when they referred to 'certain disabilities peculiar to this site'. I agree with both observations.

Lowestoft Borough Council v. Scaife (Valuation Officer)*

[An unsuccessful appeal, by the occupiers of the South Pier, Lowestoft, against a local valuation court assessment of £1,950 rateable value. One of the rents paid included payment for a Bingo hall.]

None of the witnesses, even learned counsel, would admit to any personal experience of the game of Bingo or a knowledge of the rules; but I gained the impression that Bingo is a game of chance rather than of skill, is played in a covered circular enclosure, and is profitable to the promoters.

[On the substantial issue of valuation:] Of the 52 piers in England and Wales, 34 were occupied and operated at the material date by commercial undertakings. The other 18 were operated by local authorities. In general, the commercially occupied piers showed a profit and, because a pleasure pier is a purpose-built hereditament, Mr Stiles [the respondent's expert witness] valued these piers on the profits basis. But of the 18 municipally operated piers, only 7 were run at sufficient profit to justify, in his opinion, a profits basis valuation. The remaining 11, which included the South Pier, Lowestoft, were either run at a loss or showed so small a profit that a valuation on the profits basis would have produced an absurdly low result. He valued these piers on the unit basis.

Whether a local authority makes a substantial profit on its pier,

* Decided, 16 June 1960.

or a small profit, or incurs a loss, does not necessarily depend upon the skill of the local authority as impresario. It may depend upon its policy. And the policy of a local authority, dictated by the situation, characteristics and tradition of its town, may be highbrow, or 'popular' – or something between the two. A local authority with a popular policy will tend to operate its pier in much the same way as a commercial concern. It will afford every possible attraction to those whom Mr Stiles described as '*hoi polloi*' – which expression the Oxford dictionary defines as 'the masses' or 'the rabble'. I think Mr Stiles was referring to those whom today – euphemistically if inaccurately – we call 'the lower income group'. To them the attractions of a pier are the whelk stalls, the dodg'em cars, the fortune-teller, the rifle range, the slot machines – and all those other forms of entertainment which, according to the evidence, are most profitable to the promoters. The people who enjoy these things – why shouldn't they enjoy them? – are the same people whom a local authority with a popular policy seeks to attract not only to its pier but to its town. And if in the outcome the pier yields a reasonable profit, Mr Stiles sees no reason why it should not be valued on the profits basis, like any other pier conducted by private enterprise on similar lines.

But a local authority with a highbrow policy may have a good reason for running its pier differently. It may concern itself less to show a profit than to provide in the pier an amenity which will attract to the town, in the interests of the town generally, a different class of person. Elderly ladies, retired naval and military officers, retired gentlemen of the professional classes, are unlikely to revel in those forms of entertainment which upon the evidence tend to make a pier profitable. They are too old for the dodg'em cars, too sceptical for the fortune-teller, too blind for the rifle range, and they don't eat whelks. Their taste is for a different kind of pier, less profitable to the operators: to provide such a pier, even if it is unprofitable, may be the motive which actuates the local authority in making its notional bid ... It is not surprising if a pier, run by a local authority pursuing a highbrow policy, yields no profit or shows a loss. In that case, says Mr Stiles, it is clearly impossible to value the pier on the profits basis and some other method must be found ...

Footnote

[Space may perhaps be spared here for two small extracts from Mr John Watson's later decision in *Brighton Palace Pier Co.* v. *Rees* (Valuation Officer): 31 July 1961:]

To sew a new button on an old shirt . . . is clearly a repair; to sew a new shirt on an old button is clearly a replacement . . .

[Mr Dixon, expert witness for the appellants, had claimed that the hypothetical tenant would have to find £15,000 for cash floats and contingencies: and] 'Contingencies', said Mr Dixon, 'are whatever may arise outside those things that have been envisaged.' Counsel for the appellants had difficulty in adducing evidence about the kind of thing that had not been envisaged, but which the hypothetical tenant ought to envisage and provide for; but he made up for this deficiency by his own interesting suggestions. They included the expense of receiving a royal visit; damages awarded a film actress who for publicity purposes tripped herself up on the pier and sued the company; damage to the pier itself by a steamer hitting it in a fog; and the high cost to the ratepayer of professional advice upon a proposal to increase the rating assessment. I agree with counsel for the appellants that any of these expensive contingencies might arise, of which only the royal visit would seem likely to afford any compensating advantage. But I also agree with Mr Stiles that 'in the case of some exceptional contingency the tenant would make exceptional arrangements'. No precedent was cited for an allowance of this nature and I must reject it.

In the matter of an application by K. & C.
*Bhavnani (Holdings) Limited**

This is an application under Section 84 of the Law of Property Act 1925 to modify or discharge restrictions upon land at Heathfield in the County of Sussex.

The land in question . . . is bounded on the east by the garden of a house now known as South Ridge Cottage, which is owned by the first objector. Immediately to the north and west is other land belonging to the applicants. To the north is a plot upon which they recently built eight bungalows and eight garages. To the west is a plot of about the same size which for convenience I shall call 'the blue land'. There is no fence or other physical boundary between the subject land and the blue land, and the

* Decided, 4th August 1960.

applicants have prepared a scheme for the development of the combined site. Their plan is to build upon it six detached bungalows and six garages. Three of the bungalows, one block of garages and the central footway will be sited on the blue land which is free of any restriction. The applicants desire to build the other three bungalows and the other block of garages on the subject land. Planning consent has been obtained for what they propose.

The restrictions were imposed in a conveyance, dated 1 December 1910 and are as follows:

(1) No building or any part of a building shall be erected on [the subject land] nearer than 20 feet to the road boundary or nearer than 20 feet to the eastern boundary. . . . (2) No building other than one detached dwelling house shall be built on [the subject land].

The applicants pray for a modification of these restrictions to permit the erection of the three bungalows and the three garages to be sited east of the central footway. The grounds of the application are that it falls within paragraphs (a) and/or (c) of subsection (1) of section 84. . . . I have viewed the subject land and the surrounding neighbourhood. A notice board, overlooking the High Street, announces the intentions of the applicant company. It proposes to build, it says, 'modern regency chalet bungalows' and to sell them for £2,700 each. What, it may be asked, is a modern regency chalet bungalow? I can only think it is a modern house likely to have been approved by the Prince Regent, reincarnate as a kind of town planning authority, if in the meantime he had studied domestic architecture, first in Geneva and then in Bengal.

But the Lands Tribunal is not a town planning authority; nor, in emulation of the Prince Regent, am I an arbiter of public taste. Therefore I will say no more than that in my opinion, if there has been a deterioration in the tone of this neighbourhood, the modern regency chalet bungalows which the applicant company has already built in Mutton Lane are to a considerable extent responsible for it. And I say that after inspecting two pleasant little houses which are being built on the south side of the High Street, and the other development in Mutton Lane which includes some perfectly well-mannered council houses.

This part of the High Street nevertheless remains a good class residential neighbourhood. I have no doubt that the objectors would suffer injury by the development proposed; it was precisely to guard against such injury that the restrictions were imposed in 1910. I find no grounds for their modification; on the contrary, having regard to what is threatened, it seems to me there is every reason why they should be enforced. The application is dismissed.

Envoi—Judicial Infelicity

[In *Fikes* v. *Alabama*, 352 U.S. 191, 199 (1957), Mr Justice Frankfurter (whose forename was Felix), in a concurring opinion, said this: 'No single one of these circumstances alone would in my opinion justify a reversal [of the judgment in the court below]. I cannot escape the conclusion, however, that in combination they bring the result below the Plimsoll line of "due process".' The following poem, which appeared in the Harvard Law Review of 1957, indicates that even Homer nods, and that a Felix can also be guilty of an infelicity]

> Due process, once a slippery slope,†
> Is now a Plimsoll line,
> Of rigid and invariant scope
> And easy to define.
>
> The quickly curried horse‡ is gone –
> Too late to lock that door –
> So let us concentrate upon
> This latest metaphor.
>
> We don't decry the vivid phrase,
> The erudite bravura,
> That gives judicial mayonnaise
> A touch of Angostura.||

---

* Professor of Law, Harvard Law School. A.B., Harvard, 1926, LL.B., 1929.

† 'I have thus reached the slippery slope of due process.' FRANKFURTER, *John Marshall and the Judicial Function*, in *Government under Law* 6, 18 (Sutherland ed. 1956) (the opening address of the Conference at the Harvard Law School on the Occasion of the Bicentennial of John Marshall).

‡ Frankfurter, J., in Olberding *v.* Illinois Cent. R.R., 346 U.S. 338, 340 (1953). The substitution of 'quickly' for 'soon' is dictated by the exigencies of the metre.

|| Frankfurter, J., is not responsible for this figure of speech.

And if we do not understand
   'Horse-shedding'* of a witness,
When written by a master hand
   We presuppose its fitness.

When he lays bare our ignorance,
   'Twould be at least ungallant
Should we presume to look askance
   Upon his fictive† talent.

But when his meaning's made obscure
   By fancy verbal playing,
'Tis only fair that he be sure
   He means just what he's saying.

To try to prove the great man failed –
   An almost fright'ning thesis –
Has very naturally entailed
   A bit of exegesis.‡

*

When Britain really ruled the waves,
   In good Queen Bess's reign,‖
Her seamen oft found wat'ry graves
   Through folly or chicane.

---

* Frankfurter, J., in Fikes v. Alabama, 352 U.S. 191, 199 (1957). Superficial research has brought little enlightenment. We find that in the days when American lawyers followed the judges on circuit the horse-shed beside the court house was a favourite place for the preparing of one's own witnesses for their testimony, but this usage is hardly apposite here. It may be that Frankfurter, J., has in mind the use of the phrase by J. F. Cooper (in e.g., *The Redskin*) and others to describe the preliminary negotiations towards a bargain made in the horse-shed before or after church services at a time when contracts made on Sunday were illegal.

† Frankfurter, J., in, e.g., Keifer & Keifer v. RFC, 306 U.S. 381, 395 (1939).

‡ This being a household word, no footnote is necessary, although it has been used by Frankfurter, J., and has thus caused some dictionary-thumbing by semi-literates.

‖ Sir William Gilbert's *Iolanthe* is now in the public domain.

When overloaded ships were wrecked,
  The owners bore the onus;
But nonetheless they would collect
  A rich insurance bonus.

In time some legal myrmidon
  With learned hems and haws
Would figure out the damage done,
  And try to find the cause,

As lawyers used what means availed
  To hide in legal tosh
The fact that when the vessel sailed
  Its scuppers* were awash.

For proof of unseaworthiness
  The lawyers used to grope;
The concept must have been, I guess,
  A sort of slippery slope.

Though someone now and then would say
  This state of things was wrong,
Most Britons looked the other way
  Till Plimsoll came along.

Sam Plimsoll† was the seaman's friend,
  A Liberal M.P.;
'The day of "coffinships" must end,'‡
  He swore repeatedly.

---

* Even those non-seafaring folk unfamiliar with the Plimsoll line ought to know about scuppers.

† Samuel Plimsoll (1824–1898) was born in Bristol and elected to Parliament in 1868 from Derby.

‡ A secondary source has been resorted to for this phrase since Plimsoll's *Our Seamen* (1872) was missing from the shelves and the law clerk was in a hurry. It is, however, believed to be accurate. See 18 *Encyclopædia Britannica* 77 (14th edn. 1955).

'What boots it,' old Sam Plimsoll said,
   'To see who'll pay the cost,
When British mariners are dead,
   And British cargoes lost?

'I'm sick to death of sophistry,
   In case-by-case decision,
I want responsibility,
   Determined with precision.

'We need a bright clear line to show
   The safety mark in loading,
So that a British tar can go
   To sea without foreboding.'*

Sam Plimsoll was so eloquent†
   That Parliament gave heed,
And sought this evil to prevent,
   With all deliberate speed.‡

---

* It is to be understood that the quotation is fictive, but it fairly reflects
Plimsoll's views. See note † *supra.*

† More than eloquent, Plimsoll was choleric. When Disraeli announced that
the government was dropping Plimsoll's bill, Plimsoll called the opposition
'villains' and shook his fist under the Speaker's nose. He later apologised.
18 *Encyclopædia Britannica* 77 (14th edn. 1955).

‡ In this case it was eight years. First proposed in 1868, Plimsoll's bill was
enacted in 1876. The delay tactic of appointing a Royal Commission was
resorted to in 1873. *Cf.* HERBERT, *The Sad Fate of a Royal Commission*, in
Mild and Bitter 280 (1937):

> I am the Royal Commission on Kissing
>   Appointed by Gladstone in '74;
> The rest of my colleagues are buried or missing;
>   Our minutes were lost in the Last Great War.
> But still I'm a Royal Commission.
>   My work I intend to see through,
> Though I know, as an old politician,
>   Not a thing will be done if I do.

With fervent popular support*
It passed the law he urged,
Forbidding ships to sail from port
With Plimsoll's line submerged.†

*

So if for metaphor you yearn,
You'd better find a new one
To help your readers to discern
The process that is due one.

A line that's etched upon the sand
When tidal waters shrink?
Or one drawn by a palsied hand
With disappearing ink?

An edict whispered in the dark
Behind the Iron Curtain?
But not, oh not! a Plimsoll mark
So definite and certain.‡

Words are the skin of living thought,‖
But here's an overstuffed one.
This time the mark you overshot;
Indeed, you simply muffed one,**

---

* Popular uproar, including charges that unscrupulous shipowners had brought pressure upon the government, forced Disraeli to reverse his position. See note ‖ *supra*; authority cited note † *supra*.

† Act To Amend the Merchant Shipping Acts 1876, 39 & 40 Vict. c. 80, § 28.

‡ The possibility has been explored that Frankfurter, J., was relying on the fact that a ship has two Plimsoll marks, one for summer and the other for winter. And a ship sailing on both salt and fresh water has a pair for each. On reflection, however, this appears merely to augment the difficulties.

‖ Holmes, J., in Towne *v.* Eisner, 245 U.S. 418, 425 (1918).

** It has been urged that in any case 'above' rather than 'below' the Plimsoll line would be the proper phraseology to indicate that due process was not satisfied, but Goddard, J., a distinguished admiralty judge, refers to a ship being loaded below the Plimsoll mark when it is plain from the context that it was overloaded. See The Vestris, 60 F. 2d 273, 279 (S.D.N.Y. 1932). Both

Unless perchance we find the key
  In some sly Freudian twist:
A yearning for the certainty
  You say cannot exist.*

If with this thought you disagree,
  There is at least one other:
In this a subtle parody
  Of some more rigid brother?

This fall from grace we should not mock;
  The truth has always been
That he who aims at twelve o'clock
  Will sometimes strike thirteen.

But Burbank† is not brought to book
  For one imperfect calyx;
So we're prepared to overlook
  One metaphor *infelix*.

the Plimsoll statute and 45 Stat. 1493 (1929), 46 U.S.C. § 85c (1952), use another wording: 'to be so loaded as to submerge ... the load line ....' Possibly resort to the language of the statute would eliminate the hazard of ambiguity. One might say that ' ... in combination they submerge the Plimsoll line of due process.'

* *Cf.* FRANKFURTER, *John Marshall and the Judicial Function*, in *Government Under Law* 6, 20 (Sutherland ed. 1956): 'Like all legal provisions without a fixed technical meaning, they [provisions such as due process] are ambulant, adaptable to changes of time.'

† We could display some learning about Luther Burbank (1849–1926), but we must leave something to the reader. See the opinions of Frankfurter, J., *passim*.

Notes on Contributors

ASQUITH OF BISHOPSTONE, CYRIL, LORD (1890-1954)

Balliol College, Oxford
Fellow of Magdalen College, Oxford, 1913
Captain in Winchester Rifles, 1914-19
Called to Bar by Middle Temple, 1920
KC, 1936
Recorder of Salisbury, 1937-8
Judge of King's Bench Division, 1938-46
Lord Justice of Appeal, 1946-51
Lord of Appeal in Ordinary, 1951-4
> *Some aspects of the work of the Court of Appeal*, from the
> Journal of the Society of Public Teachers of Law (1950)
> 350, p. 29

ATKIN OF ABERDOVEY, JAMES RICHARD, LORD (1867-1944)

Magdalen College, Oxford, 1887
Called to Bar by Gray's Inn, 1891
KC, 1906
Judge of King's Bench Division, 1913-19
Lord Justice of Appeal, 1919-28
Lord of Appeal in Ordinary, 1928-44
> Speech in *Perrin* v. *Morgan* [1943] A.C. 399, 411, p. 254

BACON, FRANCIS, BARON OF VERULAM and VISCOUNT ST. ALBANS (1561-1626)

Trinity College, Cambridge, 1573-5
Called to Bar by Gray's Inn, 1582
MP for Taunton, and Bencher of Gray's Inn, 1586

MP for Liverpool, 1589
MP for Middlesex, 1591
QC, 1596
MP for Southampton; 'Essays', 1597
Knighted, 1604
Solicitor-General, 1607
Attorney-General, 1613
Privy Councillor, 1616
Lord Keeper, 1617
Lord Chancellor, 1618–21
Charged with bribery 1622. Confined during the King's Pleasure
   (for a few days) and fined
      Of Judicature: Essays or Counsels Civil and Moral, p. 3

BLACK, HUGO LA FAYETTE, MR JUSTICE
(1886–   )

LLB University of Alabama, 1906
Entered practice, 1907
Police judge, 1910–11
Solicitor (prosecuting attorney), Jefferson County, Alabama,
   1915–17
US Senator from Alabama, 1919–37
Associate Justice, US Supreme Court, 1937–
      Dissenting opinion in *Beauharnais* v. *Illinois*, 343 US 250,
      267 (1952), p. 198

BLAGDEN, JOHN BASIL, JUDGE
(1901–1964)

Brasenose College, Oxford, 1924
Fellow of All Souls, 1924–31
Called to Bar by Inner Temple, 1925
Puisne Judge, High Court of Rangoon, 1940–4 and 1946–8
Puisne Judge, High Court of Bombay, 1941–8
Officiating Judge, High Court of Calcutta, 1942
Officiating Judge, High Court of Bombay, 1942–4
English County Court Judge, 1948–64 (retired)
      Judgment in *Mayr* v. *Riva.* [1943] 1 Cal. 250, p. 243

BOWEN OF COLWOOD, CHARLES SYNGE CHRISTOPHER, LORD (1835–1894)

Balliol College, Oxford 1857 (elected a Fellow while still an undergraduate)
Called to Bar by Lincoln's Inn, 1861
Junior Treasury Counsel, 1872
Judge of Queen's Bench Division, 1879
Lord Justice of Appeal, 1888–93
Lord of Appeal in Ordinary, 1893–4
  Judgment in *Mogul Steamship Co.* v. *McGregor, Gow and Co.*
  (1889) 23 Q.B.D. 593, 611, p. 185

BRANDEIS, LOUIS DEMBITZ, MR JUSTICE (1856–1941)

LLB Harvard, 1877
Practised at Bar of St Louis, Missouri, 1878–80
Practised in Boston with Samuel D. Warren Jnr.
Chairman of Provincial Committee for Zionist Affairs, 1914–16
Associate Justice, Supreme Court of US (The first Jewish judge on the Court), 1916–39
  Dissenting opinion in *Olmstead* v. *US*, 277 US 438, 471 (1928), p. 107

CARDOZO, BENJAMIN NATHAN, MR JUSTICE (1870–1938)

Columbia University, 1889
LLB Columbia Law School, 1891
Admitted to New York Bar and entered practice, 1891
Elected Justice of New York State, Supreme Court, Temporary Associate Judge of New York State Court of Appeals, 1913
Permanent appointment as Judge of New York State Court of Appeals, 1917
Chief Judge, New York State Court of Appeals, 1927–32
Associate Justice, US Supreme Court 1932–8 (succeeding Mr Justice Holmes)
Important writings: 'The Nature of the Judicial Process', 1921;

'The Growth of Law', 1923; 'The Paradoxes of Legal Science', 1928; 'Law and Literature and Other Essays and Addresses', 1931

   A Ministry of Justice, from 35 Harvard Law Review (1921) 120, p. 47

   Judgment in *Wagner* v. *International Railway Co.*, 232 N.Y. 176 (1921), p. 339

COOPER OF CULROSS, THOMAS MACKAY, LORD (1892–1955)

MA University of Edinburgh
Admitted to Scottish Bar, 1915
OBE, 1919
Junior Legal Assessor to City of Edinburgh, 1922
KC, 1927
MP for Edinburgh West, 1935–41
Solicitor-General for Scotland, 1935
Lord Advocate, 1935–41
Lord Justice-Clerk, 1941–6
Lord Justice-General and Lord President of Court of Session, 1947–54

   Judgment in *Macleod* v. *Mackenzie*, 1947 S.L.T. 335, 336, p. 91

CREWE (or CREW), SIR RANDOLPH (or RANULPHE), (1558–1646)

Called to the Bar by Lincoln's Inn, 1584
MP, 1587
Bencher of Lincoln's Inn, 1600
Speaker of House of Commons; knighted, 1614
Serjeant-at-law, 1615
King's Serjeant, 1624
Chief Justice of the King's Bench 1624–6, removed on political grounds, and stayed in retirement until his death

   Judgment in *Earl of Oxford's Peerage Claim* (1626) Jones (W.M.) 97, 101; 82 E.R. 50, 53, p. 295

DENNING OF WHITCHURCH, ALFRED THOMAS, LORD (1899–   )

Took first class honours in mathematics and law, Magdalen College, Oxford

Called to the Bar by Lincoln's Inn, 1923

KC, 1938

Recorder of Plymouth, 1944

High Court Judge, 1944–8 (Divorce Division 1944–5 and Queen's Bench Division 1945–8)

Lord Justice of Appeal, 1948–57

Lord of Appeal in Ordinary, 1957–62

Master of the Rolls, 1962–

    Judgment in *Jones* v. *National Coal Board* [1957] 2 Q.B. 55, 61, p. 315

DEVLIN OF WEST WICK, PATRICK ARTHUR, LORD (1905–   )

Christ's College, Cambridge

Called to the Bar by Gray's Inn, 1929

KC, 1945

Bencher of Gray's Inn, 1947

Judge of Queen's Bench Division, 1948–60

President of the Restrictive Practices Court, 1956–60

Lord Justice of Appeal, 1960–1

Lord of Appeal in Ordinary, 1961–4

Chairman of Nyasaland Inquiry Commission, 1959

Chairman of the Press Council, 1964–

Chairman of the Committee of Inquiry into Certain Matters concerning the Port Transport Industry, 1965

    Judgment in *Hughes* v. *Architects' Registration Council of the United Kingdom* [1957] 2 Q.B. 550, 560, p. 319

DOUGLAS, WILLIAM ORVILLE, MR JUSTICE (1898–   )

BA Whitman College, 1920

LLB Columbia University, 1925; commenced teaching in the Law Faculty

Admitted to New York Bar, 1926

Joined Yale Law Faculty, 1928–34

In Government service, 1934–9
Associate Justice, US Supreme Court 1939–
> Dissenting opinion in *Scales* v. *US*, 367 US 203, 262 (1961),
> p. 216
> Dissenting opinion in *Pollak* v. *Public Utilities Commission*,
> 343 US 451, 467 (1951), p. 324

DYSART, ANDREW KNOX, MR JUSTICE
(1875–1952)

BA St Joseph's University, New Brunswick, 1900
Entered journalism for a year
LLB Harvard, 1904
Spent a year at Oxford, 1905
Joined Bar of New Brunswick, 1905
Joined Bar of Manitoba, 1906
Judge of Manitoba King's Bench, 1921–47
Sat for a year as *ad hoc* member of Supreme Court of Canada,
  1935
Judge of Manitoba Court of Appeal for one year, 1047
> Judgment in *Mitchell* v. *Martin and Rose* [1925] 1 D.L.R.
> 260, 261, p. 349

EVATT, HERBERT VERE, CHIEF JUSTICE
(1894–   )

BA, MA, University of Sydney
LLD; admitted to Bar, 1924
Member of Legislative Assembly of New South Wales, 1925
QC, 1929
Judge of High Court of Australia, 1930–40. Resigned in 1940
Attorney-General and then Minister for External Affairs, 1940
While leading an Australian mission in the war, sat as a member
  of the British War Cabinet
Led Australian Delegation to the Paris Peace Conference, 1946
Australian Delegate to General Assembly of UN until 1948
Session President of General Assembly 1948–9
Leader of Federal Opposition (Labour Party), 1951–60
Chief Justice of Supreme Court of New South Wales 1960–2
> Judgment in *R.* v. *Hush; ex parte Devanny* (1932) 48 C.L.R.
> 510, p. 206

FIELD, RICHARD H., PROFESSOR (1903-   )
AB Phillips Exeter Academy, 1922
LLB Harvard, 1926
Joined Massachusetts State Bar, 1929
Regional Attorney, Office of Price Administration, Boston, Mass., 1937–43
Chief Legal Adviser to Administration and Acting General Counsel, Washington DC, 1942–3
General Counsel, Washington DC, 1944–6
Visiting Professor, Harvard Law School, 1946–7
Professor, Harvard Law School, 1947–
Consultant, Economic Stabilisation Administration, 1950–51
> Poem, *Frankfurter, J., concurring* ... from 71 Harvard Law Review (1957) 77, p. 373

FORTESCUE or ALAND, SIR JOHN (1670–1746)
Called to the Bar by Inner Temple, 1712
Reader at the Inner Temple, 1716
Solicitor-General to the Prince of Wales, 1714
Solicitor-General to the King, 1715
Baron of the Exchequer, 1717
Judge of Court of King's Bench, 1718–28
Judge of Court of Common Pleas, 1728–46
> Judgment in *R.* v. *Chancellor, Masters and Scholars of Cambridge University* (1723) 1 Str. 557, 564; 93 E.R. 698, 702, p. 297

FRANK, JEROME N., JUDGE (1889–1957)
PhD University of Chicago, 1909
JD University of Chicago, 1912
Joined the Illinois Bar, 1912
Practised in Chicago, 1912–29
Practised in New York, 1929–33
In Government service, 1933–41
Judge of US Court of Appeals, Second Circuit, 1941–57
> Judgment in *US; ex rel. Caminito* v. *Murphy*, 222 F. 2d 698 (1955), p. 100

FRANKFURTER, FELIX, MR JUSTICE
(1882–1965)

Arrived in America from Austria, 1894
AB City of New York College, 1902
LLB Harvard, 1906
Assistant US Attorney, Southern District, New York, 1906–10
Law Officer, Bureau of Insular Affairs, War Dept., 1911–14
Professor, Harvard Law School, 1914–39
Declined nomination to Massachusetts Supreme Court, 1932
Associate Justice, US Supreme Court, 1939–62
> Dissenting opinion in *On Lee* v. *US*, 343 US 747, 758
> (1952), p. 118
> Personal Statement in *Pollak* v. *Public Utilities Commission*
> 343 US 451, 466 (1951), p. 324
> A letter, *Advice to a Young Man interested in going into law*
> (1954), p. 357

GRESSON, SIR KENNETH
MACFARLANE (1891–   )

LLB University of New Zealand, 1914
Barrister and Solicitor, Christchurch, 1918–47
Dean of Faculty of Law, Canterbury University, 1936–47
Judge of Supreme Court of New Zealand, 1947–63
President of Court of Appeal, 1957–63; retired
Chairman of the Indecent Publications Tribunal, 1963–
> Dissenting judgment in *Re Lolita* [1961] N.Z.L.R. 54
> 548, p. 261

HAND, AUGUSTUS NOBLE, JUDGE (1869–1954)

AB Harvard, 1890
AM, LLB, Harvard, 1894
Entered practice, New York City, 1895
Judge of US District Court (Southern District), New York,
1914–27
Judge of US Circuit Court, 1927–53
> Judgment in *US* v. *Ulysses*, 72 F. 2d 705 (1934), p. 229

HAND, LEARNED, JUDGE (1872–1962)

AB Harvard, 1893
AM Harvard, 1894
LLB Harvard, 1896
Admitted to New York Bar and entered practice, 1897
US District Judge (Southern District), New York, 1909–24
Judge, US Second Circuit Court 1924–51; retired
> Judgment in *US* v. *Dennis*, 183 F. 2d 201 (1950), p. 209

HARLAN, JOHN MARSHALL, MR JUSTICE (1833–1911)

AB Center College, Kentucky
Subsequently studied law at Transylvania University and prac-
tised at Frankfort, Kentucky
County Judge, 1858–61
Colonel in Union Army, 1861–3
Attorney-General of Kentucky, 1863–7
Went to practise in Louisville, 1867
Was Republican nominee for Vice-President of US, Republican
Convention, 1872
Associate Justice, US Supreme Court, 1877–1911
Professor of Constitutional Law, George Washington University,
1889
> Dissenting opinion in *Plessy* v. *Ferguson*, 163 US 537, 552
> (1896), p. 166

HARMAN, SIR CHARLES EUSTACE, LORD JUSTICE (1894–   )

King's College, Cambridge
Called to the Bar by Lincoln's Inn, 1921
KC, 1935
Judge of Chancery Division, 1947–59
Lord Justice of Appeal, 1959–
> Dissenting Judgment in *Gollins* v. *Gollins* [1964] P. 32, 54,
> p. 155

HIEMSTRA, VICTOR GUSTAV, MR JUSTICE
(1914-   )

Educated at the Universities of Stellenbosch (BA) and Cape Town (LLB)

Subsequently, for some while, was a journalist.

Advocate at the Pretoria Bar, 1943-56

QC, 1955

Judge of Supreme Court, Transvaal Provincial Division, 1956–
   Judgment in *Potgieter* v. *Potgieter and another*, 1959 (1) S.A.
   194, p. 152

HOLMES, GEORGE NEVILLE, MR JUSTICE

Spent many years at the Bar in Durban, South Africa

Served in the army, 1939-45 War

QC, 1947

Judge of South African Supreme Court, Natal Provincial Division, 1952-9

Judge of South African Supreme Court, Appellate Division, 1959–
   Judgment in *Dreyer* v. *Naidoo*, 1958 (2) S.A. 628, p. 352

HOLMES, OLIVER WENDELL JNR, MR JUSTICE (1841-1935)

Son of Dr Oliver Wendell Holmes, poet and essayist

AB Harvard, 1861

Fought in Civil War with Unionists

LLB Harvard, 1867

Joined Massachusetts Bar, 1867

Taught at Harvard, 1870-1

Editor, *American Law Review*, 1870-3

Lecturer on Common Law, Lowell Institute, 1880-2

Published 'The Common Law', 1881

Professor, Harvard Law School, 1882

Associate Justice, Supreme Judicial Court of Massachusetts, 1882-99

Chief Justice, Supreme Judicial Court of Massachusetts, 1899-1902

Associate Justice, Supreme Court of US, 1902–32
    Dissenting opinion in *Olmstead* v. *US*, 277 US 438, 489
        (1928), p. 107
    Dissenting opinion in *US* v. *Schwimmer*, 279 US 644, 653
        (1929), p. 181
    Dissenting opinion in *Tyson and Brother United Ticket
        Offices* v. *Banton*, 273 US 418, 445 (1926), p. 204
    Dissenting opinion in *Abrams* v. *US*, 250 US 616, 624
        (1919), p. 219
    Dissenting opinion in *Gitlow* v. *New York*, 268 US 652, 672
        (1924), p. 224
    Dissenting opinion in *Southern Pacific Co.* v. *Jensen*, 244 US
        205, 218 (1917), p. 301

INGLIS, JOHN, LORD GLENCORSE (1810–1891)
Balliol, Oxford, 1834
Admitted to Faculty of Advocates, Edinburgh, 1835
Solicitor-General of Scotland, then Lord Advocate until Govern-
    ment defeated, 1852
Elected Dean of Faculty of Advocates, 1852
MP and Lord Advocate for short while until becoming Lord
    Justice-Clerk and President of Second Division of Court of
    Session, 1858
Lord Justice-General of Scotland, Lord President of Court of
    Session, 1867
        Final speech to the jury in the case of Madeline Smith,
        Notable Scottish Trials, 211, p. 82

ISAACS, SIR ISAAC ALFRED, CHIEF JUSTICE
(1855–1948)
LLM Melbourne University, 1880
Called to Victoria Bar, 1881
Member of Legislative Assembly of Victoria, 1892–1901
QC, 1899
Solicitor-General for Victoria, 1893–4
Attorney-General for Victoria, 1894–1901

Member of Federal Convention to Draft Commonwealth Con-
stitution, 1897
Member of House of Representatives, 1901
Federal Attorney-General, 1905
Judge of High Court of Australia, 1906–31
Acting Chief Justice, 1925 and 1927
Chief Justice of Australia, 1930–1
Governor-General of Australia, 1931–36; retired. He was the
first native-born Governor-General
  Dissenting judgment in *Wright* v. *Cedzich* (1930) 43 C.L.R.
  493, 500, p. 143

JAMES, SIR WILLIAM MILBOURNE,
LORD JUSTICE (1807–81)

Educated at Glasgow University, MA
Called to the Bar by Lincoln's Inn, 1831
QC, Vice-Chancellor of the Duchy of Lancaster, 1853
Vice-Chancellor of Court of Chancery, 1869
Lord Justice of Appeal, 1870–81
  Judgment in *Re Goodman's Trusts* (1881) 17 Ch.D. 296,
  p. 136

KRAUSE, FREDERICK EDWARD TRAUGOTT,
MR JUSTICE (1868–1959)

BA Cape Town University, 1885
Called to the Bar by Middle Temple, 1893
Advocate of South African Republic, 1893
First State Prosecutor for Johannesburg, 1896
Advocate of Cape Supreme Court, 1899
Fought in Boer War on the side of the Boers
KC, 1912
Judge of South African Supreme Court, Orange Free State
Provincial Division, 1923–33
Judge President of the South African Supreme Court, Orange
Free State Provincial Division 1933–8; retired

Acting Judge of the South African Supreme Court, Natal Provincial Division and elsewhere, 1944–9
Acting Judge of the South African Supreme Court, Natal Provincial Division and elsewhere, 1944–9
Judgment in *R.* v. *Chondi and another*, 1933 O.P.D. 267, p. 305

McLEAN, ARCHIBALD, CHIEF JUSTICE
(1791–1865)

Served in British army, 1812–15 War between US and Great Britain
Called to the Bar of Upper Canada and entered practice, 1815
Representative for Stormont in Legislative Assembly of Upper Canada, 1820–36
Puisne judge of Court of Queen's Bench, 1837–50, 1856–60
Puisne judge of Court of Common Pleas, 1850–6
Chief Justice of Court of Queen's Bench, 1862
President of Court of Appeal, 1863–5
Dissenting judgment in *Re John Anderson* (1860) 20 Upper Canada Q.B. Reports 124, p. 161

MACNAGHTEN, EDWARD, LORD (*4th Bart. and Baron*) (1830–1913)

Trinity College, Dublin and Trinity College, Cambridge, classical scholar and oarsman
Won the Diamond Sculls at Henley, 1852
Fellow of Trinity College, Cambridge, 1853
Called to the Bar by Lincoln's Inn, 1857
MP for County Antrim, QC, 1880
Declined judgeship, 1883 and 1887
Declined office of Home Secretary, 1886
Lord of Appeal in Ordinary, 1887–1913
Speech in *Gluckstein* v. *Barnes* (*Official Receiver and Official Liquidator of Olympia Ltd.*) [1900] A.C. 240, 248, p. 86
Speech in *Bunch* v. *Great Western Railway* (1888) 13 App. Cas. 31, 55, p. 331

MANTON, MARTIN THOMAS, JUDGE (1880–1946)

Appointed to the Federal Bench, 1916

Appointed to the Circuit Bench, 1916

In 1939 he was the Senior Judge of the Second Circuit Court of Appeal, ranking in authority only below the nine justices of the Supreme Court. He was then convicted of selling justice, fined, and sentenced to two years' imprisonment—the maximum sentence

Dissenting opinion in *US* v. *Ulysses*, 72 F. 2d 705 (1934), p. 229

MILLIN, PHILLIP, MR JUSTICE (1888–1952)

BA, LLB Cape of Good Hope University

Then worked as a journalist for a few years on the *South African News*

Called to Transvaal Bar, 1913

KC, 1927

Judge of South African Supreme Court, Transvaal Provincial Division, 1937–52

Husband of Sarah Gertrude Millin, the biographer of Smuts

Judgment in *Verwoerd* v. *Paver and others*, 1943 W.L.D. 153, p. 235

O'BRIEN OF KILFENORA, PETER, LORD
(1842–1914)

MA of Trinity College, Dublin

Barrister of King's Inn

QC, 1880

Junior Crown Counsel, 1881

Senior Crown Counsel, 1882

Third Serjeant, 1884

Second Serjeant, 1885

Solicitor-General for Ireland, 1887–8

Attorney-General for Ireland, 1888–9

Lord Chief Justice of Ireland, 1889–1913

Judgment in *Barrett* v. *Irvine* [1907] 2 I.R. 462, 467, p. 139

Judgment in *R.* v. *Drury* [1894] 2 I.R. 489, 496, p. 345

O'BRIEN, WILLIAM, MR JUSTICE (1832–1899)
Admitted to Bar of Ireland, 1855
QC, 1872
Judge of Court of Common Pleas of Ireland, 1882
Transferred to become Judge of Court of Queen's Bench of
Ireland, 1883–99
> Judgment in *Walker* v. *Great Northern Railway Co. of Ireland*
> (1891) 28 L.R. Ir. 69, 86, p. 335

PARRY, SIR EDWARD ABBOTT, JUDGE
(1863–1943)
Called to the Bar by Middle Temple, 1885
County Court Judge, Manchester 1894–1911; Lambeth 1911–27
Chairman, West Kent Appeals Tribunal, 1916
Industrial Unrest Commissioner, NW Area, 1917
President, Pensions Appeal Tribunal, 1917–18
> From *Judgments in Vacation* (1911) 52, p. 16

*PEARCE OF SWEETHAWS, EDWARD
HOLROYD, LORD* (1901–)
Corpus Christi College, Oxford
Called to the Bar by Lincoln's Inn, 1925
KC, 1945
Deputy Chairman, East Sussex Quarter Sessions, 1947–8
Judge of Probate, Divorce and Admiralty Division, 1948–54
Judge of Queen's Bench Division, 1954–7
Lord Justice of Appeal, 1957–62
Lord of Appeal in Ordinary 1962–
> Judgment in *Meek* v. *Fleming* [1960] 2 Q.B. 366, 373, p. 93

PRATT, SIR JOHN, CHIEF JUSTICE (1657–1725)
Scholar of Magdalen Hall, Oxford
Fellow of Wadham College, Oxford, 1678
Called to the Bar by Inner Temple, 1682
MP for Midhurst, 1711–15
Chief Justice of the Court of King's Bench, 1718–25
> Judgment in *R.* v. *Chancellor, Masters and Scholars of
> Cambridge University* (1723) 1 Str. 557, 564; 93 E.R.
> 698, 702, p. 297

PRICE, NORMAN CLEMENT BOLD, MR JUSTICE
(1887-)

Attorney in Johannesburg, 1908
Called to the English Bar (Middle Temple) and South African Bar, 1923
Judge of South African Supreme Court, Transvaal Provincial Division, 1945-55
Judge President of the Eastern District Local Division 1955-57; retired
Acting Judge, Appellate Division of the South African Supreme Court, 1957-8

> Judgment in *Wood N. O. and another* v. *Branson*, 1952 (3) S.A. 369, p. 256

RADCLIFFE OF HAMPTON LUCY, CYRIL JOHN, VISCOUNT (1899-)

Educated, New College, Oxford
Fellow of All Souls, Oxford, 1922-37
Called to the Bar by Inner Temple, 1924
QC, 1935
Lord of Appeal in Ordinary, 1949-64
Sat on many Government Committees, including: Chairman, Royal Commission on Taxation of Profits and Income; Chairman, Tribunal of Inquiry into the Vassall Case, 1963
Created Viscount, 1962

> Speech in *Smith* v. *East Elloe Rural District Council* [1956] A.C. 736, 766, p. 310

RICH, SIR GEORGE EDWARD, MR JUSTICE
(1863-1956)

MA University of Sydney, 1885
Admitted to Bar of New South Wales, 1887; commenced practice on Chancery side of the Bar
Judge of Supreme Court of New South Wales, 1912
Justice of High Court of Australia, 1913-50
Acting Chief Justice of Australia, 1940-1

> Judgment in *James* v. *Cowan* (1930) 43 C.L.R. 386, 422, p. 194

SIMON, SIR JOCELYN EDWARD SALIS
(1911–)

Educated at Trinity Hall, Cambridge
Called to the Bar by Middle Temple, 1934
Served in the war; rank of Lieutenant-Colonel
QC, 1951
Conservative MP for Middlesbrough, 1951–62
Solicitor-General, 1959–62
President of Probate, Divorce and Admiralty Division, 1962–
  English Idioms from the Penal Law from 81 L.Q.R. (1965)
  52, p. 266

STEPHEN, SIR JAMES FITZJAMES,
MR JUSTICE (1829–1894)

Educated at Eton, King's College London, 1847–8; graduated
  from Trinity College, Cambridge, 1851
Called to the Bar by Inner Temple, 1854
Entered journalism
Wrote in 1863 *General View of the Criminal Law*
QC, 1868
Succeeded Sir Henry Maine as the Legal Member of the Council
  in India. Helped in the codification of Indian Criminal Law,
  1869–72
Judge of Queen's Bench Division, 1879–91
Published 'History of Criminal Law', 1883
  The Punishment of Convicts, 7 Cornhill Magazine (1863) 189,
  p. 63

STOWELL OF STOWELL PARK, LORD
(WILLIAM SCOTT) (1745–1836)

Corpus Christi College, Oxford, 1764
Elected Reader in Ancient History, Oxford, 1773
1779, DCL, Oxford, Member of Faculty of Advocates, Doctors
  Commons
Called to the Bar by Middle Temple, 1780
Advocate-General for Lord High Admiral, 1782
Registrar, Court of Faculties, 1783

Vicar-General for Province of Canterbury, Commissary of City and Diocese of Canterbury, Judge of Consistory Court of London, 1788
Chancellor of Diocese of London, Master of Faculties, M.P. 1790
Judge of High Court of Admiralty, 1798–1828
MP for Oxford University, 1801
Created Baron, 1821
He was the elder brother of Lord Eldon, Lord Chancellor
> Judgment in *Evans* v. *Evans* (1790) 1 Hag. Con. 34; 161 E.R. 466, p. 125

SULLIVAN, ALEXANDER MARTIN SERJEANT
(1871–1959)

At first he was a journalist
Called to the Irish Bar, 1892
Called to the English Bar, 1899
KC of Ireland, 1908
Serjeant-at-law, 1920
He was the last of the Order of Serjeants-at-law
> *The last forty years of the Irish Bar* from 3 Cambridge Law Journal (1927), p. 7

THOMSON, GEORGE REID, LORD (1893–1962)

Educated at South African College, Cape Town
Rhodes Scholar at Corpus Christi College, Oxford
Edinburgh University
Served in 1914–18 War
Admitted to Scottish Bar, 1922
KC, 1936
Advocate-Depute, 1940–5
Lord Advocate, 1945–7
MP (Lab.) East Edinburgh, 1945–7
Lord Justice-Clerk 1947–62
> Judgment in *Blaikie* v. *British Transport Commission*, 1961 S.L.T. 190, 191; 1961 S.C. 44, 48, p. 343

VAN DEN HEEVER, FRANÇOIS PETRUS, MR JUSTICE (1894–1956)

Called to the South African Bar, 1921
Secretary for Justice and later Government Law Advisor, 1931
Appointed Judge of High Court of South West Africa, 1933–8
Judge of South African Supreme Court, 1938–48
Judge President of Orange Free State Provincial Division, 1948
Judge of Appellate Division of South African Supreme Court, 1948–56
> Judgment in *Minister of the Interior* v. *Harris and others*, 1952 (4) S.A. 769, 789, p. 173
> Dissenting judgment in *Rex* v. *X*, 1938 O.P.D. 155, 156, p. 354

WATSON, JOHN ARTHUR FERGUS (1903–   )

Chartered Surveyor, 1924
Chairman Metropolitan Juvenile Courts, 1936
Vice-President of National Association of Prison Visitors, 1939
Chairman, National Association of Prison Visitors, 1940–1
President of Royal Institution of Chartered Surveyors, 1949–50
Member of several Government Committees, including: Inter-Departmental Committee on New Towns; Royal Commission on JPs, 1946–8
> *Collection from judgments given in the Lands Tribunal*, p. 361

WILSON, DEREK FINLAY (1914–   )

Called to the South Australian Bar, 1937
Judges Associate and Clerk of Arraigns, 1937–47
Associate to Chief Justice, 1940–7
Solicitor, South Australian Crown Law Office, 1947–50
Special Magistrate, Adelaide Police Court, 1950–
> *Judgment in a prosecution in Adelaide Police Court* (1961), p. 358